ARCHITECTURAL EDUCATION THROUGH MATERIALITY

What kind of architectural knowledge was cultivated through drawings, models, design-build experimental houses and learning environments in the 20th century? And, did new teaching techniques and tools foster pedagogical, institutional and even cultural renewal? *Architectural Education Through Materiality: Pedagogies of 20th Century Design* brings together a collection of illustrated essays dedicated to exploring the complex processes that transformed architecture's pedagogies in the 20th century.

The last decade has seen a substantial increase in interest in the history of architectural education. This book widens the geographical scope beyond local school histories and sets out to discover the very distinct materialities and technologies of schooling as active agents in the making of architectural schools. *Architectural Education Through Materiality* argues that knowledge transmission cannot be reduced to 'software', the relatively easily detectable ideas in course notes and handbooks, but also has to be studied in close relation to the 'hardware' of, for instance, wall pictures, textiles, campus designs, slide projectors and even bodies.

Presenting illustrated case studies of works by architects, educators and theorists including Dalibor Vesely, Dom Hans van der Laan, the Global Tools group Heinrich Wölfflin, Alfons Hoppenbrouwers, Joseph Rykwert, Pancho Guedes and Robert Cummings, and focusing on student-led educational initiatives in Europe, the UK, North America and Australia, the book will inspire students, educators and professionals with an interest in the many ways architectural knowledge is produced and taught.

Elke Couchez is an FWO Senior Postdoctoral Research Fellow at the University of Hasselt, Belgium.

Rajesh Heynickx is a Professor in Architectural Theory and Intellectual History at the Faculty of Architecture, KU Leuven, Belgium.

"This is a remarkable collection of essays that demonstrate for both teachers and students that pedagogy is a dynamic process—one that must constantly evolve its methods, aims and media."

Ines Weizman, *Head of PhD Programme, School of Architecture,*
Royal College of Art, UK

"Methodologically speaking, *Architectural Education Through Materiality* has emerged as any powerful pedagogic prototype is inclined to do: through discussion, exchange, collaboration, transposition, provocation, iteration, reflection, and proposition. This deeply reflective endeavour offers the epistemological archaeology work needed to ensure architectural pedagogies can evolve equitably and inclusively."

Harriet Harriss, *Dean of the School of Architecture,*
Pratt Institute, New York, USA

"Now, as we find ourselves in a world that begs for reconsidering the way we build, we may want to review the way we educate architects too. Hence, a book that looks back at 20th-century architectural education in a fresh and insightful manner—shifting attention from the ends to the means—seems to be timely indeed. By presenting many episodes worth studying and re-evaluating, this book not only shows how architecture was taught—it also offers a plethora of new insights and ideas for how it could be taught. In short: there is much to be learned from this book."

Jasper Cepl, *Bauhaus-Universität Weimar, Germany*

"This welcome addition to the library on architectural education elevates the stuff of the studio, the lecture hall, the seminar, and the site visit. The question of what one could see, hear, or touch is in these pages traded for that of how students and teachers encountered and activated images, ideas, models and experiences. More than a medaition on pedagogy, this book captures a series of views on what architecture is, at precise moments, as something to impress upon its students."

Andrew Leach, *University of Sydney, Australia*

ARCHITECTURAL EDUCATION THROUGH MATERIALITY

Pedagogies of 20th Century Design

Edited by
Elke Couchez and Rajesh Heynickx

LONDON AND NEW YORK

First published 2022
by Routledge
2 Park Square, Milton Park, Abingdon, Oxon OX14 4RN

and by Routledge
605 Third Avenue, New York, NY 10158

Routledge is an imprint of the Taylor & Francis Group, an informa business

© 2022 selection and editorial matter, Elke Couchez and Rajesh Heynickx;
individual chapters, the contributors

The right of Elke Couchez and Rajesh Heynickx to be identified as the authors of the
editorial material, and of the authors for their individual chapters, has been asserted in
accordance with sections 77 and 78 of the Copyright, Designs and Patents Act 1988.

All rights reserved. No part of this book may be reprinted or reproduced or utilised in
any form or by any electronic, mechanical, or other means, now known or hereafter
invented, including photocopying and recording, or in any information storage or
retrieval system, without permission in writing from the publishers.

Trademark notice: Product or corporate names may be trademarks or registered
trademarks, and are used only for identification and explanation without intent to
infringe.

Every effort has been made to contact copyright-holders. Please advise the publisher
of any errors or omissions, and these will be corrected in subsequent editions.

British Library Cataloguing-in-Publication Data
A catalogue record for this book is available from the British Library

Library of Congress Cataloging-in-Publication Data
Names: Couchez, Elke, editor. | Heynickx, Rajesh, 1977- editor.
Title: Architectural education through materiality : pedagogies of 20th century
design / edited by Elke Couchez and Rajesh Heynickx.
Description: Abingdon, Oxon ; New York : Routledge, 2022. |
Includes bibliographical references and index.
Identifiers: LCCN 2021023633 (print) | LCCN 2021023634 (ebook) |
ISBN 9781032062082 (hardback) | ISBN 9781032062099 (paperback) |
ISBN 9781003201205 (ebook)
Subjects: LCSH: Architecture—Study and teaching—History—20th century. |
Learning, Psychology of—History—20th century.
Classification: LCC NA2005 .A65 2022 (print) | LCC NA2005 (ebook) |
DDC 720.71—dc23
LC record available at https://lccn.loc.gov/2021023633
LC ebook record available at https://lccn.loc.gov/2021023634

ISBN: 978-1-032-06208-2 (hbk)
ISBN: 978-1-032-06209-9 (pbk)
ISBN: 978-1-003-20120-5 (ebk)

DOI: 10.4324/9781003201205

Typeset in Bembo
by codeMantra

CONTENTS

List of contributors	*vii*
Acknowledgements	*xi*

Introduction: a passage to material hermeneutics *Elke Couchez and Rajesh Heynickx*	1

PART I
Objects on display: learning through looking   17

1 From wooden blocks to Scottish Tartans. Dom Hans van der Laan's reconciliation of rational patterns and spatial experience *Caroline Voet*	19
2 A walking exhibit: Alfons Hoppenbrouwers's visual pedagogy *Elke Couchez*	38
3 Clashing perspectives: Joseph Rykwert's object lesson at the Ulm school of design *Paul James*	53
4 Pancho's passages: framing transitional objects for decolonial education in 1980s South Africa *Hannah le Roux*	68

vi Contents

PART II
Hands-on: learning through manual work

83

5 Planning problems: data graphics in the education of architects and
   planners at the Harvard Graduate School of Design, the 1940s
   Anna Vallye

85

6 The Cambridge collage: Dalibor Vesely, phenomenology, and
   architectural design method
   Joseph Bedford

106

7 Little living labs: 1970s student design-build projects and the objects
   of experimental lifestyles
   Lee Stickells

126

PART III
Bodies in space: synesthetic learning

147

8 The body as an ultimate form of architecture: global tools
   body workshops
   Silvia Franceschini

149

9 Parallel narratives of disciplinary disruption: the bush campus as
   design and pedagogical concept
   Susan Holden

164

10 Revisiting environmental learning: cities, issues and bodies
   Isabelle Doucet

189

PART IV
Learning by technologies: audio-visual transmissions

203

11 In the eye of the projector: Wölfflin, slides and architecture in
   postwar America
   Rajesh Heynickx

205

12 Wireless architecture: Robert Cummings's early radio broadcasts
   John Macarthur and Deborah van der Plaat

221

13 The captive lecturer
   James Benedict Brown

235

Index

249

CONTRIBUTORS

Joseph Bedford is an assistant professor of history and theory and coordinator of thesis at Virginia Tech. His scholarship explores the intellectual history of architectural thought in the later third of the 20th century through the encounter between philosophy, theory and architectural education. He holds a PhD in history, theory and criticism of architecture from Princeton University and was the recipient of the 2008–2009 Rome Scholarship at the British School in Rome. He has taught at Princeton University, Pratt Institute and Columbia University and is the founding director of the *Architecture Exchange*, a platform for theoretical exchange between architecture and other fields, which houses an audio journal, books, workshops, oral history projects and curricula projects. He has published numerous book chapters and articles in journals such as *ARQ, AA Files, OASE, NYRA* and *Log*.

James Benedict Brown is an associate professor at Umeå University, Sweden. His PhD (Queen's University Belfast, 2012) developed a pedagogical critique of the live project in architectural education. He writes about architecture education, live projects, architectural media and representation. Prior to emigrating to Sweden, he taught at De Montfort University, the Royal College of Art, the University of Nottingham and Norwich University of the Arts.

Elke Couchez explores the intersections between intellectual history of architecture and urban design, visual studies and pedagogy. In 2018 and 2019, she worked as a postdoctoral fellow on the project "Is Architecture Art?" at the University of Queensland's Centre for Architecture, Theory, Criticism and History. As an FWO senior postdoctoral fellow at UHasselt, she teaches art and architecture history and is currently working on a research project entitled *Pedagogical Tools and Design Strategies for Urban Regeneration. International Laboratory for Architecture & Urban Design (1976–2015)*.

Isabelle Doucet is a professor of theory and history of architecture at Chalmers University of Technology, Sweden. Through a focus on resistant practices and conceptual-methodological inquiries, her research centres on the relationship between architecture, (urban) politics and social/environmental responsibility. Her recent books include *The Practice Turn in Architecture: Brussels after 1968* (2015), and the volume jointly edited with Janina Gosseye: *Activism at Home: Architects Dwelling between Politics, Aesthetics, and Resistance* (2021).

Silvia Franceschini is a curator, editor and researcher working across the disciplines of visual arts, design and architecture. She is a curator at Z33, House of Contemporary Art, Design & Architecture in Hasselt, Belgium. She holds a PhD in design and visual cultures from the Politecnico di Milano (Polytechnic University of Milan). She was a research fellow at Liverpool John Moores University and at the Strelka Institute for Media, Architecture and Design in Moscow. She is the co-author of *Global Tools 1973–1975. When education coincides with life*, a monograph on Global Tools, a multidisciplinary experimental programme of art and design education (Nero Editions, 2018). In 2015, she was a member of the curatorial team of the School of Kyiv. Kyiv Biennial 2015.

Rajesh Heynickx is a professor in architectural theory and intellectual history at the KU Leuven (Faculty of Architecture) in Belgium. He has published in *Modern Intellectual History*, *Modernist Cultures, Environment and History* and co-edited special issues of *Interiors: Design/ Architecture/Culture* and *The European Legacy*. In 2018, he acted, together with Stéphane Symons, as co-editor of *So What's New About Scholasticism? How Neo-Thomism Helped Shape the Twentieth Century*. Current research topics are 20th-century architectural theory and art philosophy; and architectural pedagogy and knowledge transfer. Recent volumes he co-edited in 2020–2021 are *Architecture Thinking across Boundaries. Epistemological Transfers in the Postwar World (1965–1995)* and *The Figure of Knowledge. Conditioning Architectural Theory, 1960s-1990s*.

Susan Holden is an architect and senior lecturer in the School of Architecture at the University of Queensland, where she teaches history, theory and design. Between 2016 and 2020, she was a chief investigator on the cross-disciplinary Australian Research Council Discovery Project examining modern Australian campus design and is a contributing author to *Campus: Building Modern Australian Universities* (UWA Publishing). Susan's research explores architecture and urban design histories; architecture in cultural policy and design governance; and the commissioning, curating and collecting of architecture by cultural institutions. Recent book publications include *Pavilion Propositions: Nine Points on an Architectural Phenomenon* (2018), *Trading Between Architecture and Art: Strategies and Practices of Exchange* (2019) and *Valuing Architecture: Heritage and the Economics of Culture* (2020). She has also published in the *Journal of Architecture, Leonardo* and *AA Files*. Susan is a fellow of the Australian Institute of Architects and contributes to the professional journal *Architecture Australia*.

Paul James is a PhD candidate connected to ATCH at the University of Queensland.

John Macarthur, FAHA, is a professor of architecture at the University of Queensland, where he teaches history, theory and design. He was the founding director of the research centre for Architecture, Theory, Criticism and History (ATCH) and remains an active member of the Centre. His research on the intellectual history of architecture has focused on the conceptual framework of the relation of architecture and the visual arts from the Picturesque to the present.

Contributors **ix**

Deborah van der Plaat is a senior lecturer at the School of Architecture, University of Queensland (Australia) and former manager of Architecture Theory Criticism History Research Centre (ATCH). Her research examines the architecture of 19th- and 20th-century Australia and its intersection with theories of artistic agency, climate, place, migration and race. Writing histories of Queensland architecture is also a focus within her work. Recent publications include *Hot Modernism Queensland Architecture 1945–1975* (edited with Macarthur, Gosseye and Wilson: Artifice, 2015) and *Speaking of Buildings: Oral History Methods in Architecture* (edited with Gosseye and Stead, Princeton Architectural Press, 2019, in press).

Hannah le Roux is an associate professor at the University of the Witwatersrand. As an architect, educator and theorist, she considers the modernist project in architecture in Africa, and how its transformation through the agency of Africa presents a model for collective and post-consumerist design. Her first degree was at Wits in the 1980s under Pancho Guedes. Her recent projects have engaged with Habesha diaspora coffee ceremonies in transforming inner city high rises, the soccer culture of earth fields in townships and the complicity of modern architects in distributing asbestos-cement to the global South.

Lee Stickells is an associate professor and head of Architecture in the School of Architecture, Planning and Design at the University of Sydney. His historical research on international countercultural and ecological design experimentation has been published widely across scholarly, professional and popular media. He contributes to the *Architectural Theory Review* editorial committee and the international advisory board for *Counterculture Studies*. Current projects include *Design Radicals: Spaces of Bay Area Counterculture*, edited with Greg Castillo for the University of Minnesota Press. Whenever he gets the chance, he can be found riding a bike.

Anna Vallye is an assistant professor of art history and architectural studies at Connecticut College. She is the editor of *Léger: Modern Art and the Metropolis* (Philadelphia Museum of Art and Yale University Press, 2013) and *Urban Renewal and Highway Construction in New London, 1945–1975* (New London County Historical Society, 2021). She is currently at work on a monograph titled *Model Territories: German Architects and the Shaping of America's Welfare State*, about the American careers of émigré architects Walter Gropius, Martin Wagner and Ludwig Hilberseimer, particularly their contributions to urban planning.

Caroline Voet is an assistant professor at KU Leuven, Faculty of Architecture, where she is part of the research group "Architectural Cultures of the Recent Past". She supervises PhD's and coordinates the research-based Masters environment 'Structural Contingencies'. She holds degrees in Architecture and Arts from the AA in London and the Henry van de Velde Institute in Antwerp. Through the dissection of (un)built heritage, architectural drawings and teaching material, she scans and reconstructs new paths of knowledge transferal. Her research and teaching focus on young architectural heritage, spatial systematics and design history and has been published in, for example, *ARQ and Interiors* Routledge. After working for Zaha Hadid and Christian Kieckens, Voet started her own practice VOET architectuur in Antwerp. They focus on heritage, reconversions and the design of public interiors and scenography.

ACKNOWLEDGEMENTS

The secret to a sourdough with tangy flavour, chewy texture and a crisp crust is time.

We consider this volume as a slow rise and fermented bread. As a starter, we organized the travelling workshop series *Objects and Technologies of Schooling*, a collaboration between KU Leuven – *SRN Texts-Buildings* and the University of Queensland's *Architecture Theory Criticism and History Research Group* (ATCH).

We organized a first workshop on 3 April 2015 in Leuven, a second one on 16 June 2016 in Brussels and a last one on 17 April 2019 at the University of Queensland in Australia. All participants set out to discover the very distinct materialities and technologies which generated architectural schools. *Architectural Education Through Materiality: Pedagogies of 20th Century Design* includes the extended versions of a selection of papers presented during these workshops. A number of papers were added later on in the process.

We are thankful to the many hands that kneaded our ideas since our initial meeting in 2015 and whose combined efforts made this volume possible. We especially wish to thank our immediate colleagues at the KU Leuven: Hilde Heynen, Yves Schoonjans, Sebastiaan Loosen and Ricardo Agarez; the colleagues at the University of Queensland: John Macarthur, Susan Holden, Ashley Paine and Macarena de la Vega; all the participants to the workshop series; the anonymous reviewers and the entire editorial and publication team at Routledge. They all fed the starter and added pinches of salt to the dough. We hope it crumbs.

INTRODUCTION

A passage to material hermeneutics

Elke Couchez and Rajesh Heynickx

In a recent edited volume *Materiality and Architecture*, Sandra Karina Loschke argued that – prompted by developments in digital fabrication – the impact of materiality is being widely reassessed in the contemporary disciplines of architecture and design (Loschke 2016). Looking at recent practices such as those by Herzog & De Meuron, MVRDV and Lacaton & Vassal, she notices that material and surface have become the preferred modes of representation and that they challenge 'traditional considerations such as form, geometry and style'. Materialisation is pertinent to the representation of architecture and appears to saturate the research on production processes in architecture and design. The German design theorist, Christian Gänshirt, for instance, pointed to the expanse of research into the tools of creative design – including sketches, drawings, models, graphs, tables, design guidelines and writing, and even shotguns used to transform clay bricks (Gänshirt 2018). A powerful attempt to historicise and theorise the role of technology and tools in architectural design was recently also conducted by Zeynep Çelik Alexander and John May. What started as an analysis of the artefacts used by designers – from the T-square to the French curve and design software – resulted in a plea to make technics a central line of inquiry in the architecture discipline (Çelik Alexander and May 2020).

One field in which the potential and the challenges of the material have not yet been fully considered is that of architectural education. There is, notwithstanding, a growing interest in the history of architectural education: in the US and Europe, studies (such as Crinson and Lubbock 1994; Ockman and Williamson 2012; De Vos and Lombaerde 2013; Stern and Stamp 2016) have addressed three centuries of educating architects, while in Australasia, many architecture schools were celebrating centennials or gold/diamond anniversaries, which gave rise to a wide range of exhibitions, conferences and book publications between 2012 and 2018 (some of the more recent projects are Murray 2015; Gatley and Treep 2017; Leach and Stickells 2018). Sensitivity to architecture and pedagogy has been increasing since Beatriz Colomina launched her collaborative research project *Radical Pedagogies* in Venice (2015), and the eponymous book by Harriet Harriss and Daisy Froud was published that same year.[1] Yet, essential as they have been, most of these efforts focus on institutional

DOI: 10.4324/9781003201205-1

changes and key educational figures; *how* the material takes part in educational processes is rarely considered in architecture and design teaching.

When working on this volume, our main question has been how educational practices in architecture and design are affected *and* shaped by materials. We turned to recent work by historians of education, who, during the past two decades, started to incorporate the scientific findings of the 'material turn' in their studies on past schooling practices, showing that materials can provide a valuable source to study the history of education, alongside texts and oral history. Knowledge transmission, they demonstrated with confidence, should no longer be only reduced to 'software', the relatively easily detectable ideas in course notes and handbooks, but also studied in close relation to the 'hardware' of globes and wall pictures, desks, chalkboards and slide collections.[2] Ian Grosvenor, in a seminal study, drew attention to what he called the 'materialities of schooling', meaning 'the ways that materials are given meaning, how they are used, and how they are linked into heterogeneous active networks, in which people, objects and routines are closely connected' (Lawn and Grosvenor 2005: 7).

The present volume found a powerful foundation in Grosvenor's anatomy of the material in educational practices. Yet, it also results from a travelling workshop series organised in Belgium and Brisbane between 2015 and 2019 which accumulated cases by which the complex, under-theorised combinations of learning materials and design theories that transformed architecture and design pedagogies from mid to late 20th century can be tackled. The present volume includes cases from Europe, North America, Australia and South Africa and aims to shift the focus from the canonical institutional narratives to Grosvenor's 'materialities of schooling' in architecture and design contexts. It does this by dissecting the models, maps, slide projectors, technologies and paintings used in the studio or the classroom and disclosing the specific products of learning processes such as student-built houses and the physical settings in which learning took place. All authors have been invited to consider how these materialities allow us to widen our geographical scope beyond local institutional histories and to discover some distinct architectural pedagogies as active agents in the making of architectural schools.

Material hermeneutics

Studying materials and their varied uses in architectural and design education comes with a challenge. In a popular student's guide to historical sources that is currently in use, the historian Giorgio Riello explicitly warns his students about the problematic heuristic nature of materials:

> Historians tend to present history as a well-woven tablecloth, covering all corners. Objects show how history is instead a rather loosely woven net that sometimes retains – but often is unable to 'catch' – concepts, people, events and explanations. Material artefacts with their multifarious meanings, their innate opaqueness and their difficult heuristic nature remind us that history is always producing but has still a great deal more to do before covering all the corners of human experience.
>
> *(Riello 2009: 43)*

Riello was not only hinting at the practical difficulty of using objects as alternative sources to grasp ideas and actions. On a more general level, he also questioned the set of interpretive methods or principles historians almost automatically resort to. Or, to phrase it abstractly: he pointed at the limits of our hermeneutics.

Hermeneutics, the theory of interpretation dealing with meaningful human actions, has indeed too often and exclusively focused on texts. As Riello argues, the *interpretanda*, or the entries to understanding human activity, are much more diverse than we tend to accept. Yet, as materials do not unveil themselves, this volume addresses some basic questions: how can one read the 'materialities of schooling' in architecture and design education, let alone decode their accumulated meanings? Is it even possible to localise knowledge in these materials and understand the agency of things? As we are well aware, the French philosopher, anthropologist and sociologist Bruno Latour tackled these difficult questions from the end of the nineteen seventies onwards by considering the histories of (inter)relationships between artefacts and knowledge.[3] Similarly, the American philosopher Don Ihde attempted to broaden the reach of hermeneutics by emphasising the role of instruments and technologies over written theoretical work. Coining the terms 'expanded hermeneutics' or 'material hermeneutics', he aspired to modify our understanding of the material remnants of the past.

Ihde's criticism of hermeneutics is comparable to Latour's. He too considered hermeneutics and its persistent focus on texts as partial and ignorant of the potential hermeneutics of things or how things play a role in the storied world. Ihde therefore provided some parameters for reframing material hermeneutics; instead of reducing the study of material culture to the *interpretation* of artefacts (while heavily relying on textual information), he encouraged *encounters* with artefacts. His goal was to 'find ways to give voices to things, to let them speak for themselves' (Idhe 1998: 139).[4] Or, as he explained in larger terms: 'A material hermeneutics is a hermeneutics which gives things voices where there had been silence and brings to sight that which was invisible' (Idhe 2009: 80).

This volume has no ambition to step into the complex theoretical debate of how a 'return to things' should destabilise classical hermeneutics. Still, Ihde's call for a material hermeneutics, consciously interrogating the too narrow postulates of interpretation, reveals an utmost attractive path to approach the persistent motive of 'silence' in discussions on historical pedagogy.[5] More precisely, when studying the recent past of architectural education, we are faced with a double silence. First of all, the classrooms and studios of the past – once places for active interaction between student and teacher – have now become inaccessible or silenced, and a lot of testimonies of former teachers and students are either mythologised or coloured with nostalgia. Second, as Stephen Lubar and David W. Kingery – much in the line of Don Ihde – rightly noticed, it is challenging to read history from things as 'they are illegible to those who know how to read only writing. They are mute to those who listen only for pronouncements from the past' (Lubar and Kingery 2013: 8). To sift through silence and cultivate an attentive reader's attitude, therefore, requires attention to 'fragments and shadows of evidence, to recurring echoes of meaning and thinly connected patterns' (Rousmaniere 2001: 8).[6]

In this volume, we intend to scrutinise precisely those patterns in order to unpack different layers of meaning over time. By combining multiple hermeneutical strategies – visual studies, textual analysis, educational history – and by fleshing out the emergence and dissemination of architectural concepts and pedagogical practices into a set of geographically wide-ranging case studies, the 13 authors disclose how, between the late 1940s until the early 1990s, single objects, existing or new sites and emerging technologies became devices to gather, group, shape, attack or transform facts, descriptions and even skills in the field of architecture. Rather than covering an entire range of materialities of schooling or to make a comprehensive coverage, the chapters collected in this volume will present a set of 'samples', all generating a richer understanding of schooling practices in architecture and design cultures. Moreover, by concentrating on the various materialities of schooling, this volume sets out to develop a material hermeneutics that will help scrutinise the understudied links between traditional institutional and disciplinary studies on the one hand and intellectual history and visual studies on the other.

Converging subjects and objects of knowledge

Before the rise of Actor-Network Theory and Science and Technology Studies, materials were often seen as subordinate and faithful to human agency and – in educational practices – as mere instruments to advance academic performances. The authors in this volume have been wary not to invoke such instrumental views on materiality, in which materials are seen as passive conveyors of knowledge or truthful representations of the past (Dussel 2013: 32). They have therefore been careful to avoid what Zeynep Çelik Alexander and John May called a 'master-and-slave dialectic familiar to Enlightenment discourses' implying that 'if humans were the master, instruments were nothing but neutral, passive tools, applying human intentions to a compliant nature' (Çelik Alexander and May 2020). But is there a middle ground between the material and its user or between objectivity and subjectivity?

Lorraine Daston and Peter Gallison have tackled this question in their book *Objectivity*, studying the discourse on scientific images and how scientists turned to mechanical reproduction in the 19th century in search for images that were more 'true-to-nature' or liberated from human – therefore subjective – interference. In its traditional interpretation, the scientific image or object – a word derived from the Latin *obiectus* [lying before, opposite] – is a tangible thing that is perceived with the senses. Often used in diametric opposition to the word 'subjectivity' in Western philosophy, objectivity is the idea that 'truth' or 'essence' can be known as such.[7] But as Lorraine Daston and Peter Gallison have shown, this essence is a human construct, and scientific images are far from neutral conveyors of knowledge:

> [Scientific images] shape the subjects as well as the objects of science. To pursue objectivity – or truth-to-nature or trained judgment – is simultaneously to cultivate a distinctive scientific self, in which knowing and knower converge.
>
> *(Daston and Galison 2007)[8]*

Materials do not transparently reflect their creator's or owners' intentions nor are they unmediated representations of the real. Rather than focusing on what materials might represent and then condemning them to mere illustrations of classroom practices, materialities of schooling can be considered as accumulation points of different meanings and relations.[9] They continually 'enter into relationships with new contexts and audiences', moving 'through time and space, from context to context', as Ian Grosvenor repeatedly demonstrated.[10]

By allowing subjects and objects to converge, this volume also wants to challenge a prevailing educational determinism, in which scientific or educational results are seen as nothing but the 'blind recapitulation of previously learned methods' (Kaiser 2005: 4). The materialities of schooling cannot be just considered to be part and parcel of the transfer of theoretical ideas to future practitioners; they also show the contingencies of architectural thought and enable a shift from a strict notion of theory as a written and codified canon of texts, to a broader understanding of 'architectural intellectuality' (Otero-Pailos 2013: 1), which also includes tacit forms of knowing. Instead of focusing solely on the peer-to-peer interactions among scholarly giants, the chapters in this volume also look at how architect-educators grappled with what Andrew Pickering called 'the mangle of practice' (Pickering 1995). Clear-cut ideas, intellectual historians warned, have always been favoured over timely, contingent and tacit efforts of theoretical production. The materialities studied in this volume allow us to venture into a complex tangle of thought and to add anomalies and ambiguities to the project of historicising architectural knowledge.

In this volume, the chapters disclose the mindsets of educators, unpack subversive pedagogical practices and trace forgotten theories developed in once noisy classrooms or studios. A projected image on the wall, a piece of textile, a studio exercise with a chair, abstract paintings, urban settings, bodily exercises, a collage or a drawing, radio and television broadcasts are scrutinised. What will be uncovered is therefore a type of concrete, even personal, architectural knowledge, produced in day-to-day work and in often small but familiar contexts, in which numerous methods, strategic assumptions and knowledge structures were at play. The different cases reveal that precisely the capricious processes of tinkering and improvisation are involved in forming and transmitting architectural knowledge. All cases therefore redirect the dominant focus from the outcomes or effects of specific pedagogical actions in the long term to the active, contingent and dialogical processes of forming and disseminating knowledge. As Beatriz Colomina correctly noted, these pedagogies occupy a unique place between direct instrumentality and conceptual speculation (Colomina et al. 2012: 81).

A pedagogical turn: objects absorbed into processes

The chapters in this volume broadly cover the period between the 1940s and 1990s; an 'interregnum' period between modernism and the rise of the digital. Mapping and dissecting architectural knowledge in this period remains a challenging task. From the early 1950s onwards, architectural knowledge appeared to be less consistent than ever. There were two significant reasons for that. First, architectural theory accommodated many coexisting and even contradictory paradigms, none of which could claim a monopolist position. Phenomenology, structuralism, neo-Marxism or rationalism, to name the most widely spread ones, marked how architecture's aesthetic, technological and societal challenges were defined and commented.[11] Second, in the post-1945 world, the impact of two major pedagogical models – the Beaux-Arts system and the Bauhaus model – was eroding. Both educational systems emphasised the formal training of architecture through studio work. Such a formalist approach was seen as too narrow, even obsolete in the second half of the 20th century.[12]

Underlying all these intense transformations of architectural teaching models was an anxiety about the disciplinary boundaries of architecture practice itself. Educators and practitioners alike started to ask what students should learn to equip them for a continually changing architectural profession. As Beatrice Colomina noted, this 'disciplinary self-reflexivity interrogated not only the historical and formal bases of modernist traditions but also the *means* by which they were disseminated in academic and institutional contexts' (Colomina et al. 2012: 81). In the second half of the 20th century, the studio and its focus on 'design', rather than on building, increasingly came to be perceived as an inadequate vehicle for preparing students for professional practice. As the architectural historians Spiro Kostof and Dana Cuff observed, the studio was criticised because it 'oversimplified architectural processes' and maintained a divide between the classroom and 'real life' that was becoming more technological, faced socio-economic challenges and saw the rise of a youth culture preferring non-authoritarian educational processes (Kostof 1986; Cuff 1992). The 1960s and 1970s, as a consequence, witnessed a proliferation of pedagogical experiments in and beyond architectural schools – often undergirded by popular treatises such as Ivan Illich's *De-schooling Society* (1971) and Paolo Freire's *Pedagogy of the Oppressed* (1970).[13] Together with the persisting influence of the learning-by-doing idea professed by individuals such as John Dewey (1859–1952), these treatises created a readiness of mind to expand institutional boundaries, to eradicate the confines of the classroom and to investigate the possibilities of mobile and situational learning. Schools were no longer considered neutral sites, isolated from societal phenomena, but as places where society was (re)produced, challenged and criticised.

Not only the contours of institutional learning were redrawn but also the educational processes. From the 1960s to the 1970s, educators and students initiated small-scale, grass-root experiments and thereby directly engaged with people and acted upon the urban environment in order to (re)shape political or cultural consciousness (Dutton and Mann 1996: 173). In many of these experiments, architecture was not seen as an isolated phenomenon or as the autonomous expression of the architect, but as a service – for example, finding solutions for low-cost housing, offering strategies for community development and user participation. Yet, in the 1970s and 1980s, this role of the architect as a social engineer was also deemed suspicious by some educators, as it reminded them of modernism's unkept promise of social change. Some architect-educators, therefore, called for individual authorship and returned to the paper as a site for spatial exploration. Though both approaches could not be more different, a research and problem-solving attitude – studying for instance use and inhabitation or testing the possibilities of spatial organisation on the 2D paper surface – now prevailed over formulating answers to pre-established solutions.

This preference for processes over finished products in educational practices coincided with a general distrust of objects in architectural discourse. For example, in his 1968 *Theories and History of Architecture*, the architectural critic Manfredo Tafuri reformulated Walter Benjamin's premise that the rise of mechanisation, industrial production and consumer culture compromised the 'aura' of the object (Tafuri 1981 [1968]). As the architectural object lost its 'absolute value' in this process of modernisation, 'meaning lies in the eyes of the observer-user, now a participant', as Tafuri wrote (Tafuri 1981: 84).[14] 'When paintings and architecture are "absorb[ed] into behaviour," they can no longer be spoken of as objects but, have become happenings [...]' (Ibid.). In her analysis of Tafuri's writings, Hilde Heynen argued that what is implicit in this mistrust of the object was a changing attitude towards aesthetic experience (Heynen 2000: 135). Emilio Ambasz, the initiator of the *Universitas* conference – which gathered leading international voices in the field of architectural pedagogy at the MoMA in New York in 1972 – observed a similar bias towards the object in his 1969 article entitled *The Formulation of a Design Discourse* (Ambasz).[15] According to Ambasz, a paradigm shift had occurred in design: 'Configuration and formal proportions' had given way to 'processes' (behaviours, operations, tendencies, relations, changes, etc.) (Ibid.: 58). The consensus was growing that architecture no longer had to produce objects but should give form to a set of recurrent or periodic activities in which results are obtained through interaction, offering a dynamic experience to its viewers and users. The connection of these debates to architecture and design education can hardly be ignored.[16] Instead of determining a design's aesthetic form or manufacturing functional tools and objects, many pedagogic exercises set out to test the *operational performance* of objects.

Organisation of the volume

The chapters in this volume consider how students were schooled in spatial and material processes and how they learned *through* materials. This volume does not offer an exhaustive overview of the materials used in educational contexts in the second half of the 20th century, but instead sets out to show that anything can be a tool or instrument for learning in many different modes. In order to organise these different materialities, we made a tentative 'taxonomy of materialities of schooling', based on Christian Gänshirt's classification of design tools (Gänshirt 2018: 110). Rather than ranking the different case studies based on the different types of materials – objects, tools, sites and technologies of schooling – as we did in the first stage of this project, it 'seems rather the use we make of something, more than the thing we use', that defines the ways we learn (Ibid.). Like Ihde, who stressed the importance of *encounters* with artefacts, Gänshirt described haptic, acoustic, olfactory and gustatory experiences when cataloguing his design tools. We make a similar distinction between visual, manual, synesthetic and audio/visual ways of learning and teaching through materials in this volume.[17]

The most self-evident and most extensive section in this book, that of the visual, entails the study of educational materials – mainly objects or representations – that are perceived through looking. The second section focuses on manual ways of learning. As discussed in the third section, the synesthetic group involves all senses and contributes to an architectural and atmospheric experience for both teacher and student. The body is an essential tool in this group, as it 'carries the organs to perceive a situation simultaneously with the five Aristotelian senses' (Ibid.: 111). The last group is the audiovisual one, which engages the learner through listening (and watching). What the present collection of chapters fully demonstrates is that both explicit theory (in its written form or verbally articulated by the teacher) and implicit theory (such as those gestures, skills and experiences that may remain unarticulated) took an active part in the production and dissemination of architectural knowledge.

Part 1: Objects on display: learning through looking

The chapters in this section deal with so-called 'object lessons'. The term was introduced in the 19th century by the Swiss pedagogue, Johann Heinrich Pestalozzi, to indicate a pedagogy based on *Anschauung* [to look at]. Pestalozzi believed that a child could better understand his or her world most of all by perceiving an object with its senses rather than through words.[18] In this section, the educators discussed all used objects in their teaching practice as a means to demonstrate and visualise architectural and design principles and comment on institutional, pedagogical, cultural and political values.

In his 1969 course, the Dutch architect and Benedictine monk Dom Hans van der Laan (1904–1991) unfolded an 18th-century piece of fabric: the Douglas Tartan. As Caroline Voet shows in *From wooden blocks to Scottish tartans. Dom Hans van der Laan's reconciliation of rational patterns and spatial experience*, Van der Laan asked his students to 'purify their immediate visual environment by surrounding themselves with good examples'. The Tartan became Van der Laan's first urban diagrammatic model to highlight the connection between architectonic space and spatial experience. For Van der Laan, the Tartan pattern incarnated a most objective vision on urbanism, not to say the city's ontology. For him, the Tartan was a *Bild des Wissens*, a conveyer of an abstract architectural syntax, helpful to incorporate the experience of dwelling as well.

In her chapter, *A Walking exhibit. Alfons Hoppenbrouwers's visual pedagogy* Elke Couchez looks at an abstract painting series that was put on display in the architecture theory classroom in the Sint Lucas Institute for Architecture in Brussels by the architect-educator Alfons Hoppenbrouwers (1930–2001) at the end of his career in the 1990s. Hoppenbrouwers's paintings, she demonstrates, were pedagogical vehicles by which he taught his students not only how to understand space perceptually, but foremost how to read architectural history. As such, this chapter sheds light on the tactile, yet tacit production of architectural knowledge in the theory classroom and thus locates architectural history at the intersection of architectural, visual and educational cultures.

In his 1958 lecture at the Ulm School of Design, *The sitting position: A question of method,* the architectural historian, Joseph Rykwert, deployed the chair as part of an object lesson to illustrate central issues associated with design. Paul James argues in his chapter *Clashing perspectives: Joseph Rykwert's object lesson at the Ulm School of Design* that this lecture challenged the ideological underpinnings of the Ulm school and, by extension, the legacy of the Bauhaus. Rykwert identified the limitations of the empirical approach to design research associated with functionalist design. He attacked the anti-historical stance of the Ulm school in favour of a greater engagement with cultural memory and the affective dimensions of design. Next to bringing that explicit message, Rykwert also produced a more covert message. As a dog whistle, scattered throughout the lecture, there were veiled references to the methods associated with the Warburg School where Rykwert had received a part of his training. From one object, a chair, many lessons could be derived.

In *Pancho's passages: framing transitional objects for decolonial education in 1980s South Africa,* the last chapter in this section, Hannah Le Roux interprets objects on display in a school setting. She looks at the material markers left by Amâncio d'Alpoim Miranda 'Pancho' Guedes, professor at the South African architecture school of the University of the Witwatersrand from 1975 to 1990. Nearly 30 years after Pancho retired to Portugal, many of the drawings he had framed and placed in passages on the first floor of a building that housed the Department of Architecture remain. Le Roux argues that the narratives explicitly curated by Pancho in the corridors made public his obsession with collecting. He confronted drawings from discrete colonial and modernist archives with newly commissioned images and models in ways that usurped conventional categories. Le Roux reconstructs and maps the objects' inventory on display and reads their inherent and unstable commentary on colonial and apartheid divisions as a mute but radical strategy of re-education.

Part 2: Hands-on: learning through manual work

In this section, all chapters explore how the student's hand – preparing presentation materials, collages and drawings, and even provisional houses – was the main instrument in acquiring new architecture and design skills.

Anna Vallye examines in her text *Planning problems: data graphics in the education of architects and planners at the Harvard Graduate School of Design, the 1940s,* the student-made presentation materials, and takes us back to the mid-20th-century Graduate School of Design (GSD) which was established in 1936. Here, a set of disciplinary negotiations between design and planning took place during the 1940s. The data visualisation strategies employed by the students, she argues, ultimately served to accommodate within the rubric of 'design' the imperatives of an evolving American planning profession, reoriented to the ends of public administration and the methodology of the social sciences. The Harvard student's mastery of rhetorical and graphic techniques was both a vivid material demonstration of a new language shared by architects and planners and a response to the waning of 'physical planning,' which had previously legitimised connections between the two disciplines.

The text *The Cambridge collage: Dalibor Vesely, phenomenology and architectural design method,* written by Joseph Bedford, explores drawing and collage-making in the studio and in the seminars given at various English institutes by the Czech-born architectural historian, Dalibor Vesely, and positions his educational practice within the theory of representation and the broader debates on the topic unfolding since the 1980s. In particular, Bedford dissects Vesely's poetic theory, which defended the role of drawings as able to unlock a deeper cultural and historical meaning, in the light of the instrumental theory, which was more prominent at that time and which treated the drawing as unable to communicate cultural intentions, being best understood as an instrument for action. Moreover, by examining the studio briefs and work produced by students as the means through which Vesely developed his theoretical position, Bedford discloses the balance Vesely tried to obtain between abstract and communicative expressions in architectural representations. Furthermore, he argues that such analysis reveals how Vesely's conception of representation possessed a political imprint, namely that of a dissident underground art movement in neo-Stalinist Prague, which had a formative influence on Vesely.

In *Little living labs: 1970s student design-build projects and the objects of experimental lifestyles,* Lee Stickells examines five experimental houses, designed and built by students during the 1970s, which sought to reshape architectural education as more operative in post-war environmental and socio-technological debates in the UK, North America and Australia. The UC Berkeley 'Energy Pavilion,' the University of Sydney 'Autonomous House,' the Architectural Association 'Eco-House,' the McGill University 'ECOL Operation' and the University of Minnesota 'Project Ouroboros' were all designed to generate energy, collect and recycle water, treat household wastes and even grow food on site. The basic concept of an infrastructurally autonomous dwelling harboured a range of experimental practices, objects and ambitions. Beginning with the resultant material artefacts, the chapter explores how – beyond the attraction of experiential learning and a heightened familiarity with building construction – these houses allowed students to actively reimagine architecture's scope and their professional agency.

Part 3: Bodies in space: synesthetic learning

In this part of the volume, the authors discover a range of educational practices and settings involving different senses at once, ranging from the body as a tool, to the campus building and the urban fabric. They ask to which extent the environment can function as a 'third teacher', how pedagogies are reflected in educational environments, and how learning was transposed to new contexts outside of the classroom or studio.

The human body is central to all processes of synesthetic learning. In *The body as an ultimate form of architecture. Global Tools Body Workshops,* Silvia Franceschini addresses the body's role as a pedagogical device in the workshops of Global Tools, an experimental design programme founded in Italy in 1973 by the members of the Radical Architecture movement in conversation with members of Arte Povera and Conceptual Art movements. The educational workshops, organised in Milan in 1975 by the architects Alessandro Mendini, Nazareno Noia, Gaetano Pesce and Franco Raggi, considered the body as a principal topic of architecture, as the centre of all the environmental experiences and therefore as a parameter for the planning process. Their performative exercises aimed to subvert the canon of spatial education through the idea of a reverse ergonomics, one fit to cope with ecological and political crises.

In *Parallel narratives of disciplinary disruption: The bush campus as design and pedagogical concept*, Susan Holden analyses the campus as a material setting for learning and as an object through which environmental subjectivity was negotiated. She analyses the innovative pedagogical agenda and distinctive campus design of Griffith University. Established in 1971, this university was part of the coordinated expansion of tertiary education in Australia in the post-WWII decades. Whereas most of the new campuses built in Australia after WWII were in peri-urban locations on greenfield sites, Griffith's bush campus was established in a remnant eucalypt forest, which became an important setting for the pioneering School of Australian Environment Studies. Holden contextualises the history of the bush campus in relation to the development of environmentalism and environmental education in Australia, and alongside the evolution of the concept of environmental design in architecture.

In the last chapter in this section, *Environmental learning revisited: cities, issues and bodies,* Isabelle Doucet argues in the line with feminist scholars that the subjectivities displayed in urban studies have often been ambivalent at best. This chapter considers issues of empowerment, subjectivity, and embodied perspectives when revisiting the fascinating proposals for 'environmental education' as developed by Colin Ward and Tony Fyson, and as published in, among others, *Streetwork. The exploding school* (Ward and Fyson 1973), and *The Child in the City* (Ward 1978). The chapter takes two aspects of environmental education (its material make-up and gender/subjectivity) as a starting point to speculate on the empowering potential of environmental learning for architectural pedagogy, also today.

Part 4: Learning by technologies: audiovisual transmissions

The chapters in this last section trace the impact of technology on the production and dissemination of architectural knowledge. How did technology change the understanding of architecture and enable new pedagogical experiments? In this last part, three authors show that projectors, radios and television broadcasts served specific didactic agendas and, at the same time, were entangled in (shifting) epistemologies.

What the microscope was for biologists, the projector was for art historians. This claim is made by Rajesh Heynickx, who focuses in *In the eye of the projector: Wölfflin, slides and architecture in postwar America* on post-1945 teaching of architectural history by looking at the imprint left by the slide projector. Already around 1900, lantern projectors were part and parcel of art history's efforts to become an ordered, systematic discipline. Specifically, the dual slide projection, popularized by the Swiss art historian Heinrich Wölfflin, made it possible to develop a formal analysis of artworks from different periods. This comparison of illuminated reproductions helped determine the prevailing style of a given period and might even be seen as 'art history's complimentary technological protocol' (Karen Lang). And the double projector marked architectural historiography. The comparative analyses cherished by prolific architectural historians as Sigfried Giedion, Rudolf Wittkower and Colin Rowe, all rooted in the side-by-side images from Wölfflin's apparatus. Yet, this chapter not just unravels how the projector was a linchpin of methodological premises among Wölfflin's admirers. It mostly pays attention to how it affected the discursive economy of those developing alternative views on architectural history, such as the historian and theoretician, Paul Zucker. By doing that, Heynickx reveals how the projector generated a space within which varied discourses could be elaborated and transmitted, launched and modified.

John Macarthur and Deborah van der Plaat focus on the unpublished talks (1930–1970) by the Australian architect and educator Robert Percy Cummings. In *Wireless architecture: Robert Cummings's early radio broadcasts*, they demonstrate how, from the 1930s through to the late 1970s, Robert Percy Cummings (1900–1989), the founding Professor of Architecture at The University of Queensland (1937–1966), wrote and presented a comprehensive series of lectures and radio talks. Aimed primarily at the general public, these considered diverse topics including the role of art in education, climate and architecture, the role of modern architecture in Queensland, architecture as art and the importance of the regions. Consisting of approximately 60 papers/talks, these works remain unpublished. The authors critically examine this body of work and position it within the current understandings of Queensland modernism. This examination will focus on the different audiences for Queensland architecture that Cummings addressed, including the general public, the architectural student and the profession. These 'educational writings', made with a specific media tool in mind, can also inform a larger discussion of his founding of the School of Architecture at UQ in 1937 and its relationship to earlier systems of architecture within Australia (Central Technical College in Brisbane and foundational schools in Melbourne and Sydney) and abroad (AA in London).

The final chapter of this volume, *The captive lecturer*, points to some future education challenges in architecture and design. James Benedict Brown zooms in on a technology to record, archive and replay the content of teaching in higher education: lecture capture. While audiovisual lecture capture has existed for as long as reel-to-reel tape recorders, the tipping point for its penetration into the University came in the last decade of the 20th century, when digital video storage and audio became more cost-effective and space-efficient than analogue recording. Amidst emerging pedagogical research that variously attributes either increased student attainment or reduced student engagement to lecture capture, and in the context of managerial impetus to demonstrate agenda of widening participation, the implementation of lecture capture has become a point of confrontation between the academic and the academy. Borrowing technologies from fly-on-the-wall television, notably pan/tilt/ zoom (PTZ) cameras that can be remotely or automatically controlled to record 'content' in the lecture theatre, lecture capture assumes some of the techniques and cultural implications of Big Brother, in the conceptions of both George Orwell and the hit reality TV show. Brown argues that complaints from academics and trades union representatives posit that recordings may be used not only for educational purposes but also for disciplinary procedures or performance evaluation. The principle of unknowing observation and therefore self-policing of behaviour draws parallels with Bentham's *panopticon*, an analogy strengthened by the name of the market leader in lecture capture, Panopto.

To better understand the origins of lecture capture in the university, Brown unravels the evolution of the technology and explores how both technology and pedagogy have, at different times, driven forward the creation of new hybrid learning spaces. According to Brown, the recent critical reappraisal of distance learning institutions, such as the retrospective of the Open University in the United Kingdom by the Canadian Centre for Architecture (CCA) in 2018, prompts historians of architectural education to explore the formative role of lecture capture and its precedents in design education.

The chapters presented in this volume take a historical approach to understand the way architecture and design educators have involved materialities in their pedagogical practices and how students were schooled in and through matter. The authors sketch a transition from educational practices focused on objects to processes, experimentation, behaviour and research. This understanding of the historical transitions in education becomes all the more pressing in a climate, in which architecture education has become the main player in a knowledge economy, and its pedagogies are often eclipsed by a focus on research and the quest for funding. As Joan Ockman noted, architecture schools model themselves on 'academic-administrative environments in fields such as medicine and social sciences' making optimisation, performance and delivery the main measures to test outcomes:

> The buzzwords of innovation, creativity, sustainability, resilience, and "design thinking" have put architecture departments in the centre of the game, making their research eminently fundable.[19]

This volume calls for an understanding of changing arrangements of knowledge and pedagogy's role in this shifting system of values. Pedagogy can not only be seen as a distinct tool serving academic or monetised agendas, but as a collection of multi-layered, encoded data both dismantling orthodoxies, confirming and contesting epistemological fashions, classroom practices and institutional or ideological agendas. Or to use David Kaiser's words: 'Pedagogy is where the intellectual rubber meets the politico-cultural road' (Kaiser 2005: 2).

Notes

1 The project website can be accessed here: https://radical-pedagogies.com
   Harriet Harriss and Daisy Froud, eds., *Radical Pedagogies: Architectural Education and the British Tradition*, 1st edition (Newcastle upon Tyne: RIBA Publishing, 2015).
2 Seminal in this regard is the volume *Materialities of schooling: Design-technology-object-routines* (Lawn and Grosvenor 2005), especially the introduction on pages 7 to 17. Scholars found a stable footing in this landmark study, and they started to move in terrains diverse as memory studies or gender theory. Following inspiring studies might illustrate this: (O'Donoghue 2010; Fenwick and Landri 2012; Rasmussen 2012; A. Taylor 2013).
3 For more on how the ANT theory might be implemented in research on architecture, one can look at the article (Latour and Yaneva 2008).

Introduction **13**

4 See also Don Ihde. "Material hermeneutics", accessed 10 April 2020, http://humanitieslab. stanford.edu/23/746.
5 This is insightfully discussed in (Grosvenor and Lawn 2001: 105).
6 Rousmaniere's plea for sneaking into the silenced classroom through an analysis of 'fragments and shadows of evidence', formed the methodological premise of an influential volume co-edited by her (Grosvenor, Lang and Rousmaniere 1999).
7 Tucker (2005: 1657).
8 Stated in the blurb on the book's jacket.
9 For a strong evocation of that idea, see (Domanska 2006).
10 The following case study is very illuminating (I. Grosvenor 2010). For a broader view, consult (Grosvenor, Lang and Rousmaniere 1999).
11 See, for instance, Kruft (1994); Nesbitt (1996); Ockman (2000); Hays (2000).
12 This criticism was uttered in, for instance, Banham (1980: 276) and Bannister (1954). See also: Salama (1995: 39).
13 A first Portuguese version was published in 1968.
14 See also Lipstadt and Mendelsohn (1993: 58–103).
15 For further reading on the *Universitas Conference*, see a more recent analysis by Scott (2004).
16 These pedagogic experiments carried out in the 1970s are discussed in two recent books: Stein et al. (2016); Borasi (2016). The latter focuses on the educational experiments of for instance Urban Innovation Group, ILAUD, AMO, IAUS, CUP, ARAU, Kommunen in der Neuen Welt, AD/AA/Polyark and Global Tools.
17 With these four sections, we far from cover all learning experiences in the studio or the classroom. Haptic, olfactory and even gustatory experiences were, for instance, not included. Further study can be done in these areas.
18 This is discussed in Ogata (2013: xiii).
19 Joan Ockman, 'Slashed', *e-flux architecture*, accessed 3 March 2020, https://www.e-flux.com/ architecture/history-theory/159236/slashed/.

References

Ambasz, E. (1969), 'The Formulation of a Design Discourse,' *Perspecta*, 12: 57–70.
Anderson, C. and K. Koehler (2002), *The Built Surface: Architecture and the Visual Arts from Romanticism to the Twenty-First Century*. Ashgate: London.
Banham, R. (1980), *Theory and Design in the First Machine Age*. 1st edition. MIT Press: Cambridge, MA.
Bannister, Turpin C. (1954), *The Architect at Mid-Century: Report. Evolution and Achievement*. Reinhold Publishing: New York.
Borasi, G. (2016), *The Other Architect*. Spector Books: Leipzig.
Çelik Alexander, Z. and J. May (2020), *Design Technics: Archaeologies of Architectural Practice*, University of Minnesota Press: Minneapolis.
Colomina, B., E. Choi, I. Gonzalez Galan and A.M. Meister (2012), 'Radical Pedagogies,' *The Architectural Review*, 232 (1388): 78–82.
Crinson, M. and J. Lubbock (1994), *Architecture: Art or Profession? Three Hundred Years of Architectural Education in Britain*. Manchester University Press: Manchester.
Cuff, D. (1992), *Architecture: The Story of Practice*. MIT: Cambridge, MA.
Daston, L. and P. Galison (2007), *Objectivity*. Zone Books: Brooklyn.
De Vos, E. and P. Lombaerde, eds. (2013), *Van academie tot universiteit: 350 jaar architectuur in Antwerpen*. UPA: Antwerpen.
Domanska, E. (2006), 'The Material Presence of the Past,' *History and Theory*, 45 (3): 337–348.
Dussel, I. (2013), 'The Visual Turn in the History of Education: Four Comments for a Historiographical Discussion,' in T. Popkewitz (ed.), *Rethinking the History of Education: Transnational Perspectives on Its Questions, Methods, and Knowledge*, 29–49, Palgrave Macmillan: New York.
Dutton, T. A. and L. Hurst Mann (1996), *Reconstructing Architecture: Critical Discourses and Social Practices*. University of Minnesota Press: Minneapolis.

Fenwick, T. and P. Landri. (2012), 'Introduction: Materialities, Textures and Pedagogies: Socio-Material Assemblages in Education,' *Pedagogy, Culture & Society*, 20 (1): 1–8.

Gänshirt, C. (2018), 'Drawing Is Not Enough: Design Tools for the Reuse of Modernist Buildings,' *Joelho - Journal of Architectural Culture*, 9: 99–117.

Gatley, J., and L. Treep (2017). *The Auckland School: 100 Years of Architecture and Planning*, School of Architecture and Planning, Faculty of Creative Arts and Industries, University of Auckland: Auckland.

Grosvenor, I. and M. Lawn, K. Rousmaniere, eds. (1999), *Silences and Images: The Social History of the Classroom*. Lang: New York.

Grosvenor, I. (2010), 'The School Album: Images, Insights and Inequalities. L'àlbum de l'escola: Imatges, Introspecció i Desigualtats,' *Educació i Història: Revista d'història de l'educació*, 15: 149–164.

Grosvenor, I. and M. Lawn (2001), *Ways of Seeing Education and Schooling: Emerging Historiographies*. Taylor and Francis: London.

Hays, K. M. (2000), *Architecture Theory Since 1968*. MIT Press: Cambridge, MA.

Heynen, H. (2000), *Architecture and Modernity: A Critique*, MIT Press: Cambridge, MA.

Idhe, D. (1998), *Expanding Hermeneutics: Visualism in Science*. Northwestern University Press: Evanston, IL.

Idhe, D. (2009), *Postphenomenology and Technoscience: The Peking University Lectures*. SUNY Press: New York.

Kaiser, D., ed. (2005), *Pedagogy and the Practice of Science: Historical and Contemporary Perspectives*. MIT Press: Cambridge, MA.

Kostof, S. (1986), 'The Education of the Muslim Architect,' In *Architectural Education in the Islamic World*. Aga Khan: Geneva.

Kruft, H.W. (1994), *History of Architectural Theory*. Princeton Architectural Press: New York.

Latour, B. and A. Yaneva (2008), '"Give Me a Gun and I Will Make All Buildings Move": An ANT's View of Architecture,' In R. Geiso (ed.), *Explorations in Architecture: Teaching, Design, Research*, 80–89, Birkhäuser: Basel.

Lawn, M. and I. Grosvenor, eds. (2005), *Materialities of Schooling: Design, Technology, Objects, Routines*, Symposium Books: Oxford.

Leach, A. and L. Stickells (2018), *Sydney School: Formative Moments in Architecture, Design and Planning at the University of Sydney*, Uro Publications: Melbourne.

Lipstadt, H. and H. Mendelsohn (1993), 'Philosophy, History, and Autobiography: Manfredo Tafuri and the "Unsurpassed Lesson" of Le Corbusier,' *Assemblage*, 22: 58–103.

Loschke, S. K. (2016), *Materiality and Architecture*. Routledge: London.

Lubar, S. and DW Kingery (2013), *History from Things: Essays on Material Culture*. Smithsonian Institution: Washington, DC.

Murray, A. (2015), *Architecture by Hand and Mind: 60 Years of Architecture at UNSW*. University of New South Wales: Sydney.

Nesbitt, K. (1996), *Theorising a New Agenda for Architecture: An Anthology of Architectural Theory, 1965–1995*, 1st edition. Princeton Architectural Press: New York.

Ockman, J. (2000), *Architecture Culture 1943–1968: A Documentary Anthology*. Rizzoli: New York.

Ockman, J. and R. Williamson (2012), *Architecture School: Three Centuries of Educating Architects in North America*. MIT Press: Cambridge, MA.

O'Donoghue, D. (2010), 'Classrooms as Installations: A Conceptual Framework for Analysing Classroom Photographs from the Past,' *History of Education*, 39 (3): 401–415.

Ogata, A. F. (2013), *Designing the Creative Child. Playthings and Places in Midcentury America*, University of Minnesota Press: Minneapolis.

Otero-Pailos, J. (2013), *Architecture's Historical Turn: Phenomenology and the Rise of the Postmodern*, University of Minnesota Press: Minneapolis.

Pickering, A. (1995), *The Mangle of Practice: Time, Agency, and Science*, University of Chicago Press: Chicago, IL.

Rasmussen, LR. (2012), 'Touching Materiality: Presenting the Past of Everyday School Life,' *Memory Studies,* 5 (2): 114–130.

Riello, G. (2009), 'Things That Shape History: Material Culture and Historical Narratives,' In K. Harvey (ed.), *History and Material Culture: A Student's Guide to Approaching Alternative Sources. The Routledge Guides to Using Historical Sources*, 24–49, Routledge: London.

Rousmaniere, K. (2001), 'Questioning the Visual in the History of Education,' *History of Education,* 30 (2): 109–116.

Salama, A. (1995), *New Trends in Architectural Education: Designing the Design Studio.* New Jersey.

Scott, F. D. (2004), 'On the "Counter-Design" of Institutions: Emilio Ambasz's Universitas Symposium at MoMA,' *Grey Room*, 14: 46–77.

Stein, M., L. Miller and M. Henrichs (2016), *Blueprint for Counter Education.* Inventory Press: Los Angeles, CA.

Stern, R.A.M. and J. Stamp (2016), *Pedagogy and Place: 100 Years of Architecture Education at Yale.* Yale University Press: London.

Tafuri, M. (1981), *Theories and History of Architecture.* Icon: New York.

Taylor, A. C. (2013), 'Objects, Bodies and Space: Gender and Embodied Practices of Mattering in the Classroom,' *Gender and Education*, 25 (6): 688–703.

Tucker, A. (2005), 'Objectivity,' In M. C. Horowitz (ed.), *New Dictionary of the History of Ideas*, 4, 1657–1658, Charles Scribner's Sons: Detroit.

PART I

Objects on display
Learning through looking

1
FROM WOODEN BLOCKS TO SCOTTISH TARTANS

Dom Hans van der Laan's reconciliation of rational patterns and spatial experience

Caroline Voet

On 23 November 1968, the Dutch architect and Benedictine monk, Dom Hans van der Laan (1904–1991), explained to his students that they had to 'purify their immediate visual environment by surrounding themselves with good examples', when designing (VDL L10 1968: 12–25) (Figure 1.1). He then unfolded an 18th-century piece of fabric: the Douglas Tartan, as a tool with which to explain the mechanisms of architecture and urbanism. This traditional Scottish woollen cloth, with white, black, and grey horizontal and vertical strips, was chosen as it embodied the specific architectural phenomenon of a three-dimensional spatial disposition. By the 1960s, Van der Laan was a well-known figure within Catholic architectural circles, using his Benedictine background as a foundation on which to develop philosophical concepts of architectonic space, combining these with a design methodology and a proportional system, as well as an austere and elementary architecture (Padovan 1994, Voet 2012, 2017, 2018).[1] Although Tartan patterns were a common design tool in the structuralist methodology of that time, Van der Laan went further by analysing the textile qualities of the fabric itself, as a means of experimenting with different spatial concepts.

FIGURE 1.1 Dom van der Laan giving a lecture. Photograph: Dom Xavier Botte, approx. 1965 (VDLA).

DOI: 10.4324/9781003201205-3

Moreover, as a Benedictine monk with a traditional neo-Thomist or neo-scholastic background living in a rapidly changing world, he mobilised the Tartan as a tool with which to integrate his rational ordering principles with a modern conception of space, one undergirded by sensitivity and empathy.

In what follows, I will develop a reading of the Scottish Tartan by analysing why it was introduced and how it was used as a pedagogical tool. It will be argued that by tracing Van der Laan's words in the classroom, via a broad series of sources such as letters, lecture notes, and publications, the role of the Scottish Tartan as a conveyer of an abstract architectural syntax of the city on the one hand, while enabling the incorporation of experience and dwelling on the other, can be illuminated.

The course in church architecture

Though an architectural approach through fabrics, clothing and sewing patterns might seem peculiar, for Van der Laan, it formed a natural progression from his work in the monastery's vestment workshop. After abandoning his architectural studies in Delft in 1927 to become a Benedictine monk, his initial role at the Abbey of Oosterhout was to produce large quantities of garments. The Benedictine environment of 'ora et labora' (contemplation and work) formed a fertile ground for an approach of study and contemplation in relation to the development of craftsmanship. Van der Laan designed and made several vestments that are still used today in the Netherlands, Belgium, and Italy. Even at the time, he rationalised this *process of making*, by unravelling the origins of clothing through the analysis of traditional Greek garments, redrawing them according to strict proportions. From 1948 onwards, he published his findings in the Benedictine journals *L' Artisan et les Arts Liturgiques* and *L'Ouvrier Liturgique* (1948–1953) (Voet, 2009).[2] Van der Laan gave technical descriptions and guidelines for the application of the correct method for the fabrication of the main liturgical garments such as the alb, the chasuble, the surplice, and the tunic, all following the *Façon Classique*. The pattern designs testify a rationalist approach towards the establishment of autonomous formal principles. In search of the original concept of Thomas Aquinas' concept of 'habitus', Van der Laan aimed to define a timeless primitiveness and austerity. 'Habitus' – or habit – translates as 'to wear', but also 'to have'. Both relate to 'being'. As Van der Laan observed, 'We are as we are dressed' (VDL L5 1950: 2). It is from this perspective that Van der Laan's architectural theories grew, taking 'habitus' as the central analogy of the elemental house. As such, the house as a work of art became itself a source of knowledge (Padovan 1999: 36).

As he had been studying original Greek garments to define general principles, Van der Laan studied Old Syrian basilicas, trying to decode their spatial hierarchy and proportion. His quest to return to the origins of religious architecture was fuelled by an ontology of being, rooted in his neo-Thomist background, which promulgated the belief that formal principles can be grasped by an objective rational ordering principle. Van der Laan regarded the knowing and applying of these universal principles as the general task of the designer, and it defined the architect's craftsmanship. He forcefully opposed the more subjective, phenomenological approach and embraced the *Nouvelle théologie* (French for "new theology"), a school of thought in Catholic theology that arose in the mid-20th century, most notably among certain circles of French and German theologians. The shared objective of these theologians was a fundamental reform of the dominance of Catholic neo-scholastic theology, by replacing an ontology of being with an ontology of becoming, one firmly grounded in experiential feelings (Heynickx 2018).[3] When he started teaching in 1946, Van der Laan told his students that they had to use 'the demands of our ratio when realizing architectural form', as the only means to bring forward 'an objective aspect of a form'. In other words: he remained with his ontology of being, and the rational, deductive path of thinking it was undergirded by. By using one's rational mind, all things coming from God ('exitus') and, in different ways, returning to him ('reditus') could be understood. Nature, as God's creation, remained a mystery and could only be grasped from an architecture that renders suitable for dwelling through its order. This is far removed from a reality that resulted from, or was based on, a mixture of feelings or impressions and therefore caught up in a process of becoming. Above all, Van der Laan's thinking was that of a designing architect, combining rationality with a longing to create order. The built form as such was decipherable and makeable via men's rational capacity (VDL L3 1946: 2).

A quest for rational forms was the driving force behind all of Van der Laan's lectures at Breda and 's Hertogenbosch, where he taught a three-year course on religious architecture in the light of the resurrection of the many destroyed churches.[4] His topics were not the history of religious architecture and liturgy, but the unfolding of a theory of the reading and ordering of space. He would teach several generations of architects until the course stopped in 1973. His lectures, as well as the other courses, exercised a considerable influence on Dutch religious post-war architecture, a style that was referred to as the *Bossche School*. The course took place mainly in the evening or on weekends. Young architects would gather and discuss, and try to define, following Dom Hans van der Laan, the ultimate form suitable for a church through the study of the first Christian religious buildings. Through the course, Van der Laan embarked on his quest for 'fundamental architectural laws' (VDL C3 1946: 2):

> The fact that we gather here, nor to discuss technical aspects, nor liturgical questions, but only to face the pure architectonic side of church building, is already without any doubt a clue for the direction that we shall take in our discussions. (…) What is it about when we build a house?
>
> *(VDL L1 1946: 1)*[5]

The structure and approach of the scholastic framework initiated in his first lectures fulfilled the role of a blueprint for all of his following writings. Every lecture was structured according to 10–15 theorems. In 1960, this series was published as *Le Nombre Plastique*, and in 1977, it resulted in the publication of *Architectonic Space* (VDL 1960, 1977). For Van der Laan, only a well-proportioned building could induce 'a sense of immanence' fitted for prayer, and this essence needed to be taught (Voet 2017). Aiming to define architectural fundamentals, the initial lectures dealt with spatial concepts as inside and outside, and solid and void. He linked these to four principles identified by Vitruvius: order (ordination), arrangement (disposition), proportion (eurythmia), and symmetry (symmetria). In ancient times, symmetry by no means referred to mirror symmetry, as we know it now. It pointed to a certain mathematical harmony and measurable proportions between the sizes of the parts of a building, from the smallest up to the whole. Architecture had to be expressive by defining a clear order: building elements related to each other and to the building through whole numbers, clearly readable and countable through its disposition.

Van der Laan set out to formulate a proportional framework that could enable this symmetry. For him, the decimal system based on the number 10, which could then be divided into a literally symmetrical 5 + 5, proved to be inadequate to design spatial compositions as the ancients defined it. In order to achieve that, he chose the number 7 and divided it into 3 + 4, as the difference between 3 and 4 for him proved sufficient in order to perceive it as a composition of two clearly distinctive forms (Voet 2012). He named the 3 : 4 ratio the 'Plastic Number'; the rational proportion that was fundamental to our discernment and our reading of space. Van der Laan defined the difference between 1 and 7 as the maximum between two forms, so that they still could be related to each other. With these numbers 1, 3, 4, and 7, he started composing hierarchical series. This all remained fairly abstract, until, in 1940, Van der Laan used two wooden blocks with sides that hierarchically interrelate as 3 : 4, his first official teaching tool (VDL C2 1940)[6] (Figure 1.2a). The two wooden blocks are the first of a series of teaching aids that were used as tools in order to explain how space works, and how it can be composed through interrelated whole numbers.

In order to train the architect's discernment, Van der Laan developed a box with a continuous series of 144 bars (Figure 1.2b). With this, he could demonstrate the relations of the plastic number.[7] The first model of a wooden box with ivory sticks was made in April 1952. He introduced it officially as in his lectures in December 1953, comparing it to the ancient Greek and Roman abacus that was used for their calculations (VDL L6 1953: 5). A manual of this abacus was added to the 1960 publication *Le Nombre Plastic*. The only way in which Van der Laan's design methodology could be understood, was by practising it, as learning to play the piano. In the afternoons of the CKA, Early Christian basilicas were analysed (Figure 1.2c) (Butler 1929 and Laprade 1940–1950). Van der Laan and his students went on study trips to France and Italy and measured monuments on site, redrawing them according to the plastic number. They made several analytical models and used them to explain the spatial hierarchy. With these examples in mind, Van der Laan's students had to build up a portfolio, and from that work towards their own designs, which they equally discussed in the afternoon classes. They used charts to translate the series into concrete building measures (Figure 1.2d). All of this training aimed at rationalising the design process itself, the result being a copy of the traditional basilica. Yet, it was not the hierarchically ordered blocks and bars that informed the fluid and perspectival spaces we see pop up in the buildings by Van der Laan and his students from 1955 onwards. For that development, other examples and teaching tools, in which the Tartan played a key role, had paved the way.

Teaching spatial superposition

In 1955, Van der Laan gave his students the assignment to draw up mosques and study the relation between the whole and its parts in three-dimensional axonometric views and series of plans (Figure 1.4). The plans of these monuments are different from the previous analysis by Laprade and Butler. They show interlocking patterns with repetitive figures, seemingly symmetrical but in detail asymmetrical. They formed layers of galleries, surrounding open courtyards or centralised vaults and copulas. In his 1955 lecture, Van der Laan showed a diagram of the Hagia Sophia, interpreting it through its hierarchical architectonic ordinance (Figure 1.3). He denoted two plastic extensions: the thickness of the wall and the overall

From wooden blocks to Scottish Tartans 23

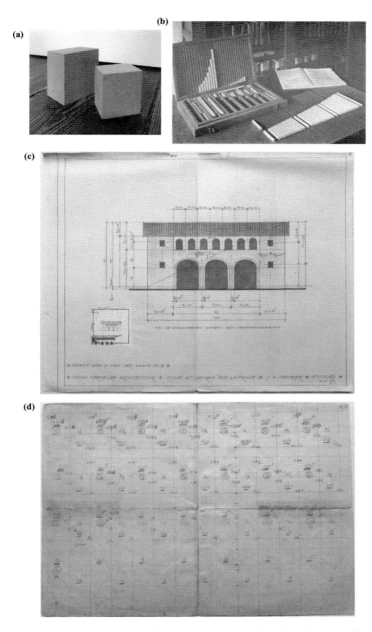

FIGURE 1.2 (a) Dom Hans van der Laan's first study tool to explain the plastic number. Two blocks where length, width, and height interrelate as 3 : 4. The largest measure of the smallest block is the smallest measure of the largest block (Cees Pouderoyen Privite Archives, photograph Caroline Voet). (b) The abacus, the first tool to test the student's discernment, 1967 (VDLA). (c) Course on Church Architecture, Study from 'Croquis' by student architect J. A. Doncker, August 1953, teacher architect Cees Pouderoyen (Cees Pouderoyen Private Archives, photograph Caroline Voet). (d) Scheme with different orders of size with the plastic number, used on the drawing board of teacher architect Cees Pouderoyen (Cees Pouderoyen Private Archives, photograph Caroline Voet).

24 Caroline Voet

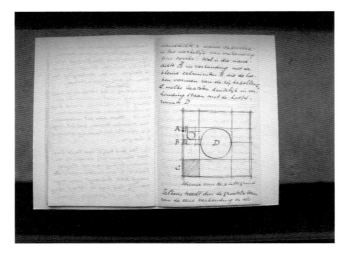

FIGURE 1.3 Notebook from lecture 14, on the Haghia Sophia, 1955, 917 (VDLA).

space. These were connected through several intermediate spaces, realised by side chapels and the cellular column groups:

> Only through the introduction of intermediate terms, it will be possible to achieve this relationship. If the wall as wall has a thickness that cannot enter into relation with its surface, this wall has no plastic value, so that it cannot enter into a plastic relationship with the three-dimensional inner space.
>
> *(VDL L7 1955)*

Van der Laan called this concept of interlocking spaces superposition. He immediately tested it in his own realisation of the crypt for the Abbey St. Benedictusberg in Vaals (1960) (Figures 1.5a–d). Nevertheless, in 1968, he explained to his students why the crypt did not fully achieve the relations of spatial superposition as a three-dimensional effect. In that year, his extension of the church and atrium in Vaals had been completed, and he had taken his students there on an excursion to explain his most recent insights in architectural disposition and the spatial phenomenon of three-dimensionality.

The students experienced the monumental new abbey spaces, which were built out of rough and elementary building blocks without any ornamentation. Series of columns and window rows formed sequences of porticos and in-between spaces, connecting the crypt to the atrium, church, and new entrance area with guest quarters. Wooden finishing and furniture in grey complementary colours complimented thick walls in concrete and masonry. In his guided tour, Van de Laan spoke to his students about the necessity for architecture to be expressive (VDL L10 1968: 4). Architectural design was not about designing in a two-dimensional plan but then to add sections and façades. Designing, he argued, needed to address the relation between mass and space. Architectonic space was not about relating solids to each other; it arose through the spaces that come into being through the solids.

From wooden blocks to Scottish Tartans 25

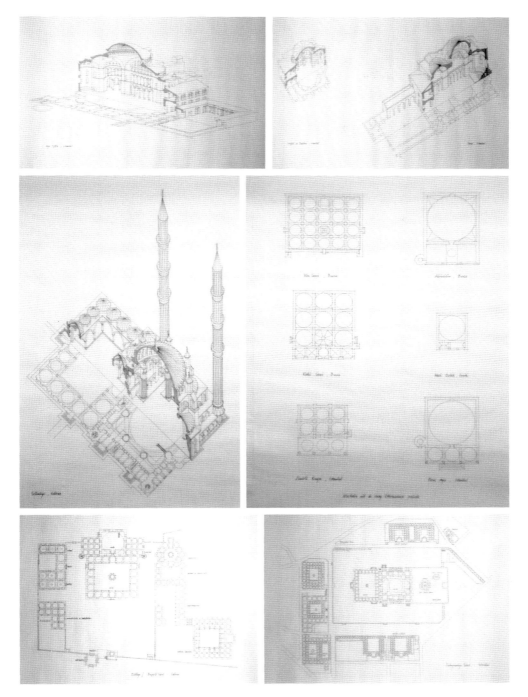

FIGURE 1.4 A series of drawings from mosques. Student architect Jos Naalden, approx. 1960–1965 (VDLA).

26 Caroline Voet

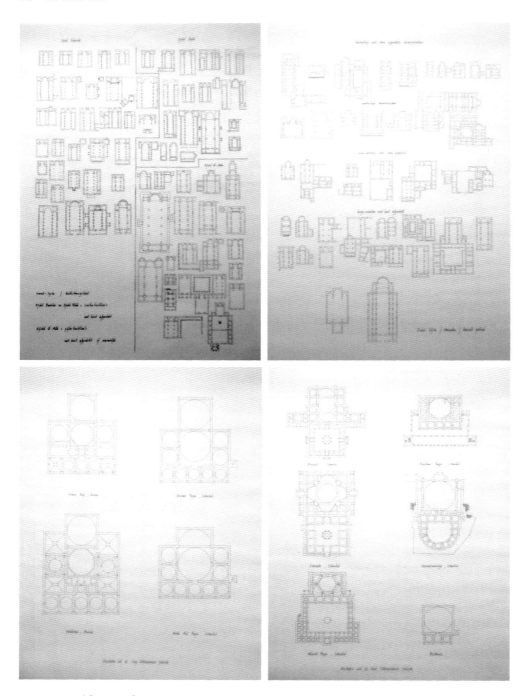

FIGURE 1.4 (*Continued*)

From wooden blocks to Scottish Tartans 27

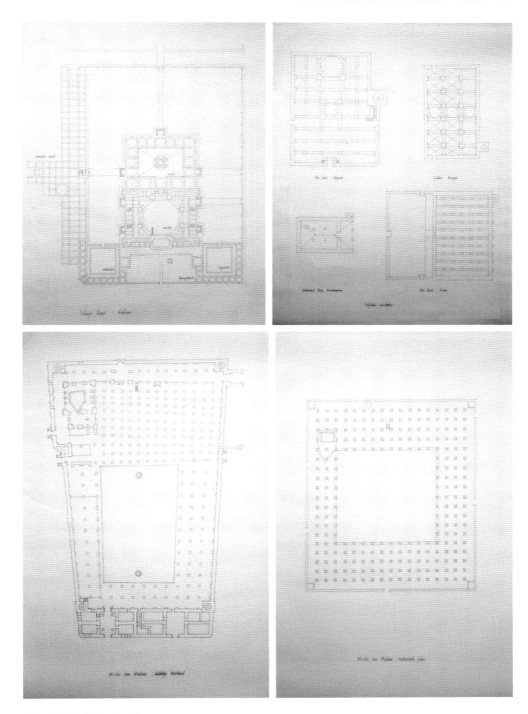

FIGURE 1.4 (*Continued*)

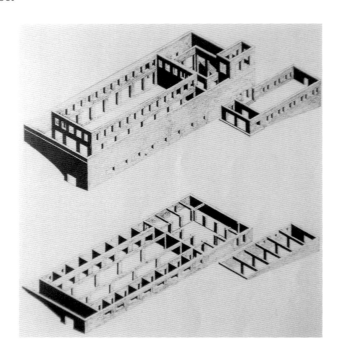

FIGURES 1.5 Abbey St. Benedictusberg, Vaals: crypt (1960), atrium and church (1968). Photograph Caroline Voet, 2008. Isometric drawing of the new extension in Vaals. Dom Hans van der Laan [Source: Dom H. van der Laan, "beschouwingen over het huis," Plan 6 (1972), 55, (VDLA)].

Architects needed to address this three-dimensionality of space by first considering length and width as 'a superior spatial extension', which could then come into contact with the height.

To explain this concept of 'a superior spatial extension', Van der Laan compared the new 1968 realisation to the earlier 1960 crypt. According to him, the crypt was still nothing more than 'a juxtaposition of spaces, as no spaces between spaces come into being'. Within the atrium, this was the case; nonetheless, here, the space was determined in a horizontal sense through galleries. But, in the church, the larger space was 'truly called upon by other spaces' (VDL L10 1968: 9). Here, a series of first spatial embryos arose through the 'standing threshold-space' defined between the pillars, their bay rhythms and lintels, and the back wall. This, in its turn, was repeated on a higher level: the series of spatial cells formed a gallery, and as they were formed, in their turn, they defined a central space. It had two dimensions that accord with the length of the galleries and their mutual position, while the third dimension was that of the height of the spatial cell.

What happened between the intercolumnium and the back wall also arose between this flat 'lying central space' and the higher flat ceiling: it was the formation of the full architectonic space with its three-dimensional definition. 'As such you see the three possibilities, realised one besides the other', Van der Laan explained to his students: 'a juxtaposition of galleries, a frame by galleries and finally a superposition of a total space with a space framed by galleries. The secret of the interplay of three spaces exactly lies within these diverse stages of development' (VDL L9 1968: 17).[8] With this approach, Van der Laan attempted at conveying spatial dynamics that operate on the level of empathy and experience as in the interplay of the spaces a subjective induction seemed to outplay a strict deduction. As a consequence, one could say, Van der Laan went beyond his own rational ordering principle of the Plastic Number. The Plastic Number had perfectly lined up with the ontology of being he had been ingrained with as a student and, that also, he had harshly defended in his course on church architecture. It was an ontological framework he did not want to drop or to replace by the opposite, an ontology of becoming, so present within phenomenological frameworks. Yet, as he wanted to operate outside a strict neo-Thomist ontology, by dismissing subjectivism and presenting his ideas as objective laws, he had to develop a reconciliation. Concretely, he needed a tool, one that would help him to rationalise his concept of an experience driven juxtaposition or superposition of spaces.

The Scottish Tartan

The Tartan cloth enabled Van der Laan to translate a series of empirical findings into more general and abstract principles. It was first introduced in 1966 as an analogy to architecture. In a lecture on architectonic disposition, he explained how a Tartan embodied a whole architecture, as a kind of urbanism, in the plane of the cloth (VDL L8 1966). He claimed that a whole city could be deducted from the primitiveness of its woven threads. He later explained to his students that architecture is as one big game of backgrounds, as can be seen in the Scottish Tartan where the coloured, intersecting bands silhouetted against the background of the 'ground colour' in their turn becoming background for smaller bands (VDL L13 1973: 9). In 1968, six months after the completion of the church in Vaals, he devoted an entire lecture to the analysis of a piece of the Grey Douglas Tartan. He explained the weaving process by comparing it to building:

> The technique of weaving consists in the making of a supple, flat stuff that we call cloth or textile, and this is done with threads that are crossed under and over each other. Thus we make flat clothes out of threads just as an architect puts together walls out of building materials: walls in order to shield living-spaces, cloths in order to cover the body. We therefore create smooth cloth from threads, just as an architect joins together walls from building materials; walls to enclose dwelling spaces, cloths to cover the body (...) Fiber, thread and cloth are the three stages of the technical process; the fiber vanishes into the thread, and the thread in its turn into the cloth. The fiber is derived from nature, the cloth must clothe the human body. This exactly parallels the analysis of the building process we developed in earlier lectures. In each case, the mediating role of the product between the natural and the human is clear. Both the cloth and the house bring about a harmony between man and nature – a harmony that is reflected in the internal harmony of their respective making-processes.
>
> *(VDL L10 1968: 15)*

Nevertheless, his interest reached further than that of an analogue relationship; he addressed the Tartan as a generic pattern, analysing its rhythm and density. He specifically chose the Douglas Tartan, one of the 200 authentic Tartans, for this analysis, as this pattern proved exceptionally strong due to its ambivalence (Figure 1.6a). The ratio of the width of the white to the width of the black strips was 3 : 4, and because of this, Van der Laan claimed that they appeared equal to the eye, testifying of a unique figure-ground relationship. This was in contrast to, for example, the 'Rob Roy', a Tartan of the McGregor clan with equal bands of red and black. Van der Laan explained that one inevitably saw this as a red Tartan with overlaid black strips. However hard he tried, the opposite interpretation, red on black, seemed impossible. The Plastic Number ratio solved this: 'For if we make the dark strip 1/7th wider and the light one 1/7th narrower, so that the ratio of their widths becomes 4 : 3, then the tendency of the light to serve as ground disappears' (VDL L10 1968: 17).

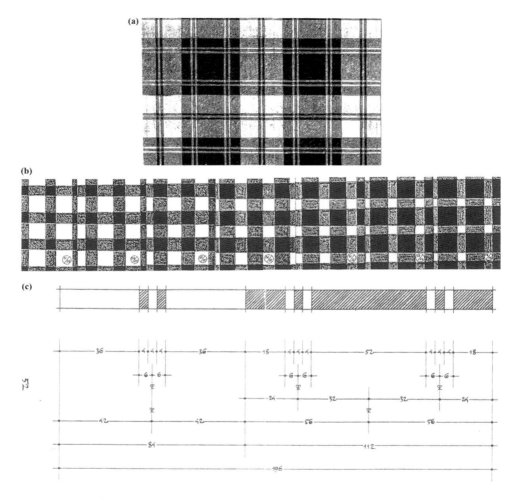

FIGURE 1.6 (a) The Douglas Tartan (VDLA). (b) Analysis of the different layers of the Douglas Tartan (VDLA). (c) Seven compositions of Tartan patterns, changing 1:7th in proportion to each other. The middle one is the Douglas Tartan where the white strips are 24: 56 of the pattern: the most ambivalent for Dom van der Laan, as white and black are equally represented. White : black = 24 : 32 = 3 : 4 (VDLA).

From wooden blocks to Scottish Tartans **31**

To exemplify this effect, he showed a series of Tartan patterns (Figure 1.6b) from left to right, and the white strips were reduced by one-seventh. The ambivalent contrast could be seen in the middle drawing with a proportion between the width of the white strips and their distance centre to centre as 24 : 56 or 3 : 7. White and black then relate as 24 : 32 or 3 : 4. Moving to the left, the dark strips become narrower from 28 : 56, 24 : 56 to 21 : 56. Moving to the right, the white strips become narrower from 24 : 56, 18 : 56 to 16 : 56. From the middle to left and right, the reductions by one-seventh occurred three times, so the figure-ground contrast strengthened equally in both directions. Van der Laan concluded that with a constant centre-to-centre distance of 56 mm, black bands of 21 mm on a light ground had the same strength as light bands of 16 mm on a dark ground. This ambivalence is exactly captured in the Douglas Tartan. It is based on the basic proportion of 3 : 4 for the initial partition into light and dark (Figure 1.6c). The width of the grey is 3/4 of that of the dark, so that the figure-ground relation remains 'undecided'.

So, for Van der Laan, a Tartan showed itself as 'an architecture in miniature', in which several stages could be distinguished. It embodied inside and outside, hollow and solid, and open and closed. Strips that appeared as figure in the first stage could now act as ground for a further partitioning. The figure-ground character of the first stage could be weakened or strengthened by this new partitioning. For Van der Laan, this introduced an interesting potential. In the Douglas Tartan, he detected a second stage created by two pairs of grey strips over the black and of a single pair of black strips over the grey. The ambivalence of the first partition is thereby decisively changed in favour of the black as figure and the grey as ground. This, for Van der Laan, constituted the whole beauty of the Tartan, which he aimed to put forward as a classic example: the power of this change being achieved by a minimum of means.

The black owes its figure-character to the fact that two pairs of grey stripes subdivided it in such a manner that the centre becomes a ground, with around it a border as figure. The pair of black strips divided the grey into two equal halves, which retain their former function as ground. Therefore, in the black zone, two distinct compositions were superimposed, which did not happen in the grey. For Van der Laan, this acquired a stronger value as figure. He also detected a third composition formed by the grey and black lines. Both sets of lines were separated by strips of equal breath to their own, which seemed to be just enough to allow this middle strip to be identified with the original ground, ensuring that the two lines appeared as two adjacent strips and not as a single broad band with a narrower strip superposed. As such, Van der Laan analysed how the exact positions and breaths of the strips played a decisive role in the layered character of the Douglas Tartan.

The Douglas Tartan did not entail a column as its starting point, as did the model of the Haghia Sophia. It was about the crossing of lines and strips, as such offering a multitude of readings through different superpositions. It was not about superimposing space with matter per se, but about superimposing space with space. In a lecture to the Society of Latin Liturgy, Van der Laan confined that by 1969, he mainly used the Scottish Tartan, as it proved an even more direct object than the human habitat with which to clarify to architects that designing was about superposing inside and outside on different scales simultaneously. For him, composing spaces had a profound meaning, comparing it to the Genesis:

> The Genesis of one day needs to be seen as the background of the work for the next day and so on, as the last bright line does with the composition of the Tartan. In

32 Caroline Voet

this vision lies the secret of the unity that arises between the different layers, in the Tartan as in our human existence. It is the unity man seeks in vain when he rejects dualism. They identify the layers as one and the same plane and as the Tartan falls apart in an endless amount of coloured squares, also of our human existence nothing remains.

(VDL L11 1969)[9]

Experiencing architecture and the city

After the blocks and the Tartan, Van der Laan developed a third kind of teaching tool. In order to come closer to rationalising the design of a human architecture, he literally translated the Tartan principle into architectonic spaces, approaching them through human scale in relation to the experience of spatial hierarchy. Although several of his students openly would turn towards phenomenology to reconcile their building practice with a more experience-based approach, Van der Laan never promoted that in his lectures or writings. He only admitted to incorporating one, the book *Mensch und Raum (Human and Space)* by the phenomenologist Otto Friedrich Bollnow (1903–1991), which allowed him to recharge his Tartan concept with experience (Bollnow 1963).[10] Van der Laan claimed to have read Bollnow's book in 1966. It was given to him by his mentor Granpré Molière, who must have recognised that Bollnow's rational models of experience space would potentially be of interest to Van der Laan. Only in 1972 were these concepts introduced in a series of lectures on the human habitat from the scale of dwelling to that of the city (VDL L12 1972).[11]

Van der Laan started out from Bollnow's concept of *Erlebte Raum (Experienced Space)*, and especially his definition of 'experience space' as three interlocking spheres surrounding one's body: the action radius (a sphere around one's body with a radius of the body's length, about 3.5–3.4 metres), the walking field (approx. 25 metres), and the field of eyesight (approx. 175m) (Figure 1.7a). Van der Laan translated these 'experience spaces' literally into architectonic space. The first spatial cell became a cell surrounding one's body (the room), and from that, it grew into larger courts (the building) and domains (terrain or city quarter). This hierarchy related the intimate human scale, defined by Bollnow as the space of one's own body, to the scale of a larger building complex or urban ensemble. Van der Laan's diagrams embodied experience by abstract architectonic elements: cella – court – domain, and he developed a series of nine possibilities, where one became part of the other. The peripheral disposition seemed to be the most interesting condition of superposition: the domain being formed by courts that in turn were formed by cellas.

It is exactly at this point that we see the Tartan as well as the initial diagrams of the Hagia Sophia reappear in an abstract manner, so they could be extended into different urban generic schemes. The Tartan pattern enabled the methodology to extend the human scape of experienced space beyond the borders of a building towards the city. He proved his point for his ideas on peripheral disposition with two city models ordering 144 blocks, which he presented in the exhibition on his work in the Bonnefanten Museum in Maastricht in 1982 (Figures 1.7b and c). Although they both had the same number of building blocks, the peripheral disposition provided more open space through squares than the centrally organised one, in which the open space is more residual. Domains then developed into city quarters around city squares (Figure 1.7d). For Van der Laan, the Tartan pattern therefore helped to formulate a most objective vision on urbanism, representing an architectural ontology of

From wooden blocks to Scottish Tartans   33

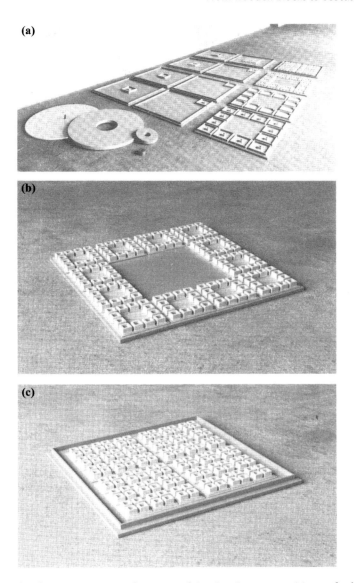

FIGURE 1.7 (a) The three experience spheres, resulting in nine compositions of cella, court, and domain. (b and c) Models 10 and 13. Two urban models, each with the same amount of 144 blocks. (d) Model 46: Several domains grow into bigger city districts around a central town square. (d and e) Model 44b and 45: Extention of House Naalden (1982) into a generic urban piece of fabric. (f) VDL, Architectuur, modellen en meubels, exhibition, and catalogue (Lemiers: Abdij St. Benedictusberg, 1982) (VDLA).

the city. When, in 1983, he reflected on his book *Architectonic Space*, he wrote to his biographer Richard Padovan:

> When the book ends with a city map as a Scottish Tartan, I know very well that such a city in our society could be built nowhere and that I at most can dream of a

FIGURE 1.7 (*Continued*)

monk- settlement in that spirit. Such a plan will always have to bend and deform itself into the circumstances that will occur, like the Tartan is subjected to the falling fold of the outfit. In order to come to that general city plan I had to take all steps of the line of thought one by one, processing again and again all subjective data to a new objective given. So I finally arrived at the objectivity of the number, to then share all previous steps in this highest objectivity.

(VDL C5)

An example of this 'bending and forming' of such a generic plan can be seen in the development of the House Naalden (Best, The Netherlands, 1982) into a generic urban block

(Figures 1.7e and f). The model shows the future development possibilities into a group of houses around courtyards. These schemes, based on the patterns of the Scottish Tartan, would later inform him when he constructed three new convents in Belgium (1975 and 1985) and Sweden (1991).

The Scottish Tartan, one can conclude, can be seen as an important hinging point in a series of attempts to incorporate empathy within a rational and objective ordering principle. It would be Van der Laan's first diagrammatic model, connecting the experience of space through its immediate and human scale to architecture and the city. As an abstract tool, it was used in the classroom to initiate his students into the formation of architectonic space and to mediate ideas on spatial experience and dwelling. All this without giving up an ontology of being. Therefore, a two-dimensional piece of fabric helped Van der Laan to rationalise both spatial three-dimensionality and, not to forget, man's experience.

Abbreviations

AS	*Architectonic Space*
CKA	Cursus Kerkelijke Architectuur (Course on church architecture)
VDL	Dom Hans van der Laan
VDLA	Van der Laan Archief St. Benedictusberg, Vaals (Van der Laan Archives St. Benedictusberg, Vaals)
VDLA C	correspondence of dom Hans Van der Laan, Van der Laan Archives St. Benedictusberg, Vaals
VDLA L	unpublished lectures by dom Hans Van der Laan, Van der Laan Archives St. Benedictusberg, Vaals

Notes

1 Van der Laan studied architecture for three years at Delft before entering the Abbey of St. Paul in Oosterhout. He built four convents and a house: extensions at the Abbey Sint-Benedcitusberg, Vaals, The Netherlands, 1957–1986 (crypt, church, guest wing, atrium, library, gallery), Abbey Roosenberg of the Mariazusters of Franciscus, Waasmunster, Belgium, 1972–1975, Motherhouse of the Mariazusters of Franciscus, Waasmunster centre, Belgium, 1978–1985, Jesu Moder Marias Kloster, Mariavall, Tomelilla, Sweden, 1991–1995 (only first part was realised) and House Naalden in Best, 1982.
2 For example: Van der Laan, Dom H., 'Façon Clasique du vêtement sacré', in *L' Artisan et les Arts Liturgiques*, n4, Abbaye Saint-André-Lez-Bruges, 1948, pp. 265–295, and 'La chasuble pliée ou <plicata>', in *L'Ouvrier Liturgique nr12*, supplement with *L' Art d' Eglise*, nr3, 1952–1951, pp. 55–58 and 'Les linges d' autel', in *L'Ouvrier liturgique,* nr17, supplement with *L' Art d' Eglise*, nr4, 1953, pp. 79–82.
3 For an in-depth study of the role of neo-Thomism in 20th-century art and architecture, more specifically within the Belgian-Dutch Benedictine context, see: Heynickx, 2018.
4 After the liberation of the south of the Netherlands, Dom Hans van der Laan was asked by Bishop Baeten of Breda to lead a group of architects in the building or restoration of churches. After the north of the country was liberated half a year later, Nico van der Laan was asked by Archbishop de Jong to become a study master for a course on religious architecture in 's Hertogenbosch. Together with Kees Pouderoyen, he would be study master.
5 VDL L1. VDL, Werkgroep Kerkelijke Architectuur Breda, Inleiding, 6 April 1946 [Unp. VDLA], 1. 'Het feit dat wij hier bij elkaar komen, niet om over technische zaken, noch om over liturgische aangelegenheden te spreken, maar enkel en alleen om de zuiver architectonische zijde van de

36 Caroline Voet

kerkbouw onder ogen te zien, is zonder meer al een aanwijzing van de richting die wij in onze besprekingen in zullen slaan. (…) Waar gaat het vooral om bij het bouwen van een huis?' English translation by C. Voet.

6 VDL, letter to his brother Nico, 1940 [VDLA]. They express the complex mathematical equation in a simple three-dimensional shape: the sum of two sides is not the next in the series, but the one after that. As such, with two numbers, three numbers in the series are interrelated. For Van der Laan, it embodied the origin of space, the foundation of three-dimensionality.

7 Already, in 1951, he wrote to his brother Nico: 'Through the clarification with the box and the bars, I found the proper manner of explication'. VDL C4. VDL, letter to his brother Nico, 25 November 1951 [VDLA].

8 VDL L9. VDL, Excursie naar de abdijkerk van Vaals, 6 July 1968, Cursus Kerkelijke Architectuur 6, Kruithuis, Den Bosch, p. 17.

> Zo ziet u dus de drie mogelijkheden, die hier naast elkaar gerealiseerd zijn; een juxtapositie van galerijen, een omlijsting door galerijen en dan tenslotte een superpositie van de totale ruimte met een door galerijen omlijstte ruimte. Het geheim van het samenspel van de drie ruimtes zit juist in die diverse stadia van ontwikkeling.
>
> Translation by the author

9 VDL L11. VDL, lezing voor de Vereniging voor Latijnse Liturgie, Amsterdam, 4 February 1969.

> Het scheppingsverhaal van de ene dag moeten wij zien als de achtergrond van het werk van de volgende dag en zo steeds door totdat de mens de hele schepping voltooit, zoals het laatste felle lijntje dat doet bij de compositie van de Tartan. In deze wijze van zien ligt het geheim van de eenheid die tussen de verschillende lagen tot stand komt, zowel in de Tartan als in ons menselijk bestaan. Het is de eenheid die de mensen tevergeefs zoeken als zij het dualisme afwijzen. Zij identificeren de lagen tot een en hetzelfde vlak en zoals een Tartan dan uiteen valt in een oneindig aantal gekleurde vlakjes zo blijft er ook van de eenheid van ons menselijk bestaan niets over.
>
> Translation by the author

10 Van der Laan had read the book in 1966. He explains this in a letter to Richard Padovan, dated 26 October 1983 [VDLA]. He wrote to Padovan that he had received the book in 1966 from Granpré Molière. The author used: Bollnow, Otto Friedrich, *Human Space*, translated by Christine Shuttleworth, Joseph Kohlmaier (ed.) (London: Hyphen Press, 2011), 267.

11 VDL, CKA 7, Het menselijke verblijf in stedelijk verband, 21 October 1972.

References

Unpublished sources

Van der Laan, dom Hans, correspondence (VDLA C):

VDL C2. VDL, letter to his brother Nico, 1940 [VDLA].
VDL C3. VDL, letter to his brother Nico, 9 September 1946 [VDLA].
VDL C4. VDL, letter to his brother Nico, 25 November 1951 [VDLA].
VDL C5. VDL, letter to Richard Padovan, 15 August 1983 [VDLA].

Van der Laan, dom Hans, unpublished lectures and course material for CKA (VDLA L):

VDL L1. VDL, Werkgroep Kerkelijke Architectuur Breda, Inleiding, 6 April 1946 [Unp. VDLA].
VDL L3. VDL, Werkgroep Kerkelijke Architectuur Breda, vijfde les, De verhouding, 25 May 1946 [unp. VDLA]: 1–2.
VDL L5. VDL, Report of a talk between Father Talma and VDL, 7 July 1950 [unp. VDLA]: 2.
VDL L6. VDL, CKA2, Het type van grootte, 12 December 1953 [unp. VDLA]: 5.
VDL L7. VDL, Veertiende les over het plastische getal of de architectonische ordonnantie: expressiviteit, Kruithuis, 7 and 21 May 1955 [unp. VDLA].

VDL L8. VDL, CKA 4, Vierde les over de architectonische dispositie, 5 March 1966 [unp. VDLA].
VDL L9. VDL, Excursie naar de abdijkerk van Vaals, 6 July 1968, Cursus Kerkelijke Architectuur 6, Kruithuis, Den Bosch: 4, 9, 17 [unp. VDLA].
VDL L10. VDL, Over een Schotse Tartan, 23 November 1968, Cursus Kerkelijke Architectuur 6, Kruithuis, Den Bosch, p1. English translation also published in: Dom Hans van der Laan ea, Living and Correspondences, From a Conference Held at the Royal Botanic Garden, Edinburgh, on 17 an 18 November 2000 in Consideration of the Work of Dom Hans van der Laan, Henry Moore Foundation External Programs, Abdij Sint – Benedictusberg Vaals and Inverleith House: 12–25.
VDL L11. VDL, lezing voor de Vereniging voor Latijnse Liturgie, Amsterdam, 4 February 1969 [unp. VDLA].
VDL L12. CKA 7, Het menselijke verblijf in stedelijk verband, 21 October 1972 [unp. VDLA].
VDL L13. VDL, Algemene lesdag 16 juni 1973: ruimte, vorm en kwantiteit: 9 [unp. VDLA].

Published sources

Bollnow, O. F. (1963), *Mensch und Raum*, Stuttgart: W. Kohlhammer GmbH.
Butler, H. C. (1929), *Early Churches in Syria, Fourth to Seventh Centuries*, Leiden: Brill.
Heynickx, R. (2018), Epistemological Tracks: On Religion, Words, and Buildings in 1950's Belgium, in: Rajesh Heynickx and Stéphane Symons (eds.), *So what's New about Scholasticism? How Neo-Thomism Helped Shape the Twentieth Century*, 48–59, Berlin: De Gruyter.
Laprade, A. (1940–1950), *Architectures de France à travers les croquis d'Albert Laprade*, Paris: Vincent Fréal et Cie (des albums différents par région).
Padovan R. (1999), Abstraction and empathy, in: Padovan, R. (ed.) *Proportion, Science, Philosophy, Architecture*, London: Spon Press.
Padovan, R. (1994), *Dom Hans van der Laan, Modern Primitive*, Amsterdam: Architectura & Natura.
Van der Laan, H. (1960), *Le Nombre Plastique, Quinze leçons sur l' ordonnance architectonique*, Translated by Dom Xavier Botte, Leiden: Brill.
Van der Laan, H. (1977, 1983 (2, revised), 1992 (3, revised), 1997 (4)), *De Architectonische Ruimte. Vijftien Lessen over de Dispositie van het Menselijk Verblijf*, Leiden: Brill. (VDL, AS).
Voet, C. (2009), Dom Hans van der Laan en zijn publicaties over kerkelijke architectuur in *L' Art d'Eglise*, in: Dominique Bauer and Mikael Bauer (eds.), *Cum tanta sit in amicitia vera perfectio, (Liber Amicorum for Prof. Em. Raoul Bauer)*, 102–133, Kapellen, 2009.
Voet, C. (2012), The Poetics of Order. Dom Hans van der Laan, *Architectural Research Quarterly 16*(2): 137–154.
Voet, C. (2017), Dom Hans van der Laan's Architectonic Space: A peculiar Blend of Architectural Modernity and Religious Tradition, *MIT Press 22*(3): 318–338.
Voet, C. (2018), Between Looking and Making: Unravelling Dom Hans van der Laan's Plastic Number, in: Matthew A. Cohen and Maarten Delbeke (eds.), *Proportional Systems in the History of Architecture. New Approaches and Considerations, Architectural Histories*, 463–492, Leiden: Leiden University Press, 2018.

2

A WALKING EXHIBIT

Alfons Hoppenbrouwers's visual pedagogy

Elke Couchez

Introduction

On spring days in the year 2000, one could at set times see a man with a firm posture and silver threads among his grey hair going up the Rue Rogier in Brussels with a painting under his arm. Alfons Hoppenbrouwers (1930–2001), an engineer architect-painter, now and then, selected an abstract geometric painting in his studio and discretely carried it outside on the streets (Figure 2.1). Every painting carried along by Hoppenbrouwers was characterised by a colourful, considered abstract play of geometrical forms and lines. An onlooker could have made references to the hard-edge painting style and geometric abstraction, which were popular in Belgium in the 1960s (Mertens, Geirlandt and Warie 2001).[1] Another passer-by could have detected visual parallels with the early 20th-century compositions created by Bauhaus masters such as El Lissitzky, László Moholy-Nagy and Josef Albers for whom geometrical shapes were instrumental in an ongoing investigation into the perceptual organisation of space.

As an inveterate smoker at the end of his career, Hoppenbrouwers had to take a short break at the crossroads when climbing Rue Rogier, pausing in between the two educational institutes where he developed his personal and professional activities. Looking in the direction he came from, he saw a neo-Gothic brick building: Sint Lukas Institute's signature style in its start-up phase. As a member of the congregation *Broeders van de Christelijke Scholen* [Brothers of the Christian Schools], he had his private apartment and studio in this secondary school for the arts. After finishing his architectural engineering studies at the KU Leuven in 1959, he configured the curriculum for the newly established Sint-Lukas Secondary School for the Arts [Artistieke Humaniora], housed in this neo-Gothic building. In the post-war period, this school disengaged from its neo-Gothic legacy and, under the direction of Brother Urbain, took careful steps towards a 'mild modernism'.[2] Hoppenbrouwers joined this train of reform by introducing modernist and avant-garde architects to his pupils and establishing a new course called 'Vormleer' that was part of an introductory course on the plastic arts.[3] This course had strong similarities to Johannes Itten's preliminary course or *Vorkurs* at the Bauhaus (1919–1923).

DOI: 10.4324/9781003201205-4

FIGURE 2.1 Picture of Alfons Hoppenbrouwers. CIVA Brussels - Sint-Lukas Archief.

Looking across the street, Hoppenbrouwers saw the former functionalist modernist Meurop furniture store, which recently had been reconverted into an architecture school for the Higher Sint Lucas Education (Coomans 2012: 81). After catching his breath at the crossroads, Hoppenbrouwers entered this six-storey concrete building and carried his painting into his architecture theory class, where he placed it on the floor, leaning to a table leg. During these classes – which he taught from 1972 until he died in 2001 – Hoppenbrouwers discussed the colours and the constructive principles of his paintings. Many of Hoppenbrouwers's former students still remember him as a mentor and a man of few words, who, if he spoke, often used enigmatic sentences. His peers and former students often described him as a somewhat eccentric and strong-willed friar *and* scholar, always searching for a theoretical approach to architecture.

A social biography of the object

Though Hoppenbrouwers was a colourful and memorable figure, it remains a significant challenge to analyse in greater detail the mechanisms of knowledge transfer in the intimate context of the studio and the theory classroom. This chapter aims to find an entrance to a past place of knowledge transfer, not only by studying written documents and oral testimonies but also by looking at the objects carried into and used in the classroom. As this chapter will demonstrate, these are material witnesses of the different knowledge production and dissemination processes. But how to study these objects?

My analysis of Hoppenbrouwers's paintings will move beyond an iconographic approach that mainly focuses on interpreting content of artistic images, or on tracing stylistic influences. Moreover, an iconographic approach could not fully explain the shifting functions and layered meanings of Hoppenbrouwers's painted objects. As Ian Grosvenor (2010: 155) noted, objects accumulate different meanings during the course of their existence and enter into relationships with new contexts and audiences. As they are moving through time and space and from context to context, these objects need a 'social biography'. This chapter proposes constructing such a social biography of the paintings by following them in two different productive contexts: (1) by going into Hoppenbrouwers's painting studio in the convent and (2) by entering into the theory classroom. The first part zooms in on Hoppenbrouwers's studio, in which the architect-painter created more than 600 paintings between 1993 and 2001. And by entering the theory class in the second part of this chapter this artistic endeavour will be situated within Hoppenbrouwers's broader theoretical and pedagogical project.

A studio visit

Being an attendant, Hoppenbrouwers or Friar Veron, as he was renamed after entering the congregation, moved into a room in the complex near Rue Rogier, immediately after obtaining his engineering diploma at the Faculty of Applied Science of the University in Leuven in 1959. His room in the convent facilitated all sorts of activities. It was a personal flat, a working room and a painting studio. Hoppenbrouwers gathered his confidants in this intimate setting: colleagues and some of his favourite students, from whom he bought the best works. Being part of the same intellectual community, and sharing the same prior knowledge, they discussed mathematic principles and aesthetic concepts. A studio visit in the 1990s was a celebration of the senses: watching and discussing new paintings, listening to some late-polyphonic music and sipping a glass of wine in a halo of smoke (interview with Guy van Kerckhoven, 26.06.2013). With one of his regular visitors, the gallery owner Marleen van Waeyenberghe, Hoppenbrouwers discussed the formal characteristics of his paintings and they agreed that the paintings could be labelled as 'neo-geometric'.[4]

A researcher today, who wants to know why Hoppenbrouwers was compulsively painting after having developed a career as an architect, does not have the benefit of lively conversation in the studio. However, some photographs kept at the Sint-Lukas archives in Brussels afford a glimpse into the studio's productive place (Figure 2.2). Though a photograph can

FIGURE 2.2 Alfons Hoppenbrouwers's painting studio. CIVA Brussels – Sint-Lukas Archief.

never enable the researcher to re-enter a past space completely, it can, as Mary Jane Jacob wrote in *The Studio Reader* (2010: xi), show the traces of artistic activity: 'Even when the making is not so visible, it is always present'. From this picture, which shows the studio as a space for making and displaying, we can sense the presence of an artist, who was deeply engaged in his artistic practice. Central in the photograph is Hoppenbrouwers' painting table. It holds the brushes and tins of paint and accumulates the residues of a thorough search of the artist for a well-balanced composition. On this table, the painter delineated his composition in tape with almost mechanic accuracy. The uncovered areas were subsequently opaquely coloured in acrylic paint, enabling the total conflation of figure and ground. Each painting hanging on the studio wall was part of a larger series by which Hoppenbrouwers explored, tested and developed spatial relations on the flat surface. In some paintings, he was looking for a harmonious composition, whereas, in other ones, he tried to expand the principles of order and organisation utilising different superposing planes. One can see how Hoppenbrouwers was struggling in each painting with how to translate spatial constellations onto a 2D surface. He used contrasting colours, and played with opaque and transparent fields by mixing colours. And he applied and tested basic rules of perspective or on the contrary, strove for absolute flatness.

Painting as searching

Hoppenbrouwers developed a 'research' mentality through painting. At least, this shows from his letter correspondence and his sketchbook annotations. The artist Lieven de Boeck, trained as an architect at the Sint Lucas Institute in Schaerbeek in the period between 1989 and 1994, reflected on the paintings in a letter to his former mentor Hoppenbrouwers:

> I take the liberty, without giving a value judgement, to interpret your work as research schemes instead of thinking about it as paintings. This observation enables me to take a distance and see the aims of the new geometry more clearly. I think it is a pity, but I also understand that you do not make annotations. The writing of a book may take a lot of time but can also give time.
>
> *(Letter of Lieven de Boeck, 13.04.1998. CIVA Brussels – Sint-Lukasarchief)*

At the very start of his painting career, in an exhibition yearbook of 1993, Hoppenbrouwers wrote that form is not merely substance. Painting for him was a 'possibility, an emanation of something that potentially can become something else'.[5] This searching mentality also surfaces in his sketchbooks which are filled with mathematical procedures. The compositions of his paintings are generated by the repetition, extension and translation of existing mathematical formulas that he found in music scores (Goossens and Labarque 2002) and in the canonical architectural plans of Palladio Perrault, Le Corbusier and Eisenman (Figure 2.3).

In the final years of his life, Hoppenbrouwers reflected on his trajectory as a painter in a letter correspondence with the Belgian composer Frans Geysen (°1936) known for his repetitive rhythmic structures. Looking at his painted oeuvre in retrospect, Hoppenbrouwers wrote to Geysen that all visual experiments contributed to one mission: the visualisation and testing of a new spatial concept that he called the 'discoherent' space. This space was no

42 Elke Couchez

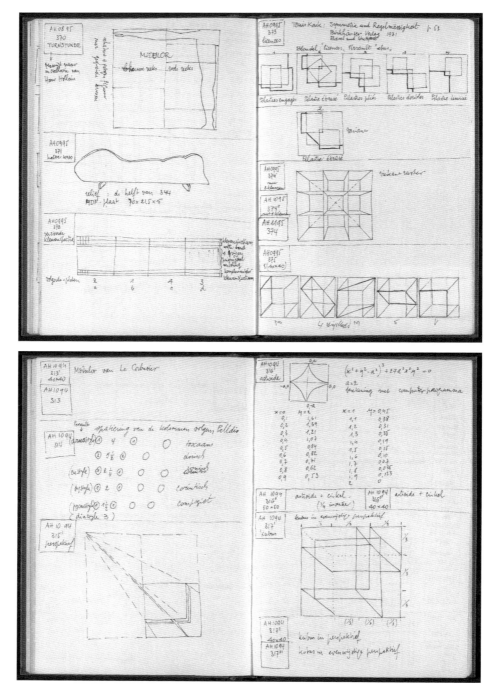

FIGURE 2.3 Calculations after canonical works. Sketchbooks are kept at Sint Lukas Archives Brussels.

longer governed by the 'hierarchic' and 'obstructing' logic of Euclidean forms but embraced chaos as an organisational principle. The painter concluded his letter with an open question:

> Under the influence of your music, I did a couple of repetitive works. I see them as intermediate steps towards the discoherent space that I have been searching for. But how to reach discoherence through rational systematics? That is still not clear to me.
> *(Letter from Hoppenbrouwers to Frans Geysen, 21.07.1998.*
> *CIVA Brussels – Sint Lukasarchief)*

Rather than offering an escape route from his religious life, Hoppenbrouwers's artistic project seems to be a continuation and reformulation of his earlier trajectory.[6] Working in the convent's dense climate, Hoppenbrouwers for a long time suppressed his artistic ambitions but ultimately found in painting a way to strengthen his religious practice.[7] Looking at the careful and devoted execution of the displayed artworks in the studio, we can assume that the painting activity functioned as a kind of spiritual silent time, part of the convent's daily routine. The exercises in scale and proportion, in which Hoppenbrouwers searched for universal – transcendental even – spatial constellations on the flat surface, might thus be seen as spiritual gymnastics. Hoppenbrouwers's studio can thus be considered as a laboratory for generating and testing spatial concepts. Consequently, the artist studio also began to function as an antechamber for his pedagogy based on these spatial concepts. Hoppenbrouwers wanted to bring into the classroom and pass on to his students this specific mentality of exploring and testing spatial concepts through design.

Into the classroom

Hoppenbrouwers's paintings played a central role in his final theory course, taught in the year 2000. Pointing to one of his paintings, the teacher asked his students if they liked the colour or the composition of the painting. He drew constructional drawings in chalk on the blackboard to explain its organisational principles (Heynickx 2012: 22). But how were these formal explorations on the two-dimensional canvas of assistance in the architecture theory class? Wim Goossens, a former student and current teacher at the institute, recalled:

> After the first lesson, most of the students believed that this discussion of the painting was a passionate, yet informal explanation about the artworks' construction and perception. Yet, throughout the course, these paintings were illustrative of something that we can call an "ontological approach of architectural space".
> *(Interview with Wim Goossens, 04.02.2015)*

In his theory course, Hoppenbrouwers discussed modernist buildings and talked about recent architectural realisations.[8] A list of case studies included Le Corbusier's early works, the space-place contradiction in Aldo Van Eyck's works and the Aronoff Center by Eisenman.[9] In a memorandum of 1978, Hoppenbrouwers explained the goals and methods of this theory course. He regarded architectural theory as an autonomous discipline that could offer a broad and systematic knowledge of the field.[10] For him, theory of architecture was 'more

44 Elke Couchez

than a theory of architecture. [...] It is meta-architecture. It both involves information, programming and politics'.[11] The only way to understand and change the current context, he argued, is by seeing it as a continuation of the past. Therefore, he started his course by discussing the evolution – he called it 'revolution' – of modernist avant-garde space concepts such as the idea of 'space-time' to postmodernist space concepts in which notions such as 'fragmentation' and 'dislocation' were central.

A 'revolution' of spatial concepts

To summarise his theory course, Hoppenbrouwers produced a quick little diagram, as we can see in the student notes[12] (Figure 2.4). Architectural modernism seemingly indicated a 'turning point' in architectural history. Modernism was the phase that followed upon classicist architecture and at its turn was eclipsed by the moment of the 'ongoing now', the time of postmodern thinking. In Hoppenbrouwers's diagram, each rough time slot brought forth a specific space concept, propagated by an agent-architect. The sixteenth century classicist architect Andrea Palladio stood for the idea of 'place'. Le Corbusier's *Villa Stein* (1927) in Garches was put forward as a paragon of modernism, propagating the modernist concept of 'space-time'. And the postmodern architect Peter Eisenman got identified with the deconstruction of previous space concepts (Figure 2.4).

Whether we cannot say with any certainty that Hoppenbrouwers's artistic production ran in parallel to his theory courses, it developed along a similar three-phase historical sequence. A glance through his notebooks shows that he had been testing out this sequence of spatial concepts in his painting practice since 1993. The painted oeuvre can be organised into three major categories, each materialising a specific space-concept: the classical place, the modernist time-space and the postmodern dissipative space.

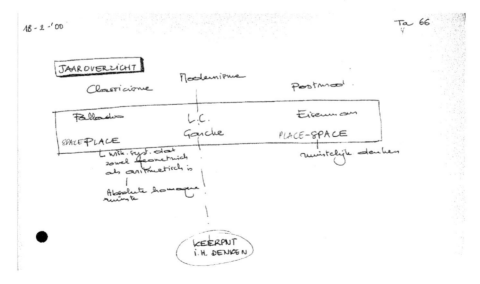

FIGURE 2.4 Diagram from the course on Architectural Theory, 2000. Personal Archives Wim Goossens.

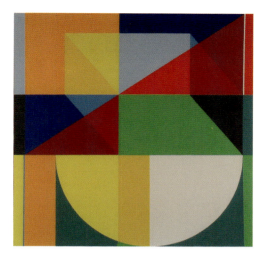

FIGURE 2.5 Alfons Hoppenbrouwers, AH 1093 no. 0254 (1993). 100 × 100. Picture by Bart Hollanders. CIVA Brussels - Sint-Lukas Archief.

Both Hoppenbrouwers's theory course and his artistic production started with exploring the so-called 'classical space', celebrating the beauty of proportion and symmetry. In a sketchbook of 1993, Hoppenbrouwers tried to trace musical sequences and intervals in Palladio's designs after having read Rudolf Wittkower's ([1949] 1998) *Architectural Principles in the Age of Humanism*. In this study, Wittkower studied how Palladio 'translated' harmonical musical ratios into architectural proportions. The results of this reading are geometrical paintings based on the quint interval (Figure 2.5). Colin Rowe's seminal essay *The Mathematics of the Ideal Villa* instigated the revival of Palladio in the 20th century. This text, in which Rowe ([1976] 1982) traced the harmonious rhythm of mathematical units in modern architecture back to Palladio's neoclassical designs, ultimately led to the reassessment of history in architectural design. Hoppenbrouwers's numerous sketches and painted interpretations of Palladio's *Villa Rotunda* (1567) illustrate this search for the organisational principle of proportion.

In another series of works, Hoppenbrouwers developed his ideas on the perceptual organisation of space and connected them to the prevailing discourse on 'transparency'. In some of his paintings, he questioned the characteristics of the mid-century modern art and architecture by exploring the concepts of 'interpenetration', 'superposition' and 'space-time'. He picked up these terms from Robert Slutzky's and Colin Rowe's influential essay *Transparency: Literal and Phenomenal* (1963) in which they analysed how space is implied in architectural form and painting.[13] In his works from 1993 to 1998, Hoppenbrouwers tested some basic perceptual principles by overlaying or superimposing planes. By layering geometrical figures on top of each other, the paintings created an idea of simultaneity of vision (Figure 2.6). Literal visual references to the Bauhaus master, Josef Albers, and more specifically to his 1950s *Homage to the Square* painting series, should come as no surprise in this context (Figure 2.7). Albers's referential book *Interaction of Color* ([1963] 2006) was a significant resource on colour for art educators and, most probably, offered theoretical support for Hoppenbrouwers's plastic experiments on figure-ground relations.

FIGURE 2.6 Alfons Hoppenbrouwers, AH 1092 no. 0216 2/3 (1992). 100 × 100. Picture by Bart Hollanders. CIVA Brussels - Sint-Lukas Archief.

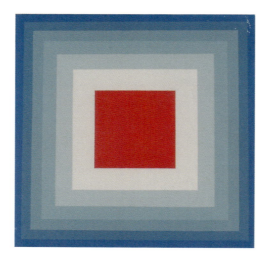

FIGURE 2.7 Alfons Hoppenbrouwers, AH 0500 no. 0595' (2000). 40 × 40. Picture by BartHollanders. CIVA Brussels - Sint-Lukas Archief.

The scheme at the end of Hoppenbrouwers's theory course demonstrates his belief that the ordered classic space and the modernist time-space were both entirely overshadowed by a new, 'potential' visual regime. Already, in 1993, he made the work *A.H.10.93 257 Contra-construction for Palladio* (Figure 2.8). This painting, as he wrote in his notebook, criticised the 'classical mechanics of the Newton-world'.[14] Using and inverting Peter Eisenman's *L-shapes*, Hoppenbrouwers wanted to gain control over this spatial concept that was still under development.

Abandoning the idea of the universality of vision propagated in modernist architecture, the new architectural space resulted from a deformation process. Basic geometric shapes, such as the square, were subjected to the dynamics of compression and inversion. In 1998, Hoppenbrouwers noted down a question in his sketchbook: 'Is it possible to paint a 'dissipative' space, a space beyond the realm of the visible?'.[15] From then on, he tried to push the limits of spatial representation even more by using concepts such as 'multilinearity', 'the fold' and 'discoherence' (Figures 2.9–2.11). He was looking to express 'a non-unitary space' and further explained: 'this dissipative space is a complex, unearthed, decentred space that only becomes visible and readable in the abstract image'.[16]

FIGURE 2.8 A.H.10.93 257 Alfons Hoppenbrouwers, AH 0500 no. 0595', Contra-construction for Palladio (2000). 40 × 40. Picture by Bart Hollanders. CIVA Brussels - Sint-Lukas Archief.

FIGURE 2.9 Name unknown. 40 × 40. Picture by Bart Hollanders. CIVA Brussels - Sint-Lukas Archief.

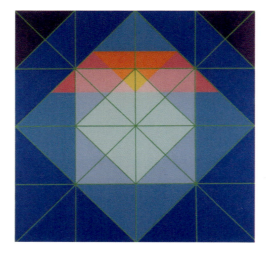

FIGURE 2.10 Alfons Hoppenbrouwers, AH 0000 no. 0141 (2000). 100 × 100. Unfolded paper boat. Picture by Bart Hollanders. CIVA Brussels – Sint-Lukas Archief.

FIGURE 2.11 Alfons Hoppenbrouwers, AH 0797 no. 0475 (1997). 100 × 100. Picture by Bart Hollanders. CIVA Brussels – Sint-Lukas Archief.

Rethinking space and time

As Nancy Stieber (2006) and Łukasz Stanek (2012) argued in their dialoguing texts, architectural discourse struggled to reach a consensus about the centrality of the concept of space as a guideline for architectural knowledge in the 20th century. Whereas space was an essential feature of architecture in the interwar period, 1960s voices influenced by the so-called 'spatial turn' questioned the abstract space concept of the Modern Movement. These voices borrowed from French theory and social studies and claimed that space is not a homogenous, passive entity governed by universal laws, but is socially produced by various practices.[17] Whereas Hoppenbrouwers at no point explicitly referred to these debates, his artistic project and design pedagogy give testimony to this struggle of coming to grips with these charged notions of space and time.

In line with the ongoing criticism on the space concept of the Modern Movement, Hoppenbrouwers sought to express a spatial regime resulting from many interacting forces. Hoppenbrouwers's course notes and sketchbooks show that the conceptual driving force that brought Hoppenbrouwers to depict a new spatial shift was the notion of 'dissipative structures'. This concept was developed by the Russian–Belgian physical chemist Ilya Prigogine and described how chaos, chance and unpredictability are at the base of specific structures (Nicolis and Prigogine 1977). Prigogine's nomination for the Nobel Prize and his collaboration with the Belgian philosopher Isabelle Stengers created a knock-on effect in 20th-century science (Prigogine and Stengers 1988). Nature was no longer considered governed by modernity's absolute laws but as a relative, dynamic and uncertain phenomenon. By borrowing ideas from Prigogine's complexity and chaos theory, Hoppenbrouwers acknowledged the 'multiple, the temporal and the complex', which were landmarks for postmodern science in general (Gaus and Kukathas 2004). Nonetheless, this idea of 'multiplicity' is only expressed intuitively and through a formal play. The painter never fully engaged with the debates on the spatial turn by, for instance, analysing how architecture is interrelated with social and political phenomena.

Hoppenbrouwers's paintings can be approached as pedagogical vehicles with which to understand space perceptually and rekindle time in the theory class. By referring to historical precedents, the painter–educator implicitly broke with a dominant rationale in architectural education. Unlike the Bauhaus pedagogues, his pedagogical project was not based on the training of the 'innocent eye and hand', but on nourishing the 'knowing mind'. Hoppenbrouwers thereby contradicted the modernist idea that the abstract painting could refer to nothing but itself and instead put forward history as a reference point for artistic production.

It must come as no surprise that Hoppenbrouwers took part in postmodernist discourses that gave rise to such historical awareness in the late 1970s and 1980s and which impacted architectural education at large. The Texas Rangers, for instance, hired Colin Rowe to teach a history course *in* the design studio (Stanford 1999; Heynen and Jonge 2002; Keyvanian 2011). As Hilde Heynen (2002: 339) noticed, this new historical consciousness played out 'as a reconsideration of the modernist heritage, in buildings and teaching methods' by which students were told that 'there is not one but rather many traditions, and that there is not one way of looking at history but many'. In his manifest *Complexity and Contradiction* ([1966] 1977), Robert Venturi likewise advocated an architecture which was 'more historically informed but not addressed to history per se'.[18] Different architectural histories became essential sources of inspiration for the designing architect. Here again, Prigogine's idea of 'multiple, the temporal and the complex' had permeated human sciences. Time had entered all equations; it had 'fused, bound, embedded and broke out', thus wrote the American architectural theorist Charles Jencks (1997) in his analysis of Ilya Prigogine's *Order out of Chaos*.

Hoppenbrouwers's retrospective attempt to historicise architecture's autonomous line of development holds a contradiction. The very idea of defining an era's characteristics by attributing distinct spatial attributes to it is, in essence, a modernist endeavour (Stieber 2006; Stanek 2012). In his study *Space, Time and Architecture*, Sigfried Giedion ([1941] 1967, lvi) stated that the Modern Movement's self-consciousness was expressed through a new conception of space: the space-time. In Le Corbusier and Mies van der Rohe's works, Giedion detected an architecture which was based on the interpenetration of hovering vertical and horizontal planes, and of inner and outer space. Hoppenbrouwers quite literally embraced this modernist spatial concept as an intermediate stage in architectural history. By following the idea that architecture history can be studied as sequences of visual regimes, Hoppenbrouwers, like Giedion, thus inscribed his project in the 19th-century *Zeitgeist* idea. Hoppenbrouwers's so-called 'revolution' of spatial concepts was an attempt to build a grand narrative of successive, yet distinct phases leading up to a culmination point. This progressive idea of history divulges the teleological and spiritual undergirdings of his life's work. Today, a researcher might encounter difficulties in reconciling this striving for universal truths with the postmodern preference for the so-called 'weak thought and weak form' (Borasi 1987; Corbo 2016). Hoppenbrouwers's design pedagogy therefore consisted of a muddling of modernist and postmodernist traditions. Yet, instead of writing off his practice based on his ideas' inconsistency and incompatibility, we can best understand him as an 'intermediate figure' who negotiated both traditions in a very personal way.

Conclusion

Hoppenbrouwers's paintings were more than pedagogical props or silent witnesses to the theory course. They were an exemplum of how to practice theory in the architecture classroom. In a way, painting functioned as a prescript to the theory course. Students turning to the first page of their syllabuses in 1999, entitled *After Modernism* could find a key to understand their teachers' pedagogic intentions in a quote from Marcel Proust (2003): 'An artwork in which there are theories is like an object on which one has left the price tag'. In *Les contemporains* (1998), Jacques Derrida (1930–2004) interpreted this sentence as resistance to theory, even as an aggravating case of theoretical asceticism (Bennington 1998; Fabbri 2008). Hoppenbrouwers, notwithstanding, did not reject architectural theory; he even managed to give it a prominent place in the curriculum.[19] Yet, like many of his contemporaries, Hoppenbrouwers fought the dominant teaching style of the 'old guard' of art historians and theoreticians who approached theory and history as descriptive disciplines that merely illustrated architectural realisations (Otero-Pailos 2010).

It seems that, by referring to Proust as a prelude to his theoretical course, Hoppenbrouwers was critiquing the object to which theory was attached as an additional value. Hoppenbrouwers wanted to establish a critical attitude and redefine theory as an 'explicit architectural thinking' by making the detour of painting in his last version of the course.[20] A painting, professedly, could explore the architectural theoretical principles from inside out and not merely illustrated theoretical principles. In other words, looking at paintings attributed to an architectural literacy and prioritised the ability to communicate and understand through visual means. Therefore, we could say that Hoppenbrouwers claimed his 'rights to theory', which, for a long time, had been held by historians of art and theoreticians at architectural schools (Kostof 1990; Stanford 1999).

This chapter considered Hoppenbrouwers's paintings as tailpieces of an architectural career, as institutional vectors that incorporated the raging two-front battle between architecture as science and architecture as art and indicators of epistemological leaps and changes. In this chapter, the paintings became tools to reflect on the instability and contingency of architectural history and theory. These artefacts unexpectedly emerged as sites, in which theoretical and pedagogical principles were appropriated, re-articulated and remodelled. They allow us to venture into a complex tangle of thoughts and to add these anomalies and ambiguities to the project of historicising architectural theory.

Notes

1 Hard-edged and geometric abstraction already had its heydays in the post-war period. In Belgium, geometric abstraction was promoted in the 1950s and 1960s by the painters Gaston Bertrain, Anne Bonnet, Jo Delahaut, Luc Peire and Guy Vandenbranden.
2 Between 1950 and 1980, the school was more open to society. Modernism had its heyday at the institute between 1955 and 1965. See (Perre 2003; Janssens 2012)
3 See the document 'Beschouwingen over de artistieke humanioria Schaarbeek' by Hoppenbrouwers, Mertens, Smeyers and Huet. Date unknown. CIVA Brussels – Sint-Lukasarchief.
4 As a protégé of the gallery owner Marleen van Wayenberghe, Hoppenbrouwers exhibited his work at the gallery Lineair Art Transfer in Dilbeek in 1993 and 1998. His first exhibition at Lineair Art Transfer was entitled '27 Acryl Paintings of Alfons Hoppenbrouwers' (25.08.1993–24.12.1993). In 1998, they organised the exhibition 'Hip Hop. Een selectie van 9 jaar neo-geometrisch werk' (19.11.1997–31.01.1998). Other exhibitions that were organised were: *27 Acrylschilderijen* at AKZO, Brussels (1993); *Neo Geo. Acrylschilderijen* at Sint-Lukas Brussels (1995); *Retoriek. Acrylschilderijen* at Lemmensinstituut in Leuven (1996). In 1979, Hoppenbrouwers established the Sint-Lukas-gallery to promote contemporary art at the institute. Leaflets kept at CIVA Brussels – Sint Lukasarchief.
5 Alfons Hoppenbrouwers, *V Filosofie*, Jaarboek Tentoonstellingen 1993 – Hedendaagse Kunst, AKZO Belgium International NV, 1993.
6 The question of how painting related to his architectural work is beyond the scope of this chapter. According to Jos Vandenbreeden, this search for a dissipative space was also present in his built oeuvre. E-mail correspondence with Jos Vandenbreeden, 29.01.2015.
7 This is expressed in a letter from his sister Monique in which she writes: 'It was Hoppenbrouwers first ambition to become a painter when he entered the convent of the Brothers of the Christian Schools. However, they were more in need of an architect than a painter' Quoted in the unpublished manuscript 'Project jonge ontwerpers en het spook van Hoppenbrouwers', project Jul Debrouw (June 2006). CIVA Brussels – Sint Lukasarchief.
8 An early version of the theory course was entitled 'After Modernism' (1990) and only contained post-modernist manifestoes. The last course was renamed 'Theory of Architecture' (1999).
9 Course book 'Theory of Architecture' (1999) CIVA Brussels – Sint Lukasarchief.
10 Manuscript: 'Theorie van de architectuur, Optievak 2u/week. 5e architectuur.' October 1978. CIVA Brussels – Sint Lukasarchief.
11 Ibid.
12 Course notes of a student (18.02.2000). Kept in Wim Goosens's personal archives.
13 Slutzky, a painter and educator himself, used the painting to talk about spatial organisation to his architectural students and was highly influenced by Josef Albers, who had been his teacher at Yale. Hoppenbrouwers made mention of this text in his course of 1999 on page 43. Course notes of a student.18.02.2000. Kept in Wim Goosens's personal archives.
14 Notebook of Hoppenbrouwers. 1993. CIVA Brussels – Sint Lukasarchief.
15 Sketchbook of Hoppenbrouwers.1998. CIVA Brussels – Sint Lukasarchief.
16 Course book 'Theory of Architecture'. 1999. CIVA Brussels – Sint Lukasarchief.
17 Central in this 'spatial turn' were Henri Lefebvre's texts *The Right to the City* (1968) and *The Production of Space* (1974). As Lukasz Stanek pointed out, Lefebvre's works were inscribed into a revision of the space concept of the Modern Movement. Stanek, *Architecture as Space,* 61.
18 This attitude was only one amongst a diversity of attitudes towards the past, as became clear during the Venice Biennale *Presence of the Past* of 1980. For a further reading, see (Szacka 2011).
19 Letter to the school management concerning the course of architectural theory. 18.03.1974. CIVA Brussels – Sint Lukasarchief.
20 Letter from Hoppenbrouwers to the board of directors about the course of architectural theory. 18 March 1974. CIVA Brussels – Sint Lukasarchief.

References

Anderson, C. and K. Koehler (2002), *The Built Surface: Architecture and the Visual Arts from Romanticism to the Twenty-First Century*, Farnham: Ashgate.

Bennington, G. (1998), *Jacques Derrida*, Paris: Editions du Seuil.

Borasi, G. (1987), 'Weak Thought' and Postmodernism: The Italian Departure from Deconstruction', *Social Text*, 18:39–49.

Coomans, T. (2012), 'Van 'Scheepke' tot 'vliegdekschip'. Een verhaal van veelzijdige gebouwen', in R. Heynickx, Y. Schoonjans, and S. Sterken (eds.), *Tekenen & Betekenen. Opstellen over het architectuurinstituut Sint-Lucas, 1862–2012*, 80–88, Leuven: Universitaire pers Leuven.

Corbo, S. (2016), *From Formalism to Weak Form: The Architecture and Philosophy of Peter Eisenman*, London: Routledge.

Fabbri, L. (2008), *The Domestication of Derrida: Rorty, Pragmatism and Deconstruction*, London: A&C Black.

Gaus, G. F. and C. Kukathas (2004), *Handbook of Political Theory*, London: SAGE.

Goossens, W. and P. Labarque (2002), *Alfons Hoppenbrouwers*, Unpublished document.

Grosvenor, I. (2010), 'The School Album: Images, Insights, and Inequalities', *Educació i Història. Revista d'Història de l'Educació*, 15:149–164.

Heynen, H. and K. de Jonge (2002), 'The Teaching of Architectural History and Theory in Belgium and the Netherlands', *Journal of the Society of Architectural Historians*, 61(3):335–345.

Janssens, A. L. (2012), *Sint Lucas 150*, Ghent / Brussels, unpublished document.

Jencks, C. (1997), 'Post-Modern Architecture and Time Fusion', *International Postmodernism: Theory and Literary Practice*, 123.

Keyvanian, C. (2011), 'Teaching History to Architects', *Journal of Architectural Education*, 64(2): 25–36.

Kostof, S. (1990), 'The Shape of Time at Yale, Circa 1960', in G. Wright and J. Parks (eds.), *The History of History in American Schools of Architecture, 1865–1975*, Princeton, NJ: Princeton Architectural Press.

Mertens, P., J.K. Geirlandt and J. Warie (2001), *Kunst in België na 1945*, Brussels: Mercatorfonds.

Nicolis, G., and I. Prigogine (1977), *Self-Organization in Nonequilibrium Systems: From Dissipative Structures to Order through Fluctuations*, Hoboken, NJ: Wiley.

Otero-Pailos, J. (2010), *Architecture's Historical Turn: Phenomenology and the Rise of the Postmodern*, Minneapolis: University of Minnesota Press.

Perre, Dirk van de (2003), *Op de grens van twee werelden: beeld van het architectuuronderwijs aan het Sint-Lucasinstituut te Gent in de periode 1919–1965/1974*, Gent: Provinciebestuur Oost-Vlaanderen.

Pour une politique de rénovation urbaine à Bruxelles: propositions de l'ARAU. 1978. Bruxelles: Atelier de recherche et d'action urbaines ARAU.

Prigogine, I. and I. Stengers (1988), *Order out of Chaos: Man's New Dialogue with Nature*, London: Fontana Books.

Proust, M. (2003), *In Search of Lost Time: Finding Time Again*, London: Penguin.

Rowe, C. (1982), *The Mathematics of the Ideal Villa and Other Essays*, Massachusetts: MIT Press.

Rowe, C. and R. Slutzky (1963), 'Transparency: Literal and Phenomenal', *Perspecta*, 8:45–54.

Stanek, L. (2012), 'Architecture as Space, Again? Notes on the "Spatial Turn"', *Le Journal Spéciale 'Z*, (4):48–53.

Stanford, A. (1999), 'Architectural History in Schools of Architecture', *Journal of the Society of Architectural Historians*, 58(3):282–290.

Stieber, N. (2006), 'Space, Time and Architectural History', in D. Arnold (ed.), *Rethinking Architectural Historiography*, 171–182, New York: Routledge.

Szacka, L-C. (2011), 'Historicism Versus Communication: The Basic Debate of the 1980 Biennale', *Architectural Design*, 81(5):98–105.

Venturi, R. (1977), *Complexity and Contradiction in Architecture*, New York: The Museum of Modern Art.

Wittkower, R. (1998), *Architectural Principles in the Age of Humanism*, Hoboken, NJ: Wiley.

3

CLASHING PERSPECTIVES

Joseph Rykwert's object lesson at the Ulm school of design

Paul James

In the winter semester of 1957–1958, the Jewish architectural historian Joseph Rykwert (born 1926) was an academic visitor at the Ulm School of Design (Hochschule für Gestaltung), located at Ulm in Germany. He had travelled there with a certain trepidation. His arrival coincided with a marked increase in the scientization of Ulm's design program. Conscious that he was unlikely to fit well within this culture, he chose to travel with only essentials, storing most of his possessions back in England (Rykwert 2017: 181). Rykwert selected the chair as the subject for his lecture. In the canonical talk 'The Sitting Position. A Question of Method', he deployed this seemingly innocuous topic to deliver a covert critique of the pedagogy and methods of Ulm School of Design. It is therefore not surprising that Rykwert's connection to Ulm turned out to be brief and tenuous. At the same time, it was also pivotal to his academic career. In his memoir, Rykwert stated that his experiences at Ulm were instrumental for his subsequent academic appointments (Rykwert 2017: 183).

Next to challenging the rationalist neofunctionalism of the Ulm School of Design, Rykwert questioned something else during his lecture: the interpretive procedures of the Warburg Institute in London. While he only ever had an informal connection to the Warburg Institute (where he attended the German architectural historian Rudolf Wittkower's weekly seminars), he awarded central importance to Wittkower in his intellectual development (Thomas 2013: 55; Rykwert 2017: 134).[1]

A critique on both institutions, so I will demonstrate, gave the lecture a specific focus. Talking about the value of emotion, aesthetics, symbolism and memory within the formation and reception of design, Rykwert introduced these notions into the central pedagogical and methodological debates present at Ulm School of Design and the Warburg Institute.

While Rykwert didn't explicitly refer to both institutions in his lecture, I contend that his argument was formed covertly in relationship to the positions and priorities favoured by these schools. At the same time, I will argue that, through a series of oblique jibes and the idiosyncratic combination of historical and anthropological interpretive procedures, Rykwert also offered an alternative understanding of the cultural relationship to objects and design methods. Much to Rykwert's disappointment, both Ulm and the Warburg had

DOI: 10.4324/9781003201205-5

marginalised the role of the sensual experience of objects in favour of intellectual ideas. In fact, by confronting the holistic vision of the Warburg Institute – one grounded in history and humanistic culture – with the rationalising programme of design at Ulm, Rykwert critically navigated between two clashing perspectives. The critical subtitle of Rykwert's lecture – 'a question of method' – therefore entailed a major concern: how could design contribute to the regeneration of post-war culture? What was the appropriate 'object lesson' to be given?

Alienation at Ulm

Rykwert's intellectual antagonism to the pedagogical priorities of Ulm School of Design originated, in part, from his academic training. He read architecture at the Bartlett School of Architecture (University College, London) (1942–1944) and at the Architectural Association in London (1944–1947). Rykwert's description of his architectural education explains his antagonism to the rationalist pedagogy advanced at Ulm:

> My mentors had brought me up to admire 'utility' and frugality [...] If the governing manner was a kindly and scaled down realism, the only outside models allowed were Scandinavian.
>
> *(Franklin 2007: 2–3).*

Following his studies at the AA he attended, as mentioned, Rudolf Wittkower's seminars at the Warburg Institute for two years (Thomas 2013: 55). These, he stated, 'were my true introduction to the history of art' (Rykwert 2017: 134).

While he had a natural affinity with Wittkower's approach to architectural history and the emphasis placed on the relationship between art and its cultural context within the Warburg institute, Rykwert's relationship to the Ulm School of Design's pedagogy was at best ambivalent.[2] Rykwert's critical stance in relationship to functionalism was forged prior to his time at Ulm. The central points of the Ulm lecture were developed from his earlier text 'Meaning in Building' written in the mid-1950s. It was commissioned to commemorate the 45th anniversary of the *Schweizer Werkbund* and subsequently rejected for its provocative content and published in *Zodiac* in 1957 (Baird 2002: 5). Foreshadowing the polemic made within his Ulm lecture, he observed the overemphasis on rational criteria within the design process and argued for greater recognition of the emotional and referential content of werkbund designers' work (Baird 2002: 5). Rykwert's argument within 'Meaning and Building' was relatively measured in comparison to the partisanal stance he was to make within his lecture at Ulm.

Ulm's founding mission was to carry forward the original aims of the Bauhaus (O'Briens 1964: 36). However, the school wasn't intended to function as a replica. Significantly, many members of its academic staff rejected the idealism of the Bauhaus' art-based model on the grounds that post-war conditions required an alternative framework to meet post-war everyday matters (Aicher and Stock 2015: 85–86). Still, the school became associated with a systematic rationalist approach to design. This constituted a break from the holistic approach that Walter Gropius, the former director of the Bauhaus, advocated within his 1955 inaugural speech at Ulm. Gropius believed that design schools should educate both the intellect and the senses (Bürdek 2015: 37). Rykwert's engagement with the cultural understanding of comfort within his lecture resonated with Gropius's aspirations for the school.

The design of the Ulm campus was undertaken by the school's first rector, the Swiss architect Max Bill, who, being a Bauhaus alumnus, had conceptualised the project as a Gesamtkunstwerk ('a total work of art'). Inaugurated in 1955, the campus was designed in accord with the pedagogical principles the institution sought to advance. At a large scale, the campus design conveyed the collectivist relationship to the community by repressing any hierarchy between the five wings of the building and by resisting the creation of a monumental principal view of the campus that could be surveyed from a privileged viewing position. Maintaining the original desire to create a school that was both responsive and relevant to post-war conditions, its material selection was governed by a tight budget with materials donated by industry. The modernist dictum of truth to materials was adhered to within the material palette that comprised exposed concrete, wood and brick (HfG Ulm 2021).

Significantly in context of attributes that Rykwert's valorised in his lecture, the aesthetic principles informing the campus design were formed out of an act of negation of the building conventions and rhetorical language of traditional architecture. The ideals of practical value and objectivity governed the design (HfG Ulm 2021).

Within this larger architectural frame was Max Bill's wooden Ulm stool (1954) that students carried with them between classes (Figure 3.1). Bound by the values informing the building design, it was made from an inexpensive material, its design was governed by strict rational criteria, and it was self-consciously modest in its formal expression. Turned on its side, the Ulm stool served as an academic's lectern. Rykwert's selection of the chair as a subject can therefore be seen as significant given the emblematic role of this stool within Bill's Gesamtkunstwerk and the diminished status of objects that was occurring within the evolving pedagogy of the institution.

FIGURE 3.1 'Max Bill teaching in 1956'.

Haptic experience within educational settings

In his lecture, Rykwert attended to the concept of comfort from a variety of cultural perspectives, drawing on examples from anthropology and other disciplines (Figure 3.2). It might be productive to consider how his engagement with the sensual, material

FIGURE 3.2 Spread from Joseph Rykwerts 1982 *The Necessity of Artifice* in which he published the lecture on the chair. The particular use of images reveals his link with the Warburg school. Rykwerts montage-collision of the image of two prehistoric skeletons and a 1930 sports hero is reminiscent of the method developed by Aby Warburg in his *Mnemosyne Atlas* (1925–1929). Warburg (1866–1929), best known as the founder of the institute that bears his name, brought together images culled from different time periods and arranged them into startling juxtapositions.

dimensions of objects sat within the pedagogical practice of 'object lessons' that occurred in science museums in Britain in the early 20th century. These lessons attended to the social and historical significance of artefacts within a museum's collection. On class trips, students were encouraged to physically interact with objects, which suggests that there was some educational value invested within the haptic experience of these items. This sub-conscious level of engagement is of interest with respect to Rykwert's emphasis on the intersection of rational and unconscious levels of comprehension of design in his lecture (Morton 2012: 374).

While Rykwert didn't refer to the architectural setting within his lecture, the pedagogical principles represented through the design of the Ulm campus had already exposed students to an alternative ideological framework to that of Rykwert. The setting and the objects within the performance of his lecture (including the Ulm stool) were silent components that communicated through an alternative form of intelligibility. The significance of the Rykwert's argument was made more intelligible when read in relationship to the students' haptic experience of the setting.

There had been conflicts over pedagogical direction since the time of the Ulm school's formation in 1955. Some staff aligned with former Bauhaus alumnus Max Bill, who was committed to maintaining links to the Dessau Bauhaus model of art-based design education, while others aligned with the Argentinian designer and theorist Tomás Maldonado who wanted to shift towards a science-based model. Maldonado was central to Ulm becoming, in Rykwert's terms, the 'epicenter of systematic rationality' (Rykwert 2017: 180). So, it was ironic then that it was Maldonaldo who invited Rykwert to teach at Ulm. Reflecting on their early meeting, Rykwert wrote:

> When Maldonado discussed the appointment with me, I inevitably inquired what I would be expected to teach. 'Cultural integration' was the title I was offered: though when I asked for an explanation of it, it did seem to me a bit like 'art history'. Not history! The very word it seemed was taboo – since the programme of the school imposed a rationality that relied on first principles alone. Scientific method and a positive rationality would guide the designers and were to be the basis of all teaching: insofar as an aesthetic was formulated there, it claimed to derive entirely from experiments in visual perception
> *(Rykwert 2017: 180).*

This encounter set the tone of Rykwert's experience at Ulm. In his autobiography, he expressed the sense of alienation he experienced as a Jewish person in post-war Germany when 'only just over a decade separated us from the opening of the concentration camps' (Rykwert 2017: 181). This was despite the reassurance he had initially gained from the fact that the school had been funded from a foundation formed as a memorial to the Scholl family members who were executed by the Nazis for their non-violent resistance as part of the White Rose Group (Rykwert 2017: 181).

The spectre of German history is implicit within Rykwert's speech to the students. As previously noted, Rykwert and the Ulm School of Design exhibited contrasting visions of the role of objects within cultural construction. Rykwert's wariness about systematic rationality and technology wasn't unique to him; his concerns were also shared by many West German intellectuals after the Second World War (Betts 2004: 157). His identification with the Jewish émigré academics at the Warburg Institute added another layer of complexity to his relationship with German history and its intellectual traditions. The terms through which he defended the study of history in his Ulm lecture resonated with the way that

Covert references

On first sight, Rykwert's selection of the chair as topic for his lecture, 'The Sitting Position – A Question of Method', seems a conventional, if not banal, topic to discuss at a design school, given the elevated place that chairs had as an area for artistic experimentation within the modernist period. To appreciate why the lecture was provocative, one must consider that Rykwert's arrival at Ulm coincided with a period of transformation within the school's pedagogy, which was marked by a shift of focus from *design objects* towards *design systems*. Johannes Itten's teaching at the Bauhaus had emphasised the expressive qualities of objects over functional requirements (Lerner 2005: 215). In contrast, Ulm instructors such as the German graphic designer Otl Aicher – who was aligned with Max Bill and a co-founder of Ulm – emphasised the development of design systems, which centred on inventing basic forms that could be utilised for a variety of purposes (O'Brien 1964: 36). Design objects were further conceived by Ulm's teachers, such as Maldonaldo, as material information (Betts 2004: 156).

To comprehend the specificity of Rykwert's critical analysis of the chair as a material and cultural object, it is necessary to uncover his covert references to the pedagogy and methods of both the Ulm School of Design and the Warburg Institute. Through his critique of functionalist design methods, Rykwert's lecture emphasised the cultural value of emotion, symbolism and memory. These terms align with the partisanal positions adopted by key figures within the institutional history of both the Ulm School of Design and the Warburg Institute. Rykwert's preamble to the paper, 'The Sitting Position – A Question of Method', provides a useful synopsis of the intent of his argument. It is worth quoting in full as his wording signposts particular positions to which I will return:

> It seemed to me that a comparison of the material from different periods and cultures would allow me to focus accurately on the relative importance of human comfort, methods of production and of cultural associations as parameters – both conscious and unconscious – of the design process. The last factor seemed to me consistently, even insistently repressed by many teachers and theorists; I was therefore concerned to show how its repression in some ways strengthened its controlling power
>
> *(Rykwert 1982a: 23).*

Rykwert contended that comfort varied from group to group and between stages of a person's lifespan. Comfort was selected as a concept because it was subjective and culturally/ historically contingent. He argued that the connection between comfort and social convention evaded the narrow framework used in ergonomics. Therefore, Rykwert contrasted the exclusive attention to the mechanics of the sitting position within ergonomic studies with the cultural and psychological relationships to comfort. He argued that attending exclusively to the mechanics involved in the sitting position fails to address the wider meaning of the term 'comfort' in the context of the whole personality.[3+]

Rykwert identified earlier examples of anthropometric measurement to demonstrate that advances in scientific measurement had not radically altered the recommended measurements for furniture developed centuries earlier. This was an obvious challenge to the focus at Ulm. Noting the persistence of traditional shapes, he highlighted the limited impact of scientific measurement. He simply postulated that it was a utopian dream that data alone could provide all the information required to determine the design of a chair. To emphasise the failings in the functionalist theoreticians' assumptions about the design process, he surmised that, as ergonomic studies were permissive, they should not overdetermine aesthetic choices. Similarly, he contended that studies of materials and manufacture offered little help for design decisions relating to form. Rykwert thus implicitly argued that the parameters for study prioritised at Ulm only provided part of the answer to design solutions and constituted a narrow vision of human requirements.

To further reinforce his position that product selection by consumers is not exclusively determined by practical requirement, he cited the example of the Hardoy chair (B.K.F. chair) that had been designed by architects Antonio Bonet, Juan Kurchan and Jorge Ferrari Hardoy in 1938 (Figure 3.3). This chair was composed of a thin metal rod frame upon which a fabric or leather sling was suspended (MOMA 2009). Noting the functional failings of the design did not diminish its commercial success, Rykwert contented that its selection was based upon irrational criteria. He itemised the factors at play within the reception of design situated outside the framework associated with functionalist theoreticians: the list included symbolism, unconscious associations and existential resonance. Rykwert awarded particular importance to the impact of memory on the perception of design. Collective memory and historical reference, he asserted, are particularly valuable to society. He wove these factors that he elevated into a critique of a narrowed vision of the design process and of the reception of objects within the functionalist model. Provocatively, he contended that the designed environment was fundamentally symbolic in nature. He closed the lecture with a discussion on historiography before finally asserting that the study of history is part of the designer's equipment and method.

Critique on the Ulm institute

The lecture as a whole was a challenge to the narrowing of the framework for design methods and to how consumers – and by extension communities – relate to objects. The attributes Rykwert valued were those that evaded a purely rational understanding of design and connected to the complex intersection of rational and subjective dimensions of its reception. Yet, his object lesson was also an indirect critique of the pedagogical traditions of both the Ulm School and the Warburg Institute. While he identified broadly with the Warburg circle's approach to interpreting art in relationship to cultural history, he maintained a critical relationship to the methods associated with the institute. On the other hand, his relationship to the pedagogy and methods at the Ulm School of Design was, as we noticed, largely combatant.

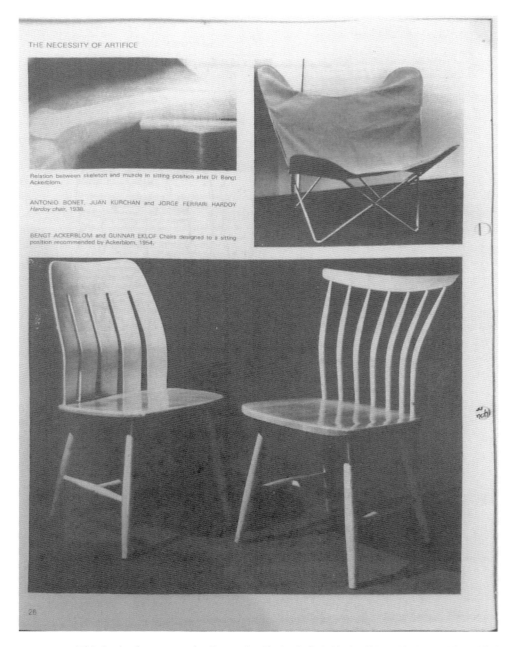

FIGURE 3.3 This is also known as the Butterfly Chair, Safari Chair, Sling Chair or Wing Chair (MOMA 2009).

Former Ulm student and design theorist, Bernhard E. Bürdek, identified three phases in the pedagogical development of Ulm. During the first phase (1954–1955), the founding members of the school conceived its social purpose in alignment with the wider postwar movement that sought to achieve political reform through progressive pedagogy.

The curriculum therefore adhered to the Dessau Bauhaus model of art-based design education. Max Bill, in his capacity as Ulm School of Design's first rector, was instrumental in recruiting former Bauhaus staff to teach at the school (Bürdek 2015: 39–40).

During the second phase (1956–1958), new scientific disciplines were added to the curriculum with the school's educational model being developed to reinforce the relationship between design, science and technology (Bürdek 2015: 40). By the end of this period, the feud between Bill and Maldonado had divided the school over its pedagogical direction; Bill resigned in 1957 and Maldonado's science-based model won (Betts 1998: 77). Bill described the school as becoming a 'technoid degeneration of its once good idea' (Betts 1998: 77). His departure signalled the rejection of the art-based heritage of Ulm's design education and led to the re-evaluation of its relationship to its Bauhaus heritage. In turn, the Meyer-led period of the Bauhaus became the favoured historical foundation at Ulm (Betts 1998: 75–76). Rykwert arrived at the very end of this second phase. Significantly, in light of Rykwert's lecture, it was during this period of transformation that the school attempted to distance the designer from the legacy of aesthetics and history of artistic production (Betts 1998: 77).

By the time of Rykwert's appointment, Maldonaldo had become the acting rector. In stark contrast to Johannes Itten's teaching at the Bauhaus, where he emphasised the expressive qualities of objects, Bürdek recalled at Ulm, 'Objects that possessed an artistic or craft character were more or less taboo' (Bürdek 2015: 45). In this context, Rykwert's attentiveness to the affective qualities of the chair gains greater significance.

Rykwert must have observed the curriculum's increasing emphasis on disciplines including semiotics, ergonomics and economics. Through the influence of semiotics, design at Ulm was increasingly seen as information in a way that was analogous to mathematical representation. For Maldonado, 'scientific operationalism' required design to become divorced from aesthetics and to be conceived as no more than material information and production coordination (Betts 2004: 156). Seen in this light, the values and priorities of design that Rykwert identified in his Sitting Position lecture were a stand against the rationalising of design processes that the school had committed to and perhaps a sympathetic gesture towards the founding vision of Ulm that had recently faded.

While there certainly wasn't a lot of common ground between Rykwert's and Maldonado's relationship to design, there was a more complex relationship between his priorities and those associated with the first phase at Ulm led by Max Bill. The values that Rykwert advanced in his lecture share some common ground with the key pedagogical principles associated with Max Bill. Following Bauhaus principles, Bill argued that design education should be linked to art because art and artists were the primary means of cultural and political regeneration (Betts 1998: 76). He felt that design work should be in accordance with the spiritual substance of modern art (Betts 2004: 143).

Max Bill's and Rykwert's positions on the value of aesthetics also overlapped. Bill introduced the concept of beauty into modernist design discourse. He observed that beauty could not be developed exclusively from functional requirements. In order to resurrect the concept of beauty, which was repressed within functionalism due to its association with aesthetics, he classified it as a 'function'. Bill argued for beauty to be awarded equal value as other functional demands (Gimmi 2010: 12). This is compatible with Rykwert's position within the Ulm lecture where he contended that, 'In spite, then, of the promise which the "functionalist" theoreticians of the last generation made, the functional solution

62 Paul James

of problems will not lead to an ideal situation where the arbitrary aesthetic choices with relegated to a marginal exercise' (Rykwert 1982a: 24).

Still, Rykwert and Bill shared less common ground in their relationship to cultural memory. Rykwert asserted in the Ulm lecture

> There is no humanity without memory and there is no architecture without historical reference. In a critical situation such as ours where collective memory is continually being denied and its relevance to the contemporary situation questioned, we approach (collectively) the malaise of the psychologist's patient who repressed his past in order to justify his irrational behaviour in the present
>
> *(Rykwert 1982a: 31).*

Rykwert's comment may well have been directed to Max Bill's design of the campus at Ulm. Bill repressed all traces of emotional sentiment, symbolism and subjectivity in the design of the Ulm's buildings to distance the school from the legacy of Nazi emotional manipulation. This design decision embodied the mission of the school's founders to undertake cultural renewal by evading links to the culture associated with recent German history (Betts 2004: 145, 148). Rykwert and Bill tried to come to terms with the past through two opposing models. For Rykwert, the study of history was redemptive and part of the restoration of humanist culture; for Bill, recent historical memory was too present – unclean and painful, it needed it to be repressed through a form of psychic disavowal.

Interest in the design of expressive and unique objects eroded over time at Ulm. Bill had viewed industrial design as part of a totalising artistic programme. Whereas Ulm, after the rise of the scientific model, favoured the development of product systems. Maldonado was engaged with semiotics and information theory. As for others at Ulm, these areas of knowledge appealed due to 'its putative methodological objectivity, its rejection of humanism and moral values in the name of scientific inquiry and "value free" analysis' (Betts 2004: 157). The status of the object, as a material entity, was further diminished within the foundation course that Maldonado designed. Maldonado emphasised methodology by starting with theory and mathematical concepts rather than making references to practical design (Leopold 2013: 369).

Rykwert's lecture was a demonstration of sympathy for the ideology of the earlier stages of the Bauhaus exorcised at Ulm in favour of the Meyer-led Bauhaus model. Rykwert's polemical presentation, however, concealed the extent to which his framework for design aligned with the holistic approach favoured by Gropius and Bill. He also failed to acknowledge the social objectives of neo-functionalism at Ulm.

Critique on Warburg institute

Despite the informality of Rykwert's connection to the Warburg Institute, his attendance of Wittkower's seminars over a two-year period was to have an enduring impact on his relationship to interpretative procedures within architectural history (Baird 2002: 13). The M.A. course at the University of Essex that he was to develop many years later was even viewed as Warburgian in spirit (Onians 2015: 179).

At the Warburg Institute 'the question of method' was just as central to its institutional identity as it was at Ulm. Its first director in England, the art historian Fritz Saxl, defined the role of the Warburg by way of contrast to the Courtauld Institute of Art (Sears 2018).

He said that the role of the Courtauld was to teach art history, whereas the Warburg's central role was to provide practical instruction to individual researchers in how to deploy a variety of historical methods.[4]

Rykwert ended his lecture at Ulm with a veiled criticism of the German art historical tradition associated with the Warburg. While he did not mention the institute by name, his allusions were clear: first, he identified the limitation of iconology which has been defined by some as the 'Warburg Method'; and second, he speculated that the 'grand perspectives and the metaphysical speculations of a Riegl or a Wölfflin will decrease in relevance'. This was a challenge to the academic foundation of the Warburg institute and the intellectual lineage of academics associated with it (Saxl was a student of Heinrich Wölfflin, whereas Vienna-trained Ernst Gombrich drew on Alois Riegl's work).[5] Third, he referenced the 'pseudo-objectivities of our contemporaries'. This is a charge Rykwert levelled against Gombrich in his memoir when he reflected on his time at the Institute (Rykwert 2017: 133).

Rykwert presents his critique of the Warburg Method obliquely through his use of historical method and communication style. The approach to argumentation in the lecture was inconsistent. The first half of the lecture was written in a conventional academic manner, with a linear, logical argument. In the second half, Rykwert presented his argument in a far more fragmented, associative style. Positioned strategically, prior to his explicit concluding comments on historical method, Rykwert included an extended passage of text that, viewed in context of his body of work, appears to be an experiment in the associative style that would become a feature of his writing in later decades. Within this fragment of text, prior to launching into a wild display of free association of cultural precedents, Rykwert cited the work of the social anthropologist, Gordon W. Hewes, who had studied human postures that were perceived to be comfortable within diverse cultures. Rykwert collaged examples of different cultures' relationships to the sitting position together, in a manner that implied that the concept of 'comfort' operated like a palimpsest through which conflicting understandings could be drawn out. This section of Rykwert's essay demonstrates a performative relationship to the material of writing that is distinct from the rest of his lecture.

Inserting the associative method prior to his critique of approaches to history associated with the Warburg was significant. The combination of direct and oblique modes of argumentation may demonstrate the influence of philosophical hermeneutics. Yet, prior to his explicit comments on historical method, Rykwert reflected upon his own use of history anticipating criticism from his distractors, writing, 'my elaborate analysis of an agreeable if arbitrary shape will seem gratuitous to some, absurdly over-literary to others' (Rykwert 1982a: 30). His self-reflective wording anticipates the reception of his work by historians associated with both the Warburg Institute and the Courtauld Institute of Art. By the 1960s, the associative style of presentation in its dawning in the Sitting Position lecture had developed into a dominant feature of Rykwert's writing and teaching. In 1973, Gombrich wrote a scathing review of Rykwert's book *On Adam's House in Paradise: The Idea of the Primitive Hut in Architectural History* where he was critical of Rykwert's methods (Gombrich 1973).

Several of Gombrich's criticisms could be extended to the associative section of Rykwert's lecture at Ulm. Towards the end of his lecture Rykwert stated the following:

> The whole of the environment, from the moment we name it and think of it as such, is a tissue of symbolic forms: the whole of environment is symbol. To understand how the situation can be managed we are forced to look to the past; no contemporary

guide can offer any real help here. This burdens the historian with the task to which
he is not altogether used: that of acting as a psychoanalyst to society

(Rykwert 1982a: 31).

Rykwert's call for the historian to act like a psychoanalyst of society was curiously, perhaps
knowingly, signalled in Gombrich's observation on Rykwert's method within his book
review. Gombrich wrote, 'To track down and to map this cluster of associations the author
adopts the methods of the psychoanalyst rather than those of the historian' (Gombrich 1973).
He further argued that Rykwert 'prefers suggestive allusion to systematic presentation', and
that he was 'not really concerned with the history of an idea'; rather, he was 'concerned with
memories or fantasies of an archetypal dwelling'. He also accused Rykwert of motif hunt-
ing, stating that this practice was no longer supported by anthropologists' (Gombrich 1973).

In defence of Gombrich's criticism of Rykwert's use of sources, the architectural historian Helen Thomas argued that Rykwert's disinterest in linear structures was a critical
strategy that he used to unbind the meaning of cultural artefacts from the Warburgian history of an idea (Thomas 2013: 57–58). Thomas identified several key points of distinction
between Rykwert's use of history and that of the Warburgian academics. She noted that, for
Rykwert, 'Meaning is not held in the object itself (as with the Warburg method), but instead derives from the object's relationship to other things, minds and times' (Thomas 2013:
54). She also viewed his use of 'non-linear and associative structures' within his academic
writing as a challenge to German academic thinking that was associated with 'rationalising
tendencies and convenient genealogies' (Thomas 2013: 55).

Rykwert and Gombrich had conflicting positions on the value of emotion and objectivity in historical research. Gombrich, in an interview with the French philosopher Didier
Eribon, expressed his disinterest in aesthetics and art criticism because they were centred on
the expression of emotional responses to art.[6] He argued for the central importance of facts
to support claims. Rykwert, on the other hand, in line with Hans-Georg Gadamer's philosophical hermeneutics, refused the assumption that the prejudice could be suspended in
'objective' art history. In his memoir, Rykwert noted that 'E.H. Gombrich (later Sir Ernst),
supposedly engaged on an intellectual biography of Warburg, but in fact writing learnedly
on various aspects of the Renaissance from a perversely positivist perspective while the
biography waited' (Rykwert 2017: 133). The conflict over method with Gombrich relates
to the influence of positivism and rationalism within the German art historical tradition
associated with the Warburg Institute. It was certainly something Rykwert argued against
in his 1958 lecture.

Conclusion

Rykwert's object lesson, pointedly on the subject of the chair, sits within a critical dialogue
with both the Ulm School of Design and the Warburg Institute despite the fact that he
didn't make any explicit references to either of these institutions in his lecture. The primary
focus of his lecture was directed towards scientifically orientated design methods that were
strongly, if not emblematically, championed by Ulm School of Design. His implicit critique
of the 'Warburgian method' is primarily presented through his alternate use of history and
his method of argumentation. The subtitle of his lecture 'a question of method' clearly

resonates with the central influence of the two institutions on methods of design and humanities research, centred on objects, during the late 1950s.

Rykwert's criteria for the appraisal of objects and their reception were in direct contrast with those associated with Maldonaldo's 'scientific operationalism' which repressed these criteria in favour of those that lent themselves to a narrowly defined rational system that was compatible with a mathematical representation of reality. Rykwert's lecture was a demonstration of sympathy for the ideology of the earlier stages of the Bauhaus exorcised at Ulm in favour of the Hans Meyer-led Bauhaus model. It signalled the other side of the origins of functionalist design. In some regards, Rykwert's lecture echoes the inaugural speech given by Walter Gropius at the Ulm School of Design in 1955, where he 'rejected the charge that the Bauhaus had promoted a one-sided rationalism. In his work, Gropius said, 'he was searching for a new equilibrium between the practical and the aesthetic, psychological demands of the age' (Bürdek 2015: 37).

The values held by Gropius and his fellow Bauhaus member, Bill, bear a more sympathetic relationship to the values that Rykwert defended. The polemical stance presented in Rykwert's Ulm lecture provided a reductive representation of the functionalist agenda and concealed his ambiguous relationship to its social objectives. Rykwert's relationship to Warburgian methods of interpreting objects was more ambiguous and conflicted. He acknowledged his debt to Wittkower for his intellectual development and shared the institute's engagement with the symbolic dimensions of objects. He differed in the hierarchical weight that he awarded the object. In contrast to the Warburg method, he did not think that meaning was held in the object itself; rather, he deferred its meaning to the network of relations with other objects and contexts.

The status of the chair as a pedagogical tool is complex in Rykwert's lecture as it exists as an example of material history, motif, illustration of theoretical positions and the outcome of methodologies. Ironically, it was Max Bill's *Gesamtkunstwerk* which overdetermined the haptic experience of Rykwert's earnest students. The Ulm campus was a vital element within the performance of Rykwert's object lesson. The student's subconscious experience of the pedagogical principles overdetermining the design of the setting animated the alternative ideological framework that Rykwert espoused.[7] Moreover, the unyielding form of the emblematic Ulm stool emphasised the experience of duration, reminding the audience that their bodies and the objects that contributed to the formation of their horizons of existence were insinuated within modern life and overflowed mathematical models of understanding.

Notes

1 Wittkower disposed of the purely aesthetic theory of Renaissance architecture.
2 Prior to his post as an academic visitor at the Ulm School of Design (1957–1958), Rykwert had taught at the Hammersmith School of Arts and Crafts (1951–1953). Prestigious academic positions were enabled by the aura of Ulm including his role in establishing the MA in the History and Theory of Architecture at Essex University (1968) and his Professorship at the University of Cambridge in 1980 (Franklin 2007: 3–4). His course at Essex was Warburgian in spirit and demonstrated the lingering influence of Wittkower's seminars on his intellectual orientation and development (Onians 2015: 179).
3 The term 'whole personality' is of particular significance as Rykwert's tenure at Ulm coincided with the shift to the scientification of its design pedagogy and methods. Attention to the 'whole personality' was an aspiration of the earlier phase of the school when it was led by staff formally associated with the Bauhaus.

4 Whether a specific 'Warburg Method' existed is highly contested. Space limitations prevent detailed discussion of this matter although the following characterisation of the 'Warburg Method' is useful as Rykwert's critique of the approaches to art historical research connect to this representation of the method. Creighton Gilbert stated:

> One of the most effective [methods and schools of art history] (and one of the few to have been somewhat self-analytical) is iconology—or the Warburg method, after its promulgator...This method in simple essence is to study the work of art as a carrier of the interests of its culture and its social myths. Iconologists show and define the attitudes in a work of art by analyzing its technique, its design and style, and most obviously its subject matter, or iconography, and further those details in which this work varies from earlier and later presentations of the same subject matter. This last has been the most triumphant and illuminating Warburg technique...
>
> (Woodfield 2001: 289)

5 Heinrich Wölfflin (1864–1945) focused on the formal organization of art works and aligned the development of art with the succession of styles. This approach is in contrast to art historians working at the Warburg Institute who were engaged with iconographic analysis, which placed emphasis on the way that art communicates ideas. Alois Riegl (1858–1905) was engaged with the relationship between style and cultural history.

6 On his approach to history, Gombrich wrote:

> If you take the writings of my colleagues, particularly the critics or the art historians, many of the things they say are untranslatable, they are metaphors, like poetry. Nothing but emotion. Let me use a figure of speech drawn from banking. The old banknotes always carried the promise that you could exchange them for gold. So with our statements, we ought always to be able to go to the bank and say: give me a fact for it. Therefore I am not very interested in aesthetics or in art criticism, because so much of what these people write is just an expression of their own emotions.
>
> (Gombrich 1993: 169)

7 The way that Rykwert exploited the setting in his Ulm lecture resonates with Baird's description of Rykwert's life long intellectual project:

> Indeed, I would be inclined to argue that is has been his lifelong intellectual project to employ the distinctive analytic methods he has devised, to bring to the conscious awareness of his contemporaries, the implications and potential consequences of the assumptions lying within the beliefs, social forms, and artifacts that form their horizon of existence, however individualized or however collective those forms may at first seem to be.
>
> (Baird 2002: 22)

Works cited

Aicher, O. & Stock, W.J. (2015), *The World as Design*, 2nd edition, Berlin: Ernst & Sohn.

Baird, G. (2002), 'Introduction: "A Promise as Well as Memory" Toward an Intellectual Biography of Joseph Rykwert', in George Dobbs and Robert Tavernor (eds.), *Body and Building: Essays on the Changing Relation of Body and Architecture*, 2–27, Cambridge, MA: MIT Press.

Betts, P. (1998), 'Semiotics and Society: The Ulm Hochschule für Gestaltung in Retrospect', *Design Issues*, 14(2): 67–68.

Betts, P. (2004), *The Authority of Everyday Objects*, Berkley: University of California Press.

Bürdek, B.E. (2015), *Design: History, Theory and Practice of Product Design*, 2nd revised ed. Basel: Birkhäuser.

Franklin, G. (2007), *Inner Court, 48 Old Church Street, London Borough of Kensington and Chelsea Historic Building Report Research*, Research Department Report Series 22/2007, Swindon: English Heritage.

Gimmi, K. (2010), 'On Bill', in Brett Steele (ed.), *Form, Function, Beauty = Gestalt*, 3–19, London: AA Publications.

Gombrich, E. (1973), 'Dream Houses', *New York Review of Books*.

Gombrich, E. (1993), *A Lifelong Interest: Conversations on Art and Science with Didier Eribon*, London: Thames and Hudson Ltd.

HfG ULM. (2021). *Spiegel der Pädagogik (Mirror of Education)*. Available online: https://www.hfg-ulm.de/de/hfg-ulm/architektur-der-hfg-ulm/ (accessed 25 March 2021).

Leopold, C. (2013), 'Precise Experiments: Relations between Mathematics, Philosophy and Design at Ulm School of Design', *Nexus Network Journal*, 15(2): 363–380.

Lerner, F. (2005), 'Foundations for Design Education: Continuing the Bauhaus *Vorkurs* Vision', *Studies in Art Education*, 46(3): 211–226.

Levine, E. (2013), *Dreamland of Humanists. Warburg, Cassirer, Panofsky, and the Hamburg School*. Chicago, IL/London: The University of Chicago Press.

MOMA (2009), Antonio Bonet, Juan Kurchan, Jorge Ferrari Hardoy, B.K.F. Chair, 1938. Available online: https://www.moma.org/collection/works/4393 (accessed 25 March 2021).

Morton, C. (2012), 'Photography and the Comparative Method: the Construction of an Anthropological Archive', *The Journal of the Royal Anthropological Institute*, 18(2): 369–396.

O'Briens, G. (1964), 'Ulm School Carries on Bauhaus Aims', *New York Times*, 4 February. Available online: https://www.nytimes.com/1964/02/04/archives/ulm-school-carries-on-bauhaus-aims.html/ (accessed 31 January 2019).

Onians, J. (2015), 'Fruitful Intellectual Exchanges: The Warburg Institute's Impact on Britain and Britain's Impact on the Warburg Institute', in Uwe Fleckner and Peter Mack (eds.), *The Afterlife of the Kulturwissenschaftliche Bibliothek Warburg: The Emigration and the Early Years of the Warburg Institute in London*, 175–186, Berlin: Walter de Gruyter & Co.

Rykwert, J. (1982a), 'The Sitting Position – a Question of Method', in Charles A. Jencks (ed.), *The Necessity of Artifice*, 23–32, London: Academy Editions.

Rykwert, J. (1982b), 'Meaning and Building', in Charles A. Jencks (ed.), *The Necessity of Artifice*, 9–16, London: Academy Editions.

Rykwert, J. (2017), *Remembering Places: A Memoir*, London: Routledge.

Sears, E. (2018), *The Courtauld and the Warburg: Complementarities*. From YouTube. Video, 46.47. Posted by the Courtauld Institute, [Online]. Available online: https://www.youtube.com/watch?v=9O1ROr1zdTM (accessed 25 March 2021).

Thomas, H. (2013), 'Joseph Rykwert and the Use of History', *AA Files*, 66: 54–58.

Woodfield, R. (2001), 'Warburg's "Method"', in Richard Woodfield (ed.), *Art History as Cultural History: Warburg's Projects*, 259–293, Amsterdam: G+B Arts International.

4

PANCHO'S PASSAGES

Framing transitional objects for decolonial education in 1980s South Africa

Hannah le Roux

> These objects remind me that there are other living cultures, other ways of being and expressing oneself. They provide me with a passage into these other worlds.
>
> Amancio d'Alpoim Guedes (2009: 165)

Passing Pancho

On the first floor of the John Moffat Building that houses the architecture programme in the University of the Witwatersrand – 'Wits' – in Johannesburg, two pairs of images face off against each other (Figure 4.1). One pair are blueprints of the elevations of the Johannesburg Art Gallery, designed by Edwin Lutyens in 1910 following a bequest from the Randlords

FIGURE 4.1 Isa Kabini, acrylic paintings, circa 1981, and Edwin Lutyens, Johannesburg Art Gallery, 1910, on display in John Moffat Building, 2021.

DOI: 10.4324/9781003201205-6

who had made enormous profits from mining the rich gold reserves of the region. Opposite them, across a passage, are two acrylic paintings by Isa Kabini, one of the Ndebele women whose painted geometric murals on their rural homes that had caught the imagination of some South African architects since the 1940s.[1] In this conceptually provocative pairing, a Neoclassical pavilion, built to enclose colonial cultural objects, is confronted by the resistant visual culture that African women, doubly dispossessed by colonisation, encoded in the maintenance of their homes. The women painted to welcome home their men whose underpaid migrant labour enabled Johannesburg's mining economy, and to make visible their settlements in the face of evictions by colonial and apartheid governments.

The curatorial placement of these images is clearly political, read against the dynamics of South African spatial inequity that was encoded in the policy of racial apartheid between 1948 and 1994. Works by white and black artists would not normally be co-displayed, and these structures they represent would be located in segregated districts. But the images are also mute things, barely noticed today due to their familiarity and setting in a neglected interior passage that leads to staff offices. They remain as a trace of the object-centred pedagogy of Amâncio d'Alpoim Miranda 'Pancho' Guedes,[2] architect, artist and head of Architecture from 1975 to 1990, some 30 years after he retired to Portugal (Figure 4.2). They are just some of a few dozen architectural artefacts that he framed and hung in the passages on the first floor of the John Moffat Building during his tenure (Figure 4.3), all carefully placed in relation to each other, to the city of Johannesburg and to his wide circle of architectural connections.

The narratives that emerge from the objects that Guedes explicitly curated in the Wits passages are an unexamined public face of his private obsession with collecting. The homes he shared with his wife Dorothy and their family in Lourenço Marques – now Maputo – from 1950 to 1975, Melville, Johannesburg (1976–1990), and at Eugaria near Sintra, Portugal (1972–1990, and 1982–2006) were all filled with artworks as well as objects from Southern

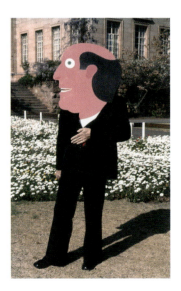

FIGURE 4.2 Self-portrait by and with Adam A. d'Amancio Guedes outside the John Moffat Building, 1981. Source: collection of Pedro Guedes.

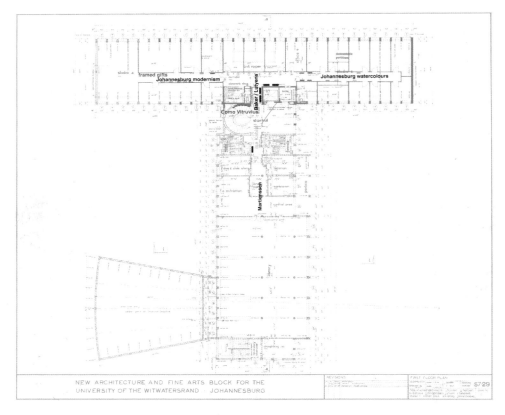

FIGURE 4.3 Positions of image sets in the first floor passages. Drawing by author over 1956 plan by studio 7. Source: Architecture archives, University of the Witwatersrand.

Africa created for rituals, as curios, or commissioned by Guedes. They are evidence of his personal trajectory from Portugal as a child to its colonies, to Mozambique, where his father was a medical doctor, and his uncle a lawyer who had been exiled by Portugal's Salazar regime for Socialist agitation in Brazil. Guedes went to Johannesburg for high school and university, then back to Mozambique where he built a practice over 25 years, to exile in Johannesburg and eventually back to Portugal after his academic retirement (Guedes and Guedes 2003; Green 2006).

The Guedes' personal collection has been catalogued and displayed on various occasions and related to Pancho's creative path (Pomar and Pereira 2010; Guedes, 2017). As formal arrangements, these objects were experimental referents for his creative work. He was curious about the 'other worlds' that preceded, or co-existed, on the margins of colonial space. Within their material cultures, he believed ways might exist from which to develop de-colonial forms. Paradoxically, given this ambition, Guedes was able to access these objects due to his privileged position in a colony. Unlike collectors based in Europe, whose practices of collection were mediated by dealers,[3] Guedes was able to retrieve masks and markers that had been used in rituals and was aware of their relation to other ontological worlds. Other objects were colonial trade objects, toys or curios, and some were produced within modern media of communication.

When political change brought him to Wits as a professor in 1975, Guedes extended his personal curatorial practices into a critical pedagogic strategy. He added African material to the department's collection of classical and modern architectural ephemera that included student work, competition renderings, blueprints and study sketches. This expanded and reorganised collection reflected Guedes' understanding of drawing as a process of producing liminal material between the imagination and concrete reality. The presentation of the artefacts that he discovered, commissioned, reprinted or added to this collection was ritualised. He ceremonially unveiled them – once literally pulling a new item out of a paper bag, but more usually showing them in a slide – to colleagues and students at the regular 'School Talks' and then placed them in the department's passages with curatorial purpose. Over and above securing their presence, he considered their interrelations, reframing the drawings from discrete colonial and modernist archives and then placing them alongside new images and models in combinations that usurped conventional categories. These displays were a commentary on colonial, racial and gendered divisions that were deeply scripted in the curriculum and practices of the profession. They functioned as Guedes' mute but radical strategy of the re-education of his colleagues and students who came out of late apartheid's racially segregated, deeply unequal and Eurocentric education system (Cross 1986; Elk 1986), while implicitly critiquing the supremacy of the colonial archive. The passages where he hung them can be considered an interim site that suggested other futures both for architecture and the material on display.

The passage

The John Moffat Building had been built in 1957, between Guedes' studies at Wits until 1949, and his return as a professor following the Mozambican revolution that forced Portuguese settlers, regardless of their affiliations, to leave the country in 1974. Pancho's fixed property was confiscated, and he hastily left Lourenço Marques with possessions that could fit on two trucks. He also lost his practice in Rua de Nevala, which combined a productive business and an atelier and formed the base for extensive connections to other creative minds (Green 2006; Pomar and Pereira 2010). Pancho used wood carvers and carpenters to build models and was the patron of the artists Malangatana Ngwenya Valente and Alberto Mati. Despite the colony's relative isolation, he remained connected to networks beyond Mozambique (Beinart 1961; Levin 2016). He would join several of the Team 10 meetings starting with Royaumont in 1962, and Alison and Peter Smithson were photographed with him at the site of the 'clandestine' crèche in the Caniço. Pancho also represented Mozambique at the seminal 1961 São Paulo Biennale where the Neo-Concrete art movement including Lygia Clark and Helio Oiticica presented their manifesto and work, and he played a significant role in the 1962 First International Congress of African Culture arranged by Frank McEwen in Salisbury (Green 2006).

Guedes' collection strategy had much in common with that of his friend and fellow member of Team 10, Aldo van Eyck. Like Guedes, Van Eyck used his home as a physical museum for African artefacts and saw them as a conceptual supply for his personal *museé imaginaire* (Uribe 2018). Inspired by vernacular architecture, and as a way to critique the exclusions of international modernism, Van Eyck prepared a diagram, which came to be known as the Otterlo Circles, for the CIAM conference of 1959 (Fabrizi 2020). In its annotations, Van Eyck proposed that authorship 'by us' should encircle three architectural referents, namely 'vernacular of the heart', 'immutability and rest', exemplified by classical monuments, and the 'change and movement' of the experimental modern movement. This triadic view of architecture must have resonated with Pancho, who was carrying out studies of the housing built by Mozambicans in the area of Lourenço Marques called the Caniço (Guedes 1963), expanding his frame of reference beyond the classical studies of an architecture student under colonial rule and the normative modernism that was practiced in Southern Africa.

In the immediate period after his exile to Johannesburg, Guedes travelled on several occasions to Europe and the USA (Green 2006). By the late 1970s, stung by some student criticism of his absences from Wits, he moved into an office on the north wing of the John Moffat Building. This 'harmonious' and carefully detailed late modernist building was designed for up to 320 students by seven of its lecturers (Herbert and Donchin 2013; Keeling 2014). The building allowed for various forms of low key, functional display. Apart from student work pinned to the hessian and cork inner wall of the foyer for reviews (Figure 4.4), there was a materials museum on the top floor and an art display area next to the library. A photo from 1960 shows that small, framed paintings were also hung on the blank ends of library shelving units and wall. The building was completed in 1957 and housed – from the top of four floors down – fine arts studios, architecture studios, a library, lecture halls and a graduate programme in town and regional planning, quantity surveying, lecture rooms and staff offices. The overall scheme was an exercise in restraint and the product of consensus, with individual expression tightly contained. The building had two larger-scaled

FIGURE 4.4 Foyer of the John Moffat Building, c1960. Source: Architecture archives, University of the Witwatersrand.

decorative projects in public areas that grew from the affiliations of the Fine Arts and Architecture chairs, respectively: an oval, abstract mosaic by South the African artist Cecily Sash (1924–2019) at the base of the staircase, and Perret-influenced glazed grille that ran the height of a southern staircase. An oval staircase, the building's most striking feature, links the common spaces.

The seven lecturers who co-designed it allocated a zone for their 'studio seven' below the auditorium, separately accessible from the carport to allow site or client visits between their teaching work. The students were arrayed in neat rows of wide tables, with the windows to their left, in five studios from the basement to the first floor. Modernist order prevailed – on plan, at least. In 1975, the Fine Arts department moved away to another site, and its studios were converted to a studio for a planning programme that was growing in size and autonomy. The original studios were partitioned over time into double-banked offices, upsetting the modernist clarity of the original scheme and its close relations between studio masters and students. Only the foyer and shared lecture rooms remained largely as built in 1957, without any new fixtures, and continue to be so today. The vinyl-clad gypsum board passage walls that carved up the open plan first floor studios were functional installations without any heritage significance, and Guedes treated them as support structures for secondary layers of display material.

The John Moffat Building's tight scripting of spatial order was disrupted in other ways in the period leading up to Guedes' arrival. The former head of Department, John Fassler, who died in 1971, had faced nearly a decade of challenges to his empiricist approach, which was manifest in his taste for Perret and Festival of Britain architecture (Walker, n.d.). The most overt challenge to his directorship was a 1962 exhibition and catalogue entitled 'For Us': a homage to Van Eyck's term that students and young staff, including Julian Beinhart and Ivor Prinsloo, put out as an anti-aesthetic statement with Brutalist influences (Jones 1963). The project, for which they asked Pancho to contribute a text from Mozambique, was hung with clips in the foyer on scaffolding, using unframed black and white photographs and *sans serif* statements on craft card. Their rebellion was taken forward by the Urban Action Group, a collective of young architects who had pursued post-graduate studies at the University of Pennsylvania and shared a chair in the department in 1971 and 1972. They funded visits by Robert Venturi and Alison and Peter Smithson for lectures and pursued engagement with city planners to influence growth and renewal projects (Cooke n.d). Their antipathy towards the John Moffat Building's order was also manifest in an unrealised proposal for a prefabricated extension to the east, clad in lightweight panels and poised above the entrance and boldly embossed using Letratone onto the existing plan. Having disrupted the conservatism of the earlier generation, Ivor Prinsloo moved away to head the architecture school at University of Cape Town in 1974, leaving a vacuum for transformative education that Guedes' arrival was to fill.

Introducing Eclectica

The objects that Guedes had managed to bring from Mozambique were re-homed between his Wits office, the pair of semi-detached houses he renovated for his family in Melville and a small cottage in Eugaria near Sintra, Portugal, that he transformed incrementally during the annual break. He also generated new material, including a significant number of models made in the workshop by a woodworker, Ernie de Witt, and drew posters for each visiting speaker at the school. He hired two photographers, Alpheus Chuene and Henrietta Johnson, and built up a well-equipped darkroom to produce images for his projects and teaching (Department of Architecture 1989). Photos of Guedes' office taken around 1980 (Figure 4.5) show a space with the walls nearly full of framed drawings, alongside a small drawing board, plan drawers, books and a bank of slide trays, and racks added to hold sculptures, models and toys. There were also a set of chairs around his desk that Charles Rennie Mackintosh designed for the Hill House in 1905, reproduced by de Witt and a round table that was often covered with the material for projects in progress.

In Guedes' inaugural lecture that took place in 1977, a usually formal event where new professors introduce their area of expertise to the university at large, he showed 100 slides of works he had completed in Mozambique, as well as an exhibition in Venice and the Waterford School in Swaziland, dividing his 'styles' into 12 categories which resembled nothing canonical.[4] Later, he introduced the idea of a utopian archipelago called 'Eclectica'. He imagined that it lay off the African coast, where, his biographer Cedric Green notes,

FIGURE 4.5 Guedes' office, John Moffat Building, c1980. Source: collection of Pedro Guedes.

he had spent three happy years as child on the island of São Tomé e Príncipe (Green 2006): 'Eclectica ... is not an "ideal city" – there would be a mixture of good and bad architecture, and buildings inherited from the past by anonymous builders' (Green 2006). Acknowledging that Wits was an eclectic campus in physical terms, in the few opportunities he was given for design on campus, Guedes engaged with the adjacent structures with exceptional respect. These projects – the Sanctuary renovation, Sutton Close and Physics landscaping, and the unbuilt architecture archive proposed below the fishpond outside John Moffat – took an approach of drawing attention to the work of earlier architects and working with geometrical orders implicit in their form (Figure 4.6).

The array of names on the slide collection in Guedes' office reflects the more dispersed set of projects by architects that he would sometimes refer to as his friends, regardless of whether they were alive or long dead. He interrogated the evolution of their creative projects through the joint viewing of images with students in unscripted lectures. These trays of images were hand-labelled in appropriately aestheticised fonts and arranged alphabetically, creating surprising adjacencies: Alberti's Ten Books, Alberti, Aldo Van Eyck, Aalto, Americo Egipcio, Amsterdam brickwork, Aspen, Auguste Perret, Baldassare Peruzzi, Beaux Arts, Brancusi, Bruce Goff, Brunelleschi, C.H. Townsend, C. Moore Piazza N.O, C. Sitte, Casa Battlo, Casa Dos Bicos, Cassiano Branco, Cazal dos Olhos, Chagall, Chirico, CIAM, Colosseum Escom and Conceição Velha Misericórdia.[5] Some share established categories – early modern architects, Arts and Crafts, modern movement, Surrealists and postmodernists – but there were also curiosities in the form of buildings that fell between categories in their artisanal inventiveness.

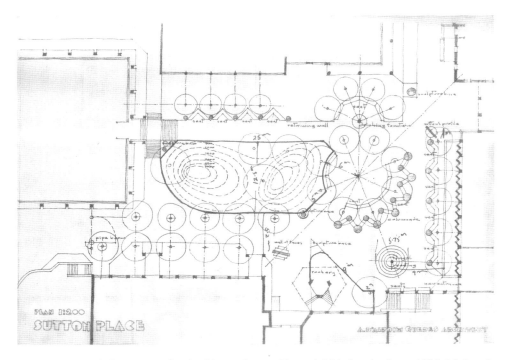

FIGURE 4.6 A. D'Alpoim Guedes Architect, Sutton Place. 1:200 sketch plan, c1980. University of the Witwatersrand PIMD collection.

The categorisation of his slides, which were either images from his own work, books or travels, began to extend over to a concern with disrupting and renewing the Wits drawing archives. He commissioned cabinets for the collections and began the practice of displaying some drawings on the walls of the passages of the first floor. There is no timeline of these images' placement, and it is likely that some have been moved. The long passage runs east–west, and the shorter one north–south from the library to the long passage. Two of the walls where these passages crossed were altered in the early 2000s, and there is no record of displays before then. The remaining images represent a wide selection of architects and genres. The images fall into three categories: those from the department's archives, gifts to the school and those commissioned by Guedes. The modernist archive, as he inherited it, held work of former students dating back to the 1930s, culminating around 1950, as well as some of the modernist architect and editor Rex Martienssen's drawings, correspondence and photos of buildings designed by his circle. Guedes admired the cosmopolitanism of Martienssen, who had been invited into CIRPAC by virtue of his overtures to European modernists to contribute work to the journal that he edited from 1931, *The South African Architectural Record* (Herbert 1975). The letters between Martienssen and his friend Norman Hanson were preserved and one very joyful one, noting Le Corbusier's dedication in his *oeuvre complète* to the 'Groupe Transvaal', (le Corbusier 1935) was framed in the library.[6]

Guedes secured the study collection amassed by Greig (1970) of drawings by the British neo-classical architect, Herbert Baker, and his contemporaries. In a rough inventory, he listed the framed watercolour renderings of Johannesburg buildings in the Department's holdings, including several from the collection of Kallenbach, Kennedy and Furner, dating from the 1920s to 1950s. There were drawings by Willem Dudok, Gordon Cullen and Michael Graves. In the 1980s, Guedes was supervising at least two dissertations (Frescura 1985; Rich 1991) on Ndebele architecture which led to the commissioning of the set of six acrylic paintings by Isa Kabini. Apart from some older watercolours, these works all had new frames created to Pancho's designs by Mr de Witt in the workshop. Along with these bespoke frames, Mr de Witt crafted wooden objects in the workshop from drawings including a set of scale models of Macintosh chairs.

Passages as relations

The use of the passage to present images in frames that resembled windows, the emphasis on street views of buildings and the commissioning of Ndebele wall decorations suggests that Guedes saw the passage as a street in the imaginary town, Eclectica. The act of viewing them would be tangential, giving unconscious impressions rather than the scrutiny of a gallery, unless driven by curiosity. Within this changing scape, he set specific images in challenging relations. For instance, as one exits the women's rest rooms, the facing image is a blueprint of a plan of the Union Buildings from the office of Herbert Baker (Baker 1910c). This less than sanctified location that places the seat of the joint British and Boer government of 1910, the capital building of the country, between two sets of toilet seats can be read as an act of deep disrespect of the building's symbolic value. Yet, the framing and preservation of the drawing signals a clear act of care for it that also acts to sever the associational power of the building from its materiality. Available for close reading – it is placed at the eye level of a squatting viewer – the labels of room functions provide an instructive diagram of the extractive bureaucracies of the new state.

Around 1980, Guedes instructed Mr de Witt to reproduce a set of pilasters representing the six orders in the Como Vitruvius (Vitruvius Pollio and Cesariano 1521) that were hung against the wall of the oval staircase (Figure 4.7). The location is a possible allusion to Bramante's 1505 spiral staircase in the Vatican that is considered to be the first conscious articulation of orders, but it is also quite central in the building's circulation (Ackerman 1983: 25). It could be read as a didactic display and coincides in time with the inaugural Venice Biennale of Architecture that resuscitated interest in the classical orders through the installation of postmodern facades along the Strada Novissima in the Arsenale (Szacka 2017). But the six Como orders that Guedes displayed are ornamental oddities compared to the subsequent and more restrained set of five orders that Serlio, Vignola and Palladio would codify in their respective treatises. The stair pilasters, two with foliar carvings and one capital with a face, are likely a dissident statement in relation to such received orders. The established neo-classical orders were, unsurprisingly, those taught in colonial schools and used in the older buildings on the Wits campus. Excluded from the canon, the ornamental variations that the Como order represents

FIGURE 4.7 Wooden pilasters commissioned by Guedes following the Orders of Architecture according to Cesare Cesariano, Como Vitruvius, 1521.

were closer to those widely found in popular and peripheral architecture beyond the circulation of sanctioned texts. In other words, Guedes was promoting an order of, or for, the New World.

This use of 'ironic' thought that Guedes articulated in his inaugural speech also engaged with the paradoxical nature of Wits, a university formed as a School of Mines to support the mining industry but transformed through social scientists and other academics to become the most progressive outpost of the white left. In the architecture department, this orientation was reflected in the influence of Kurt Jonas, a Jewish student who returned to South Africa in the mid-1930s after his studies in Frankfurt and Berlin. Jonas ran a series of extramural lectures to other students on Marxism and public culture and collaborated on a thesis on black housing (Connell et al. 1939). While Jonas' student drawings were kept in the drawers, a few of the colleagues he influenced are represented in the passage. One, of an apartment building resembling Jonas' design for Radoma Court, is a 1938 drawing by Betty Spence, a third-year student who would go on to become an important researcher and activist for black housing in the 1950s (le Roux and Woudstra 2020).

Along with displaying the work of Kabini and Spence, Guedes also designed a female counterpart to the Modular man figure that was etched into the glass doors of the John Moffat Building, along with the Vitruvian man. The gendered binary implicit in these pairings – Kabini opposite Lutyens, the Ladies toilet facing the gentlemen of the state, and Spence's inclusion amongst the all-male membership of the 'Groupe Transvaal' – was almost certainly a challenge to the architecture profession that had very few female figures of prominence in the 1980s.

Read in relation to its context, placing images in the passage constituted a quietly critical act in relation to the male supremacy that was commonplace in the profession. But the racial content of the display had troubling methods. Kabini's six panels came from acts of research, collecting and display that were not party to scrutiny in terms of their ethics. Although most of Guedes' personal collection was bought from living artists, between 1974 and 1975, he came across Mbali grave markers in an abandoned cemetery in Mocamedes, Angola, which he removed and kept (Pomar and Pereira 2010). In the context of a contested zone, soon to be the site of war, he saw this act as rescuing the wooden forms from further decay.[7] While these markers were never part of the Wits displays, their shapes, cut out of flat planks, seems to have inspired some of the frames designed for the Wits drawings. Guedes designed an elaborate frame to house an editioned sketch from Michael Graves evoking a wordplay that is likely to have been intentional.

The celebration of Ndebele art also overlapped with some of the tactics of apartheid cultural policies in relation to the homelands at that time. The state promoted the cultural values exemplified by mural artwork and women's dress as a justification for the creation of an ethnic "homeland" called KwaNdebele. In reality, this policy entailed the removal of families from dispersed ancestral settlements on farms, their homesteads demolished and their salvaged belongings dumped on small plots in settlements far from work or social infrastructure (Lekgoathi 2009). The forced removals lent some justification to the projects of the lecturers Peter Rich and Franco Frescura of recording these homesteads, sometimes with student help, in the course of writing on this architecture. However, in line with Wits' political binaries, at the same time, activist students in the department were actively protesting these removals or participating in relief missions to the bleak new resettlement camps.

Postpassage

The last five years of Guedes' career at Wits continued to be interrupted by political events, as the ever more beleaguered apartheid state clamped down with violence on political opposition within and beyond the national borders. On campus, the lecturers of the Department were not visible at the protests at which several architecture students were arrested by the police. Nor was Guedes heard to articulate a politically aligned position during the Metropolis conference of 1986 that highlighted the activism of emerging community planners and activists (Elk 1986), most of whom supported the African National Congress-aligned, anti-apartheid Civic associations. However, he prepared the last and significant object for that event in the form of a large-scale model – possibly 1:20 – of Aldo van Eyck's unbuilt 1963 competition design of the Protestant 'Wheels of Heaven' church for Driebergen. Raised on legs, and with circles cut into its base, the model allowed students to insert their heads into the church's interlinked gathering spaces from below.

Read as a didactic object in relation to the moment of its arrival in the foyer of John Moffat, the model could be seen to propose ways of coming together without a centre or a cluster of African buildings offset with a structural grid. It also suggested that architecture, however minimal, had an agential value in political negotiations. The return to Team 10 as a referent for this provocative object was not unconscious: Guedes reminded the students in the conference that he had only ever been associated with a group that had no formal membership. The other politics embedded in his material hermeneutics, including the very question of whether to build under apartheid, however, went unspoken. Designed to be engaged within different ways, as a canonical work, a homage, a design probe or as a failure, this final object placed by Pancho left the narrative open.

Guedes' investment in curating these objects, and their continued precarity, in turn, challenge us to return to them to consider how they might again talk to context. What are their potentials in relation to the contemporary call for decolonial architectural education (Mbembe 2015; Tayob and Hall 2019) as harbingers of change and markers of the durée of certain forms of Western knowledge? In their state of near-loss, they suggest a further pedagogic project through their re-animation as object references for new rituals of change in Africa, so linking the past with creative futures.

Notes

1 The architect-written articles on this architecture include (Spence 1940; Spence and Biermann 1954; Guedes 1962; Rich 1984).
2 Guedes had quite complex self-naming strategies which appear in 'An explanation of sorts' in (Guedes 1980). In line with his identification of A. d'Alpoim Guedes as the 'keeper of all the surviving drawings, paintings. sculptures, photographs, toys, embroideries, models, slides and words' he is named Guedes here when referring to his period at Wits, even though his colleagues and students in the department still called him Pancho.
3 Most famously Picasso, but also Tristan Tzara, whom Guedes would befriend. Guedes was aware of the European use of African art through journals he subscribed to, but was at pains to support living African artists as equivalent to others in their transformative work. From emails with Pedro Guedes and Alexandre Pomar, 2019–2021.
4 The 12 styles that Guedes described included Stiloguedes, the 'American Egyptian style', 'a tropical bush style' and an 'arched and somewhat Roman manner' (Guedes 1977).
5 From images of slide tray labels from Pedro Guedes' collection, 2019.

6   The framed letter to Hanson has been removed from the library to an unknown location. There are also missing artefacts from the Martienssen collection, including a page from a letter of praise by Le Corbusier, and two letters and an inscribed book from Walter Gropius.
7   Communication with Pedro Guedes, 2021. The Mbali were freed slaves from Brazil and Angola who developed hybrid material cultures. According to a 1930s anthropology report, these crosses and silhouettes were placed on graves by widows or widowers in a ritual of dissociation that would allow them to remarry. See (Estermann 1939: 74–86).

Bibliography

Ackerman, J. S. (1983), 'The Tuscan/Rustic Order: A Study in the Metaphorical Language of Architecture', *Journal of the Society of Architectural Historians*, 42, 15–34.

Baker, H. (1910c), New Union Buildings Pretoria. General Plan, First Floor.

Beinart, J. (1961). 'Amâncio Guedes. Architect of Lourenço Marques', *The Architectural Review*, 129, 240–260.

Connell, P. H., Irvine-Smith, C., Jonas, K., Kantorowich, R. & Wepener, F. J. (1939), *Native Housing*. (Bachelor of Architecture thesis). University of the Witwatersrand, Johannesburg.

Cooke, J. (n.d.) *Ivor Prinsloo*. Artefacts. Available online: https://www.artefacts.co.za/main/Buildings/archframes.php?archid=3029 (accessed 25 March 2021).

Cross, M. (1986), 'A Historical Review of Education in South Africa: Towards an Assessment', *Comparative Education*, 22, 185–200.

Department of Architecture (1989), *Periodic Review Report*, Johannesburg: University of the Witwatersrand.

Elk, C. (ed) (1986). *Metropolis Student Congress Architecture Wits, 30 March–4 April 1986*, Johannesburg: National Architecture Students Union.

Estermann, C. (1939), 'Coutumes des Mbali du sud d'Angola', *Africa: Journal of the International African Institute*, 12, 74–86.

Fabrizi, M. (2020), 'The Otterlo Circles by Aldo van Eyck. Collage as Condensed Theory', *piano b. Arti e culture visive*, 4, 1–15.

Frescura, F. (1985), *Major developments in the rural indigenous architecture of southern Africa of the post-Difaqane period*. (Unpublished master's thesis). Department of Architecture, University of the Witwatersrand, Johannesburg.

Green, C. (2006), 'A Biographical Essay'. In: R. Jacinto (ed.), *Lisboscopio*, Lisbon: Instituto das Artes.

Greig, D. E. (1970), *Herbert Baker in South Africa*, Cape Town, etc., Purnell.

Guedes, A. (1980), *Amancio Guedes*, London: The Architectural Assocation.

Guedes, A. D. A. (1962), 'Les Mapoga', *Aujourd'hui: Art et Architecture*, no 37, June. 58–65.

Guedes, A. D. A. (1963), 'A Cidade Doente - Varias receitas para curer o mal do caniço e o manual do vogal sem mestre', *A Tribuna*, 6–7.

Guedes, A. D. A. (1977), *Fragments from an Ironic Autobiography Inaugural Lecture by Amancio d'Alpoim Guedes Professor and Head of the Department of Architecture University of the Witwatersrand Johannesburg Delivered on the Twenty Fourth of August Nineteen Seventy Six*, Johannesburg, Witwatersrand University Press.

Guedes, A. D. A. & Guedes, P. (2009), *Pancho Guedes: Vitruvius Mozambicanus*, Lisbon, Museu Colecção Berardo.

Guedes, L. & Guedes, P. (eds.) (2003), *Viva Pancho*, Durban: Total Cad Academy.

Guedes, N. (2017), Available online: https://wrongwrong.net/article/pancho-guedes-the-memory-of-a-collector (accessed 25 March 2021).

Herbert, G. (1975), *Martienssen and the International Style: The Modern Movement in South African Architecture*, Cape Town-Rotterdam, AA Balkema.

Herbert, G. & Donchin, M. (2013), *The Collaborators: Interactions in the Architectural Design Process*, Farnham, Ashgate.

Jones, P. (1963), For Us; Johannesburg Department of Architecture, University of the WItwatersrand.

Keeling, C. (2014), *The John Moffat Building: A Conservation Report*, Johannesburg: University of the Witwatersrand.

Le Corbusier (1935), *Le Corbusier et Pierre Jeanneret – Oeuvre complète de 1929–1934*, Zurich, H. Girsberger.

Le Roux, H. & Woudstra, R. (2020), 'Build Your Own House': Betty Spence's Design Research in 1950s South Africa. *SAHGB Architectural History Seminar*, online event.

Lekgoathi, S. P. (2009), 'Colonial'experts, local interlocutors, informants and the making of an archive on the "Transvaal Ndebele" 1930–1989', *The Journal of African History*, 50, 61–80.

Levin, A. (2016). 'Basic Design and the Semiotics of Citizenship: Julian Beinart's Educational Experiments and Research on Wall Decoration in Early 1960s Nigeria and South Africa', *Abe Journal: Architecture beyond Europe*, 9–10. Retrieved from https://abe.revues.org/3180

Mbembe, A. (2015), *Decolonizing Knowledge and the Question of the Archive*. New York: Africaisacountry.

Pomar, A. & Pereira, R. M. (2010), The Africas of Pancho Guedes. In: C. M. D. Lisboa (ed.), Lisbon: Sextante Editora.

Rich, P. (1984), 'The Hybrid "palaces"of the Mapogga', *Space and Society*, 26, 6–25.

Rich, P. (1991), *The Architecture of the Southern Ndebele*. (Unpublished master's thesis). Department of Architecture, University of the Witwatersrand, Johannesburg.

Spence, B. (1940.), 'Native Architecture', *South African Architectural Record*, 25, 387–391.

Spence, B. & Biermann, B. (1954), 'M'Pogga', *Architectural Review*, 116, 34–40.

Szacka, L.-C. (2017), *Exhibiting the Postmodern: The 1980 Venice Architecture Biennale*, Venice, Marsilio Editori.

Tayob, H., & Hall, S. (2019). *Race, space and architecture: towards and open-access curriculum*. Retrieved from http://eprints.lse.ac.uk/100993/

Uribe, A. C. (2018), *Aldo van Eyck: le Musée imaginaire,* Doctorate, Escuela Técnica Superior de Arquitectura de Valencia.

Vitruvius Pollio, M. & Cesariano, C. (1521), *De Architectura Libri Decem*, Como, Agostino Gallo and Luigi Pirovano.

Walker, J. (n.d.), *Fassler John*, Pretoria: Artefact. Available online: https://www.artefacts.co.za/main/Buildings/archframes.php?archid=493 (accessed 20 February 2021).

PART 2
Hands-on
Learning through manual work

5

PLANNING PROBLEMS

Data graphics in the education of architects and planners at the Harvard Graduate School of Design, the 1940s

Anna Vallye

In June 1937, the National Resources Committee (later renamed and better known as the National Resources Planning Board, or NRPB), the headquarters of New Deal public planning policy, published its landmark study, *Our Cities, Their Role in the National Economy* (Figure 5.1).

Our Cities was the inaugural product of the NRPB Urbanism Committee, formed in 1935 with a mandate to define the relationship between cities and national planning (Hancock 1988: 197–230). The report called for direct federal investment in cities, on everything from taxation policy, to welfare assistance, to urban land policy and public works. For architects, it augured grand building opportunities to come.[1] It also elevated urban planning to a new national prominence.

The cover design of *Our Cities* features, in the foreground, groupings of high-, medium-, and low-rise buildings, suggesting a cross-section of urban skylines. Clouds in the middle ground part to reveal a diagram of urban locations across the nation, each denoted by a circle that represents the city's relative population size. The graphic's message is correspondingly layered. It is showing American cities first as they may be seen by the layperson's eye and then again comprehended more deeply through the transformative lens of demographic analysis. More than representing the report's contents, the cover communicates the nature of urban planning as a discipline of knowledge with new relevance for both state and citizen.

The task of establishing cities as targets of federal action pivoted on a redefinition of 'national resource'. The early years of the New Deal were chiefly preoccupied with rural and agricultural areas and their 'physical resources of water, land, and minerals', but now, the 'Nation ha[d] wisely begun to concern itself with the conservation of its human and social resources as well' (National Resources Committee 1937: v). The object of governance was, thus, recalibrated along a logical chain: from rural areas to urban areas, from 'natural resource' to 'human resource', from the land to the population, from massive physical structures like Tennessee Valley Authority dams to the more abstract entity, 'human life' (National Resources Committee 1937: 1). Within the purview of federal governance, indicated the report, the methods and tools employed in the study of cities were those of the

DOI: 10.4324/9781003201205-8

86 Anna Vallye

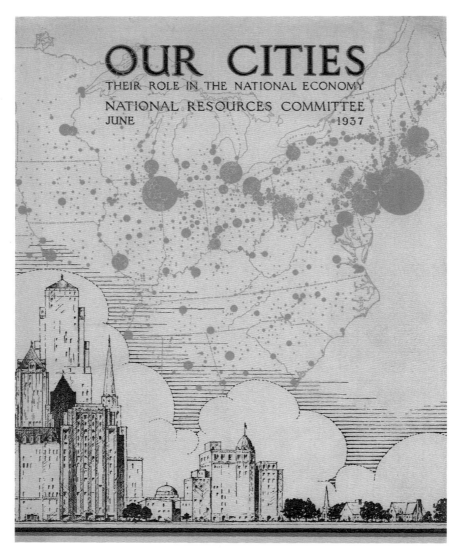

FIGURE 5.1 Cover. National Resources Committee, Our Cities: Their Role in the National Economy (June 1937).

social sciences, grounded in statistical analysis and trend projection.[2] The report's cover graphically represented that focal shift within the planning discipline from the physical environment to the immaterial order of data.

For architects, the decade to come would be marked by 'a culture of planning', of thinking building on a vaster scale and bold visions for life in '194X'.[3] But that fervid imaginary was buttressed and ultimately confined by a powerful, if more prosaic, technology, evolving on its parallel course within the discipline of planning defined as a function of governance. This presented a quandary for architecture. The methods and objects of planning were distanced to an unprecedented degree from built structures, the traditional ends of architectural expertise. The art of planning for cities of 'human resources' was rather understood to be a science of 'public administration'. What place would there be for architecture's tools of spatial design and its languages of visual communication within a discipline focused on increasingly immaterial terrain?

In the decade that followed the publication of *Our Cities*, the Harvard University Graduate School of Design (GSD) developed an influential approach to that problem. The issues of knowledge and practice raised at the intersection of architecture and planning, this chapter argues, were registered in the artefacts produced by GSD students in the course of collaborative problems that combined the programs of architecture, landscape architecture, and urban planning. Statistical diagrams and maps, infographics, and other graphics meant to illustrate the research conclusions of students were important pedagogical 'materials' at the GSD, and a premium was placed on acquiring the skills necessary to design and execute them.

In the first half of the 20th century, statistical data graphics were ubiquitous in a wide range of contexts on both sides of the Atlantic, embraced by amateurs as well as experts, and officially recognised and adopted by government agencies (Funkhouser 1937). Modern architects, eager to impart to their practice the authority of science, made frequent use of statistical representations. They were commonly found especially at the intersection of architectural and planning studies, most famously in the analyses of cities carried out under the auspices of Congrès International de l'Architecture Moderne (CIAM) (Weiss et al. 2014). The 1942 publication *Can Our Cities Survive?*, which popularised CIAM ideas in America, featured data graphics among its illustrations (Sert 1942). With Walter Gropius, Martin Wagner, and Marcel Breuer on the faculty, the European modernist approach was well represented at Harvard. Wagner, in particular, as I have shown elsewhere, was conceptually invested in data visualisation (Vallye 2020). But, American architects and planners employed a broad spectrum of visual persuasion strategies in the 1940s, creatively borrowed from fields like photography, advertising, and art (Shanken 2006, 2018).[4]

The emphasis at Harvard was placed specifically on the visualisation of statistical information. GSD demonstration materials, I argue, were products of curricular transformation that aimed to re-negotiate the disciplinary juncture of architecture and planning. Like the image on the cover of *Our Cities*, GSD graphics communicated, beyond their immediate content, the claims to authority and organising structures of professional knowledge. The visual language they developed prioritised clear translations between two-dimensional representation (coded as the order of data) and three-dimensional representation (the order of space). The pedagogical value of such graphics thus resided in developing habits of eye and assumptions of mind that would prepare students for a professional world in which architecture was envisioned to operate at the core of planning and planning likewise at the core of architecture.

Curriculum reform at Harvard

Harvard was the cradle of planning education in the United States. The first city planning course was taught there in 1909, and Harvard's School of City Planning, established in 1929, was the first educational institution of its kind in America (Alofsin 2002: 41–46, 64–72). Soon thereafter, in 1936, the University amalgamated the previously separate schools of architecture, city planning, and landscape architecture into a single school of design under the leadership of Dean Joseph Hudnut. Together with his most significant hire, Walter Gropius, who arrived in 1937, Hudnut elaborated a capacious pedagogy of 'design' that understood the architectural and territorial scales of organisation to exist along a single continuum of expertise – an architecture that, as Gropius envisioned it in 1935, grows 'from the house to… the street; from the street to the town; and finally to the still vaster implications of regional and national planning' (Gropius 1935: 98–99; see also Alofsin 2002: 112–195; Pearlman 2007).

But, by 1940, their curricular platform was threatened when the University raised the possibility of transferring planning education from the GSD to the new Littauer School of Public Administration, also established in 1936.[5] Through that motion, the Harvard administration aimed to remain at the forefront of the planning discipline. It also threatened the GSD's cultivated assumption of basic compatibility between the professional competencies of architects and planners. While planning education was ultimately retained as part of the GSD, the curricular, conceptual, and personnel changes that followed into the mid-1940s amounted to a fraught, if highly productive, negotiation between approaches derived from modern architecture and American planning – mediated, ultimately, by the needs and logics of US governance (Vallye [manuscript]).

'The staffs of the planning commissions today', wrote GSD planning department chair George Holmes Perkins in 1950, 'bear faint resemblance to those of the 1920s when engineer and architect were almost the sole participants' (Perkins 1950: 316). Accordingly, the question animating Harvard's curricular reforms a few years earlier: if planning was increasingly becoming a social science and governmental practice, what relationship could it still have to design? Political scientist John Merriman Gaus, hired to oversee the transition, outlined Harvard's new program in his 1943 report *The Graduate School of Design and the Education of Planners*. The study became something of a bible of 1940s planning pedagogy, referred to in professional circles as 'the little red book' of Chairman Gaus (Isaacs and Serageldin 1973: 18). Gaus started from the premise that the historical trajectory of planning had led from its origins in architecture to current 'administrative planning', a matter of coordinating 'social research' into a complex of goals and procedures dedicated to guiding governmental policy (Gaus 1943: 27). Yet, in the end, he asserted, the role of the architect 'ha[d] only become more important' because the operations of governance must 'of necessity be registered in physical change' (Gaus 1943: 39). Reviewing the ongoing planning education reforms at several US universities two years later, Gaus again noted a widespread 'reaction against the more uncritical criticism of the early city planners as being too concerned with architecture… as the social scientist discovers how *tangible* the end result of his own contribution must be' (Gaus 1945: 308–309 [emphasis added]). The question of architecture's role in planning was placed at that juncture between processes of governance, informed by social-scientific research and material interventions in physical space. As planning education translated disciplinary structures into teachable skills, traditional architectural competencies in spatial design and graphic representation became a significant register of conceptual shifts within the planning discipline.

In a 1942 survey conducted by the American Institute of Planners (AIP), 43% of the respondents believed that graduates of planning schools must 'at least acquire a respectable competence in graphical representation of their ideas if they are to be recipients of a planning degree', and only 2% felt otherwise. While the AIP assumed that a lack of 'competence in physical design', or even of 'potential ability to design', would not disqualify an aspirant from entering the field, 'graphic representation' was still believed to be necessary as 'the physical interpretation of [a planner's] ideas' (Committee on Education and Personnel Standards 1942: 12). In 1948, the AIP Committee on Planning Education concluded more forcefully that, while a senior planning official 'may not touch pencil to drafting board... for months on end', both graphic 'presentation techniques' and 'design techniques' were to be among the 'basic tools' or skills in a planning curriculum. 'Since the subject matter of his planning,' wrote the Committee about the planning professional, deals largely with spatial relationships, he needs also some skill in graphic expression – freehand sketching and mechanical drafting. [And the planner also] needs technical competence in and understanding of the use and limitations of spatial design. Design training in architecture, landscape architecture, or engineering is relevant, (Committee on Planning Education 1948: 12).

Much about the professional meaning and social agency of planning in fact rested on the products of those design and presentation techniques – and therefore, in a sense, on architecture. Architecture thus became *more* important to planning the more planning moved in the direction of administrative governance and away from physical design.

Objects and objectives in Harvard planning problems.

The showcase results of Harvard's curricular reorganisation of 1942–1943 were so-called 'collaborative research problems'. Collaborative coursework across departments was encouraged at Harvard since the turn of the century (Alofsin 2002: 23–29) and under Hudnut was elaborated as a key educational precept. What distinguished the courses conducted in the second half of the 1940s was their expanded emphasis on social-scientific research and their likewise spectacularly intensified efforts to visualise the products of that research through graphic design strategies. The students continued to produce more conventional drawings, site plans, and models, but now, they were also required to generate substantial numbers of statistical graphs, maps, and other visualisations. Arguably, such materials were the chief physical products of Harvard's planning education reform.

The collaborative problems of the 1940s ranged from courses taught by two or three professors to massive undertakings that focused the attention of the entire school. As described by Gropius in a 1946 meeting of the school council, a typical problem of the latter type would open with an all-school meeting and introductory discussion at the beginning of the semester. The planning department would then prepare a 'skeleton scheme, [including] all necessary data'. During that 'preparatory stage', planning students would conduct weekly meetings with architecture and landscape architecture students (Report of Council Luncheon 1946). All three departments would then join together to prepare design proposals, complete with models and drawings. After jury review, there would be another all-school meeting to discuss the results.

Using the example of a 'housing study' done in the spring semester of 1945, Perkins gave this close-up view of the collaborative problem process:

> A housing market analysis was prepared into which went the contributions of economists, sociologists, public administrators, and architects – both students and professors. From this analysis was developed a program from which, in turn, grew designs for the redevelopment of a large city area complete to [sic] methods of public and private financing, architectural plans, and traffic proposals.
>
> *(Perkins 1945: 312)*[6]

Such problems focused on specific towns or metropolitan regions, usually in the Boston metropolitan area, and were sometimes initiated in response to competitions announced by municipal authorities. Over the course of the 1940s, the school studied the Massachusetts towns of Wayland, Hingham, Sudbury, and Framingham; as well as the rehabilitation of South Boston, East Cambridge, and other sections of Greater Boston (Hudnut 1948: 9). In essence, the all-school problems were intended to be laboratory ventures in professional planning practice. The most prominent, a fall semester 1947 study of Framingham, was actually commissioned by that city. The student report was published in February 1948 as *Framingham: Your Town, Your Problem* (Row et al. 1948) (Figure 5.2).

Widely publicised, the report was of a professional quality so notable that Perkins grew concerned about its precedent leading to competition with practicing planners.[7] A brief review in the American Society of Planning Officials Newsletter highlighted the fact that the report was 'very well illustrated, with many drawings and coloured plates' ('Review: "Framingham: Your Town – Your Problem"' 1948: 76).

A closer look at the Framingham problem reveals much about the school's approach. The students were grouped into six interdisciplinary teams. As per standard procedure, the first half of the semester (six weeks) was devoted to research, carried out by the planning students alone. Joined in November by the architects and landscape architects, the planners continued their research while working collaboratively on the remaining requirements (Perkins 24 December 1947).[8] The initial research phase of the problem consisted of studies

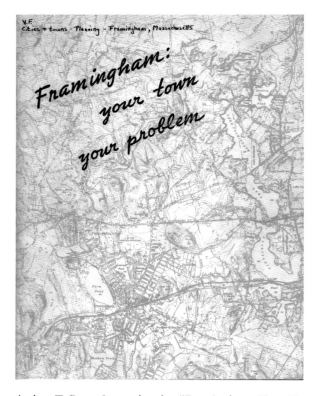

FIGURE 5.2 Cover. Arthur T. Row, Jr., et.al., eds., "Framingham: Your Town, Your Problem" (February 1948).

of population, economic base, transportation, land use, community facilities and services, and government organisation ('Problem I: Framingham' [September 1947 to January 1948]). 'The first six weeks', Perkins reported,

> were spent in a hectic push of gathering data, preparing maps, making a basic topography, and generally in getting a feel for the town. At the end of this period, we had produced more than sixty 30" x 40" charts summarising the material, and reports totalling about 300 pages.
>
> *(Perkins April 1948: 3; see also Perkins May 1948)*

While university archives preserve none of those 60 'charts', their large format conceived in view of eventual exhibition at the Framingham town hall, they are amply reproduced in the published report (Perkins April 1948: 3; see also Perkins May 1948).[9] Supplemented with some photographs of models, those graphics constitute the bulk of the report's visual program.

The Framingham study reveals a debt owed to the NRPB blueprint. In 1943, the NRPB Urbanism Committee published *Action for Cities*, a 'community planning manual' (Mallery, Blucher & Ridley 1943; for more on this publication, see Shanken 2009: 21–23). Its goal was to provide a step-by-step guide to comprehensive planning for municipal planning agencies, on the example of three 'demonstration cities': Corpus Christi, Texas; Salt Lake City, Utah; and Tacoma, Washington. The 'demonstration city' projects commenced with a quick 'reconnaissance' survey of the area to be planned, intended to 'identify key problems [and] uncover available data', and made by 'touring the area…; by examining documents, maps, and aerial photographs; and by conferring with officials, business, and civic leaders' (*A technique for accelerated planning*, 1943). Harvard plunged into the 'reconnaissance' stage already in the summer of 1947, when one of the students, Edward Heiselberg, was engaged to produce some 'base maps' of the city (Perkins 26 June 1947). Heiselberg consulted the town engineer, the school superintendent, the town accountant, and other local officials (Heiselberg 19 June 1947).[10]

An illustration in *Action for Cities* conveys the reconnaissance process by means of a circle that suggests a magnifying glass superimposed over a map of Tacoma (Figure 5.3). The urban landmarks that fall within its perimeter acquire an analytical depth, revealing factors like housing quality and traffic congestion. 'It is important', explained *Action for Cities*:

> *to look at the community as if it were being seen for the first time*, noting its important characteristics, its assets, and its difficulties. … The reconnaissance can be used to identify the salient facts and problems that will have to be dealt with now and later.
>
> *(Mallery et al. 1943: 10 [emphasis added])*

Such preliminary studies typically employed aerial or topographic maps of the target territory. For example, in a 1954 Aero Service Corporation advertisement printed in the *Journal of the American Institute of Planners*, aerial maps provide 'answers' to urban problems like 'traffic flow, land use, [and] housing' – but not before the expert eye of the planning technician poised before the image decodes the societal patterns in play across the earth's visible surfaces. The technician's eye is in that way analogous to the 'stereo-plotting instrument' pictured on the right, which had earlier produced the aerial photograph itself (Figure 5.4). Planning knowledge is figured as a technology that peels away apparent surface phenomena to reveal a hidden social order subject to instrumental intervention.

92 Anna Vallye

Reconnaissance map of Tacoma showing conditions existing in June, 1942. Inset shows detail of area around main business section on a larger scale. The reconnaissance survey was made in a week, the map sketched and colored in three hours.

RECONNAISSANCE OF THE COMMUNITY

FIGURE 5.3   "Reconnaissance of the Community," from Earl D. Mallery, et al., Action for Cities: A Guide for Community Planning (1943), 9.

Planning problems 93

Raleigh, N. C. city officials get office answers to traffic flow, land use, housing and other problems with precise AERO photo maps.

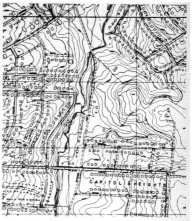

Detailed AERO topo maps speed solutions to engineering problems... help plan highways, railroads, pipe lines, industrial and mining development.

Aero can solve your mapping problem, too!

AERO maps have saved time and money for cities like New York and Philadelphia, Cleveland and Hamilton, Ohio, for Bethlehem, Pennsylvania, and Ottumwa, Iowa, and many others. Our dependable photo maps provide basic facts for planning city growth: subdivisions... playgrounds... land use... traffic. Our contour maps provide answers for sewerage and drainage problems and other engineering developments. Our engineers can bring a wealth of city mapping experience to bear on your city's problems.

Skilled technicians with complex stereo-plotting instruments produce AERO maps to the most exacting engineering standards.

No need to hire new staff engineers for your big mapping job. AERO crews can do the job faster— saving you 50 to 90 percent of ground survey costs! ▶

AERO SERVICE CORPORATION
Philadelphia 20, Pennsylvania

Oldest Flying Corporation in the World

Affiliates:
AERO SERVICE CORPORATION (Mid-Continent), TULSA
AERO SERVICE CORPORATION (Western), SALT LAKE CITY
CANADIAN AERO SERVICE, LTD., OTTAWA

AIRBORNE MAGNETOMETER SURVEYS
PRECISE AERIAL MOSAICS • TOPOGRAPHIC MAPS
PLANIMETRIC MAPS • RELIEF MODELS • SHORAN MAPPING

FIGURE 5.4 Advertisement for Aero Service Corporation, from Journal of the American Institute of Planners 20 (Fall 1954), [220].

94 Anna Vallye

FIGURE 5.5 Arial view of Framingham, Massachusetts. Frontispiece to Arthur T. Row, Jr., et al., eds., Framingham: Your Town, Your Problem (February 1948).

Opening with a topographical map on the cover and an aerial photograph on the frontispiece, the Framingham booklet records the explicit steps of the reconnaissance survey process and telegraphs the same implicit message about the nature of planning's specialised knowledge (Figure 5.5, see also Figure 5.3). Like the cover design for *Our Cities*, the Framingham study juxtaposes the putative realism of those opening views to the coded abstraction of statistical graphics that proliferate on the subsequent pages: diagrams of population distribution, land use, industrial activity, patterns of blight, etc. According to the NRPB, the preliminary survey set directions for localised in-depth studies, focused on such conditions as local demographics and population trends, industry patterns and economic base, services and facilities, traffic flow, and land use patterns, concluding with recommendations for future growth ('A technique for accelerated planning' 1942: 48). The GSD report conducted similar studies for Framingham, illustrating each with statistical visualisations.

A model of Framingham's aggregate income elegantly conveys distributed expenditure streams in a hard-edged spiralling figure, gradated in shades of grey and relative width of line (Figure 5.6). The flow of vehicular and railway freight traffic spreads like a vascular system across a map of New England, the Boston metropolitan region carved out for closer inspection (Figure 5.7). A bar chart of population statistics by employment type is organised like a cross-section of a building with floors stacked by percent share from tallest to

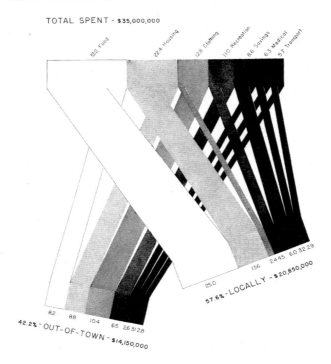

FIGURE 5.6 "Income Distribution," from Arthur T. Row, Jr., et al., eds., Framingham: Your Town, Your Problem (February 1948), 10.

shortest, each accompanied by a miniature icon clad in the uniform of its respective profession (Figure 5.8). Demonstrating an imaginative use of standard statistical graphics formats, those charts are reminiscent of the illustrations arrayed across the pages of *Our Cities*[11] (Figure 5.9). The visual language of the diagram *materialises* the abstract order of data by translating quantities into images vested with putative realism. The relative number of dollars spent is conveyed through the relative width of a line. The number of vehicles present along a traffic artery is mapped out in relation to its corresponding location in physical space. Like the eye of the planning technician scanning the surface image of a city, the statistical diagram reveals invisible patterns embedded in data. It does so through conceptual operations that navigate between two-dimensional and three-dimensional space, analogous to those of perspectival and projective drawing used by architects.

Taken together, the localised studies presented the groundwork for what the AIP Committee on Planning Education, for example, saw as planning's core procedure: 'integration', or, determining 'the relationships of things to each other'. The 'things' that planners addressed were the 'subject matters of all the social sciences', taken typically as measurable quantities (Committee on Planning Education 1948: 6). Although such 'elements of the city' were to be studied individually, they were to be 'so developed that the relationships of these elements to each other [would] be constantly brought to the student's attention',

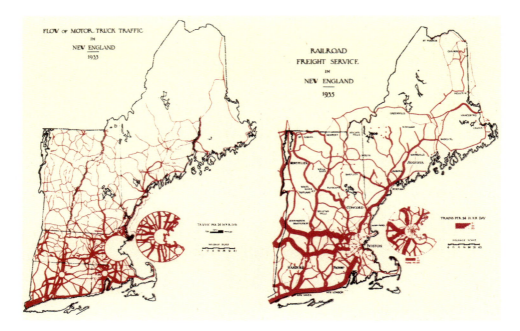

FIGURE 5.7 "Motor Truck Traffic in New England, 1933" and "Railroad Freight Service in New England, 1935," from Arthur T. Row, Jr., et al., eds., Framingham: Your Town, Your Problem (February 1948), [27].

eventually producing a 'well-coordinated, unified plan' (Committee on Planning Education 1948: 18). According to *Action for Cities*, the localised studies phase was to be followed up by 'diagramming relationships of functions (residence, work, shopping, play, etc.)' (Mallery et al. 1943: 57). The application of such diagrammatic studies to the physical territory would prompt the generation of 'desirable patterns' of development.

Planning work was the analysis, calculation, and correlation of social factors to reveal beneath the surfaces of everyday urban reality a complex and dynamic functional pattern, destined to be optimised and projected into the future. The proposed land use schema was derived from that pattern; it was the 'physical arrangement to fit those economic and social needs' ('A technique for accelerated planning' 1943: 42).[12] The GSD student drawings express an axiomatic assumption about the disciplinary foundation of planning in social-scientific method, which translates urban life as a set of quantifiable mass phenomena, accessed by means of aggregated data. The images are imaginative pictorial embodiments of that data, clothing its bloodless abstractions in a vivid material foil. As such, they script the analytical diagram's assumed eventual return, full circle, to shape the physical spaces of the city. *Action for Cities* recommended producing a 'diagram of general functional relationships' to 'dramatise in "graphic language" the essential relationships of areas and uses' (Mallery et al. 1943: 57) (Figure 5.10). Withholding any visual relationship to the physical site, the purely abstract diagram was to be used as a guide for 'alternative schemes' of physical development, a 'realistic working plan' (Mallery et al. 1943: 57). The Framingham study skipped that intermediary diagram, creating two versions of final 'sketch plans' for the city (Figure 5.11). Although shown against the actual topography and other givens of the site, the 'sketch plans' were nonetheless schematic land use studies, meant to 'suggest a direction

POPULATION

TYPE OF EMPLOYMENT 1940

Number of people in each occupation expressed as a per cent of the total workers in each community.

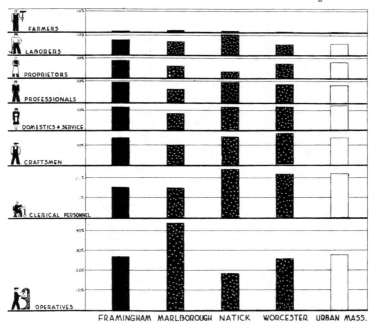

Number of people in primary and derived employment.

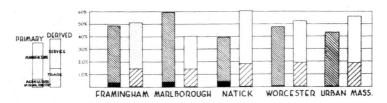

FIGURE 5.8 "Population," from Arthur T. Row, Jr., et al., eds., Framingham: Your Town, Your Problem (February 1948), 9.

for growth' (Row et al. 1948: 39).[13] They were followed up with photographs of models done in collaboration with architecture and landscape architecture students, which showed township layouts and a schematic design for a shopping centre (Figure 5.12). From the aerial photograph to the architectural model, the reference to physical space had come full circle, traversed on its path by the analytical abstraction of data.

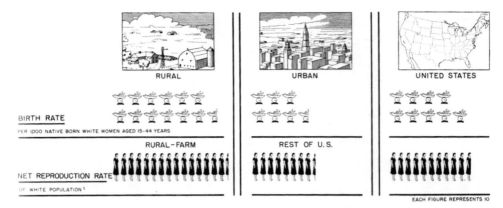

FIGURE 5.9 Births—1930," from National Resources Committee, Our Cities: Their Role in the National Economy (June 1937), 11.

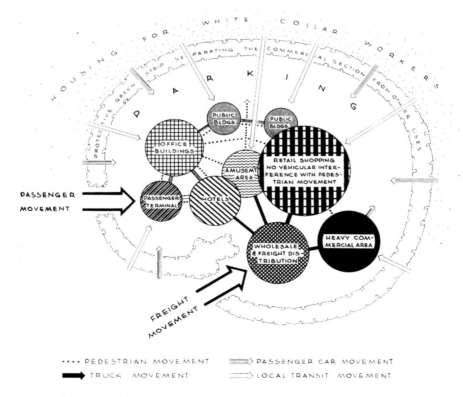

FIGURE 5.10 Diagram of the functional relationship of activities in the central commercial area of Tacoma," from "A Technique for Accelerated Planning," New Pencil Points (August 1943): 43. "[Such diagrams] bring out relationships in a way easy to comprehend and sometimes point the way to bold and useful measures of rehabilitation such as might not be suggested by the physical map itself.

FIGURE 5.11 "Sketch Plan I," from Arthur T. Row, Jr., et al., eds., Framingham: Your Town, Your Problem (February 1948), [45].

The goal of the Framingham study, explained Perkins, was 'not the adoption of a plan, but an arousing of the citizens to a point where they will see for themselves the advantages and economies of the planning process' (Perkins May 1948: 101). Ultimately, the GSD team pointed out to the citizens of Framingham, the city is 'your town and your problem'. This distancing manoeuvre was meant as a retreat from expert responsibility on behalf of a student 'laboratory' project.[14] But it also replicated a common hinge around which the disciplinary machinery of planning pivoted into the speculative dimension. The 'demonstration cities' project proved to be the swan song of the NRPB, disbanded by Congress in July 1943. While federal investment in cities continued to grow through the 1940s, the NRPB's demise decisively shut the door on a New Deal notion of planning as comprehensive design of the urban fabric. As the historian M. Christine Boyer noted, ironically, the institutionalisation of planning within the federal government did not necessarily lead to the implementation of its expert proposals (Boyer 1983: 205, 230–231). The marked contrast with the evident material productivity of European state-sponsored planning was noted at Harvard, as elsewhere. 'We haven't been able to produce', wrote Perkins to Gordon Stephenson, editor of the UK-based *Town Planning Review*, in December 1948, 'either in legislation or in fact as clear demonstrations of planning as you have. Therefore, we tend sometimes to be satisfied with research as a substitute for reality...' (Perkins 28 December 1948: 1).

The 'void' in agency, Boyer observes, was filled on the one hand through an intensification of disciplinary techniques – as planning 'turned inwards toward abstract policy

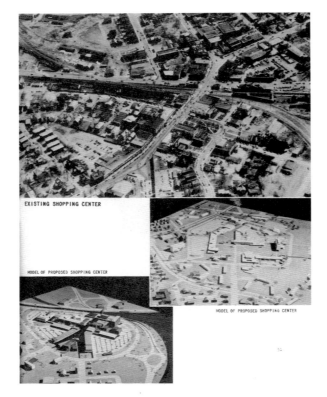

FIGURE 5.12 Existing and proposed shopping centers, from Arthur T. Row, Jr., et al., eds., Framingham: Your Town, Your Problem (February 1948), [51].

formation, research, and information collection' – and on the other hand, through efforts to generate 'popular sentiment' or 'public will' in support of official intervention (Boyer 1983: 205, 230–231). Like the 'demonstration cities' projects before it, the Framingham study stressed the importance of ensuring 'the continuing active interest and participation of leading citizens and civic groups' ('A technique of accelerated planning' 1943: 31). The informed and persuaded citizen was the implied addressee of planning's expert knowledge and the avatar of its social agency. Thus, the GSD students' work drew closer to what practicing planners identified as one of the profession's key products – the increasingly ubiquitous 'public information pamphlet' (*American Society of Planning Officials Newsletter* 1949: 16). If, as GSD planning faculty member Martin Meyerson wrote in 1946, the goal of the planner's work was to 'fuse data and insight', its medium had to 'capture the enthusiasm of the people' (Meyerson 1946: 172). Visual rhetoric did not merely accompany, but in a significant respect *actualised* the core operations of planning.

The key role of public persuasion in planning was well considered at Harvard. In 1944, for example, the school hosted meetings of the fledgling American Society of Planners and Architects, spearheaded by Hudnut, with Marcel Breuer and Walter Gropius among its faculty members. The Society listed 'public education by means of critical articles, pamphlets,

WALKING DISTANCES IN NEIGHBORSHIP

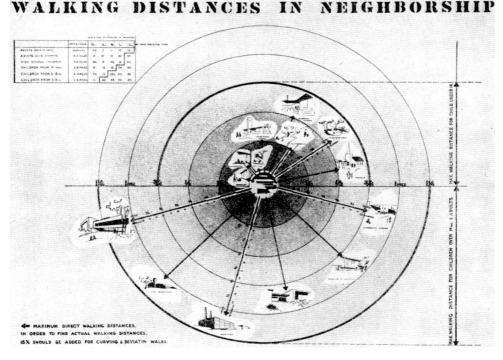

FIGURE 5.13   John Benton, "Walking Distances in Neighborship," ca. 1947. (Image source: Harvard University Archives.)

exhibitions or other related activities' among its three main objectives. The members deemed 'essential' the role of visual means in the 'true popularisation' of planning, calling on 'experts in graphic presentation' and 'first-rate graphic artist[s]' (American Society of Planners and Architects 4 March 1944: 2). Similar goals were emphasised in the first post-war issue of the GSD student-edited journal *Task* by *American City* journal associate editor C. Eric Carlson. 'The job of selling and vitalising planning to the common man', wrote Carlson, 'is the current planning frontier…' (Carlson 1948: 89).

In the 1940s, graphics became an established and increasingly codified component of GSD planning coursework. By 1951, Harvard faculty sought to build a collection of graphic standards catalogues for 'students in city planning who do an immense amount of poster work' (Creighton 12 March 1951). Like the Framingham report, GSD student work was often written about or featured in architectural and planning publications. The dissemination of those student graphics testifies to the substantial pedagogical imperative placed on fledgling planners and architects to master a new grammar of visual persuasion, tailored to the public sphere. Scholars often note the perceived need for publicity as a means to legitimise the proposals of a planning profession with an insecure foothold in the existing institutions of governance. What distinguished the graphic materials produced at Harvard was a tendency to tip the balance in favour of diagrammatic clarity over rhetorical impact and to employ abstraction as a provisionary abrogation of the urban fabric's material givens. The requirements for a 1949–1950 collaborative problem instructed, for example:

> each portion of the research [including zoning and land use, transit system, population trends and projections, the municipal budget, etc.] *must present in easily understandable graphic form the pertinent facts and data.... Three-dimensional presentations are discouraged* and whenever possible techniques, colours and symbols which are reproduceable in black and white shall be used.
>
> *([Perkins] 1949–1950; n.p. [emphasis added])*

Anticipating eventual publication, the instructions prescribe the visual language of statistical graphics. To use another example, a student's diagram of 'Walking Distances in [a] Neighborship' demonstrates the distribution of a model neighbourhood's services as a ratio of walking distance to time (Figure 5.13). It is a crisply drawn segmented circle, the outermost perimeter of which designates the maximum distance in miles to be walked within a comfortable twenty minutes by an average adult. Concrete urban space is translated into geometrical area, within which schematically drawn structures are arrayed not in relation to their actual location within a neighbourhood, but rather as a function of their distance from the circle's centre, marked 'home'. The drawing is not uniformly successful in avoiding 'three-dimensional presentation' as instructed, but it clearly attempts to build a graphic interface between urban territory and data.

In the first half of the 20th century, the broad adoption of diverse forms of data visualisation by both social scientists and public authorities rested on the assumption that images were both simpler and more compelling than words and numbers (Vallye 2020). As such, they could, in the words of a 1954 *Journal of the American Institute of Planners* article, assist in closing 'the growing gap between those who are technically competent to lead and those who must follow if the leaders are to accomplish anything' – a 'matter of vital importance' (Bair 1954: 196). Data graphics explained *and* legitimised planning proposals to the lay person. The planner's task was to achieve 'sufficiently simple forms of expression so that the public [would] understand more clearly what it is planners [were] doing, and why the results of their work [were] important' (Bair 1954: 196). But beyond any specific proposal, and more than other symbolic systems, data visualisations communicated the disciplinary structure and efficacy of planning technique as such: the process of translating projective analysis of social quantities into physical land use patterns. Architecture was understood to have a key role to play in that translation. Architectural expertise in spatial design and techniques of projective modelling closed the circuit of exchange between physical space and the planimetric order of data. The statistical graphics that dominated the Framingham report were, in that sense, architecture.[15]

Notes

1 For example, *Architectural Record* concluded in its review of *Our Cities*: 'This report advances recommendations ... which are the immediate concern of architects, town planners, and engineers' (Mikkelsen 1937: 60).
2 Social scientific methodology was always a feature of planning knowledge, but was increasingly institutionalised in American planning starting in the 1930s (e.g., Birch 1980: 32).
3 Shanken (2009) traces a 'culture of planning' that emerged during the war and penetrated deep into the American architectural profession.

4 This was not an exclusively American approach, but generally characteristic of global architectural and planning culture in the first half of the 20th century (e.g., Freestone and Amati 2014).
5 Today, the John F. Kennedy School of Government.
6 This likely describes Problem IV, 'Cambridge Housing Needs', taught by Perkins and Gropius ('Preliminary statement: Cambridge housing needs' 21 April 1945).
7 'I am somewhat of two minds', Perkins wrote in a private letter to Harold S. Buttenheim

> about the idea of repeating such a performance elsewhere. … [T]he towns for which you do the job get the impression that it is a cheap substitute for competent professional advice and, if thought of in this way, we would be put in the position of competing with consultants and specifically with our own graduates for jobs of this kind.
>
> (Perkins G H 24 March 1948)

8 See 'Problem I: Framingham' [September 1947 to January 1948]; 'Collaborative Problem: Civic and Commercial Center of Framingham' 12 November to 19 December 1947. The school also dedicated the spring semester to Framingham outside the scope of the commissioned report. Employing a similar protocol, the spring semester problem focused on the development of a model neighbourhood ('Problem III: Framingham Neighborhood' 2 February 1948).
9 The presentation materials were first exhibited at Harvard and then in February through March 1948 at the Framingham town hall. '[T]he story [of the report] is told graphically on the charts and models [on view]', reported the local newspaper ('Harvard Survey Display' 1948).
10 Other students joined in this work over the course of the fall semester. See correspondence with local agencies, collected in Harvard University Archives, UAV 322.138, Box 3.
11 More uniform in their graphic language, the illustrations in *Our Cities* consist of two main types: cartograms, with statistical information distributed across a schematic map of the territory under analysis; and charts that employ neat rows of icons or ideogrammatic figures, each conveying a quantitative unit of value. The latter were based on the 'visual dictionary' of statistical data developed by Austrian social scientist Otto Neurath. Created by designers such as Neurath's former assistant Rudolph Modley, Theodor Jung, and others, the statistical graphics in New Deal government publications often loosely adopted Neurath's Vienna method of 'pictorial statistics', without reference to the latter's broader philosophical or pedagogical aims (Charles & Giraud 2013). Likewise, although Neurath was a participant in CIAM discussions, his method was not directly adopted by the architects (Weiss et al. 2014, Vossoughian 2008). It would have been familiar to GSD faculty and students largely at a second-hand remove, through governmental and architectural publications, although Neurath's concepts were also introduced to the American architectural community directly in Neurath 1937.
12 In reporting on the 'demonstration cities' study, *New Pencil Points* put an extra emphasis on the fact that the land use pattern was derived from statistically-grounded analysis:

> City planning, up to now, has been perhaps too much limited to physical planning. Too often has only cursory attention been given to the economic and social considerations which should underlie and influence whatever physical plans were made. The procedure followed in the demonstration cities was designed to emphasise these economic and social foundations. Only after arriving at concepts of the size, character, and desirable distribution of the population, and setting goals for future employment and economic activities for the kind of community the people wanted, was the next step undertaken: i.e., to work out a physical arrangement to fit those economic and social needs.
>
> ('A technique for accelerated planning' 1943: 42)

13 Sketch I was a more daring proposal tying the community into a broad vision for regional development, premised on the construction of a belt-line railroad system for the Boston metropolitan region, to catalyse new industrial plant locations linked by a chain of residential 'neighborhood units'; Sketch II was a more conservative version that 'buil[t] upon the present community structure as the basic framework and suggest[ed] a direction of growth which in every part [was] attainable within the existing economic resources and powers of the town' (Row et al. 1948: 39).
14 The 'laboratory' model recurs in discussions of the Framingham project. For example, the town's planning committee chair John O. Fisher wrote in the contract letter, 'I believe that your students will find this to be an outstanding laboratory field for their study' (Fisher, J O 1 May 1947).
15 I discuss at length the spatial orientation of statistical graphics and outline the history of their use in the planning profession in Vallye 2020.

104 Anna Vallye

References

Alofsin, A. (2002), *The Struggle for Modernism: Architecture, Landscape Architecture, and City Planning at Harvard*, W. W. Norton: New York.

American Society of Planners and Architects (1944), Draft of minutes for the meeting held Saturday, March 4, 1944, Harvard University Archives, Cambridge, MA.

American Society of Planning Officials Newsletter, February 1949, 15, 2.

'A technique for accelerated planning' 1943, *New Pencil Points*, 24 (8): 31–50.

Bair, F. H. and Jr. Fall (1954), 'Graphic organisation of statistics,' *Journal of the American Institute of Planners*, 20 (4): 196–200.

Birch, E. L. (1980), 'Advancing the art and science of planning: Planners and their organisations 1909–1980,' *Journal of the American Planning Association*, 46 (1): 22–49.

Boyer, M. C. (1983), *Dreaming the Rational City: The Myth of American City Planning*, MIT Press: Cambridge, MA.

Carlson, C. E. (1948), 'Planning notes,' *Task*, 7/8: 89.

Charles, L. and Giraud, Y. (2013), 'Economics for the masses: The visual display of economic knowledge in the United States (1910–45),' *History of Political Economy*, 45 (4): 567–612.

'Collaborative Problem: Civic and Commercial Center of Framingham,' 12 November to 19 December 1947, Arch. 2c, Land. Arch. 2c, C.P. 2b, R.P. 2c, Harvard University Archives, Cambridge, MA, HUE 17.1147.72.

Committee on Education and Personnel Standards October-December 1942, 'Education for and in city and regional planning: Report of committee on education and personnel standards,' *The Planners' Journal*, 8 (4): 4–12.

Committee on Planning Education Winter 1948, 'The content of professional curricula in planning,' *Journal of the American Institute of Planners*, 14 (1): 4–19.

Creighton, R L, Instructor in City Planning to Paratone [sic, likely Para-Tone, Inc.] Company, Inc. 12 March 1951, Harvard University Archives, Cambridge, MA, UAV. 322. 138, Box 1.

'Harvard survey display to open in lower Nevins Hall' 19 February 1948, *Framingham News*, 102 (37): 1.

Fisher, J. O. to G. Holmes Perkins, 1 May 1947, Harvard University Archives, Cambridge, MA, UAV 322.138, Box 3.

Freestone, R. and Amati, M. (eds.) (2014), *Exhibitions and the Development of Modern Planning Culture*, Ashgate: London.

Funkhouser, H. G. (1937), 'Historical development of the graphical representation of statistical data,' *Osiris* (3): 269–404.

Gaus, J. M. (1943), *The Graduate School of Design and the Education of Planners: A Report*, The Graduate School of Design: Harvard University.

Gaus, J. M. (1945), 'The education of planners: A commentary on some current projects,' *The Journal of Land and Public Utility Economics*, 21 (4): 307–309.

Gropius, W. (1935), *The new architecture and the Bauhaus*, Faber and Faber: London.

Hancock, J. (1988), 'The new deal and American planning: The 1930s,' in D. Schaffer (ed.), *Two Centuries of American Planning*, 197–230, Johns Hopkins University Press: Baltimore, MD.

Heiselberg, E. to G. Holmes Perkins, 19 June 1947, Harvard University Archives, Cambridge, MA, UAV 322.138, Box 3.

Hudnut, J. (1948), 'Memorandum: Programs of research formulated by the School of Design,' Harvard University Archives, Cambridge, MA, UAV 322.138, Box 3.

Isaacs, R. R. and Serageldin, M. I. (1973), 'The art, education and responsibility of planners,' in *The Place of Planning: the 1971–72 Lectures in Urban and Regional Planning*, Auburn University: Auburn, AL.

Mallery, E. D., Blucher, W. H. and Ridley, C. E. (1943), *Action for Cities: A Guide for Community Planning*, Public Administration Service: Chicago, IL.

Meyerson, M. D. (1946), 'What a planner has to know,' in *Planning 1946: proceedings of the Annual Meeting of the American Society of Planning Officials, held in New York City May 6–8*, American Society of Planning Officials: Chicago, IL.

Mikkelsen, M. A. (1937), 'Have the cities reached maturity?' *Architectural Record* 82 (6): 60–64.

National Resources Committee 1937, *Our Cities: Their Role in the National Economy*, Washington, DC.

Neurath, O. (1937), 'Visual representation of architectural problems,' *Architectural Record*, 82 (1): 57–61.

Pearlman, J. (2007), *Inventing American Modernism: Joseph Hudnut, Walter Gropius, and the Bauhaus Legacy at Harvard*, University of Virginia Press: Charlottesville.

Perkins, G. H. (1945), 'The education of planners: At Harvard University,' *The Journal of Land and Public Utility Economics*, 21 (4): 311–313.

Perkins, G. H. to John O. Fisher, 26 June 1947, Harvard University Archives, Cambridge, MA, UAV 322.138, Box 3.

Perkins, G. H. 24 December 1947, Memorandum to the Council of the Department of Regional Planning, Harvard University Archives, Cambridge, MA, UAV 322.138, Box 3.

Perkins, G. H. to Harold S. Buttenheim, 24 March 1948, Harvard University Archives, Cambridge, MA, UAV 322.138, Box 3.

Perkins, G. H. April 1948, 'Framingham Report write-up for *The American City*,' draft manuscript, Harvard University Archives, Cambridge, MA, UAV 322.138, Box 3, p. 3.

Perkins, G. H. (1948), 'Harvard students conduct planning survey for Framingham,' *The American City*, 43 (5): 100–101.

Perkins, G. H. to Gordon Stephenson, 28 December 1948, Harvard University Archives, Cambridge, MA, UAV 322.138, p.1.

[Perkins, G. H.] 1949–1950, 'Collaborative problem—notes for meeting', Architecture 2b, Land. Arch. 2b & 2c, City Planning 2b, 1949–50, Harvard University Archives, Cambridge, MA, UAV 322.272.

Perkins, G. H. January 1950, 'The planning schools: 3. Harvard University', *The Town Planning Review*, 20 (4): 315–319.

'Preliminary statement: Cambridge housing needs' 21 April 1945, Problem IV, Architecture 2d, Civic Design & Techniques I, Harvard University Archives, Cambridge, MA, HUE 17.1144.72

'Problem I: Framingham' [September 1947 to January 1948], City Planning 2b, Regional Planning 2c, Harvard University Archives, Cambridge, MA, HUE 17.1147.72.

'Problem III: Framingham Neighborhood' 2 February 1948, Arch. 2b, L.A. 2b, C.P. 2b, Frances Loeb Library, Harvard University, Cambridge, MA.

Report of council luncheon, 16 January 1946, Harvard University Archives, Cambridge, MA, UAV 322.5.1.

'Review: 'Framingham: Your town – Your problem'' September 1948, *American Society of Planning Officials Newsletter*, 14 (9): 76.

Row, A. T. Jr., Dolbeare, L. P. and Tannenbaum J. eds. (1948), *Framingham: Your Town, Your Problem: Prepared by Planning Students in the Graduate School of Design, Harvard University*, Harvard Graduate School of Design: Cambridge, MA.

Shanken, A. M. (2006), 'The uncharted Kahn: The visuality of planning and promotion in the 1930s and 1940s,' *The Art Bulletin*, 88 (2): 310–327.

Shanken, A. (2009), *194X: Architecture, Planning, and Consumer Culture on the American Home Front*, University of Minnesota: Minneapolis.

Shanken, A. M. (2018), 'The visual culture of planning,' *Journal of Planning History*, 17 (4): 300–319.

Vallye, A. (2020), '"Balance-sheet" city: Martin Wagner and the visualisation of statistical data,' *Journal of Urban History*, 46 (2): 334–363.

Vallye, A. [manuscript], *Model Territories: German Architects and the Shaping of America's Welfare State*.

Vossoughian, N. (2008), *Otto Neurath: The Language of the Global Polis*, Nai/D.A.P. Distributed Art Publishers: Rotterdam.

Weiss, D., Harbusch, G., Maurer, B., van Ess, E., Somer, K. and Perez, M. (eds.) (2014), *Atlas of the Functional City: CIAM 4 and Comparative Urban Analysis*, Thoth Publishers: Amsterdam.

6

THE CAMBRIDGE COLLAGE

Dalibor Vesely, phenomenology, and architectural design method

Joseph Bedford

Dalibor Vesely

Dalibor Vesely (1934–2015) was an architectural educator unusual in his disposition towards philosophy. In contrast to many other prominent and influential architectural educators in the 1970s and 1980s, Vesely had no official training in architecture prior to his career teaching studios and seminars in schools of architecture. He had studied engineering in Prague in the 1950s and specialized in the civil engineering of bridges, but the education that mattered most to his career as a teacher in schools of architecture in the 1970s and 1980s was the informal education he had received in philosophy. This informal education was primarily gained through his attendance of the secret underground seminars of Jan Patočka for several years in the early 1960s. Patočka was one of the most important Czech philosophers of the 20th century and an heir to the phenomenological tradition, having himself studied directly with both Edmund Husserl and Martin Heidegger. Vesely augmented his education with Patočka through his own independent and autodidactic practices of reading not only in the phenomenological tradition but also in many areas of continental philosophy, including in phenomenological psychology, philosophical anthropology, modern hermeneutics, philosophies of history, and philosophies of religion.

Vesely emigrated from Czechoslovakia to Britain following the events of the Prague Spring as Warsaw Pact tanks rolled into the city in August 1968 to crush the liberalization movement there. His emigration, like so many Czechs of his generation, enabled him to reinvent himself and to present himself with the mystique and allure of a central European intellectual steeped in philosophical culture. As Peter Cook put it, writing about Vesely in the 1970s, 'he always "sounded interesting" to those who lacked both the knowledge and the intellectual stamina of his old Central European friends who could parry with him' (Cook 1983).

Vesely taught in several schools between his arrival in Britain in January 1969 and his retirement in 2002. First, he taught at Essex University where he was part of a seminal new graduate-level history and theory of architecture program established there by Joseph Rykwert. Vesely taught dedicated seminars on philosophy there, while Rykwert taught

DOI: 10.4324/9781003201205-9

historical seminars dedicated to reading architectural treatises from Vitruvius to Marc-Antoine Laugier. In parallel to his invitation by Rykwert to teach with him at Essex, Vesely had received an invitation to teach at the Architectural Association (AA) in London, beginning in Peter Cook's team-taught diploma school, and after Alvin Boyarsky became the new chair of the AA in 1972 and extended the undergraduate unit system to the diploma school, Vesely became one of the first, and soon one of the most successful of the new diploma unit masters. At the AA, Vesely's success and appeal was precisely as a new kind of teacher who placed architectural education into contact with profound philosophical and world-historical issues. As Martin Pawley put it, mockingly, Vesely's pitch to the student body in 1974 for students to join his new unit involved a 'bleaching philosophical discussion' with concepts of such 'largess' as to make 'students swoon' (Pawley 1974).

Vesely struggled, however, throughout much of the 1970s to connect his philosophical teaching to the practices of design in studio. As Vesely put it, later: 'It took me several years. I was in a state of schizophrenia' (Thomas 2006: 41). It was only at the University of Cambridge where he became a professor in 1979 and where he remained until his retirement, that he succeeded in bringing his philosophical orientation to bear on the everyday practices of design studio, such that it established a distinct and novel method of architectural design.

Vesely's philosophical orientation could be described as strongly anti-instrumental. The strength of his opposition to what he called 'instrumentality' had a great deal to do with the context of his early philosophical formation in a communist state the official doctrine of which was materialist determinism. For many years, the Czech state had, as a result, systematically persecuted the traditional aspects of Czech culture associated with idealist philosophy or religion viewing them as remnants of bourgeois society that needed to be overcome in order to bring about socialism. The clash between such soviet communist doctrines and the traditions and institutions of bourgeois society has been seen by historians as much more tragic in Czechoslovakia than anywhere else in the Soviet Union because of just how Western and how developed Czechoslovakia was prior to the cold war division of Europe (Judt 2010: 437).

As a result of this widely perceived tragedy of Czech history, phenomenology and the various other philosophies that Vesely drew from carried an especially poignant historical meaning for figures such as Jan Patočka in the 1960s (Tucker 1996). The tradition of phenomenology had been established by Edmund Husserl at the end of the 19th century, and Husserl's approach had from the outset been determined by his own reaction to the perceived ethical crisis of European thought at that moment, resulting from the dominance of science and technology. From his earliest studies of arithmetic, Husserl had been concerned with the conflict between the abstraction of mathematics and the concreteness of experience. His philosophical project sought to critique the narrowing conception of human reason as it became synonymous with the scientific method. Mathematics had come to serve in this method as a powerful means to model and predict the workings of nature and to unleash hitherto unparalleled energies and industrial productivity. Yet, for Husserl, this modern conception of reason in the West was mistakenly understood if it was thought that mathematics described what was most true about human reality or if it was thought that what counted as truly real was what could be objectively measured.

Husserl's phenomenological project called into question the trajectory of human reason as defined exclusively by the successes of modern science. The slogan of his philosophy, 'to the things themselves,' did not so much mean simply a return to empirical evidence, but rather a lifting of the accumulated mental baggage by which the modern mind had come to perceive the world around it. This modern mode of perception was, for Husserl, largely now defined by the idea of objects subject to mechanical laws and independent of their relation to consciousness and subjectivity. Returning to things thus meant 'bracketing' scientific understanding for a moment, and focusing upon how things appear in perception, to consciousness, in order to discover afresh the vast areas of reality that spring from the way objects and subjects are related to one another. By stripping the role of modern scientific objectivity in informing perception, phenomenology as a method of reflection invited philosophers to examine all the overlooked ways in which things, experiences, imaginary entities, ideas, conceptions of time, and so on, that are constituted in the very process of perception, are equally real and worthy objects of human reason despite being unmeasurable and not easily subject to instrumentality and productivity.

Living in interwar Europe, where he experienced persecution in Nazi Germany for being seen as a Jew, Husserl had already pressed his philosophical project into service as a way to diagnose and cure the perceived 'crisis' of European reason which Husserl saw as having devastating moral and ethical consequences (Husserl 1933, 1936). Jan Patočka was a direct inheritor of Husserl's conception of world-historical crisis and its moral implications. In the words of the intellectual historian Michael Gubser, phenomenology's theme of crisis 'moral decline despite technical progress, spiritual enslavement despite material freedom' was 'particularly apparent in the communist half of *Mitteleuropa*' (Gubser 2014: 133).

Recall that Vesely had discovered phenomenology in the late 1950s and early 1960s during the height of neo-Stalinism in Czechoslovakia, and in such underground spaces as Patočka's seminars, the location of which had to be kept secret and spread by word of mouth to avoid the eye of the secret police. When he did so, he discovered a philosophy of profound social, historical, political import, that contained a programmatic mission to renew the perception and consciousness of individuals and of society and to avert the moral and ethical crisis of the present. Vesely's contention as an architectural educator oriented by such philosophical sources was that architectural design practices could draw from the insights of phenomenology in order to play an active role in transforming and renewing society. The question for Vesely was how to transform the practices of architectural design in studio, to carry out that charge, such that those practices might embody and enact a form of non-instrumental reason oriented towards immeasurable dimensions of reality, and which might help to renew the moral coordinates of society.

Cambridge

Vesely considered that the loss of democracy and the subjection of all aspects of culture to planning in Eastern Bloc countries was clear evidence of the out-of-control nature of modern instrumental reason. Yet while such a loss was a more extreme symptom of what Husserl had described as 'his crisis,' other symptoms of the crisis could be equally seen in Western countries such as Britain as governments like that of Harold Wilson invested unparalleled faith in the progress of science and technology to transform society. In the 1970s, then, shortly after his arrival in the UK, Vesely was equally as engaged in reading the philosophy of members of the Frankfurt School such as Herbert Marcuse and Jurgen Habermas and began to teach these authors in his Essex seminars. The vocabulary of 'instrumentality,' 'objectification,' and 'reification,' which he drew from them in order to critique the generalized historical reduction of culture to mathematically measurable objects, would never leave him.

Vesely's phenomenological crisis discourse, then, had no clearer critical edge than when he took up his position as a professor at the University of Cambridge, which had been, and still was, one of the epicentres for the application of mathematical and computational techniques to methods of design. When Vesely arrived in Britain in 1969, the tide had already turned for an architectural education enthusiastically driven by modernist functionalist approaches to design. A perceived failure of modern architecture and town planning now dominated mainstream public discourse, and preservation movements in the West were beginning to succeed in curtailing any new tabula rasa developments in cities. Yet, when Vesely began teaching at Cambridge, he discovered design studios there being run by some of the scientific researchers in the school who were associated with its research arm, the Martin Centre, and which continued to provide him a foil against which to position his argument.

In these studios, students spent much of their time focused on the optimization of a building's performance in terms of the efficiency of circulation, spatial connectivity, floor area ratios, and natural daylighting (Griffiths 1980: i). After designing their own project for an office building on the same site, each student then spent a significant amount of time analysing their design in order to develop an understanding of the optimum way that design could respond to its environment (Figures 6.1–6.4). The context in which the design project was situated was treated largely in materialistic, technical, quantifiable, and mathematical terms. Students had come to identify the key features of architectural design with only those attributes of buildings that were measurable; the depth of the block, its geometry, and the height and density of surrounding buildings. They were not especially encouraged to pay much attention to the ways in which buildings were perceived by their occupants or how that perception was constituted by a larger cultural and historical context.

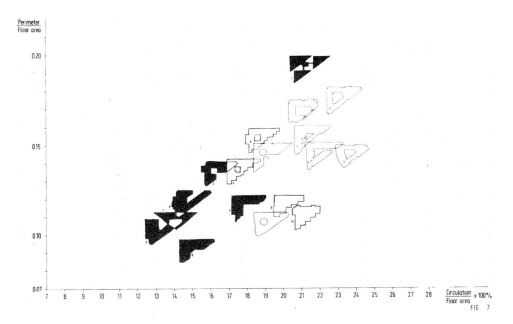

FIGURE 6.1 "City site: comparison of three variables," diagram (Image Source: from Griffiths, 1980).

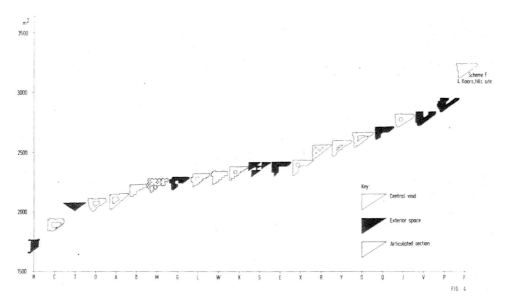

FIGURE 6.2 "City site: area ranking" diagram (Image Source: from Griffiths, 1980).

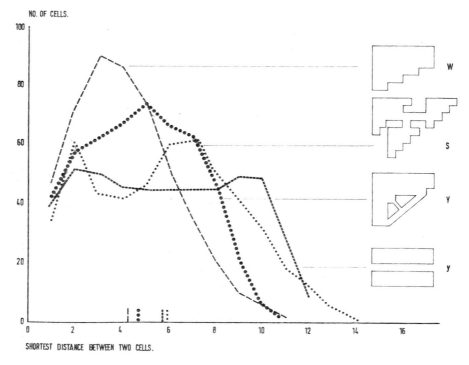

FIGURE 6.3 "Number of cells against shortest distance between them" diagram (Image Source: from Griffiths, 1980).

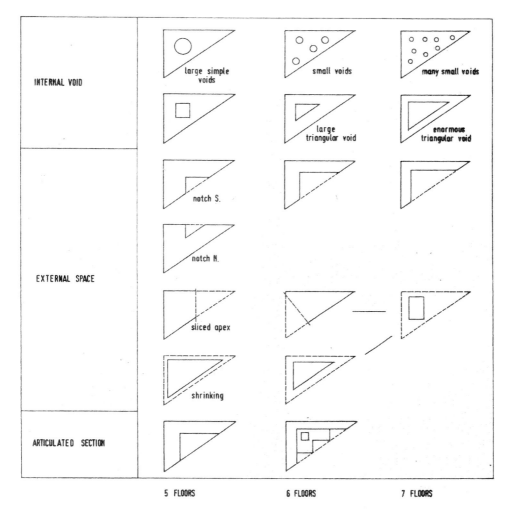

FIGURE 6.4 "Predicted generic types" diagram (Image Source: from Griffiths, 1980).

For Vesely, as well as his colleague Peter Carl whom he brought with to Cambridge in 1978, this relative lack of interest in the perceptual, cultural, and historical dimension of architecture was embodied in the choice of the mode of representations used by the students in the studio; namely monochrome, inked, orthographic line drawings, that predominantly used plans, sections, and axonometric projections to describe buildings. Such engineering drawings captured well the quantitative dimension of the object – it's true measure, geometry, and form – yet, they captured only very poorly the qualitative dimensions of perception, culture, and history. They said little about the associations a building might evoke; the metaphorical meaning of its elements and details; or the matter of decorum and ritual that affects how its rooms are used. In a sense, Vesely and Carl attributed to specific modes of representation, the capacity to manifest and propagate the functionalist and scientific attitude born of 'the crisis,' as Husserl had described it.

112 Joseph Bedford

In type-written memos to the students in 1979, Carl was explicit about the new critique of the existing functionalist approach to design offered in the school. He criticized what he called the 'residue of functionalist bubble-diagram thinking' and its tendency to treat design as a matter of problem-solving. 'Architecture is not about problems being solved,' as he put it, 'rather it is about opportunities for revelation…' (Carl 1979: 6). Criticising the exclusive use of orthographic architectural forms of drawing such as circulation diagrams and especially plans, Carl went on:

> … the plan, as an architectural document, is *not* the generator; even less are such documents as circulation diagrams – this sort of thing is fine and quite useful for plumbing, and perhaps traffic, particularly when the only concern is efficiency expressed as a function of time, distance, and volume. Whoever thinks of himself as circulating? Whenever did you draw a plan of your dreams? Of a novel you'd read? Of a movie you'd seen? Surely efficiency in the sense above is a false economy; the trade-off between methodological certitude and cultural revelation leaves the second column heavily in the red, the whole enterprise bankrupt, poverty-stricken.
>
> *(Carl 1979: 3)*

Carl thus viewed forms of architectural representation such as orthographic line drawings as being embodiments of an abstract, functionalist, problem-solving attitude; one linked to a larger spiritual crisis caused by instrumental reason. In contrast, Carl advised his students to seek opportunities by which architectural design could 'reveal the culture.' As he put it:

> The obligation of the architect resides, in the responsible revelation of the culture. … to know how to build, how to provide for easy movement the architect must be acutely sensitive to the subtle and manifold attributes of all manner of architectural situations, the places where cultural and architectural meaning coalesce. … Only a revelatory hermeneutic will permit adequate "management" of the complex and dramatic material that is the true nature of any cultural phenomenon.
>
> *(Carl 1979: 2).*

For Carl, one could start therefore anywhere within the given conditions of the context or activities or 'situations' to be accommodated by the design because every concrete thing, place, or situation had a history, and a set of associations, and refers to other things, places, and situations in an endless unfolding web. As a pedagogical device to make his point, he gave his students a two-page type-written list which contained a wide array of cultural artefacts to choose from – a *domus ecclesia*, a *scaenae frons*, the Ardabil Carpet, a Belvedere, Pythagorean musical scales, Mozart's Magic Flute, and Marcel Duchamp's The Bride Stripped Bare by Her Bachelors. Any one of these artefacts, Carl insisted, could be the basis from which to begin a deeper interpretation of the culture (Figure 6.5).

In order to reveal the historical fabric of the culture that lay latent within things, places, and situations, Carl advocated for a method which he referred to as 'exploratory, elaborative, an opening up' (Carl 1979: 2):

> The elaboration will proceed irregularly, sometimes here, sometimes there, and work in one area will sponsor associations in another. … You are concerned with

image-making as it provokes access to the imagery of the culture. … That is to say, that your drawings and models must provide the sort of opening or site for the manifestation or revelation of meanings…

(Carl 1979: 7)

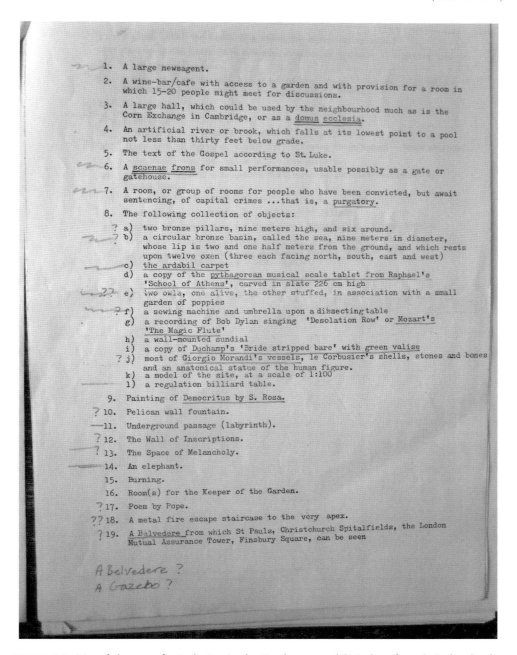

FIGURE 6.5 List of elements for inclusion in the Garden around St Lukes, from St Lukes Studio Brief 1979 (Image Source: Carolyn Steel Personal Archive).

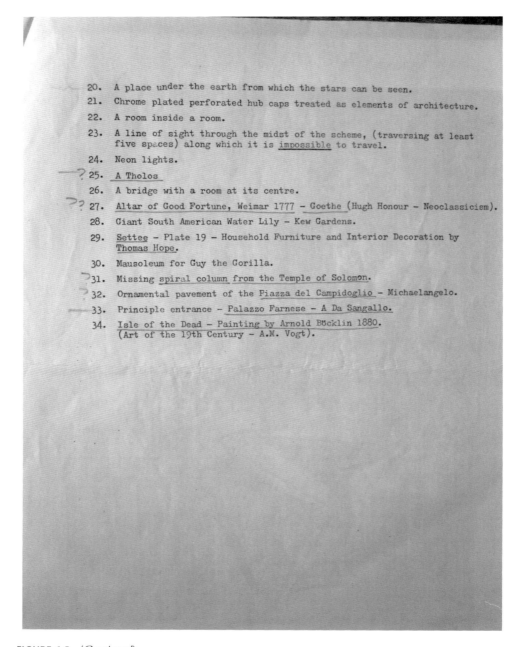

FIGURE 6.5 (*Continued*)

Carl's critique of what he perceived as the school's prior instrumental practices of studio design was clear in the late 1970s. Yet, there was not yet in place a clearly developed alternative method of representation. At this time, Carl's teaching focused upon cultivating a new attitude among the student body; one sympathetic towards the role of historical and cultural reference in architecture and upon establishing the importance of creating associations, analogies, and metaphors in one's design. Carl's work in the undergraduate school in the early 1980s was crucial in laying the groundwork for what was to come. By the time Carl's undergraduate students arrived in Vesely's studios in 1984, this clearer manifestation of everyday design practices that reflected Vesely's pedagogy began to emerge as a distinct form of representation, increasingly referred to as 'the Cambridge Collage.' By around 1988, a series of students, including among them David Dernie, Christian Frost, Elspeth Latimer, and Dean Smith, began to perfect the use of collage as a means of embodying Vesely's phenomenologically oriented philosophy of crisis and renewal and to transform it into a method of architectural design.

Collage

Prior to the late 1980s, the predominant technique used in the context of Vesely's pedagogy was still largely pencil rendering. As had been the case during his teaching at the AA during the 1970s, lumograph clutch pencils, Derwent crayons, ink washes, and pastel sticks on watercolor paper were still the prefered drawing techniques. Vesely's philosophical call to focus on what phenomenologist's like Husserl called the 'lifeworld' and its situations, rather than buildings as purely measurable material objects had been somewhat met by exploring the rendering techniques once used in the Beaux-Arts. Rendering, whether through watercolor washes or pencil strokes, had always been a way to depict the building in its more concrete manifestations, including light and occupation (Allais 2020). Following the exhibition of Beaux-Arts drawings at the Museum of Modern Art in New York in 1975 which signalled the historicist impulse central to the critique of modern architecture at the time, simply using an 18th- and 19th-century drawing technique evoked the air of this critique of the functionalist legacy of modern architecture.

Among Vesely's AA students such as Homa Fashardi and Eric Parry, pencil rendering took on a Turneresque or Impressionist degree of ambiguity, however, one that could satisfy Vesely's phenomenological discussions of perception. The grain of pencil lines, alongside a consistent orientation to the stroke, also had the effect of blurring the boundary between the building as an object and its context between the objecthood of the building as a complex assemblage of material components and its manifest appearance largely through its surface treatment and ornamentation. In the more extreme examples, the building's form appeared as if it it were merely a mirage appearing through the diagonal grain of inclement weather, and its surface embellishment was worked out down to the choice of drapery and finishings, while nothing was known about how it was to be assembled or to stand up (Figures 6.6 and 6.7).

Yet, while the pencil-rendered section enabled Vesely to begin to shift the students theoretical focus from the building as an object to the building as a background setting for various situations, it was nonetheless still felt to be limited. Such rendering was still commonly used as a finished presentation drawing, and as such, they tended towards too great a degree of clarity and completion. Pencil-rendered sections in particular still tended to objectify the building from a de-situated Archimedean point of view. They still conveyed an epic pictorialism more common to submissions to the Paris Salon. In contrast, phenomenology's discovery of the everyday lifeworld had far more in common with the break of Modern Art from impressionism to synthetic cubism, which focused on the fragmented and spatially simultaneous perception of everyday things as they were experienced. The postmodern moment in architecture could be said to have peaked circa 1980. The public success

116 Joseph Bedford

FIGURE 6.6 "Eric Parry, pencil rendered section (1979–1980)" (Image Source: Courtesy of Eric Parry Architects Archive).

FIGURE 6.7 "Hugh Locke, pencil rendered section (1979–1980)" (Image Source: Hugh Locke Personal Archive).

of neo-avant-garde architects such as Zaha Hadid, Bernard Tschumi, and Peter Eisenman with their winning competition entries for the Peak Project in Hong Kong, Park La Villette and the Wexner Center signalled a sea change towards modernist strategies drawn from Suprematism, Surrealists, and De Stijl. With this symbolic shift in the field, pencil rendering gave way to the recuperation of disjunctive modernist techniques of cutting and reassembling.

One of the breakthroughs in this recuperation could be said to have been catalysed in the mid-1980s by the photocopier. Xerography had been invented in 1938, and the first Xerox copier was marketed in 1949, but with only limited success. The first commercially successful Xerox copier went on the market in 1959, and it was not until the 1980s that Xerox copiers became standard items in schools of architecture and commonly accessible to students. Technical developments such as photography which enabled the mechanical reproduction of images have been widely discussed by critics and historians as central causal factors in determining the perceived aesthetic break of modern art. A classic thesis on this topic remains Walter Benjamin's 'The Work of Art in the Age of Mechanical Reproduction' (Benjamin 1935). It is in the same vein that the aesthetic break from perspectival and so-called homogenous and unified representations of space towards a discontinuous mode of presentation was made possible by techniques of mechanical reproducibility and that those techniques enable artists to foreground the mobile and embodied experience of the viewer (Stierli 2018: 1). The introduction of the photocopier into schools of architecture thus facilitated the historical repetition of this discovery of a fractured and yet embodied view of experience and helped facilitate the recovery of avant-garde representational techniques in the late 1980s.

Vesely's students began to combine their use of the photocopier with acetate transfer, which allowed the inked image to be freed from the surface of the copy paper after copying, using cellulose thinner, acetone, or lighter fluid to transfer the ink pattern onto another material surface – and even directly onto a model – by rubbing the back of the wetted paper. Detailed images of activities and historical references could now not only be freely sourced from popular magazines, books, or photographs but infinitely copied and manipulated without using up the students original. Students quickly built up collections of image-fragments of materials, references, conditions of light, and structural elements that could be used over and over in different collages and manipulated in different ways.

The very fact that images were now copied and used repeatedly made them into examples of a *type* rather than a singular instance. Vesely had long spoken to his students about culture being historically stratified between newer elements of culture that belong to more recent technological developments or recent fashions and older elements that persist over millenia because they relate to natural conditions or recurring drammatic patterns in human life. Vesely referred to such persistent dimensions of culture as 'typical' or (borrowing from Carl Jung) as 'achetypical.' The photocopier, in a sense, gave students a means to more easily reflect upon and collect image-fragments conceived as being indicative of archetypical situations – groups gathering and talking around a table, reading in front of a window, or children playing in the street – as well as the most appropriate architectural elements commonly used to set the scene for these archetypical situations – material surfaces and textures, furniture, equipment, artefacts, and building details (Figures 6.8 and 6.9).

FIGURE 6.8 "Elspeth Latimer, Cambridge Collage (1988)" (Image Source: Elspeth Latimer Personal Archive).

FIGURE 6.9 "Biba Dow, Cambridge Collage (1992)" (Image Source: Biba Dow Personal Archive).

Phenomenology and design method

Phenomenology and design method could be seen to come together most clearly at Cambridge around 1988 and can be viewed by looking at two simultaneous pedagogical scenes in the school in that year: Vesely's seminars, which now took place in the library on the first floor in the evening, and Vesely's studio, located in the basement one floor below. Working between these pedagogical scenes, Vesely connected his theory to a specific method of design based on the idea of the associative power of the fragment.

In his seminars, Vesely moved from a reading of Friedrich Nietzsche and the problem of nihilism to a more in-depth discussion of the 'crisis of the object.' As Vesely put it:

> The negative fragment is really a product of reification, objectification. It is really one of the typical products of instrumental effort, what we normally refer to as an object, the object that would be idealized, universal, to such an extent that it becomes independent of its context. …. It is in the 19th century where people begin to be aware of something like a universal object.
>
> *(Vesely 1989)*

The concept of fragmentation interested Vesely because it could name the process of reification in which objects became isolated and divorced from their situation. His examples were mass produced shoes and art works sold in the market, in which things treated as tradable goods were made speculatively and for no specific context.

> The beginning of the crisis of the object is non-perspectivity, the questioning of the field of an object. What the object is, is an interesting question. What is this type of object, where there is no context, where the context is arbitrary, that we are referring to? … It is not the same thing as a pair of shoes that is being produced for a particular population of people doing particular things. We may well use a better term rather than call it an object. I would call it a fragment. The fragment is a special kind of reified reality.
>
> *(Vesely 1989)*

Vesely gave this idea of the fragment the specific name of a 'negative fragment' because he viewed the attempt to dissociate things entirely from one another to be ultimately impossible. For Vesely, this impossibility had been proven historically by the very failure of the modern dream of objectification and had resulted in the revelation that the fragment also had a positive side. As Vesely put it in another seminar session that year:

> Instrumental representation is impossible to complete. There is always a moment of the symbolic in it. … The negative fragment cannot be completely negative for the same reason. There is always some kind of a field (actually or potentially present) to which it belongs. The object is never entirely dead. You can see how difficult it is to really encounter a totally meaningless thing. Even if you do not recognise it, you ask yourself: what does it look like? You can never resist that moment. It always looks *like* something... The moment you encounter the almost absoluteness of its isolation or deep object, at this point you reach something which also brings you back. …

Once you reach your limit, being concerned about reaching that limit you discover the other.

(Vesely 1989)

Despite the common perception even today that phenomenology's 'return to things' constitutes a solipsistic subjectivism, Vesely understood the significance of phenomenology – much like similar cultural movements of the time including new holistic sciences like Gestalt Psychology and artistic movements like Surrealism and Synthetic Cubism – as being due to its discovery that consciousness was imaginative and that imagination was not independent and self-generated but dependent on a larger context.

In the early years of Vesely's seminars in Essex, he would commonly teach the sources of his favoured philosophical text, Maurice Merleau-Ponty's *Phenomenology of Perception* (1945), and would go back to the work of gestalt psychologists such as Max Wertheimer, Wolfgang Köhler, and Kurt Koffka who had informed Merleau-Ponty's research in the 1940s. The principal insight of these gestalt psychologists was that perception was more than simply the passive reception of sense data, but a simultaneously active imaginative phenomenon, in which the impression made by the part depends upon the imagination of the whole (Ash 1995; Harrington 1996). When we perceive the whole prior to the part, as gestalt psychologists demonstrated in their various optical experiments, we do so precisely because what we anticipate to be the case strongly outweighs what is actually there in terms of mere sense data. The whole that one perceives prior to the part is then ultimately the whole of the context of the situation, of language, culture, history, and nature; all of which are symbolic referents in every moment of perception.

For Vesely, many 20th-century artistic movements like Surrealism and Synthetic Cubism had been premised on this historical rediscovery of the positive side of the fragment, its power to always refer through likeness, analogy, and metaphor to something else and something far larger. As he put it:

The deep motivation behind cubism is the sense of the positivity of the fragment. ... The fragment carries a field which can be revealed in the encounter with another fragment, which serves as a catalyst. ... What is happening here is that you are recovering the field by using a process of fragmentation in its positive possibility or power, following the principles of metaphor. It is a metaphorical process.

(Vesely 1989)

Vesely's seminars then brought this historical and philosophical reflection to a more practical level that spoke to the design students in the room who were simultaneously in the process of making their collages for him in studio in the basement below:

[Things such as] love, flowers, guitar, newspapers, chair, room, belong to something else, like house or city, sky, clouds, water and so on. And the way you refer and see the relation between one and the other takes place through the analogies and resemblances, which means, in other words, through a field. You can go from one to the other, which you open and, at the same time, discover and by discovering you are mapping and by mapping it you are bringing it into existence. Having brought it to existence you are restoring its reality in its situational sense against its object-like sense.

(Vesely 1989)

The Cambridge Collage

In his studio that year in 1988, Vesely was working on a site at Spitalfields Market in East London. The site itself presented an allegory of the very history of crisis and renewal that Vesely spoke about in his seminars. It was bordered to the south by a more traditional urban fabric which included a baroque church and a working-class neighbourhood based on a small-scale urban grain of terrace houses and to the north by the expanding gentrification driven by London's transformation during the Thatcher government into a hub of global financial capital. The city of London was expanding at such a rate that the towers that housed the world's leading financial institutions that were now wired together after the computerization of global markets in the late 1980s were now encroaching southward and threatening to destroy the traditional urban fabric and to replace its architectural expressions of immeasurable reality with architecture as a pure product of developer's financial calculations and the instrumental logic of capitalist production.

One student, Dean Smith, took the site at the centre of this urban conflict and proposed a joint centre for the study of computer viruses and dance therapy for mental health problems, a program that further allegorized the historical conflict between instrumental reason and more traditional forms of representation (Figure 6.10).

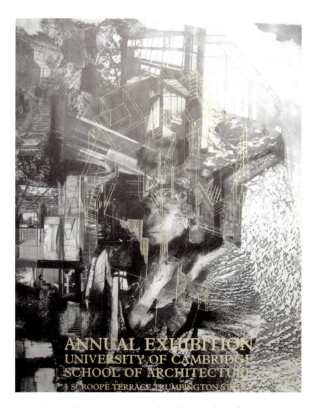

FIGURE 6.10 "Dean Smith, Collage, Institute for the study of Computer Viruses, Spitalfields Project, 1988–1989" (Image Source: Dean Smith Personal Archive).

One of Smith's central collages for his project brought together typical images of scientific experiments and more typical elements of buildings; glass vessels, trays of chemicals, a workbench with clamps, a vice and wheel, a man studying, a thick reference book, a hanging lamp, a magnifying glass, the branches and leaves of a tree, books on a bookcase, light from a glazed window, stair treads, cabinatry, corner shadows, and skylights; all of which were intended to invoke both the technical horizon of modern science and the deeper historical situation of study.

In seeking to precisely tune the metaphorical relations between the associative fields of each image-fragment, Smith drew upon a range of very particular material techniques that had begun to commonly circulate within the studio. The image-fragments were to be kept apart from one another without collapsing them into a unified perspectival alignment that would result in realistic pictorialism. They could be more or less merged or separated by way of a number of very concrete material techniques involving the copier and acetate transfer. Smith could construct more or less unified or disjunctive relationships between the fragments on the page in several ways. He could bring images into a similar sense of scale with respect to one another by reducing or increasing their size on the photocopier. He could merge their impressions on the page when transferred by pressing down harder when rubbing the back of the solvent-soaked copy or by using a common angle of his pencil strokes when rubbing to give a common grain to each image, blending them together. He could also smudge the pencil marks together with his oily finger or sharpened the edges between images with a crisp white or black crayon. Convesely, he could render each image-fragment more incongruous on the page with the same techniques.

There was always a tendency among students to over play the theme of reconciliation and to allow everything to collapse together in an increasingly synthetic and whole, losing the sharp edges of each fragment and the moment of disociation inherent to it. 'Smudgy' was a common term used by students and reviewers in describing the cambridge collage. Yet, this moment of disjunction was inherent to Vesely's philosophy of the fragment, as we have seen. It communicated the historical crisis against which the act of reconciliation became meaningful in the studio. And so, as we have seen, instrumentality was never far from any of Vesely's student's projects. They were actively encouraged to make 'instrumentality' or 'the crisis' thematic as much as possible in order to signal their own work as one of 'reconciliation.'

From this implicit requirement of the pedagogy to maintain the theme of crisis, there arose a second stage in the development of the Cambridge collage, the emergence of the so-called composite collage, in which additional layers were added to convey those modes of representation that were perceived to be more rational, instrumental, and objective. Borrowing such techniques of composite layering from other students that year such as David Dernie and Christian Frost, Smith then created a final drawing for his project that was celebrated by Vesely by being selected for the poster advertising the end of year school exhibition (Figure 6.11).

This additional composite technique involved layering the image between a base of chipboard and a sheet of glass. The chipboard would be sculpted with a chisel to embed fragments of other materials in it (wood, metal, stone), painted, and collaged with photocopied images transfered onto the materials. After resting one's drawing board flat, one could create crisp lines on glass, either with a Rotring drafting pen filled with white ink or with scored lines brushed with white chalk dust. This more advanced technique was risky, however, as one risked cracking the glass when trying to attached it to the base with pre-drilled holes,

FIGURE 6.11 "Dean Smith, 1988–89 Annual Exhibition Poster, (1989)" (Image Source: Dean Smith Personal Archive).

bolts, and nuts. Tears were shed by students after the top layer of glass slid off the chipboard and smashed on the floor. Something of the material hardness of glass and the sharpness of scored lines conveyed the perceived violence of instrumentality, now imported again in to the image.

Conclusion

In some sense, it might appear odd to focus upon Dalibor Vesely's work in terms of such a material register, focusing upon such things as the photocopier, the weight of paper or card, the sharpness of scalpels, and so on. As we noted at the outset Vesely was deeply critical of reducing reality to decontextualized 'objects', insisting instead that reality be understood as composed of 'things' situated in a continuum of historical, linguistic, and natural references. Yet, I hope it is clear from the above description of the case of Vesely's philosophy and its role in fostering a new set of material practices within the pedagogy of studio design that at each moment such materialities, tools, techniques, and objects were deeply referential and imbued with symbolic meaning for the students, such that they were as much symbolic as material instruments.

In some sense, it might seem contradictory that Vesely was so critical of instrumentality and method and yet created a method that students must have believed would function to

124 Joseph Bedford

foster a more holistic sense of vision in the world. It might seem odd to describe what occurred in Vesely's studios in the 1980s as a design method when historians are so used to using the phrase 'design methods' to describe precisely the approach to the process of design once envisioned by figures like Christopher Alexander. Yet whether one calls it simply a style, and approach, or a way, there was something consistent about the steps that Vesely's students would proceed through in their studios and there was something functional about their conviction that such steps were not for nothing, but would lead to a better design, a better building, and even a better world.

Vesely was only critical of modes of representation that he viewed as fostering an instrumental attitude, a world view that limited humanity's sense of what is real to only that which is measurable. He never rejected, however, the power of representation or the power of what one can still surely call tools of design, to constitute our individual and shared symbolic reality. Rather, it was precisely because he believed in the power of material means as simultaneously symbolic means in this way that he was so staunchly critical of some versions of them. For Vesely, a great deal was at stake historically in the way architects drew their projects because such tools and techniques co-constituted the way they perceived their projects and the intentions invested in them as cultural artefacts which might be perceived by others. Indeed, for Vesely, what we do, say, imagine, and think really does shape the reality of the world we live in. And this idea alone is what had so much consequence for architectural design in these years at the University of Cambridge because it transformed the meaning of the very method of architectural design.

Bibliography

Allais, L. (2020), 'Rendering: On Experience and Experiments', in Zeynep Çelik Alexander and John May (eds.), *Design Technics: Archaeologies of Architectural Practice*, 1–44, University of Minnesota Press: Minneapolis.

Ash, M. (1995), *Gestalt Psychology in German Culture, 1890–1967: Holism and the Quest for Objectivity*, Cambridge University Press: New York.

Benjamin, W. (1969 [1935]), 'The Work of Art in the Age of Mechanical Reproduction', in H. Arendt (ed.), *Illuminations*, translated by Harry Zohn, Schocken Books: New York, 1969. Originally published in German in 1935.

Carl, P. (1979), 'Brief St Luke's Project', Personal Archive of Carolyn Steel.

Cook, P. (1983), 'Cook's Grand Tour', *The Architectural Review*, 174 (1040): 32–43.

Gubser, M. (2014), *The Far Reaches: Phenomenology, Ethics, and Social Renewal in Central Europe*, Stanford University Press: Stanford, CA.

Griffiths, K. (1980), *Office Performance: The Design and Analysis of Fifty Schemes from the Final Year of the Diploma Course in Architecture at Cambridge University October '77 to June '78*, Diploma Publications for the Department of Architecture, University of Cambridge.

Harrington, A. (1996), *Reenchanted Science: Holism in German Culture from Wilhelm II to Hitler*, Princeton University Press: Princeton, NJ.

Husserl, E. (1933), 'Letter to Dietrich Mahnke, May 4, 1933', in K. Schuhmann and E. Schuhmann (eds.), *Briefwechsel*, Vol. III, Kluwer Academic Publishers: Dordrecht. Cited in Detmer, D. (2013), *Phenomenology Explained: From Experience to Insight*, Open Court: Chicago, IL.

Husserl, E. (1970 [1936]), *The Crisis of European Sciences and Transcendental Phenomenology: An Introduction to Phenomenological Philosophy*, trans. David Carr, Northwestern University Press: Evanston, IL.

Judt, T. (2010), *Postwar: A History of Europe Since 1945*, Vintage: London.

Merleau-Ponty, M. (2013 [1945]), *Phenomenology of Perception*, Routledge: Abingdon, Oxon; New York.

Pawley, M. (1974), 'Ghost Dance Diary,' *Ghost Dance Times*, Friday, October 19th.

Stierli, M. (2018), *Montage and the Metropolis: Architecture, Modernity, and the Representation of Space*, Yale University Press: New Haven, CT.

Thomas, H. (2006), 'Invention in the Shadow of History: Joseph Rykwert at the University of Essex,' *Journal of Architectural Education*, 58 (2): 39–45.

Tucker, A. (1996), 'Shipwrecked: Patočka's Philosophy of Czech History,' *History and Theory*, 35 (2): 196–216.

Vesely, D. (1989), MPhil, Seminar no.11, (June 20th 1989), Daphne Becket Personal Archives.

7

LITTLE LIVING LABS

1970s student design-build projects and the objects of experimental lifestyles

Lee Stickells

The heating was less than effective in the Ecological House. Its transparent double acrylic skin greenhouse (with a small paraffin heater as back up) underperformed in the cold London winter, and the occupants eventually applied for a council-supplied electric hot water system (Hunt 2014: 140). Taking a hot shower at the ECOL Operation house was unpleasant if not simply dangerous. A modified Brazilian-manufactured, combined heater/head-unit was designed for city pressure water supply, not a rainwater tank, and the heater itself was improperly grounded. The result was dribbling water and occasional electric shocks (Ortega et al. 1972: 91). A methane digester at the Sydney Autonomous House was intended to recycle organic wastes but didn't get much farther than some cut and welded steel drums. Its designers instead used a portable camp toilet, which they emptied in the bathrooms of nearby university buildings each morning (Stickells 2017: 365). The Berkeley Energy Pavilion was a victim of its own funky DIY aesthetics. A peculiar assemblage of salvaged timbers supported, amongst other devices, a homemade rooftop solar collector, barrels to collect rainwater and a wind-powered generator. It drew large crowds, but annoyed university administrators, and was demolished after accusations that it lacked proper building permission (Van der Ryn 2005: 46). At the Ouroboros South house, it blew a gale. Innovative custom-built fibreglass blades for the house's wind power generator cracked in a storm and significant redesign was required (Marcovich 1975: 111) (Figure 7.1).

The preceding litany of malfunction emerges from accounts of five buildings designed, constructed and tested by groups of students in architecture schools spread across the UK, North America and Australia between 1972 and 1978. The Ecological House (1972–1975), also known as the Street Farmhouse, was built in southeast London by the anarchist collective Street Farm, whose core members were students at the Architectural Association (AA). Some construction funding was even provided through the AA's then-chair Alvin Boyarsky, recognizing the house as a student research project as much as a home for Street Farm member Graham Caine and his family. The ECOL Operation House (1972–1973) was built in Montreal by students in McGill University's Minimum Cost Housing Group (MCHG), with support from Canadian organizations including the Sulphur Institute and

DOI: 10.4324/9781003201205-10

FIGURE 7.1 A "Utopian Fair" at the Sydney Autonomous House, in the grounds of the University of Sydney, c.1976. (Image Source: Photograph by Tone Wheeler.)

the Central Mortgage and Housing Corporation. The MCHG was founded by Colombian architect-educator Alvaro Ortega in the early 1970s and focussed on research into human settlement problems of the poor, with an emphasis on efficiency and self-reliance. MCHG student Arthur Acheson and his wife Elizabeth lived in the house for three months in 1972. The Sydney Autonomous House (1974–1978) was designed and built for academic credit by University of Sydney students, with around a dozen students residing in the house over its lifespan. Completely self-funded, it was inspired by shared interest in alternative technologies, material recycling and the encouragement of activist-educator Colin 'Col' James. The UC Berkeley Energy Pavilion (1973) prefigured the nearby Integral Urban House (IUH, 1974–1978). The pavilion was constructed on campus from salvaged and scrounged materials as a public demonstration project by students taking a 'Natural Energy Systems' studio. No students lived in the on-campus pavilion, but they did live and work in the IUH.[1] The experimental energy-conserving Ouroboros South house (1973–) was built by University of Minnesota students in Tom Bender and Dennis Holloway's environmental design classes, with the support of a grant from the Northern States Power Company, as well as donations of materials from local and national firms. Students initially lived in the house and monitored its systems before it was later occupied by a live-in house manager and even used as guest accommodation by the University of Minnesota. Each of the projects has its own fascinating history and complex individual (sometimes intersecting) stories of ambition, advance and disappointment (see, for example, Anker 2010; Kallipoliti 2012, 2018; Richards 2016; Stickells 2017). In some ways, they were intensely different. For example, Street Farmer's anarchists strongly identified with a European strand of left libertarian fraternity (focused on collectives), whereas the Berkeley group's disposition was towards a sunny, conservative Californian libertarianism of personal, spiritual and economic freedom. Here, though, they are considered together in order to draw attention to their collective signalling of a distinctive moment in the history of architectural education – one that saw its institutions co-opted towards reimagined forms of design and activism. The houses featured in this chapter involved students in an experimentally driven material engagement, focused on architectural objects that proffered the reinvention of lifestyle over technical advancement or formal innovation (Figure 7.2).

There was a shared investment in hands-on experimentation and building across the projects, but they were by no means part of a coordinated program, pedagogical or otherwise. Personal communication between the various project actors was limited. They are perhaps best thought of as situated in a broader mosaic of pedagogical experiments influenced by a global 'anti-school', as Beatriz Colomina has put it (Borgonuovo and Franceschini 2018: 5), clustered around the thinking of figures such as Buckminster Fuller, Stewart Brand, Victor Papanek and Ivan Illich. Small endeavours, often on the fringes of institutions, the connections between them came from their ties with professional architectural education programs, the accelerated global flow of architectural publishing post-World War II and a set of resonating concepts, concerns and practices. The latter included the exploration of

FIGURE 7.2 The "Natural Energy Pavilion" at UC Berkeley, 1973. A sign at its base described the structure as "autonomous life support". (Image Source: Barry Shapiro photograph archive. UC Berkeley. Bancroft Library.)

small-scale, self-sufficient living systems through design techniques marked by the popularization of ecological and cybernetic thinking in the period as well as material and technical approaches influenced by the ideas of the 'appropriate technology' movement (brought to widespread attention by E.F. Schumacher's 1973 book *Small is Beautiful*). A shared interest in domestic autonomy is most striking. The projects had overlapping ambitions to integrate technological systems and cultural practices allowing people to generate their own energy, collect and recycle water, treat their own wastes and even grow their own food. In this way, the student designers conceived the houses as a means to recalibrate the 'infrastructuring' of everyday life and reshape relationships between the household and interconnected environmental, societal and economic systems. They reflected the increasing integration of architecture schools into the culture and practices of the research-intensive post-war university, while simultaneously challenging their pedagogical traditions (Ockman and Williamson 2012; Knoblauch 2020). Architectural education was reimagined as an expanded site for situated learning that directly intervened in socio-technical debates – bridging from the personal to the urban and addressing environmental and socio-political challenges via the house and its infrastructural couplings. The resulting projects were uneven, very amateur, but ambitious experimental dwellings.

The binding thread in this chapter's weaving of these curious episodes of activist eco-bricolage is the role of the houses as living laboratories. Each, in its own register, became an experimental vehicle for the development, deployment and testing of new technologies and design strategies for actively modelling a transition to a radically different society. At a time when research in architecture schools was far more limited in scope and scale, as living labs, the projects variously intertwined the public testing of innovative materials, technical systems, architectural forms and radical lifestyles. They strayed from the orderly and professional technical testing of institutional research programs as well as developing forms of experiential learning in architecture, such as students providing design services for disadvantaged communities.[2] The students who designed, built, occupied and studied their experimental houses looked to prefigure new ways of living as much as they tried to validate discrete technologies, boost carpentry skills or build for underserved communities. The houses as labs became sites for enacting participatory environments and testing architecture's capacities as a socio-cultural and environmental control mechanism (Figure 7.3).

FIGURE 7.3 Students constructing the Ouroboros South house at the University of Minnesota, 1973. (Image Source: Photograph by Dennis Holloway.)

The objects of experimentation

The episodes recounted above – of faulty systems and faltering objects – speak to more than just the projects' shared conceptual radicalism. The experiences and outcomes of the labs were profoundly affected and shaped by their material qualities. This is foregrounded in the chapter as vital for apprehending the distinctive character of their small scale, grassroots architectural experimentation and the importance of the house as an artifact through which educators and students sought to act directly in the world. The possibilities imagined for recasting architectural education and intervening in broader socio-political debates were closely bound to the labs' material dimensions – the interconnected objects, people and routines that gave them meaning and linked them into heterogeneous networks. The status of the houses as design-build projects is a good place to begin consideration of their material qualities and interventions. The pragmatic values of experiential learning and a heightened familiarity with building construction – closely associated with student design-build projects – here underpinned experimentation that actively reimagined architecture's scope and the students' own professional agency.

During the 1960s and 1970s, architectural education came under intense pressure to transform its pedagogical practices to realign with 'real world' pressures while also being reimagined as a vehicle through which to act on, and in, that world. Architectural schools, like the universities in which they now mostly sat, were marked by phenomena such as the May 1968 student-worker protests, the civil rights movement, the rise of second wave feminism, the transnational counterculture, energy crisis, global environmentalism and the critique of the post-war university as an elitist, repressive and undemocratic institution. The fundamentals of professional architectural education and its institutions were challenged, and many students demanded a new kind of design knowledge and 'educational relevance' (Tzonis and Lefaivre 2016: 56). Architecture schools became key sites for challenging the norms of established architectural culture (see, e.g., Colomina et al. 2013). The ideas of the transnational deschooling movement fuelled this disruption and often gave shape to pedagogical counter-proposals. North American anarchist and psychotherapist Paul Goodman (1960) and the most influential anti-institutional voice of the period, Ivan Illich (1971), argued for a new style of education that informed wider arguments against credentialism and towards more libertarian, student-directed learning (Wood 1982: 370). Illich, in particular, advocated for approaching the physical environment as a freely available resource where people could learn on their own terms. Rarely were the full implications of ideas such as deschooling effected in architecture schools. However, the disposition towards de-institutionalizing education can be sensed in the many experiments with more self-directed, fluid and informal modes of pedagogy and practice, extra-institutional settings and a reenchantment of the material via an emphasis on hands-on, experiential learning. The projects discussed in this chapter point to this variety. In Sydney, following a 1972 student strike, there was a more freewheeling curriculum in place, and the autonomous house project was conceived explicitly in terms of Illich's educational philosophy (although never completely decoupled from the university). At the MCHG, a similarly freewheeling approach was taken – there were 'no classes, no grades' in the program (CCA 2006). In Minnesota, though, while Ouroboros South drew on the unconventional environmental design thinking of Tom Bender (and used dome-building retreats to bond students), it developed through a tightly directed research, design and construction program (led by Dennis Holloway) involving around 150 students.

Experiential learning in itself was not new to architectural education. It has been traced at least as far back as the 19th century, in the Arts and Crafts movement's assertion of the craftsperson as an ethical figure and its injunction to students to reengage with hand craft processes (Crook 2009).[3] It might also be identified in aesthetic systems that coalesced in Germany during the same period, focused on bodily movement, psychological impulse and feeling – what Zeynep Çelik Alexander has called 'kinaesthetic knowing' (2017). Walter Gropius's training program at the Bauhaus is perhaps the most influential example of its subsequent harnessing into a didactic regimen. Modes of embodied cognition and their pedagogical import have been a longtime concern for architecture. The design-build project, though, was a distinctive and key pedagogic development of the late 1960s and into the 1970s, emerging amongst the building occupations, strikes, teach-ins, community advocacy and zines that characterized architecture student activism of the time. A defining example (which continues to this day) is the Yale Building Project (Hayes 2007), which began with a 1967 studio in which first-year Yale University Masters of Architecture students designed and constructed a community centre in New Zion, Kentucky. The building featured on the cover of *Progressive Architecture*'s September 1967 issue, signalling to the profession an ambition for socially progressive, pragmatic education that became reinforced in similar programs developed across the United States and elsewhere. Design-build has since become a common term for architectural educational programs involving students in the active design and construction of buildings.

Design-build programs have been diverse in their motivations, forms and concerns. However, as Canizaro (2012) notes, there are recurring characteristics, and these gravitate around material engagements with architectural objects. They include the desire to enhance students' construction knowledge and tectonic awareness and to augment their professional skills (through collaboration with each other and other actors in the architectural process). The pragmatic disposition of the design-build project is also sometimes framed as a counter to a supposed idealism in design studio paper projects and a means to better develop more site-specific sensitivity in design. Enhancing understanding of material properties, extending to exploration in material innovation and fabrication techniques, has been another, connected focus. Beyond the hands-on development of professional skills, though, a prominent characteristic of design-build programs has been their organization around the provision of service to local communities (Dean 2002; Pearson 2002; Moos and Trechsel 2003; Bell and Wakeford 2008; Awan et al. 2011). The Yale Building Project reflected the strong emphasis on the social responsibilities of the architect that shaped programs developed in the late 1960s and 1970s. This aspect rivalled calls to advance students' design skills through direct engagement with material experimentation and construction. Design-build projects became important sites within which to attempt the reordering of spatial and social relations as much as they exposed students to construction techniques in situ (Dutton 1991). In this way, their pedagogical experimentation became closely associated with the wider phenomenon of 'social architecture' – loosely classed as practices aimed at challenging dominant professional models of client-dependent, capital-intensive architectural production (Jones and Card 2011; Gribat and Meireis 2017) (Figure 7.4).

The five projects discussed in this chapter can certainly be understood through the rubric of design-build education but they also offer a more complex picture. The UC Berkeley Energy Pavilion emerged from the 'Outlaw Builder' studio, taught by Sim Van der Ryn and Jim Campe, in which a group of students retreated to a forest hillside in Marin County in order to design and build a communal settlement for themselves. 'Ouroboros South' grew out of an environmental design course taught by architect-educators Tom Bender and

FIGURE 7.4 The ECOL Operation house on the Macdonald Campus of McGill University in Montreal, 1972. (Image Source: Courtesy of the Minimum Cost Housing Group, McGIll University.)

Dennis Holloway early in 1973 – extending Bender's desire to "change things and make concrete examples, not just theory and words" (T Bender 2016, interview, 10 October). The McGill University ECOL operation was the product of a Masters program led by Alvaro Ortega for developing and testing dwelling technologies deemed transferable to developing countries. The autonomous house at the University of Sydney began as a second-year design studio project, with the ambition to create a building that operated independently of all services infrastructure and was constructed primarily from recycled materials (Stickells 2017). The projects extended the ambition of design-build efforts, though, emphasizing the creation of experimental research spaces – living labs – between instrumentality and conceptual speculation. Their hybrid qualities 'cross the divide' to use Amy Kulper's expression in relation to architecture's disparate modalities of experimentation (2011) – being structured by neither simply a rigid Enlightenment empiricism nor the messy scientific fiction of an alchemical laboratory. Invoking the logics of other disciplines (such as ecology), without being overdetermined by a scientific instrumentality, the houses allowed for a speculative making as knowing. Comprehensive description is beyond the reach of this chapter, though; rather, the emphasis is on highlighting ways in which they wielded architecture as an experimental process, the building as a socio-technical apparatus, and breached the boundaries between learning, working and living (Figure 7.5).

FIGURE 7.5 The northern side of the Ouroboros South house, showing the sod roof, 1974. (Image Source: Photograph by Dennis Holloway.)

No white coat boffins

The houses were research projects as much as construction exercises. We would struggle to find a professional scientist involved, but all the projects required intensive trial and discovery as their student-creators looked to test some variant of an ecological architecture connected with politically guided forms of domestic self-reliance. The students developed, tested and reported on systems that they often designed themselves. Graham Caine, for example, became intimately acquainted with sewage biology through researching and building the anaerobic digester at Street Farmer's Ecological House (ostensibly his thesis project at the AA). The defecating and urinating human figure Caine drew at the centre of a mandala-like house diagram underscored the importance of physiology to the "life sustaining biological cycle" of the house (Caine 1972a: 140). Lydia Kallipoliti has described how this led Caine to study and repurpose NASA's (National Aeronautics and Space Administration) work on closed-cycle technologies for space flight (Kallipoliti 2011). However, Caine was staunchly anti-professional and determinedly not, as he put it, a 'white coat boffin' (Hunt 2014: 146). Rather than pursuing 'super technology to save the world' (Caine 1972a: 140), the Ecological house was to be a living example of small-scale, accessible 'peoples' technology', including a custom-built toilet designed to carefully separate liquid and solid wastes (Caine 1972b: 12) (Figure 7.6).

In Montreal, experimentation at the ECOL house was similarly hands-on and directed towards enhancing personal autonomy, although couched mainly in terms of developing self-help housing technologies for "poverty areas" (Ortega et al. 1972: 3). The house incorporated a range of building principles and technologies that MCHG students had been

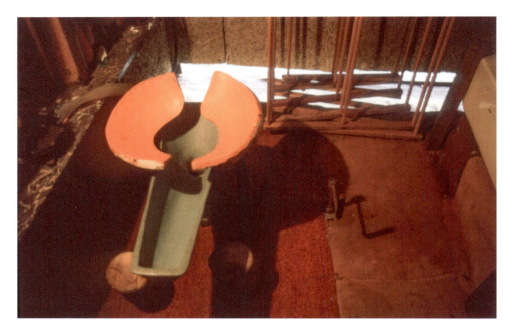

FIGURE 7.6 The Street Farm Ecological House in south London, 1973. Shown here is the toilet seat designed and built by Graham Caine to separate solid and liquid waste. (Image Source: Photograph by Tone Wheeler.)

researching and testing, particularly focused on the use of materials that were by-products of industrial processes. This included pre-cast modular sulphur concrete blocks, solar stills and cut asbestos sewer pipes as roof sheeting. The students regularly drew on expert knowledge from adjacent institutions (such as the Brace Research Institute, which had developed simple technologies for water provision in tropics), but such collaboration was incorporated into a more countercultural disposition. Regular 'Crazy Friday' experimental sessions saw students encouraged to explore their wildest ideas without fear of ridicule. Basically, Arthur Acheson recalls, 'we stopped work and did silly things in the lab' (Acheson 2017, interview, 22 February). Results included the discovery that sulphur concrete tiles could be easily imprinted with images via a transfer process from magazine and newspaper pages – offering a 'poor man's fresco' (Ortega et al. 1972, 43). The house and its experimentation was publicized via the second of the students' 'The Problem Is' books: *The ECOL Operation: Ecology + Building + Common Sense* (1972). Its cheap paper stock, cartoonish illustrations, step-by-step photography and accessible, do-it-yourself tone, bear the influence of the period's flourishing counterculture publishing scene and its arenas for nonconformist dialogues (such as the *Whole Earth Catalog*). The reflexive sidenotes scattered throughout the book emphasize that quirky pragmatism; one example offers advice on cheap casting tactics:

> We use a plastic beaker to pour the sulphur. When the sulphur in the beaker has hardened, you can squeeze the plastic to dislodge the excess sulphur (which can be recycled!) Look for it in the Kitchen Dept. of your favourite store
>
> *(Ortega et al. 1972: 33).*

The D.I.Y. publishing that went hand-in-hand with the D.I.Y. experimentation helped develop an alternative design scene. At the time, there were few readily available publications connecting the practical requirements of the technologies and materials being investigated with dwelling design – how did one actually build and incorporate anaerobic digestors and aquaculture in a house? So, when the UC Berkeley group conceived their own Energy Pavilion, it required considerable effort to simply gather the knowledge required to underpin the design and construction processes. The course reader developed by students was a scrappy 300-plus pages of hand-drawn diagrams, notes and mimeographed article reprints on topics including composting, methane digestors, water recycling, windmills, solar water hearing and 'living lightly' (Anthony et al. 1972). It included ECOL researchers' materials covering water recycling and solar stills as well as a *Mother Earth News* article on the Street Farmer Eco House. The reader was even picked up by Random House, titled the *Natural Energy Designer's Handbook* (Van der Ryn and Campe 1975) and published as one of the first mainstream handbooks on solar architecture (the publishing house was quick to recognize the mercantile potential of counterculture print offerings when retailed as trendy lifestyle manuals). Each of the houses received journalistic coverage in venues such as *Architectural Design (AD)* (e.g. Caine 1972a; James 1977), *Undercurrents* (e.g. Baxter & Grayson 1976) and *Mother Earth News* (e.g. Hughes 1973; Clark 1975; Reynolds 1976). However, the newfound publishing opportunities exploited by the various groups (the Sydney students also produced a mail-order pamphlet around 1978 – *54 Alma Street, Darlington* – and the Ouroboros group published a book in 1974) allowed more detailed knowledge of their trial and discovery, and the socio-technical practices developed in the houses, to nurture an international network of ambitious amateurism (Figure 7.7).

A process of people living together

Experimentation in the houses focused on the integration of multiple technologies into a living system. While they bore some similarities to experimental houses built by university research programs in previous decades, such as the MIT solar house series (Barber 2016), or even the determinedly anti-institutional mid-century experiments by Peter van Dresser and others (Van Dresser 1972), they differed significantly. Apart from obvious distinctions in funding, status and personnel as student projects versus formal research programs (or dropout ventures), neither did they have a focus on the isolated testing of singular technologies or materials. Their approach was more often marked by the popularization of cybernetic thinking in the period's environmental activism (especially its use in describing ecosystems) and its flow into countercultural publications such as the *Whole Earth Catalog*. Systems thinking had provided a key bridge between ecological science and the 1970s' burgeoning environmentalism. Ludwig von Bertalanffy's earlier systems theory was foundational for Eugene Odum's notion of 'Ecosystem Ecology' (Odum 1967) and permeated growing public debate from the 1960s regarding global environmental issues. This was seen, for instance, in the Club of Rome's *The Limits to Growth* (Meadows et al. 1972) or the career of Barry Commoner, whose dual role as both respected scientist and popular political leader exemplified the close relationship between the science of ecology and post-World War II North America's expanding environmental awareness (Worster 1977; Dunlap 1981).

136 Lee Stickells

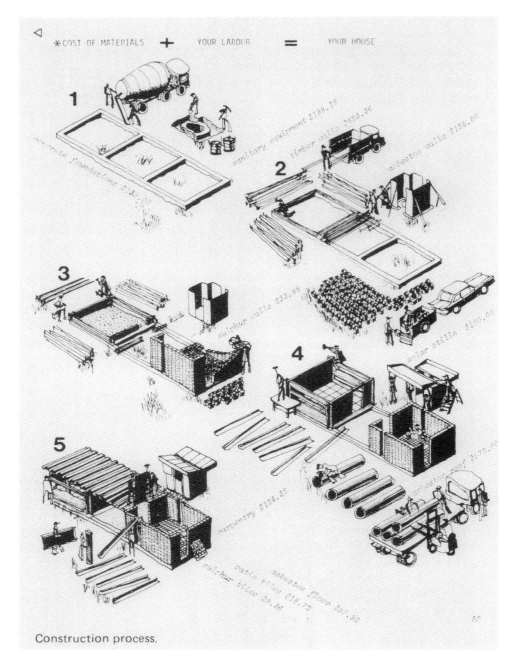

FIGURE 7.7 A drawing of the construction process for the ECOL Operation house, 1972. (Image Source: Courtesy of the Minimum Cost Housing Group, McGIll University.)

The filtration of scientific thinking into more popular forms of environmental discussion brought notions of system, cycle, network and hierarchy (and the particular role of living being in those structures) to the foreground – emphasized in the students' projects by the recurrence of mandala-like diagrams mapping energy and material flows. This kind of environmental awareness, especially when framed politically, tended towards rethinking of concepts like responsibility, limit and diversity, in the firm belief that the future of 'spaceship earth' itself was at risk (Höhler 2016). 'It is, in fact, far more than a house, it's an energy system within itself' Graham Caine claimed of the Ecological House (Caine 1972b: 12). The idea chimed with a growing disciplinary concern for transferring ecological principles to the domain of buildings and cities in the form of closed-systems design. Peder Anker and Lydia Kallipoliti have highlighted the role of military research and the experiments of NASA's space program in the evolution of this synthetic naturalism in architecture (Anker 2010; Kallipoliti 2018). Though, rather than the industrialized, high-tech integration of period programs such as the Grumman Corporation's *Integrated Household System* (with its life support technologies redirected from space research towards more environmentally benign earthbound housing products), the students' living labs were subject to much more ad-hoc processes. A range of low and hi-tech systems and materials were pieced together in scrappily pragmatic bricolage – hybrid approaches that embraced 'poor' technique and were open to collective creativity (Figure 7.8).

Across London, Berkeley, Montreal, Rosemount and Sydney, the array of material flows and systems was diverse. A noteworthy aspect of the shared approach was the combination of vernacular technologies with the period's appropriate technology fascinations. It also

FIGURE 7.8 Students at the Sydney Autonomous house built a Trombe-Michel wall from beer bottles scavenged from the surrounding neighbourhood. Shown here is a student in the process of washing the bottles, filling them with water and sealing them with new crown caps. (Image Source: Photograph by Tone Wheeler.)

manifested through building with recycled and scavenged materials. For example, provenance for the sod roof at Ouroboros South was claimed in the Scandinavian roots of many of the Minnesotan students, while the house also integrated a modern Swedish Clivus Multrum composting toilet (newly introduced to the US by Abby Rockefeller) and three iterations of a trickle-down solar collector designed and fabricated by mechanical engineering student John Ilse (Holloway 1976: 16). The interior of the rudimentary Berkeley Energy Pavilion accommodated a sink supplied with water by rooftop storage drums, a urine collection system (used for fertilizing plants) and a composting privy. A greenhouse, assembled from PVC piping and plastic covers, was attached to the southern side of the pavilion; inside, lettuce and snow peas were growing, bedded in a compost utilizing restaurant food scraps. The Sydney Autonomous House had its own student-designed solar flat plate collector and beer bottle Trombe Wall, as well as a makeshift 'Coolgardie Safe' for refrigeration (the latter device being a cupboard with wetted hessian walls for keeping food cool, invented in the late 19th-century goldfields of Western Australia). The ECOL house was roofed with asbestos cement channels cut down by hand from industrial drainage pipes, the aforementioned malfunctioning water heater was imported from Brazil but modified to fit a telephone-style shower head. A plastic 'porta-sink' was purchased for $12 from a camping store, while the house floors were paved with student-cast interlocking textured sulphur blocks (nicknamed 'orthopaedic tiles') that came from experiments in recycling the sulphur waste produced by petroleum extraction. The houses combined primitive technologies with jerry-rigged modern infrastructures. While the students' artisanal avant-gardism sometimes approached a moralistic asceticism, the overall thrust was an optimistic hands-on pragmatism.

Experimental integration and reimagining of old and new technologies was coupled with the reconfiguration of associated domestic practices of cooking, heating, bathing and defecating. This speculative redesigning of dwelling modes was often consciously open-ended rather than any simple blueprint for living. In Sydney, the students' mail-order pamphlet *54 Alma Street Darlington* declared on its cover that the house 'does not present "the answer" – it presents one specific view in a wide range of alternatives.' Later, in the pamphlet, after detailing the house's experimental systems and their ongoing modifications, a student also wrote that if the house was to be thought of as a prototype, then it was:

> A prototype not defined by engineering specifications or measured with thermometers and galvanometers but as a process of people living together and working together with the goal of living more creatively, not confining themselves to the narrower horizons of efficiency and convenience.
>
> *(p. 7)*

Dennis Holloway similarly noted of Ouroboros South that it was: 'not a prototype of the house of the future, but simply a laboratory' (Marcovich 1975: 80). Offering a correspondingly open answer to just how its systems might be applied, a hand-painted sign at the Energy Pavilion described it for visitors as an experiment in 'autonomous life support.' In Montreal, On 22 October 1972, test-subjects Arthur and Elizabeth Acheson vacated the ECOL house, observing: 'The house will stand empty until the spring, when someone else will take a turn at ecological living [...] When we drive off the windmill begins to turn in the evening breeze' (Ortega et al. 1972: 88). More than technical objects, the houses were tools for experimental lifestyles (Figure 7.9).

FIGURE 7.9 The Street Farm Ecological House as photographed by Tone Wheeler, a University of Sydney student who visited the house in 1973 on a study tour of "autonomous housing" in the UK and North America. (Image Source: Photograph by Tone Wheeler.)

Let them eat sprouted seeds

The occupation and monitoring of the houses undertaken by the students across the projects extends the point about the rethinking of dwelling practices within these living labs. The houses were vehicles for testing experimental lifestyles as much as they were for testing technologies – reflecting the 1970s' emergence of the personal as political and inflecting the tradition of the model or prototype house. The occupants, who were often also the designer-builders, mapped paths of knowledge through their interactions with the houses. They monitored the domestic technologies, recorded their personal experiences and undertook adjustments to the systems; sometimes making extensive changes and radically reconfiguring them as dwellings. The students developed complex relationships with their projects as they established domestic routines in amongst maintaining data collection, leading tours, running workshops and classes on-site, publishing pamphlets and books, fielding sometimes-intense media attention (the Street Famer Ecohouse was the subject of BBC television programs in 1973 and 1976) and entertaining visits by celebrities of various sorts (such as Buckminster Fuller visiting – and naming – the ECOL house). The participants' connections with their projects were thus public but often very intimate. For Graham Caine, Fran Stowell and their daughter Rosie, the Ecohouse was a family home. Arthur and Elizabeth Acheson were recently married when they occupied the ECOL house. Around a dozen people lived in the Sydney Autonomous House over its four-year life, but a 1977 *Sydney Morning Herald* article, titled 'Solar heat and beer bottle

140 Lee Stickells

insulation in the $1-a-week house', captured a kind of snug domestic scene that might have been repeated across all five projects:

> Dan MacNamara is playing a moving Beethoven sonata at an old piano in distinctly unclassical conditions. Beside him is a wall of 4,000 water-filled beer bottles; beneath, a floor of bricks set in the earth; above, a fluorescent light lit by a windmill generator. As the haunting melody wafts through the thin wooden walls on the other three sides, his housemate Al Wurth is washing dishes in sun-heated water collected from the roof rainwater. In the small garden outside Al's crop of tomatoes, lettuce, spinach, radishes, potatoes and assorted herbs is flourishing in well-composted black soil that two years ago was stony ground.

Project publications also conveyed ways in which the material conditions of the houses conditioned the invention being pursued through conscious lifestyle choices. The pamphlets and books that emerged adopted the hands-on approach to advice and stimulation found in 1970s' countercultural print culture and reading networks (Binkley 2007). The rustic drawings, sometimes-crude technical diagrams, hand lettering and stapled, Xeroxed pages offered reportage on the experimental lifestyles and practical advice. The ECOL Operation book included do-it-yourself tips and the Acheson's diary of their stay. The details they shared highlight the intense concern over the house systems' everyday functioning: 'Our waste system has been functioning now for more than a month, and although people have shown some scepticism, it is working very well, with no smell or discoloration of the toilet bowl' (Ortega et al. 1972: 94). Continuing the feculent theme, the Sydney Autonomous House pamphlet included similarly personal reflections on dietary modifications in response to operational complications with the methane digester. Echoing back-to-nature ideas (such as those of the early 20th-century *Lebensreform* movement) that were being reinvigorated in the 1970s counterculture, a raw food diet was advocated: 'Experiments have been conducted on our diet – eating raw vegetables and fruits, "cooking with water rather than fire" e.g. sprouting seeds and eating them' (Ibid.: 6). Ultimately, as described at the beginning of the chapter, the Sydney students relied on a portable camping toilet.

These projects were not workplace laboratories but full-time public experiments in dwelling. And while absorbing its possibilities, they also extended what had become – in the post-war period – the familiar device of the model home (Colomina 1998; Floré and Kooning 2004: 411–412). They even encompassed sites for public experimentation and educational programs. While the large crowds gathering to experience the Berkeley Energy Pavilion were a significant reason for its demolition by campus authorities, at the peak of its activity, hundreds of school children were being led through the Sydney Autonomous House each week. The ECOL house received a modest stream of guests, including filmmakers and researchers; few enough that overnight stays were sometimes accommodated. Ouroboros South operated until the early 1980s as a venue for public tours and lectures delivered by its live-in manager Scott Getty and covering topics including:

> Environmental design, climate orientation, earth-sheltered housing, high insulation-low infiltration housing, active and passive solar energy, thermal mass storage, clean efficient wood heating, wind energy, water conservation and dry

FIGURE 7.10 Elizabeth Acheson washing up in the ECOL Operation house, using the water atomiser. Elizabeth lived in the house for three months, testing its systems, with her husband Arthur (an MCHG student). (Image Source: Courtesy of the Minimum Cost Housing Group, McGIll University.)

composting, energy efficient appliances, financing energy conscious homes and current federal and state energy tax credits.

(University of Minnesota 1981: 9)

The students' living laboratories fit with a strand of architectural–environmental ambition in the 1970s, in which dwelling design was implicated in a technological politics questioning conventional frameworks of growth, progress and development (Bonnemaison and Macy 2003). In their conspicuously inventive occupation of the houses, and the earnest attention to the very quotidian details of their experimentation, they edged towards something more than the conventional organizational structures, pedagogical frameworks and architectural ambitions of design-build projects (Figure 7.10).

Pottering about to the sounds of Zappa and Lennon

To conclude, let us come back to the technical failures highlighted at the beginning of the chapter. As the students became their own experimental subjects – receiving electric shocks, reaching for extra blankets and recasting broken turbine blades – the houses became living laboratories. Highlighting those uncomfortable moments, where the force of contingency took hold, reinforces the importance in the projects of the experimental integration of technical objects as enablers of new spatial and social practices. Although they were all design-build projects validated by professional architecture programs, the projects placed relatively little emphasis on students' proficiency with conventional construction practices, the development of sophisticated, craft-based design skills or tectonic awareness, or even direct community service. This could prompt institutional concern; in Sydney, for example, the students completed a remedial set of drawings in order to avoid a Fail grade for their project. The houses held little appeal on conventional disciplinary terms and had next to no effect on insitutionalized curricula – none of the projects were repeated. While design-build projects and a range of other experimental practices have become familiar pedagogical techniques in architecture schools, the freewheeling intensity of these 1970s living labs seems far more distant.

Similarly, as models, or prototypes, the projects were of little consequence. While described as 'ecological' or 'alternative energy' houses, their declared pursuit of new technical knowledge and goals such as improving the resource efficiency of buildings and reducing their adverse environmental impacts was rarely the most prominent outcome. Rather, the intense interest in enabling various styles of self-reliance meant the often-fraught trialling of novel technical artefacts, systems and user practices (brought together in the niche conditions of the living labs) foregrounded the techno-political implications of dwelling practices. House design offered, not finished architectural objects, but a constructive and flexible ground for experiments in being human and being social while also testing ecological boundary conditions.

The students' houses resonated with a period in which prefigurative and lifestyle politics came to the fore, in their reframing of boundaries between public and private life, between pedagogical, professional and political action (Hoffman 1989; Stephens 1998; Binkley 2007; Arrow 2019). They opened a view to a mode of messy, flawed but ambitious architectural experimentation – exhibiting a sort of improvised, outlaw laboratory praxis that tried to open possibilities for exploring architecture's dynamic engagement with technology, culture and politics as well its power to materialize new ways of living on an increasingly fragile planet. The five projects discussed in the chapter offer up to us a moment in which water tanks, urine fertilizer, waste recycling, compost bins, solar photovoltaics and a diet of sprouted seeds, could be entwined as the focus of hopeful, even humorous experimentation. The students' committed engagement with the most intimate material conditions of the house-objects saw them test the possibilities of architecture as a socio-cultural and environmental control mechanism. They overreached, perhaps, but as architecture engages with the overwhelming techno-cultural challenges of mitigating and adapting to climate instability, and with its disciplinary imbrication in untenable extractive resource systems, the fumbling ambitions of those 1970s educational experiments resurface as urgent. How can architecture conjure a viable future everyday worth wanting? The last word goes to Graham Caine, describing the dream of the Ecological House:

> The environment created, that of a direct involvement with natural cycles, should project a different life style and thus expectations for the inhabitants [...] a more peaceful existence [...] a sort of pottering about to the sounds of Zappa and Lennon.
>
> *(Caine 1972b: 12)*

Notes

1 The 1973 Energy Pavilion was initially envisaged by educators Sim Van der Ryn and Jim Campe as an occupied "ecotecture house" (Van der Ryn 1972; Van der Ryn & Campe 1972). The later IUH was effectively the realization of that idea, working with systems tested in the Energy Pavilion.
2 For instance, community design had emerged in the US during the 1960s (typically referred to as community architecture in the UK). Community Design Centers (CDC) often combined teaching and training of students with a broader community service; examples included the Yale Building Project at Yale University and the Pratt Center for Community Development at the Pratt Institute. Similarly, in the UK, Community Technical Aid Centres were created, such as Support Community Building Design, a co-operative linked to the Architectural Association, and Assist, which was connected to Strathclyde University.
3 Histories of design-build education sometimes point to John Ruskin's direction of his students (who became known as 'Ruskin's diggers') to build a road as a service to a poor Oxford community as an early example (e.g., Canizaro 2012: 21; Hayes 2007: 22–23).

References

54 Alma Street, Darlington, anonymous photocopied pamphlet in possession of the author, Sydney, 1978.

Alexander, Z.C. (2017), *Kinaesthetic Knowing: Aesthetics, Epistemology, Modern Design*, University of Chicago Press: Chicago.

Anker, P. (2010), *From Bauhaus to Ecohouse: A History of Ecological Design*, Louisiana State University Press: Baton Rouge.

Anthony, C., Campe, J. and Van der Ryn, S. (1972), *Natural Energy Design Handbook*, photocopied course reader in possession of the author, Berkeley, CA.

Awan, N., Schneider, T. and Till, J. (2011), *Spatial Agency. Other Ways of Doing Architecture*, Routledge: Oxford.

Barber, D.A. (2016), *A House in the Sun: Modern Architecture and Solar Energy in the Cold War*, Oxford University Press: New York.

Baxter M. and Grayson, R. (1976), 'Bottling Up the Sun: Details of a Self-Built Autonomous House in Sydney, New South Wales,' *Undercurrents*, 8 (October–November): 28–29.

Bell, B. and Wakeford, K. (eds.) (2008), *Expanding Architecture: Design as Activism*, Metropolis Books: New York.

Bonnemaison, M. and Macy, C. (2003), *Architecture and Nature: Creating the American Landscape*, Routledge: London.

Colomina, B. (1998), 'The Exhibitionist House,' in R. Ferguson (ed.), *At the End of the Century: One Hundred Years of Architecture*, Harry N. Abrams: New York.

Colomina, B. (2018), 'Learning from Global Tools' in V. Borgonuovo and S. Franceschini (eds.), *Global Tools 1973–1975: When Education Coincides with Life*, NERO editions: Rome.

Colomina et al. (2013), 'Radical Pedagogies.' Available online: https://radical-pedagogies.com (accessed 14 September 2018).

Caine, G. (1972a), 'The Ecological House,' *Architectural Design (AD)*, 3: 140–141.

Caine, G. (1972b), 'A Revolutionary Structure,' *Oz*, November: 12–13.

Canizaro, V.B. (2012), 'Design-Build in Architectural Education: Motivations, Practices, Challenges, Successes and Failures,' *Archnet-IJAR, International Journal for Architectural Research*, 6 (3): 20–36.

Clark, W. (1975), 'Ouroboros South and Ouroboros East,' *Mother Earth News*, November–December: 93–96.

Crook, T. (2009), 'Craft and the Dialogics of Modernity: The Arts and Crafts Movement in Late-Victorian and Edwardian England,' *The Journal of Modern Craft*, 2 (1): 17–32.

Dean, A.O. and Hursley, T. (2002), *Rural Studio: Samuel Mockbee and an Architecture of Decency*, 1st ed., Princeton Architectural Press: New York.

Dunlap, T.R. (1981), *DDT: Scientists, Citizens, and Public Policy*, Princeton University Press: Princeton, NJ.

Dutton, T.A. (1991), 'The Hidden Curriculum and the Design Studio: Toward a Critical Studio Pedagogy', in T.A. Dutton (ed.), *Voices in Architectural Education*, Bergin & Garvey: New York.

Floré, F. and De Kooning, M. (2004), 'Postwar Model Homes: Introduction,' *The Journal of Architecture*, 9 (4): 411–412.

Goodman, P. (1960), *Growing Up Absurd: Problems of Youth in an Organized Society*, Vintage Books: New York.

Gribat, N. and Meireis, S. (2017), 'A Critique of the New "Social Architecture" Debate,' *City*, 2 (6): 779–788.

Hayes, R. (2007), *The Yale Building Project, the First 40 Years*, Yale School of Architecture: New Haven, CT.

Hoffman, L.M. (1989), *The Politics of Knowledge: Activist Movements in Medicine and Planning*, State University of New York Press: Albany, NY.

Höhler, S. (2016), *Spaceship Earth in the Environmental Age, 1960–1990*, Routledge: London.

Hughes, F. (1973), 'The Ecologic House,' *Mother Earth News*, 20: 62–65.

Hunt, S.E. (2014), *The Revolutionary Urbanism of Street Farm: Eco-Anarchism, Architecture and Alternative Technology in the 1970s*, Tangent Books: Bristol.

Illich, I. (1970), *Deschooling Society*, Marion Boyars: London.

James, C. (1977), 'Australian Autonomy,' *Architectural Design (AD)*, 47 (1): 15–17.

Jones, P. and Card, C. (2011), 'Constructing "Social Architecture": The Politics of Representing Practice,' *Architectural Theory Review*, 16 (3): 228–244.

Kallipoliti, L. (2011), 'Clearings in a Concrete Jungle,' *Journal of the Society of Architectural Historians*, 70 (2): 240–244.

Kallipoliti, L. (2012), 'From Shit to Food: Graham Caine's Eco-House in South London, 1972–1975,' *Buildings & Landscapes: Journal of the Vernacular Architecture Forum*, 19 (1): 87–106.

Kallipoliti, L. (2019), *The Architecture of Closed Worlds, Or, What is the Power of Shit?*, Lars Müller: Zürich.

Knoblauch, J. (2020), *The Architecture of Good Behavior: Psychology and Modern Institutional Design in Postwar America*, University of Pittsburgh Press: Pittsburgh.

Kulper, A. (2011), 'Experimental Divide: The Laboratory as Analog for Architectural Production', in Á. Moravánzky and A. Kirchengast (eds.), *Experiments: Architecture Between Sciences and the Arts*, 92–115, Berlin: Jovis.

Marcovich, S. (1975), 'Autonomous Living in the Ouroboros House,' *Popular Science Magazine*, 111 (December): 80–82.

Meadows, D.H. (1972), *The Limits to Growth*, Earth Island Ltd: London.

Moore, C. (1967), 'Departmental Reports: Department of Architecture,' *Eye: Magazine of the Yale Arts Association*, 29.

Moos, D. and Trechsel, G.A. (2003), *Samuel Mockbee and the Rural Studio: Community Architecture*, Birmingham Museum of Art: Birmingham, AL.

Ockman, J. and Williamson, R. (eds.) (2013), *Architecture School: Three Centuries of Educating Architects in North America*, MIT Press: Cambridge, MA.

Odum, E. P. (1967), *Fundamentals of Ecology*, Saunders: Philadelphia.

Olkowski, H., Olkowski, W. and Javits, T. (1979), *The Integral Urban House: Self-reliant Living in the City*, Sierra Club Books: San Francisco, CA.

Ortega, A., Rybczynski, W. and Ayad, S. (1975), *The ECOL Operation: Ecology + Building + Common Sense*, Minimum Cost Housing Group, School of Architecture: McGill University, Montréal.

Ouroboros East: Towards an Energy Conserving Urban Dwelling 1974, University of Minnesota.

Pearson, J. (2002), *University-Community Design Partnerships: Innovations in Practice*, Princeton Architectural Press: New York.

Reynolds, J. (1976), 'Urban Homesteading: The Integral Urban House,' *Mother Earth News*, November–December.

Richards, S.G. (2016), 'Inputs, Outputs, Flows: The Bio-Architecture of Whole Systems Design, the Energy Pavilion, and the Integral Urban House,' in S. Schrank and D. Ekici (eds.), *Healing Spaces, Modern Architecture, and the Body*, Routledge: London.

Schumacher, E. F. (1973), *Small is Beautiful, A Study of Economics As If People Mattered*, Blond & Briggs: London.

"Solar Heat and Beer Bottle Insulation in the $1-a-week House," *Sydney Morning Herald*, June 9 (1977): 7.

Stickells, L. (2017), 'Journeys with the Autonomous House,' *Fabrications*, 27(3): 352–375.

University of Minnesota Bulletin—Non-credit Informal Courses 1981–1982 1981, University of Minnesota, 9.

Van der Ryn, S. (1972), 'Abstract of Proposal to Build an Ecotectural House', grant application letter in possession of the author, November.

Van der Ryn, S. (2005), *Design for Life: The Architecture of Sim Van der Ryn*, Gibbs Smith: Salt Lake City.

Van der Ryn, S. and Campe, J. (1972), untitled proposal to build prototype house in possession of the author, undated.

Van der Ryn, S. and Campe, J. (1975), *Natural Energy Designer's Handbook*, Random House: New York.

Van Dresser, P. (1976), *A landscape for humans: a case study of the potentials for ecologically guided development in an uplands region*. Lightning Tree: Santa Fe.

Wood, G.H. (1982), 'The Theoretical and Political Limitations of Deschooling,' *The Journal of Education*, 164 (4): 370.

Worster, D. (1977), *Nature's Economy: A History of Ecological Ideas*, Sierra Club Books: San Fransisco, CA.

PART 3

Bodies in space
Synesthetic learning

8

THE BODY AS AN ULTIMATE FORM OF ARCHITECTURE

Global Tools body workshops

Silvia Franceschini

The body as an ultimate form of architecture

The idea of a 'system of workshops in Florence for the propagation of the use of natural techniques and materials, and related behaviours', named Global Tools, emerged in 1973 on the initiative of groups and individuals that were representatives of Italian Radical Architecture.[1] This movement reached its theoretical maturity and perhaps its exhaustion following the international recognition it obtained at the exhibition *Italy The New Domestic Landscape* at MOMA New York in 1972 (see Figure 8.1).

The announcement of the initiative in the magazine Casabella was anticipated by an article written by Andrea Branzi and entitled 'The Abolition of The School'[2]: a manifesto inspired by the writings of the philosopher and pedagogue Ivan Illich, advocating for the necessity of a radical change in the field of education. In July 1973, 'Tre note per una tipologia didattica' (Three notes on a didactic typology) was also published in Casabella and detailed the research of Global Tools, which, according to the group Superstudio, would call for 'life as permanent global education'. The text alluded to Illich's publication, *Deschooling Society* in which he stated that the training of young people is never achieved in a school context but elsewhere, in times and situations beyond the control of the school.[3]

Global Tools emerged as a reaction against the return to order which occurred inside of the faculties of architecture after the weakening of the students' movement and against the backdrop of the growing academic power of what they perceived as the architectural establishment, and particularly the Italian movement *Tendenza*. At the end of the 1960s, a wave of experimentation took place within various Faculties of Architecture in the country. In Florence, experimentation was driven by architects and intellectuals such as Leonardo Savioli, Leonardo Ricci, Gillo Dorfles and Umberto Eco, whose courses created an indispensable ground for the later experiments of the so-called 'Radicals'.[4] In Milan, the several campus occupations by the student movements from 1964 onwards moved to a more public ground in 1968 with the occupation of the XIV Milan Triennale exhibition. In Turin, in 1969, teaching assistants and students of the Architectural department at the Polytechnic

DOI: 10.4324/9781003201205-12

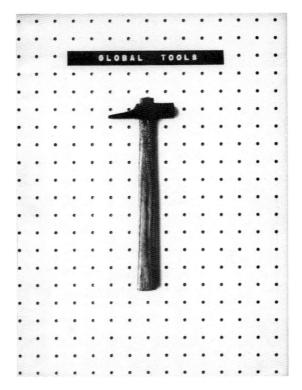

FIGURE 8.1   Global Tools Bullitin, no. 1 (cover), 1974. (Image Source: Courtesy of L'Uomo e l'Arte, Milan.)

University hosted a public meeting titled *Utopia e/o Rivoluzione* (U e/o R), questioning the teaching system of architectural education and making a case for greater involvement within society in the hope of promoting a revolution within the discipline against capitalist logic.[5] But the attempts to unite the different voices of the student movements faded in the post-1968 world, with the university's return to a conservative position. As Andrea Branzi observed, the older generation of teachers, the one which sprang up during the war and was responsible for the social failure of the university, sought to take full advantage of the student protest movement (Branzi 1973). Global Tools, however, did not aim to achieve a new academic model. On the contrary, it was conceived as a project free of formal programming, in which the results would not be read in terms of disciplinary models of reference but acquired as an act of spontaneous communication. As Franco Raggi stressed, Global Tools was conceived as a 'collective project in continuous transformation and continually subjected to verification'.[6] Its elusiveness was a conscious strategy to avoid the disciplinary divisions and to promote the role of creativity-based work within the process of education and social change. To achieve this goal, the crossover between the visual arts and different artistic strategies was crucial. Global Tools was not a school, neither in the physical meaning of the word nor in the dialectical one: the nomadic laboratories that were meant to appear in different cities in Italy – from Florence to Naples – were conceived as joint experiences to be made inside an established experimental frame. Defined as the first Italian counter-school of architecture (or non-architecture or again non-school), Global Tools was supposed to be a

FIGURE 8.2 Superstudio, construction session; first Global Tools general seminar (November 1-4 1974, Sambuca Val di Pesa, Florence). (Image Source: Courtesey Adolfo Natalini Archive, Florence.)

directory to 'provisional and private laboratories in town, an agency for the spread through society of all creative activities connected with the use of constructional techniques and of all the sub-architectonic systems for characterizing the environment'.[7] One of the first goals of Global Tools was to reconcile the distance between the minds and the hands, the practice and the theory. In the words of Franco Raggi:

> Those who founded or took part in Global Tools were interested in the construction of a program of didactic and productive research activities, with the aim of unshackling individual creativity from those cultural superstructures which prevented or hindered its expressive capacity. It was a slightly anarchic (yet organized) experimental hypothesis in the field of design, living and the construction of simple primary structures, attempting to trace the way back to a sort of primal state of action, exploiting one's own individual "tools", the instruments immediately available to us through which to interact with the outside world: our hands, brain, feet and body.[8]

The activities of Global Tools took place within a context of review and rejection of the conventional development models proposed by Western modernity that held that quality of life, environment and work are unachievable without models of continuous and exponential growth. The limits of this growth model first of all became a pressing issue in Italian factories in the 1970s, where rapid industrial production had generated revolts and strikes. In 1973, workers went on strike to obtain rights, which eventually led to a shut-down of Fiat factory in Turin, one of Italy's most important manufacturers. Second, global standards of living were challenged by the severe energy crisis that broke out as a consequence of the Arab–Israeli War – known as the Yom Kippur War – in 1973. The embargo on the export of petroleum introduced by OPEC countries heavily influenced daily life in Europe and elsewhere. This event brought the entire Western world face to face with the intrinsic fragility of the prevailing development model, which was built on the certainty of an endless supply of energy and resources. Global Tools questioned these paradigms of growth by proclaiming an anti-materialist, autarchic utopia, based on recourse to manual labour, which proposed new behaviours instead of new products and new relations between humans and their environment. This attitude was described by Simon Sadler as 'eco-ontological' in seeking a new potential for sets, instruments and epistemologies (Sadler, 2018). Within this process of revision, the role of the body as the central instrument of labour, which did not take into account its sensual and social dimension, was also called into question. The theme of the Body appeared from the outset as one of the most fertile in stimulating alternative investigations on the potentialities of human and creative expression and a departure from the narrow disciplinary field of architecture. The body theme was explored by the architects Alessandro Mendini (at that time director of the architectural magazine *Casabella*), Nazareno Noia, Gaetano Pesce and Franco Raggi together with the photographer and musician Davide Mosconi in several writings, an 'inventory of the human body' and two workshops promoted in Milan in 1975.

The body as a tool: an inventory

> Our body, considered as the principal topic of architecture, as the centre of all the environmental experiences, is the parameter for the use (ergonomics) of the whole planning experience.[9]

The human body was analysed in its ideal primordial condition: that is its state before being defined by functional goals. This was explained in the chapter dedicated to the topic of the body in the first official bulletin of Global Tools:

> Within a process of actions, deprived of their intellectual side, you can think of inquiring about the body, seen as an instrument, without considering specific cultural worlds, simulating and running again to through the process, progressively from the discovery to the finalized use or not of the body. We cannot foresee the results, but we can determine them, gradually after our operations. So doing we shall be able to develop more conscious processes about the use and the instrumental faculties of our body.[10]

If in conventional learning processes in the field of architectural education, the body was seen as an impediment or was simply overlooked, in the Global Tools workshops, the physical nature of the body and the way it related to its environment became a goal in itself.

The inquiry of the Body Group started in 1974 with an 'inventory of the human body', a preparatory list of concepts and actions which was published in the second Global Tools Bulletin and was supposed to serve as a pedagogical blueprint for future courses, in which the human body was regarded as a tool for surviving, building and communicating. The inventory considered the body as a connector which held all categories together, and the primary tool of measurement of mental and behavioural acts. The body was perceived as a physical and at the same time mental reality. The rediscovery of the body as a primary utensil emerged through a rigorous yet arbitrary 'inventory' of its parts, a cataloguing of every possible experience connected with the body, listing movements, positions, constrictions, the pursuit of unexpected relationships between bodies and object:

> A list of its various parts. Morphology anatomy, relief map of the body – The body as a built object. – Its various components: flesh, hair, nails ... - The body as a tool. The

Body as energy, (as a machine). – Ages. – The foetus. – Ageing - The Corpse. – Races. – Evolution. – The five senses (sight, hearing, smell, taste and feeling). – Pathology of the body. – The deformed body. – The body structure. – Beauty.[11]

The 'inventory of the human body' therefore focused on the classification of the possible characteristics, use and activities of the human body in relation to the research themes associated with Global Tools.

The body in the different global tools workshops

Global Tools consisted of five laboratories or research groups – Body, Theory, Communication, Construction and Survival – which prepared and offered expeditions into an unexplored layer of the human and creative resources of the city and its surrounding environment. Before studying in greater detail the works developed in the Body laboratory, it is important to understand the different approaches to the body in some of the other laboratories.

In the Theory group, the body was seen as an instrument for acquiring knowledge or for penetrating a certain reality outside of the body itself. Mental exercises (such as shock, discontinuity, casualty and emotion) as well as parapsychological conditions (drug, magic, astrology and ecstasy) and imagination techniques were hypothesized to mediate the distance between the self and objects. In the same period, the Soviet psychologist Evald Ilyenkov, who wrote about the role of bodily activity in education and human development, coined the term 'thinking body' to describe a mode of activity of the body that is not separated from the 'mind' (Lantolf and Poehner 2014). In his writings, Ilenkov aimed to overcome the mind-body dualism and to treat the thinking subject as located in material reality. Such a materialist vision of education seems relevant nowadays to frame the way in which Global Tools tried to foster a theory of education starting out from the body.

The Communication group (deeply influenced by reading McLuhan's work) saw the body as language, representation, self-representation and contemplation. But, first of all, it was analysed as an entity which could receive and assimilate information. The goal of the laboratory was to break down the mediating communication filters that separate the individual from reality by reducing the communication to direct relationships and exchanges with the interlocutors. According to the Global Tools group, the emergent domain of media communication was starting to dangerously affect the field of education and also risked confusing the idea of 'training' with the idea of 'information' (note that, in Italian, these words are very similar: *informazione* and *formazione*).[12] In 1974, a workshop from the Communication group took the form of a boat trip on the river Rhine from Dusseldorf to Basel on a boat named 'France' and was organised by Ugo La Pietra, Gianni Pettena and Franco Vaccari to study and implement the communication on different layers between individuals through the use of bodily primary instruments of communication (such as voice, gestures, touch and smell), between the individual and the tool (use of materials external to the body for communication) and between the individual and the environment (through the use of collective environments for communication such as the public spaces of the boat). This laboratory, which was held in a contained space over several days, therefore aimed to realise a coercive situation, in which spontaneous forms of communication could be broadened, amplified and extolled without destroying attention.

The research carried out by the Construction group emphasised the idea of the 'body as a tool', reassessing the lost relationships between the hands and its tools. The emphasis was placed on the activity of building as an unfunctional work, and on the bodily value of work, which was estimated by reference to activities in which the physical approach to the environment preceded the mental one – just as in the classic development of architectural projects, which start from drawing rather than from thinking. A special focus was put on 'poor techniques'. This was especially present in the experiments of the architect Riccardo Dalisi in the Rione Traiano, a satellite town close to Naples, built in the post-war era and threatened by serious problems of urban decay and organised crime. Through the building of spontaneous and ephemeral constructions and environments with the children of the area, Dalisi tried to give form to the unexplored depths of the constructive energy emerging from the singular and collective creativity.

Finally, the *Survival* workgroup conveyed the most apocalyptic and accurate image of the period of the Oil Crisis in 1973. Alessandro Mendini commented: 'I was closely connected to the Viennese, Haus-Rucker-Co., Walter Pichler, Max Peintner, Coop Himmelb(l)au; it was the moment in which this sense of drama was compelling us to reflect upon survival. The word ecology did not yet exist, and the reasoning was on the idea of 'elementary survival'.[13] The survival group promoted the first Global Tools seasonal workshop in November 1974 in an abandoned country house owned by Superstudio member Roberto Magris to test the lost ability of the body to re-adapt to rural conditions and to relate to traditional tools (see Figure 2). Here, the Global Tools pointed to the loss of skills and forms of knowledge related to traditional agricultural and material labour that was taking place as a result of the over-rapid urbanisation and the abandonment of rural areas in Italy that were ongoing in the 1970s. Organised as a group session, the meeting included real-time actions of organisation of transportation and communication, collective cooking, as well as other manual activities such as building renovation, in parallel with nightly theoretical discussions. Through elementary and somehow archaic physical activities, individual and collective conscious or unconscious actions of survival, the goal was to raise consciousness on the primary needs of the individual in relation to habitation.

Body group workshops

The first workshop of the Body group entitled 'The body and constraints' took place in the courtyard of the house of musician Davide Mosconi in Milan from the 5 to 8 June 1975. Apart from the official members of the Body group mentioned before, the seminar included friends, architects, performers and actors.[14] No material artefacts have been kept from the workshop, only a series of black and white documentary photographs of the performances and gatherings which were published in *Casabella* number 411 in 1976. The workshop consisted of exploratory analyses of the body's relationship to space through elementary movements, with the help of improbable and inexorably ephemeral objects. The products of the workshop included: tube eyeglasses to look 'only' into the eyes; arm and finger constraints; blindfold masks to display a mouth, a nose, an ear; clogs to remain immobile going uphill or downhill; elastic garments to trigger involuntary synergies in nearby persons and constraining shoes for stable and obligatory frontal juxtaposition[15] (see Figures 8.3 and 8.4). Similar to extensions or complementary parts of the body, these props tied people together or stressed the possibilities of one single body to become a tool on its own. Constructed mainly with low cost, everyday materials, such as concrete, paper, wood and textiles, they were regarded not as a 'thing', but as a form of practice to study processes of measurement of space and bodies. They were generating a logical and procedural short circuit with regard

Global Tools body workshops **155**

FIGURE 8.3 Constraining shoes for stable and obligatory frontal juxtaposition, Franco Raggi and Ettore Sotttsass Jr. Milan, 1975. First seminar of the Body Group 'Il corpe e i vincoli', 5–8 June 1975, Milan. (Image Source: Courtesy Archivio Franco Raggi, Milano.)

FIGURE 8.4 Elastic garments to trigger involuntary synergies in nearby persons, Alessandro Mendini, Milan, 1975. (Image Source: Courtesy Archivio Franco Raggi, Milano.)

to the tools of classic architectural design, keeping alive a dialogue between art and design, between the body as a tool and between objects as preparatory prosthesis to creatively re-establish the relationship between man and its environment. According to Franco Raggi:

> The methodological and operative input of the seminar "The body and constraints" was actually quite elementary in its subversive simplicity: to conceive and make, in an instantaneous way, objects with limited functions, or even dysfunctional items, starting with one's own body and its possible relations with other bodies. Objects that, by constraining, concealing or subverting the usual relationship of utility, could reveal something else, and by impeding one type of use could unpredictably generate another.[16]

In contrast to the established and accepted practice of a technological, comfortable, useful and functional design, which in those years was solidifying through the acceptance of precise ergonomic standards,[17] the intent was to posit a nomadic practice for an archaic and dysfunctional design. While ergonomics – a science created to reconcile 'labour' and 'health' in the light of a new 'cybernetic' modes of working – was reinforcing the idea of a man-machine design to extend the working hours as much as possible into the free time, the exercises of Global Tools were directed towards a voluntary anti-ergonomic practice of liberation of man from labour (see Figure 8.5). By emphasising the idea of the body as a living element deprived from alienation, a new idea of comfort was suggested based on a new 'ecology of the mind', rethinking the relationships between humanity and nature, nature and culture, theories and techniques, the hand, the machine and the brain.[18] Such philosophy of the project in which the body was at the centre of creative work was part of a critique of late-industrial society's role in fostering widespread alienation and the destruction of cultures and skills.

But the body was also being progressively and systematically denied, wounded, constrained and deformed in heavily ritualised events. This working method was reminiscent of the notion of bodily prostheses and deformations that were explored in the works of, for instance, the artists Rebecca Horn, František Lesák, Dennis Oppenheim or Walter Pichler. These artistic propositions valuing the body as primal and ancestral cockpit were interpreted by the members of Global Tools as forms of 'proto-design', which could be taken as a reference to challenge the positivism underlying the rationalist project of the inhabited environment and its objects which was at the base of architectural education in Italian academies (see Figures 8.6–8.9).

FIGURE 8.5 Blind mask to show a mouth, a nose, an ear, Franco Raggi. First seminar of the Body Group 'Il corpe e i vincoli', 5-8 June 1975, Milan. (Image Source: Courtesy Archivio Davide Mosconi e Inez Klok, Milano.)

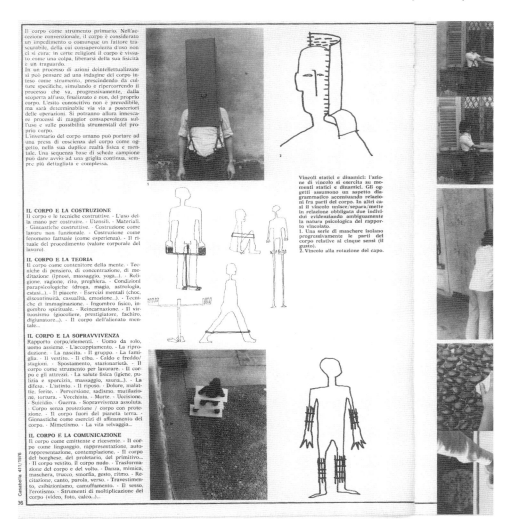

FIGURE 8.6 Global Tools Milano - giugno '7: Il corpe e i vincoli: L'uso anomalo del corpo come strumento conoscitivo. Azioni-oggetti-progetti (in)utili. Casabella n. 411, March 1976. (Image Source: Courtesy Archivio Franco Raggi, Milano.)

0The second Body group workshop was held in an empty gallery in Milan. A 'detection room' was constructed, inspired by the scientific, neutral approach with which the American photographer Edward Muybridge, at the start of the 20th century, had set up a black wall subdivided into segments with white lines to make sequential shots of human bodies in motion. It was a room for testing a new anthropometry, a measurement of the body not according to its capacity to perform optimised positions of labour – as was in the classical use of anthropometry carried out to serve the needs of industrial design – but deconstructed through unpredictable individual and collective bodily movements. Inside the room, photographic sequences were made, depicting normal actions isolated by the abstract, geometric and modular form of the space involving (among others) Marina Spreafico, Dario Sereni and Paolo Inghilleri of the *Teatro Arsenale* in Milan. These actions were loosely inspired by the

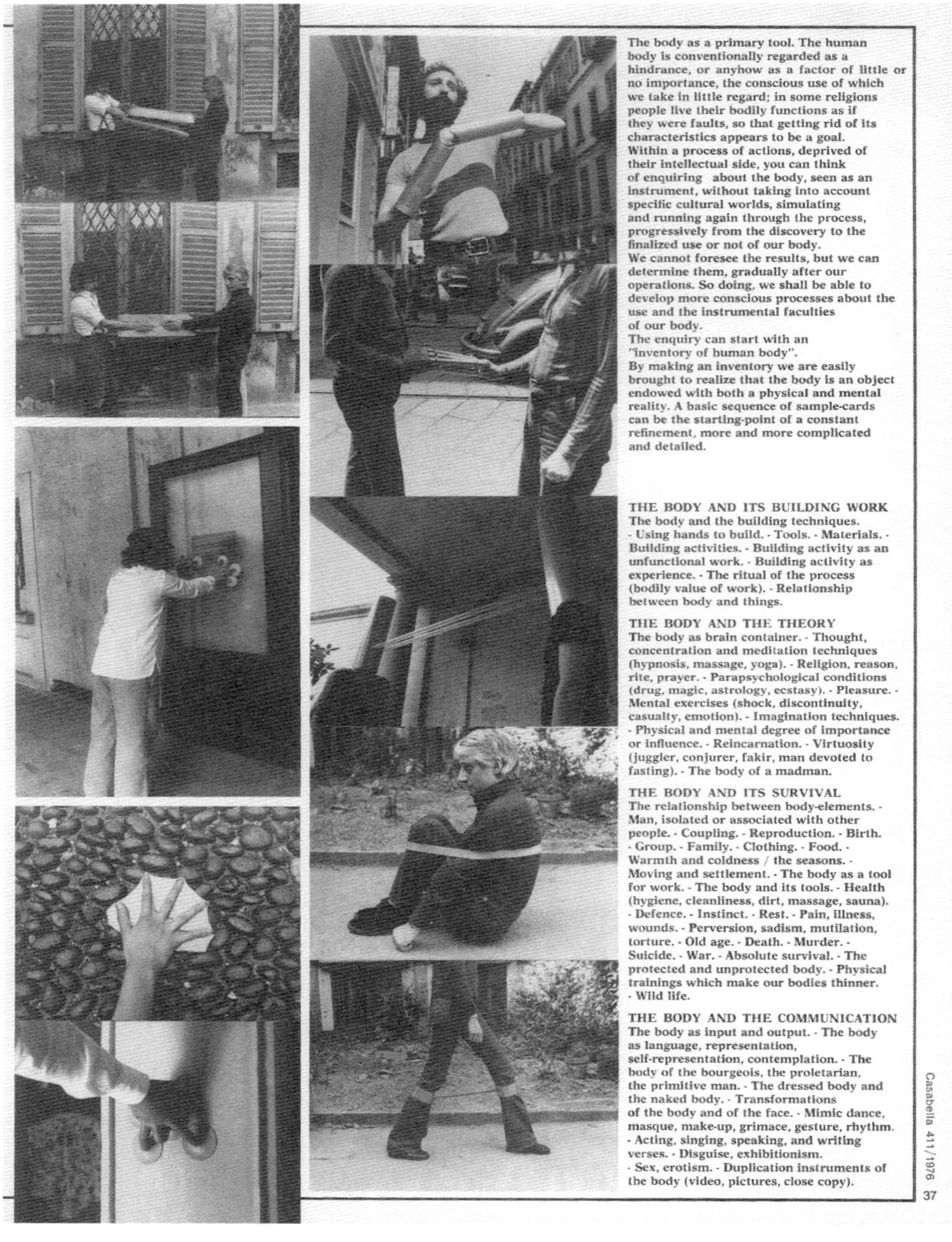

The body as a primary tool. The human body is conventionally regarded as a hindrance, or anyhow as a factor of little or no importance, the conscious use of which we take in little regard; in some religions people live their bodily functions as if they were faults, so that getting rid of its characteristics appears to be a goal. Within a process of actions, deprived of their intellectual side, you can think of enquiring about the body, seen as an instrument, without taking into account specific cultural worlds, simulating and running again through the process, progressively from the discovery to the finalized use or not of our body. We cannot foresee the results, but we can determine them, gradually after our operations. So doing, we shall be able to develop more conscious processes about the use and the instrumental faculties of our body. The enquiry can start with an "inventory of human body". By making an inventory we are easily brought to realize that the body is an object endowed with both a physical and mental reality. A basic sequence of sample-cards can be the starting-point of a constant refinement, more and more complicated and detailed.

THE BODY AND ITS BUILDING WORK
The body and the building techniques. - Using hands to build. - Tools. - Materials. - Building activities. - Building activity as an unfunctional work. - Building activity as experience. - The ritual of the process (bodily value of work). - Relationship between body and things.

THE BODY AND THE THEORY
The body as brain container. - Thought, concentration and meditation techniques (hypnosis, massage, yoga). - Religion, reason, rite, prayer. - Parapsychological conditions (drug, magic, astrology, ecstasy). - Pleasure. - Mental exercises (shock, discontinuity, casualty, emotion). - Imagination techniques. - Physical and mental degree of importance or influence. - Reincarnation. - Virtuosity (juggler, conjurer, fakir, man devoted to fasting). - The body of a madman.

THE BODY AND ITS SURVIVAL
The relationship between body-elements. - Man, isolated or associated with other people. - Coupling. - Reproduction. - Birth. - Group. - Family. - Clothing. - Food. - Warmth and coldness / the seasons. - Moving and settlement. - The body as a tool for work. - The body and its tools. - Health (hygiene, cleanliness, dirt, massage, sauna). - Defence. - Instinct. - Rest. - Pain, illness, wounds. - Perversion, sadism, mutilation, torture. - Old age. - Death. - Murder. - Suicide. - War. - Absolute survival. - The protected and unprotected body. - Physical trainings which make our bodies thinner. - Wild life.

THE BODY AND THE COMMUNICATION
The body as input and output. - The body as language, representation, self-representation, contemplation. - The body of the bourgeois, the proletarian, the primitive man. - The dressed body and the naked body. - Transformations of the body and of the face. - Mimic dance, masque, make-up, grimace, gesture, rhythm. - Acting, singing, speaking, and writing verses. - Disguise, exhibitionism. - Sex, erotism. - Duplication instruments of the body (video, pictures, close copy).

Casabella 411/1976

37

FIGURE 8.7 Global Tools Milano - giugno '7: Il corpe e i vincoli: L'uso anomalo del corpo come strumento conoscitivo. Azioni-oggetti-progetti (in)utili. Casabella n. 411, March 1976. (Image Source: Courtesy Archivio Franco Raggi, Milano.)

'accumulation' dance performances of Trisha Brown, questioning architecture by assembling and disassembling bodies in a three-dimensional space. At the same time, the use of temporary body prosthesis and ephemeral instruments to limit the actions of the body while acknowledging and measuring the space was reminiscent of a tentative deconstruction of some of the scenes of Bauhaus dance of Oskar Schlemmer (see Figure 8.10).

FIGURE 8.8 Global Tools Milano - giugno '7: Il corpe e i vincoli: L'uso anomalo del corpo come strumento conoscitivo. Azioni-oggetti-progetti (in)utili. Casabella n. 411, March 1976. (Image Source: Courtesy Archivio Franco Raggi, Milano.)

This was not the first time that performative actions and processes of this kind were appearing in the educational experiments of the Italian Radical design movement: the contribution of dance and theatre to architectural and spatial pedagogy had already been explored a few years before by the group 9999 and Superstudio within the workshops of Space Electronics and of the short-lived pedagogical initiative *S-Space, Separated School for Expanded Conceptual Architecture*.[19]

Conclusions

Within the rising perception of the body as a site of exercise from a sovereign and neoliberal capitalist power, the deconditioning from culture and the performative status of production seemed, for the members of Global Tools, to form a route towards a somatic rebellion,

FIGURE 8.9 Global Tools Milano - giugno '7: Il corpe e i vincoli: L'uso anomalo del corpo come strumento conoscitivo. Azioni-oggetti-progetti (in)utili. Casabella n. 411, March 1976. (Image Source: Courtesy Archivio Franco Raggi, Milano.)

forming part of an insurgent process of bodies. According to Pierre Bourdieu, somatic practices are 'general formulas of domination' from which bodies should emancipate. Against the formation of a newly optimised normative body, Global Tools staged a return to an idea of a man – once posited as the measure of all things – liberated from all tools until the body itself is used as a tool. Trying to tackle the dualism of the modern world, the division between mind and body, self and others, the subject and the object, Global Tools aimed to

FIGURE 8.10 The Body Group, detection room for 'corporal actions', 1975-1976, Milan. Second seminar of the Body Group, 1975-1976, Milan. (Image Source: Courtesy Archivio Franco Raggi, Milano.)

formulate a programme for a counter-pedagogy in design and architectural education, taking the cognitive procedure of design back to a primary, didactic form, while reassessing the anthropological nature of the body as a tool of physical and mental survival.

The activities of the two Global Tools body workshops took the form of existential and performative exercises aimed at a corporal and mental liberation of the artist from the physical and intellectual exploitation typical of the society of late as well as from cognitive capitalism. Through the de-intellectualisation of the design project and a focus on the phenomenology of the body as a primary medium for testing the environment and exploring the limits of the body in relation to it, Global Tools triggered processes of greater awareness 'regarding the use and the purposed possibilities of one's body'.[20] What moved the research of Global Tools was therefore a need to build experience, to explore the world according to unconventional points of view, to link the body with the new recording instruments such as photography and video recording, to employ it as a medium capable of functioning not only as a prosthesis of the senses but also the psyche, in line with the strategies in place at the Body Art, Narrative Art and Conceptual Art.

As said in the introduction, Global tools called for life as permanent global education with particular reference to *Deschooling Society* by Ivan Illich:

> The teaching and exchanges of experiences around themes like the working of iron and wood, ceramics, tailoring, music, gymnastics, singing and dance, gastronomy, photography and film, can constitute an approach to the ideal moment when education coincides with life itself.[21]

162 Silvia Franceschini

Global Tools therefore never achieved implementation as a real school, surviving in history as a spontaneous and pure life experience without students or formal heritage. The programme of activities studied at length did not lead to any specific and 'efficient' organisation of the initiatives, leaving the task of producing a remarkable number of artefacts to free aggregations of persons, thoughts and materials. However, today, 40 years later, it seems to contain a remarkable consistency of method and to assert an autonomy of the creative process that is regarded as a possible form of knowledge released from linguistic and cultural superstructures. Indeed, its ephemeral aspect was also part of its programmatic (and problematic) principle as we read in one of the bulletins:

> The problem of "funding a school" coincides this time with the problem of "freeing oneself from school", of teaching to learn, of organising, in order to guarantee discontinuity, of making contacts in order to spread one's personal case, with taking one's place in history in order to remain a pure phenomenon.[22]

Notes

1 The official founders of Global Tools were Archizoom Associati, Remo Buti, Casabella (Alessandro Mendini, Carlo Guenzi, Franco Raggi, Luciano Boschini), Riccardo Dalisi, Ugo La Pietra, 9999, Gaetano Pesce, Gianni Pettena, Rassegna (Adalberto Dal Lago), Superstudio, U.F.O., Zziggurat and Ettore Sottsass Jr. They were later joined by relevant figures from the Arte Povera, such as the founder of the movement, Germano Celant and the artist Luciano Fabro, and also by figures from the Arte Concettuale, such as Franco Vaccari and Giuseppe Chiari.
2 *Casabella*, no. 373, Milan, January 1973.
3 *Casabella*, no. 379, Milan, July 1973.
4 In his experimental classes, Leonardo Ricci was proposing the idea of the abolition of the 'urban plan' in favour of a 'creative plan' or a 'community space'. In his course titled *Spazio di coinvolgimento* (Space of involvement), which involved Adolfo Natalini (Superstudio) and Paolo Deganello (Archizoom Associati) as assistants, Leonardo Savioli focused on an artistic and performative response to the problem of mass culture, designating space as a 'continuous happening'. Umberto Eco taught courses in the semiology of visual communication.
5 See Alicia Imperiale, *Utopia e/o Rivoluzione*, Politecnico di Torino, Turin, Italy, 1969 in www.radical-pedagogies.com. The contributions to the conference by different participants are reported in the magazine Marcatré, no. 50/55, February–July 1969.
6 Franco Raggi, 'Radical Story: The History and Aim of Negative Thinking in Radical Design since 1968: The Avant-garde Role Between Disciplinary Evasion and Commitment', *Casabella*, 382 (October 1973).
7 The Chronicle, Global Tools Bulletin n°2, 1975.
8 Valerio Borgonuovo, Silvia Franceschini, *Notes on Global Tools*, conversation with Franco Raggi, Studio Puppa Raggi, Milan, September 2011 on Gizmoweb http://www.gizmoweb.org/2012/06/appunti-su-global-tools/
9 Global Tools, bulletin no. 1, *Laboratori Didattici Per La Creatività Individuale*, Edizioni L'uomo e l'arte, Milan, 1975.
10 Ibid.
11 Ibid.
12 *A School of Popular Arts and Techniques*, Unrealised document without date, Archive Ugo La Pietra, Milan.
13 Alessandro Mendini, in conversation with Silvia Franceschini and Valerie Guillaume, Studio Mendini, Milan, 27 September 2012, unpublished.
14 1. The participants in the workshop were Almerigo De Angelis, Siana Futacchi, Ines Klok, Andrea Mascardi, Alessandro Mendini, Davide Mendini, Paola Navone, Nazareno Noja, Pini Pisani, Lidia Prandi, Franco Raggi and Tareneh Yaida.
15 Ibid.

16 Ibid.
17 In 1960, the American designer, Henry Dreyfuss, published *The Measure of Man: Human Factors in Design*, a book of ergonomic reference charts providing designers with precise specifications for product designs. An American male named 'Joe' and an American female 'Josephine' were taken as models of anthropometrically detailed measurements for industrial purposes, a man-machine design with emphasis on the human size factor. The standardisation of the human body initiated a century before with the formulation of the *homme moyen* by Adolphe Quetelet (around 1835) and continued by Ernst Neufert's canonical *Architects' Data* (1936) ultimately became the main subject and target of the nascent global consumerist culture.
18 The proposal to read the activities of Global Tools through the idea formulated by Gregory Bateson in his book *Steps Towards an Ecology of the Mind* was formulated by Manola Antonioli and Alessandro Vicari in their essay *Global Tools as a war machine for an ecology of mind* in Valerio Borgonuovo, Silvia Franceschini (ed. by), *Global Tools. 1973–1975 When Education coincides with life*, Nero Editions, Rome, 2018.
19 Space Electronic was a nightclub, a hybrid space in which to experience multimedia experiments in architecture, music, theatre and technology, which was founded in Florence by the group 9999 in 1969. Live performances came from British and Italian prog rock groups as well as relevant theatre groups such as Dario Fo, Franca Rame and the New York group Living Theatre. S–Space, Separated School for Expanded Conceptual Architecture founded by 9999 and Superstudio in 1971 was a hypothesis of a theoretical–practical global system of experimental teaching for the refinement of mental strategies.
20 BODY group, report by: Andrea Branzi, Gaetano Pesce, Alessandro Mendini, Franco Raggi, Ettore Sottsass Jr, 8 October 1974. Unrealised document published in Valerio Borgonuovo, Silvia Franceschini (ed. by), *Global Tools. 1973–1975. When Education Coincides with Life*, Nero Editions, Rome, 2018.
21 Untitled Global Tools document, 1973, Adolfo Natalini Archive. Unrealised document published in Valerio Borgonuovo, Silvia Franceschini (ed. by), *Global Tools. 1973–1975. When Education Coincides with Life*, Nero Editions, 2018.
22 The Chronicle, *Global Tools Bulletin*, n°2, 1975.

References

Aa Vv. (1974), Global Tools Bulletins, no. 1 and no. 2, Milan, Edizione L'uomo e l'arte. https://www.neroeditions.com/product/global-tools-when-education-coincides-with-life/

Ambasz, E. (1972), *Italy: The New Domestic Landscape. Achievements and Problems of Italian Design*, New York, Museum of Modern Art of New York.

Borgonuovo, V., Franceschini, S. (2018), *Global Tools. When Education Coincides with Life*, Rome, Nero Editions.

Branzi, A. (1973), 'Global Tools, Radical Notes', *Casabella*, 377.

Dreyfuss, H. (1967), *The Measure of Man: Human Factors in Design*, New York, Whitney Library of Design.

Illich, I. (1971), *Deschooling Society*, New York, Harper & Row.

Lantolf, J. P., Poehner, M. E. (2014), *Sociocultural theory and the Pedagogical Imperative in L2 Education: Vygotskian Praxis and the Research/Practice Divide*, London, Routledge.

Franco R. (1973), 'Radical Story: The History and Aim of Negative Thinking in Radical Design since 1968: The Avant-garde Role Between Disciplinary Evasion and Commitment', *Casabella*, 382, 1973.

Sadler, S. (2018), 'Tool Globalism', In: Borgonuovo, V., Franceschini, S. (eds.), *Global Tools. When Education Coincides with Life*, Rome: Nero Editions.

9

PARALLEL NARRATIVES OF DISCIPLINARY DISRUPTION

The bush campus as design and pedagogical concept

Susan Holden

'Problem Solvers for our tomorrow': this was the headline in Queensland's daily newspaper on 11 June 1973, as inaugural Vice-Chancellor John Willett announced the newly established Griffith University's intentions to produce graduates that could come to grips with the problems facing 21st-century society. Griffith University was Australia's 16th University and the tenth established as a new institution in the post-WWII decades as part of a wider nation-building agenda that included the coordinated expansion of tertiary education.[1] As evident in Willett's bold statement, forming a new institution presented an opportunity to be ambitious and innovative, which those involved in shaping the University intended to pursue in all aspects of its design (see Figure 9.1).

The campuses of the new universities built in Australia in the post-WWII period certainly reflected new pedagogical agendas and a conception of the modern university institution as accessible, social and civic. Yet, Griffith was unique in coalescing an innovative pedagogical agenda with a distinctive campus design. Whereas most of the new campuses built in Australia after WWII were in peri-urban locations on greenfield sites, Griffith was established in a remnant eucalypt forest, much of which was preserved in the campus's development. As Ted Bray, Griffith's inaugural Chancellor, later reflected 'unless you're flying over the site you wouldn't know it was filled with buildings and thousands of students and staff.... It was a stroke of great genius to preserve this site and improve it in the way it's been improved' (Griffith University 1996: 26). Early academic staff members reiterated the impressive experience of arriving on campus. Roy Rickson from Minnesota was 'very impressed with a university ... in a middle of a forest' and Reg Henry from Adelaide 'fell in love with the campus straight off' (Griffith University 1996: 47 and 49).

Modern campus design can be understood as reflecting a shift in the discipline of architecture in the post-war period, in which the environment became an organising principle for the expansion of knowledge and practice through interdisciplinary encounters. As described by Sachs (2018: 8), environmental design encompassed 'an emphasis on environments rather than buildings, on collaboration with other professions, and on close attention to social and environmental constraints'. In many respects, the campus was conceived as an environmental design problem *par excellence*, bringing together planning, architecture, and landscape

DOI: 10.4324/9781003201205-13

FIGURE 9.1 The article 'Problem solvers for our tomorrow' by John Willett appeared in *The Courier Mail* 11th June 1973 and described the ambition of Brisbane's new Griffith University to focus on problem-based learning (Source: Griffith Archives, Griffith University. Johnson Papers. © Griffith University and News Corp Australia.)

architecture into a cohesive whole and introducing expertise from science and social science disciplines to address the challenge of designing for flexibility and future change.

Beyond this, Griffith's campus design was undertaken at a time of growing consciousness of socio-cultural values of the environment and awareness of environmentalism. Early recognition of the campus environment's quality accorded with Willet's and Bray's decision to introduce environmental studies as one of the University's areas of focus. As part of a second wave of new post-war universities in Australia, Griffith adopted many of the organisational and pedagogical innovations of earlier counterparts established during the 1960s, including a model of 'Schools' instead of Departments that followed traditional academic disciplines.[2] However, Griffith brought another level of innovation, formulating its Schools as interdisciplinary units that focused on pressing issues facing modern society. Griffith's first four schools included the School of Australian Environment Studies (SAES) which established the first undergraduate degree program in Environmental Studies in Australia.[3] There was a growing appreciation of the complexity of environmental problems and the necessity to understand them as resulting from the 'tremendous intensification of interaction between cultural and natural processes' (Boyden 1970: 18). The Griffith program translated curriculum and pedagogical concepts being developed in the emerging field of environmental education for school and citizen education to the higher education setting in Australia.

The parallel development of the academic program and the campus masterplan allowed the planning and architecture of the campus to reinforce the goals of interdisciplinary education. The first four schools were housed in discrete buildings where each could foster a sense of community and shared purpose. They were organised along a pedestrian circulation spine in a compact arrangement that prioritised the preservation of the remnant forest. The large expanses of surrounding bushland became a setting for teaching and research through the designation of Forest Study Areas, an initiative of the SAES supported by the University Site & Buildings Division (S&BD). Over time, Bray's identification of the campus as a tight grouping of buildings lost in the bush gave way to a strong conception of the bush itself, an island in suburbia anchored by the campus core.

This chapter explores the development of Griffith University's bush campus, as both a design and pedagogical concept. It explores how the pursuit of a problem-oriented pedagogy was the engine for interdisciplinary teaching and research, and in turn, how the campus was a vehicle through which pedagogical and institutional goals coalesced. It reflects on the different roles the campus played: as a material setting for learning and as an object through which environmental subjectivity was negotiated. This history is contextualised in relation to the development of environmentalism and environmental education in Australia and alongside the evolution of the concept of environmental design in architecture. These are presented as parallel narratives of disciplinary disruption, one in which interdisciplinary teaching and research yielded new knowledge and practices in the area of environmental studies and another in which concepts of environmental design tested the limits of architecture's professional identity.

Environmentalism and Interdisciplinary education

> Environmental problems ... are not just a matter of economics, but of geology, biology, land use, sociology and economics, as well as of politics. Therefore, the education

of problem solvers in the next century must be directed towards a multi-disciplinary and inter-disciplinary approach. That ... is what Griffith is aiming to do.

(Willett cited in 'Problem solvers for our tomorrow' 1973)

For Willett, the emerging field of environmental studies was an exemplar of the kind of interdisciplinary approach to teaching and research that Griffith intended to embrace in its organisational structure and academic programming. The campus's unique design being developed at the time, which preserved its expansive remnant eucalypt forest setting, reinforced the University's inclusion of an environmental focus. While the campus site had been decided and obtained several years earlier, the impetus to include environmental studies was also an early part of academic planning.

The initial idea that one of the University's first Schools might be focused on environmental problems had come from Ted Bray, who chaired the committee established to plan the new institution and was impressed by 'developments in environmental concerns ... and of environmental studies programs in USA and UK universities' that he observed during an international research trip undertaken in 1970–1971 (Rose et al. 2017: 59). Bray's schedule[4] included visiting the University of Michigan which had established an Environmental Education Program and, through the work of William Stapp, is credited as one of the originators of the modern concept of environmental education, which focused on developing environmental literacy and critical thinking as the basis for behaviour change (Stapp 1971: 266–267).

Bray's interest reflected growing institutional recognition of the need to better understand and respond to human impacts on the environment and the role of education in this. In the USA, the establishment of the Environmental Protection Act was mirrored by the National Environmental Education Act, both passed in 1970. Similarly, the United Nations Declaration on the Human Environment of 1972 recognised the important place of education not only to navigate the complexity of environmental problems but also for the development of a literate and responsible population (Greenall and Womersley 1977: 16). UNESCO subsequently formalised a statement on environmental education in the Belgrade Charter in 1975 (Carter and Simon 2010: 4–5) which articulated an agreed definition:

> Environmental education is a process aimed at developing a world population that is aware of and concerned about the total environment and its associated problems, and which has the knowledge, attitudes, motivations, commitments, and skills to work individually and collectively toward solutions of current problems and the prevention of new ones.

(UNESCO-UNEP 1976: 2)

Closer to home, environmental threats to the Great Barrier Reef from proposed oil exploration and mining were receiving widespread public and media attention (Trumbull: 1970). The campaign that ensued led to the 1975 Great Barrier Reef Marine Park Act. For Bray, an ex-newspaper man, this was a prime example of the growing need for new knowledge and skills to support better 'environmental management as a scientific matter' in Australia, and this became a touchstone for curriculum development in the SAES (Rose et al. 2017: 60).

In 1970, Stapp visited Australia to address the Australian Academy of Science Conference on Environmental Education (Gough 2012: 5) introducing curriculum concepts to

168 Susan Holden

Australia. While science education was seen as something of a surrogate home for environmental education, it was recognised that the urgency and complexity of environmental problems required a more integrated approach, as articulated by Stephen Boyden, a convener of the conference:

> The suggestion that all our problems will be solved through further scientific research is not only foolish, but in fact dangerous... the environmental changes of our time have arisen out of the tremendous intensification of the interaction between cultural and natural processes. They can neither be considered as problems to be left to the natural scientists, nor as problems to be left to those concerned professionally with the phenomena of culture... all sections of the community have a role to play...
>
> *(Boyden 1970: 18)*

There was also a growing focus in environmental education on learning 'outside the classroom', allowing students 'to see firsthand the forces interacting in [the] environment … to test them and ultimately to understand them' (Sullivan and Schlesinger 1972: 361). This reflected the legacy of early 20th-century nature study societies, which encouraged the appreciation of nature through direct experience, and the conservation education movement, which reacted to the problems of natural resource management after the Great Depression, in the development of environmental education in the USA (McCrea 2006: 2–4). Stapp argued the importance of 'environmental encounters' in developing both critical thinking skills and environmental values (Stapp 1970: 32). Stapp's environmental encounters also involved learners in defining environmental problems and proposing solutions and thus utilised a problem-based pedagogy to link 'relevant ecological, economic, social, technological and political information'. Furthermore, meaningful encounters were described as ones in which learners could physically explore their environment and connect with their communities to develop 'interest, awareness, understanding and respect' and 'become personally involved in positive action towards the solution' (Stapp 1970: 30). Stapp was influenced by Hess and Torney's theorisation of childhood as a critical time in the formation of citizen responsibility and later by the development of action research methodology[5] (Stapp 1971; 266; Gough 2001: 21–22).

Each of the four Schools at Griffith was 'expected to be guided by a problem-definition and problem-solving emphasis with respect to their teaching and research' (Johnson 1973a: 3). Griffith's ambition was to use the School structure as a catalyst for interdisciplinary exchange that could absorb methodological and epistemological differences and provide an anchor and purpose for student learning. This picked up on the 1970 OECD seminar on interdisciplinarity, which emphasised a 'problem-focused' approach as a foundation of interdisciplinary teaching and research (Apostel et al. 1972). In this respect, interdisciplinarity was also aligned with the aim to develop a more accessible higher education system. As noted by Franks: 'Educational reform movements sought to eliminate social barriers to learning. … As part of this, epistemological barriers (notably, the disciplinary organisation of knowledge) were also targeted, and interdisciplinarity and knowledge integration were invoked as methods of reform' (Franks et al. 2007: 17) (see Figure 9.2).

Bray's early interest in Environmental Studies aligned with Willett's focus on interdisciplinary problem-based teaching and research as the basis of Griffith's institutional organisation. The SAES would focus on the 'knowledge necessary to understand, and hopefully

School and Focus	Concentration Areas
School of Australian Environmental Studies *To foster understanding of:* *(a) the nature of the Australian environment* *(b) the interrelationship of its parts* *(c) the laws or other processes by which the* *parts influence on one another*	Urban ecology and societal processes Resources ecology Systems science and applicable mathematics
School of Humanities *To explore the notion of human values, their* *development and their communication.*	Comparative Literature History Italian Studies Communications and the media Comparative cultural studies
School of Modern Asian Studies *The development of political, commercial,* *industrial and cultural contact with Asian* *societies.*	Modern Chinese Economics Management and technology Social and political history Geography
School of Science *The theme of Material and Civilization.*	Chemistry Biological chemistry Chemical physics Physics

FIGURE 9.2 The first four Schools at Griffith University, as described in the 1973 Annual Report, had a multi-disciplinary problem-based focus. In the 1990s, Griffith introduced Faculties into its organisational structure, and the School of Australian Environmental Studies was folded into the Faculty of Environmental Science. Griffith introduced a degree program in Architecture in 2010 in the School of Environment (Source: Table by author based on information from https://griffitharchive.griffith.edu.au/items/foundation-schools/)

anticipate, the full consequences of human activities which have an impact on the natural world, and through that on the public or common good, such as on human health and well-being' (Rose et al. 2017: 60). The inaugural professors in the School – Calvin Rose who was conducting land use research at the CSIRO (Commonwealth Scientific and Industrial Research Organisation) and had first-hand understanding of the interrelated environmental and social impact of pesticide use in the USA, and Arthur Brownlea who saw Griffith as 'the next stage in the interdisciplinary approach' he had experienced at Macquarie University – determined four key concepts to guide the development of the curriculum which included a systems approach to understanding environmental concerns, the importance of an evidence base to study environmental problems, a focus on interdisciplinary linkages between social and natural science, and a focus on fieldwork (Quirk 1996: 20).

Griffith adopted a foundation-year approach, a curriculum innovation that was amplified by the challenge of bringing together diverse disciplines to define a new field of study. One of the foundation-year courses in SAES was titled 'From Environment to Habitat' and brought together bio-geographical and social-historical knowledge[6] (Willett 1983). The SAES thus played an important role in bringing together science and humanities education at Griffith. Both Bray and Rose referred to C. P. Snow's influential essay 'The Two Cultures', which significantly influenced post-war educational reform, particularly

FIGURE 9.3 Theodore Bray (Inaugural Chancellor), John Willett (Inaugural Vice-Chancellor) and Roger Johnson (campus architect-planner) on the site of Griffith University, c.1973 (Source: Griffith Archive, Griffith University. Johnson Papers).

in the UK and Australia (Rose et al. 2017). Willett later reflected that the SAES was the centre of heated interdisciplinary debate (Willett 1983). Part of this was attributed to the 'value-laden nature' of environmental studies programs (Braddock et al. 1994: 35), and the different pedagogical approaches being employed to develop both rigorous and ethical learners, which was also apparent more generally in the development of environmental education.

The early appointment of Roger Johnson in the position of university architect-planner meant that campus and academic planning happened in parallel, with the close involvement of Willett, who quickly appreciated how a distinctive campus would reinforce a distinctive institutional identity. As one of its first employees, Johnson was immersed in all aspects of the planning of the new University. He had a good understanding of the Griffith concept of Schools and expected that the missions of the Schools would inform the campus design. The development of the campus plan during 1972–1973 would become a reinforcing loop for the focus in the academic program on interdisciplinarity and study of the Australian environment (see Figure 9.3).

Bush campus as design concept

'If you went around the Australian universities you'd find that most … are either on the side of a hill, in the bottom of a creek …[or] next to a cemetery', so recalled Sam Ragusa (2017), the head of Griffith University's Site and Buildings Division from 1978 to 2007. The siting of new campuses built in Australia in the post-WWII period was largely determined by availability and affordability of large tracts of land. Griffith was no exception. A hilly site at the southern edge of Brisbane's suburban fringe, bordered by the Toohey Forest Reserve and Mt Gravatt recreational reserve and cemetery, was obtained for the new campus by the State Government from the Brisbane City Council in 1966. It was land that, as Johnson noted, 'in the past … had been regarded as poor land, the stringy iron-barks testifying to the rocky and thin top-soil cover' (Johnson 1973a: 10).

Yet, the distinctive quality of the geology and flora of the site, which included several rare species, was immediately recognised by those involved in planning the new University, reflecting a growing environmental and nationalist consciousness that was challenging the marginal conception of bushland and fringe environments.[7] The idea to leave as much of this bushland intact as possible emerged quickly as a guiding principle in the development of the campus plan by Johnson. This was supported by Bray and Willett who saw an opportunity for a unique campus that would reinforce Griffith's identity as a progressive institution and clearly distinguish it from other universities, particularly its local counterpart, the sandstone and gardenesque University of Queensland (see Figures 9.4 and 9.5).

Johnson favoured a compact arrangement of buildings forming the main academic complex. The arguments for a compact plan, as distinct from a more dispersed approach observed at bush campus precedents known to Johnson including the University of California, Santa Cruz and the University of Newcastle in Australia, were in Johnson's estimation 'overwhelming': 'short walk times, economy of roads and services and the creation of urban spaces in contrast to the bush, flexibility for future connections' (1973a: 17). UC Irvine was another important precedent in the development of post-war campuses in Australia in the 1960s, which reflected the conception of the campus as a total environment, as encapsulated in William Pereira's integrated design that included the revegetation of the greenfield site.[8] While Griffith followed modernist campus planning ideals that saw campuses developed in the post-war period as urbanistic and civic, it was also, importantly, a way to preserve as much of the bush environment in its natural state as possible and reflected a broader socio-cultural conception of the environment.

FIGURE 9.4 Aerial photograph of Griffith University campus c.1980 (Source: Griffith Archive, Griffith University).

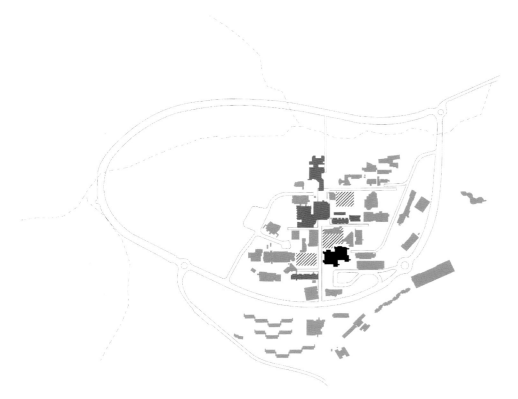

FIGURE 9.5 Diagram of the Griffith Nathan campus showing the first buildings arranged along the circulation spine (dark grey), and the School of Australian Environmental Studies (black) situated adjacent to designated Flora Reserves (hatched) which protected areas of bush at the heart of the campus during construction. Subsequent buildings (light grey) filled-in the campus core. Forest Study areas were developed beyond the campus core and the ring road (Source: Diagram drawn by Sophia Fu).

Johnson's Campus Development Plan determined the location, extent, and form of the main academic complex, which arranged buildings along a pedestrian circulation spine with the Library and University House anchoring one end. Sites for the first four Schools were determined as much by an assessment of where buildings should not be constructed, as by consideration of the site's micro-climate and the adoption of passive design principles 'to achieve well-proportioned sunny open spaces, good air movement, good internal day-lighting, and building flexibility within reasonably compact limits' (Johnson 1973a: 20). Johnson's commitment to a compact campus carried over to his strategy for managing the impact of a growing student population anticipated at the time the new University was being planned. He sought to balance expansion onto new sites with the effects of more concentrated populations on the campus environment, including the effects of trampling, identifying select sites for uncommitted expansion, but also determining a limit on the extent of car parking (Johnson, Griffith Site Planning Report 1973c: 20–21).

Landscape Architect Barbara van den Broek was commissioned in 1972 to test the idea of the 'bush setting' as a concept for the campus landscape design. As there were limited funds to do extensive re-landscaping, a strategy that worked with the existing landform and vegetation was necessary. However, van den Broek brought an aesthetic and ecological dimension to the task: 'the concept of a "bush-setting" for the University is both practical and aesthetic in origin. ... [it] is a valid concept with good chances of success provided all the relevant factors governing plant habitat are taken into account' (1972: 1 and 26). The resulting landscape report developed a design schema that classified the site into natural landscape areas to be reserved, reinforced, or reinstated and included strategies for protecting, transplanting, and cultivating plant stock (Dwyer and Associates 1972).

Johnson's and van den Broek's attention to the ecological and cultural value of the bush landscape at Griffith followed an evolving interest in the use of native Australian species in landscape architecture practice that simultaneously embraced and critiqued a romantic notion of the Australian bush through its pragmatic and responsive approach. As described by Don Watson:

> The Australian Bush is both real and imaginary. ... [It] is everything from a gum tree to any of the creatures that live in it or shelter beneath it, and it is the womb and inspiration of the national character.
>
> *(2016: 66)*

In the 1960s, the development of an environmental movement saw this nationalist conception of native bush landscapes link with emerging conservation agendas. The 1968–1970 campaign to preserve the Little Desert in north-west Victoria, in which a 'Bushlands Magna Carta' was drafted, captures the significance of this moment in shifting popular conception of the value of frontier or fringe landscapes (Robins 1998).

The designation of Flora Reserves in the Campus Development Plan was a key strategy in shaping Griffith's bush campus. Flora Reserves were areas of bushland that were to be preserved within the main academic complex and were protected during construction of the first buildings under the building contracts. The Flora Reserves reinforced van den Broek's bush campus design ethos and facilitated the preservation of bushland in close proximity to the spaces that students and academics would spend their time (see Figure 9.6).

Johnson's approach to architectural controls and building materials further reinforced this design approach. It was Johnson's intention that 'a clear cut distinction between what is landscape and what is architecture should reinforce the desired contrast between buildings and natural landscape' (1973a: 22). A palette specifying the use of predominantly white and off-white materials to maximise this contrast was set out by Johnson to guide the design of the first buildings (1973a: 33–34). Each of these buildings was designed by different architects who followed these guidelines in different ways. Highlighting the bush environment of the campus by making the built-natural interface explicit – through the proximity of the Flora Reserves and through the staging of nature in contrast with the built – constituted a valuing of the environment 'as found' and on its own terms.

The idea of a bush campus thus became an anchor for the identity of the new institution, including its academic program and aims for pedagogical innovation. Johnson's early recognition that the SAES ought to have an input into the development of the campus was facilitated by key professorial appointments of Rose and Brownlea in the early stages of the campus planning process both in early 1973.[9] As noted by Rose, in the early days: 'we felt we had a very substantial input in the planning and management' of the campus (1993) (see Figure 9.7).

FIGURE 9.6 Griffith University campus under construction, showing designated Flora Reserves preserving bushland in close proximity to buildings at the heart of the campus: between the benched SAES site and the just completed Library and Humanities building by Robin Gibson and Partners, c.1975 (top); and adjacent to the Humanities building, with University House by John Dalton in the background, c.1975 (bottom) (Source: Griffith Archive, Griffith University).

Bush campus as pedagogical concept

[T]he atmosphere ... was one of excitement, involvement, a feeling that the environmental issues were of great importance to the students, to the staff, to Australia and to the world generally and that we were in the beginning of developing programs that were addressing these kinds of issues.

(Rose and Thoms 1993)

FIGURE 9.7 (top L to R) Professor Calvin Rose and Professor Arthur Brownlea from the School of Australian Environmental Studies, (bottom L to R) Campus Architect Neil Thyer, and Curator of Grounds Colin Phillips, all supported the development of the bush campus (Source: Griffith Archive, Griffith University).

Griffith's privileging of the School as the primary organising unit of the University reflected its prioritisation of problem-based pedagogy as the driver for interdisciplinary teaching and learning. The decision that each School would have its own building was a conscious decision taken to reinforce their individual identity. For the SAES, the physical co-location of diverse disciplines in one building gave a spatial expression to the ambition to define a new interdisciplinary field of study. As described by Johnson: 'The School, in the Griffith concept, will be an intellectual, social and counselling focus for students and staff' (1973a: 3). This approach thus also served the aim of fostering 'close relationships between students and the University, both formally and informally'[10] (Johnson 1973a: 5).

John Andrews International were commissioned to design the SAES building in 1975, with John Simpson taking the role as design architect. Andrews had recently returned to Australia from Canada, where he had established a practice after undertaking graduate studies at Harvard University. He had extensive experience in educational projects, notably Scarborough College (1963–1969)[11] and Guelph University student residences (1965), two distinctive university projects completed as part of Canada's expansion of tertiary education. Both projects emphasised circulation space as a major determinant in planning, translating progressive pedagogical agendas that recognised the importance of providing opportunities for both formal and informal interaction between staff and students (Scrivano and Lobsinger

2009). One of the practice's most celebrated educational projects, Gund Hall (1968) for Harvard's Graduate School of Design, was an important precedent for designing for inter-disciplinary learning in a single building and demonstrated Andrew's appreciation of the social dimension of this. Gund Hall's dramatic stepped studio spaces gathered planning, landscape, and architecture students under a single expressive raked roof, so there was 'no separation between disciplines' (Taylor and Andrews 1982: 92). As described by Andrews, 'It is that openness to simple curiosity, to inquiry, to cross-fertilisation that the building represents' (1982: 99). The adjacent lounges on each level were imagined as a common social space that could enhance learning:

> The building had to facilitate contact by bringing students, faculty and administrators into a physical relationship with each other which provided opportunities for them to develop their own informal learning and social contact ... Everyone will have to pass the lounges, which are primarily open, comfortable spaces. The faculty member will see a colleague having coffee there and stop for a chat, a student will nail him about his last lecture, the dean will wander by with the registrar.
>
> *(Taylor and Andrews 1982: 96)*

Johnson would have encountered Andrews during his time working for the National Cap-ital Development Commission (NCDC) in Canberra (1968–1971), where he worked prior to coming to Griffith. In Canberra, Andrews had won a major commission in 1968 for the Cameron Offices, a large-scale project to accommodate 4,000 office workers that was to anchor the new town of Belconnen, which was overseen by Johnson (Taylor and Andrews 1982: 151). Andrews' own campus planning work resonated with Johnson's approach, and his design for Cameron Offices integrated a series of expansive courtyards modelled on dif-ferent Australian landscapes, a project Johnson admired.

The SAES building sat directly alongside the main pedestrian circulation spine of the campus, and at ground level, this space was integrated with the building through an open undercroft, facilitating a seamless meeting of campus and building circulation and reit-erating a planning technique common to Andrews's educational work.[12] The spatial or-ganisation and formal expression of the building are like an earlier project by the practice, Weldon Library, completed for the University of Western Ontario (1967), with its tight and compact forms recognisable as Simpson's influence (Taylor and Andrews, 1982: 133). The organisation of the SAES building also prioritised circulation, with offices and small teaching spaces arranged along the edges of the two larger demonstration spaces, and curved concrete stairwells punctuating the end of each horizontal run of circulation, and protrud-ing as strong sculptural forms into the surrounding bush. Opened in 1977, it was the fourth major building on the campus and was separated from the Humanities building by a large Flora Reserve that brought the bush landscape into close proximity to the building, echoing the landscape strategy of Cameron Offices. A shared common room for staff and students was an often-commented upon spatial feature that echoed the lounges of Gund Hall, albeit in a more prosaic way, and supported what Roger Braddock, the fourth Chair of SAES (1984–1989) later theorised as the 'lifeboat' model of interdisciplinarity (see Figure 9.8):

> Staff and students intermingled and the common room was symptomatic of the life-boat - a place to gather and discuss the traumas of interdisciplinary studies, or to

recount comparative experiences from the traditional disciplinary culture. The common room was … a place to meet disciplinary and interdisciplinary colleagues from elsewhere in the building, to discuss wider applications of a particular expertise in environmental problem solving. This social arrangement is very different from the 'them' and 'us' of traditional departmental common rooms, devoid of undergraduates and containing only one discipline, with possible subdivisions into specialised groupings.

(1994: 44)

Beyond the School building itself, the wider campus environment perhaps played a more fundamental role in environmental learning, reflecting Rose's and Brownlea's prioritising of fieldwork in the original inception of the academic program, and also the 'learning outside the classroom' that was deemed important in environmental education. Fieldwork in diverse ecosystems in the region developed as a cornerstone of the School's curriculum, including the signature Tallebudgera Orientation Exercise which involved students and staff travelling to the Gold Coast together for several days, to learn about marine processes, fluvial processes, agriculture, and urban change 'from the mangroves to the sewage works' and be inducted into problem-based learning (Griffith University 1996: 31). However, Rose and Brownlea quickly saw an opportunity for the campus to serve as a more immediate learning environment.

The establishment of Forest Study Areas was a tangible way in which the broader campus environment was utilised as a setting and resource for teaching and research. Forest Study Areas were first proposed from 1974, as the campus's first buildings were under construction a year before the commencement of teaching. The initial proposal made by the SAES to the S&BD, who were responsible for campus planning and management, set out the unique

FIGURE 9.8 School of Australian Environment Studies Building by John Andrews International c.1977, located along the campus pedestrian spine and adjacent to flora reserves. Internal planning included a common room shared by staff and students (Source: Griffith Archive, Griffith University).

opportunity offered by the bush campus environment and the convenience of being able to conduct research and teaching on the site:

> The provision of a large on-campus forested area for studying eucalypt ecosystems will be an important commitment by the University. It will provide a unique opportunity to examine over a lengthy period many factors affecting sclerophyll forest ecosystems typical of eastern Australia, and the ways in which these ecosystems function. It will be one of the few areas in Australia where a forest may be conveniently and intensively studied as a whole ecosystem….. To gain an adequate appreciation of, and training in, environmental problems, it is essential that courses contain sufficient elective field activities. [without the cost of transport associated with field excursions] … Proposed activities included: soil mapping, litter studies, soil erodibility, vegetation mapping, land surveying, microclimate studies, catchment hydrology, ecosystem cycling, animal populations, characteristics of rare plants, effects and role of fire and control burning techniques, management strategies and tactics for urban parkland.
>
> *(Griffith University Site and Buildings Committee 1974: 1–2)*

The conservation value of the Forest Study Areas was also recognised:

> Several rather rare species of plants … are found on the site … and it therefore represents a potential natural preserve for these species, which are being threatened by suburban expansion. The development of management methods for this area, especially for the preservation of rare species, will be a major contribution to the conservation movement in Queensland. Determining general management programmes for rare species is a science in its infancy and the School of Australian Environmental Studies, in conjunction with the Site and Buildings Committee, have an excellent opportunity to contribute to this aspect of land management.
>
> *(Griffith University Site and Buildings Committee 1974: 1)*

Johnson later reflected that 'Griffith ha[d] proved native plants can be used for the landscaping of a comparatively large-scale complex and … require much less maintenance than exotics' thus providing a valuable precedent 'in a resource-conscious world' (Johnson et al. 1981: 50).

In the 1980s, as student numbers grew and resourcing was rationalised, the Toohey Forest Orientation Exercise replaced the Tallebudgera Exercise as the signature orientation experience for the first-year students. This involved students undertaking a guided walk across the campus, pausing in a range of locations where they met different staff members and undertook activities related to different knowledge areas of the curriculum. Such an exercise required two-way radios, first-aid stations, and evacuation procedures, and in some cases, students would get lost (Griffith University 1996: 72). For Nicole Thornton, a student in the 1990s, this was a formative aspect of her studies:

> We cannot forget all our excursions into our beloved Toohey Forest. … Studying Casuarina species … and Xanthorroea trees; making mud cakes from soil for Soils Geomorphology; being blinded by the sun measuring canopy cover; running face-first into … spiders …
>
> *(Griffith University 1996: 126)*

Through the Flora Reserves, the Forest Study Areas and Toohey Forest Orientation Exercise, the bush campus was thus experienced at two scales: through the staging of the bush in close proximity to buildings in the academic core and through the long-term study and management of the expansive bush site. Academic staff member Carla Catterall quantified this in 1987 as follows (see Figure 9.9):

> Over 200 first-year students use the forest to gain field experience in soil science and ecology. ... some 300 students per year use the forest for various forms of fieldwork ... Local primary and secondary schools also use the forest for educational pursuits ... [and this] is expected to grow, given the expected growth in the various educational sectors.
> *(1987: 154)*

Beyond their didactic purpose, the Forest Study Areas were a catalyst for the establishment of protocols of interaction between SAES, the S&BD, and the broader university community. The publication *An Island In Suburbia: The Natural and Social History of Toohey Forest* provides a record of some of the long-range research and teaching that utilised the campus and illustrates the way the campus, in conjunction with the adjacent 262ha of the Toohey

FIGURE 9.9 Fieldwork on and off campus was an important aspect of learning for SAES students (Source: Griffith Archive, Griffith University).

Forest Park and Mt Gravatt Recreational Reserve, was valued as an important ecosystem (Catterall and Wallace 1987). Ultimately, *An Island In Suburbia* presented an argument for conservation and evidences the formation of environmental subjectivity, particularly amongst staff members from the SAES and from the S&BD.[13] Catterall's contribution explicitly tackled the question of the value of the forest and its sustainable management. Bob Coutts described his survey of the flora of Toohey Forest included in the publication, as some of his most important work. Both Catterall and Coutts refer to their involvement in the conservation of Toohey Forest as a significant part of their careers, demonstrating how the campus was a subject that linked the development of staff research expertise and their environmentalism (Griffith University 1996: 95–96). Amongst the contributors, Neil Thyer played an important role in facilitating communication between different stakeholder groups through his roles as landscape architect in the S&BD (1972–2008), member of the Forest Study Committee, and coordinator of student and community involvement in campus plan reviews in the 1980s.[14] Although further built expansion of the campus tended to be viewed as a threat to the campus environment, Catterall's analysis recognised the complexity involved in 'striking the right balance' between uses and values (Catterall and Wallace 1987: 160). Nonetheless, the university proved to be an effective custodian of the site and a mode of use that was compatible with its conservation (see Figure 9.10).

Australia's post-war campus designs provided opportunities for pioneering practitioners to test the use of native species in different climatic regions and evidence a growing environmental awareness (Saniga and Holden 2022). The characterisation of the Griffith campus as anchoring and protecting the remnant eucalypt forest in contrast to the surrounding spread of suburban development, marked a particularly potent advance on this line of thinking and practice, and embedded a conservation agenda in the way that the bush campus was mobilised as both a design and pedagogical concept. As a literal island in suburbia, the campus continues to functions as an object lesson in conservation (Figure 9.11).

Afterword: environmental design

> Dear Professor Jackson. I'm glad you received the Griffith Site Planning Report … I thought you would be interested in the idea of trying to keep much of the bush intact. … When I saw you in Berkeley I was still working full-time on Griffith but had been appointed to head the School of Environmental Design in Canberra. I was looking at other similar schools and also for staff … We take our first students next year. … I hope, if there is any chance of your coming to Australia … you will let me know.
>
> *(Johnson, 5 September 1973b)*

In 1973, Johnson exchanged correspondence with J. B. Jackson, after meeting him in Berkeley and then having sent him a copy of the Griffith campus planning report.[15] Jackson was 'greatly impressed' and noted 'how fortunate to have so large an area of … untouched land to work with' (Jackson, 27 August 1973). He said he would take the report back to Harvard where he was teaching that Fall.

J. B. Jackson was a pioneer in the development of landscape architecture and, through his *Landscape* magazine, introduced new paradigms through which to understand the cultural, social, and political processes that shaped everyday and vernacular urban and regional

FIGURE 9.10 An *Island In Suburbia: The natural and social history of Toohey Forest*, edited by C.P. Catterall and C.J. Wallace. Griffith University, Institute of Applied Environmental Research, Nathan, 1987. The cover image highlights the contrast between the campus environment and the surrounding suburban development (Source: Griffith University).

landscapes. Through his teaching at Berkeley and Harvard, Jackson also contributed to the expansion of built environment education through interdisciplinary teaching. The College of Environmental Design at Berkeley (est. 1959), where Jackson taught, was an early expression of the push towards interdisciplinary teaching. Wurster Hall, designed by CED faculty Joseph Esherick, Vernon DeMars, and Donald Olsen and completed in 1964, brought together planning, landscape, architecture, and decorative arts into one building. In its intent to foster interaction between allied disciplines, it was an influential predecessor to Andrews's Gund Hall at Harvard. In her historical study of the evolution of environmental

FIGURE 9.11 Conservation of the campus environment continues through the ongoing protection of Flora Reserves at the core of the campus and through the management and revegetation of the surrounding bushland (Source: Photographs by Susan Holden, 2017).

design in post-war America, Sachs highlights both of these institutions as playing a significant role in the early development of the concept of environmental design:

> The term *environment* … widened the purview of architects to include all aspects of the human world, including topics … which had previously been considered beyond the profession. Conveniently, *environment* could be (and was) applied to both natural and rural areas and to cities … [and] captured the notion that architecture was shaped … in the balance between humans and their surroundings.
>
> *(Sachs 2018: 10, see also 20–42)*

In the evolution of environmentalism, the built environment was also quickly recognised as a key subject in addressing environmental problems. In the 1960s, environmental design developed as an umbrella term to describe both an ambition for a new 'inter-discipline' (Ekistics 1976: 258) as well as an imperative for the built environment design disciplines to engage with environmental problems. At the University of Pennsylvania, landscape architect Ian McHarg introduced a seminar course titled 'Man and Environment' that engaged with social science and science methodologies and 'articulated an ecological imperative that evolved with the rise of the environmental movement in the 1960s' (Sachs 2018: 6). By the 1970s, the influence of behavioural science and systems theory had begun to codify environmental design. In 1976, a special issue of *Ekistics* dedicated to environmental education – in part, a response to the US Environmental Education Act – described how: 'the man-built environment has literally reordered and restructured the natural scene, but the man-built environment of human settlements also exerts its own environmental impacts on the behaviour of the inhabitants … [and] thus the ways in which humans plan, construct, and manage their settlements' (1976: 260).

In 1969, Jackson resigned as editor of *Landscape* stating that 'his "explorative and speculative approach" didn't fit the "boom" of environmental studies' (Notteboom 2017: 49) reflecting a mounting tension in the evolution of environmental design between social and physical concepts of the environment (Sachs 2018: 7). What followed in architecture was a move to recuperate formal and aesthetic aspects of architectural design and an understanding of the design process as more than just a problem-solving exercise. One way to understand this trajectory is as a tension between interdisciplinarity and professionalism. As Braddock et al. noted in their analysis of interdisciplinary teaching and research in the university context, which used Griffith SAES as a case study, 'professional insecurity is one of the greatest barriers to effective interaction among disciplinarians' (1994: 39). While the 1967 Princeton Report, commissioned by the American Institute of Architects, registered the traction of environmental design on architectural education, it also brought to a head the effects of disciplinary expansion as it encountered the politics of the profession, as can be seen in Richard Bennet's blunt response to the report: 'The Princeton Report has unfolded an umbrella far bigger than the profession it shelters. It has done so by substituting 'the process of practising environmental design' for the 'status' of being an architect' (quoted in Sachs 2018: 163). Sachs has astutely characterised this tension as a misrecognition of environmental design as a theory of architecture: 'Ultimately, architecture as environmental design was a theory of the *profession* and its role in democratic social action, or a theory of *practice*, and not a theory of architecture' (2018: 164). More generally, Linder suggests that while interdisciplinary exchanges in the first part of the 20th century didn't radically change the 'basic identity of architecture as a discipline primarily concerned with the design and construction of buildings', they did seed exchanges with other fields of knowledge that 'exacerbated the seemingly settled interdependence of architecture education and the profession' and 'initiated a period of discipline reconfiguration that continues to the present' (2012: 295–296).

More radically, the formulation of a concept of the environment that underlied the emergence of environmental studies and environmental design became a provocation for the reconceptualisation of the university institutions itself. In the same year that the Griffith campus plan was being developed, Emilio Ambasz made a more extreme, if elusive, provocation, in his Universitas project, which solicited contributions from a diversity of disciplines and looked to design as a catalyst to disrupt the very concept of the University so that a new kind of institution could emerge to address the 'environmental crisis brought on by the emergence of the postindustrial age' (Scott 2004: 51).

In presenting the Griffith campus to Jackson, Johnson was perhaps posing the bush campus as a more tangible, if modest, case study of interdisciplinary pedagogy and environmental design. Johnson's own trajectory presented an opportunity to engage more directly in environmental design education and for these parallel narratives of disciplinary disruption to converge. In 1973, he left Griffith, returning to Canberra to take up the position of Head of the new School of Environmental Design at the Canberra College of Advanced Education (later University of Canberra), attracted by the opportunity to establish the new School from first principles. Johnson had been involved in early discussions about the possibility of establishing such a school in Canberra in the late 1960s, and his selection committee included John Andrews (Richardson 1979: 185). By this time, environmental design had indeed become an accepted umbrella for the institutional organisation of architecture programs. A precedent for Canberra was the School of Environmental Design at Manchester Polytechnic which influenced the decision to include landscape architecture. Johnson developed a suite of three programs in architecture, landscape and industrial design which shared a common foundation year (Richardson 1979: 188). Eminent figures in landscape architecture contributed to the shaping of curriculum including Professor Garett Eckbo, Bruce Mackenzie and Richard Clough who had played an important role in the development to several post-war Australian campuses and was at that time working for the Design and Environment Division of the NCDC.

The Canberra campus itself also provided opportunities for teaching and learning:

> In 1974 it was agreed … that the landscape would be developed through the involvement of staff and students of the School of Environmental Design' and a 'plant materials laboratory was set up … [which] contributed to the landscaping of the … campus where the teaching work of the School was integrated with practical work undertaken by students.
>
> *(Richardson 1979: 190–191)*

Academic staff members Miss J Hendry and Mr G Wilson were experts in native plants and involved in revegetating the campus landscape (Richardson 1979: 189–191). Johnson was also involved in the design of a new building for the School, completed in 1979 with Eggleston Macdonald Secomb, which organised the building to create 'a pleasantly landscaped and tiered courtyard' (Richardson 1979: 192) and utilised expressed circulation to connect studio spaces on each level to encourage 'unity among its occupants' (The Architectural Review 1979: 302). In 1977, Johnson joined the Campus Master Plan Review Committee (Richardson 1979: 194). He remained committed to the environment, and in his book *The Green City*, Johnson reflected on the significance of the Griffith campus as an integrated environmental design (1979).

Johnson saw the value of potential connections with SAES, which he expressed to Jackson, but he does not appear to have pursued them, despite continuing as a consultant to Griffith University and contributing to campus plan reviews into the 1980s. The requirements of professional accreditation ultimately had as much influence in shaping program structures at Canberra University as the desire to develop an interdisciplinary concept of environmental design. Similarly, back at Griffith, as environmental studies matured as a field of study and graduates defined professional trajectories, the SAES also evolved. In the early 1990s, following a period of reform of higher education policy in Australia which determined new parameters for Commonwealth funding, Griffith established the Faculty of Environmental Sciences, which absorbed the SAES and introduced specialised programs in environmental engineering and environmental planning (Griffith University 1996: 80). As was common amongst many new universities established in Australia in the post-war period, Griffith did not initially include professional programs such as law, engineering and architecture as these were antithetical to the notion of interdisciplinary education. However, the focus on graduate employability and the knowledge economy that underpinned shifts in higher education in the 1990s marked a significant change in this outlook and motivated program diversification. Griffith introduced an architecture program within the School of Environment in 2010. The early formation of environmental studies at Griffith benefited from having a common goal in staking out a new field (Braddock et al. 1994: 39). But as noted by Franks et al. 'It was also likely that the growth of professional education, both inside Griffith and more broadly, was an important factor in the diminution of interdisciplinarity as an intellectual position' (Franks et al. 2007: 176).

Against the vicissitudes of tertiary education policy reform, and despite the expansion of Griffith University through institutional amalgamations and the development of new campuses, Toohey Forest endures as a bushland reserve, an ecosystem, and a learning environment. During the 1990s, Griffith established an Eco-Centre on the campus 'to serve school children, tourists and Brisbane residents interested in Toohey Forest' (Griffith University 1996: 88). It is a tangible legacy of the more ambitious goal of institutional and pedagogical reform that underpinned the formation of Griffith, which took place in part under the interdisciplinary umbrella of environmental education and ascribed a material value to the campus as a setting for situated problem-based learning and the development of environmental subjectivity.

Notes

1 Australia's higher education system is state-supported. A Commonwealth Government policy framework has existed since 1959 when the Australian Universities Commission (AUC) was established. The expansion of the higher education system in Australia in the 1950s–1970s mirrored a world-wide trend that saw the modernisation of the institution.
2 Flinders, Macquarie, and Latrobe Universities established in the 1960s in Australia all adopted a Schools model. Sussex University, one of the UK's post-war 'plateglass' universities, was a shared precedent.

186 Susan Holden

3 The other three Schools were Modern Asian Studies, Humanities, and Science. Calvin Rose, Foundation Professor of the School of Australian Environment Studies, suggests that the established universities were sceptical of the environmental movement and thought of it as a 'fad', something that could be adequately addressed in postgraduate studies. However, the new universities who were implementing a Schools structure saw an opportunity to engage with this new field at undergraduate level. It was easier for the new universities to experiment with academic structure (Rose and Thoms 1993).
4 Bray's travel schedule included ACU, UGC in the UK, State University of New York (Albany), Michigan State University (East Lansing), University of Michigan (Ann Arbor), Antioch College (Ohio), University of Illinois (Urbana), University of Illinois (Chicago Circle), Stanford University, and University of California (Berkeley). Griffith University Academic Minutes (0066/72) 2/72, 29 March 1972, p. 2.
5 Stapp had an ongoing involvement in the development of environmental education in Australia which is described by Gough. In her analysis of the development of Stapp's pedagogical approach, Gough characterised it as socially critical curriculum development (2001: 22).
6 It included: historical biogeography of the Australian-Asian region; study of biophysical environmental processes; Australian social history and social organisation; societal goals, motivations, and perceptions; political systems and administration; economic systems and the city as a system (Griffith University 1996: 16).
7 An initial evaluation of the site, made when the new campus was being planned as a satellite college of the University of Queensland, included geological and botanical surveys that recorded 139 plant species including two rare eucalypts and a xanthorea.
8 UC Irvine was particularly influential for Roy Simpson (Yuncken Freeman) who developed the masterplan for Latrobe University in 1965 (Simpson 1967).
9 This was not atypical in other Australian universities. Amongst new universities, the involvement of academic staff in campus development occurred notably at Monash University and Newcastle University.
10 Alongside the Schools, 'the replacement of the traditional Students' Union and Staff House by the one University House, has been seized on in the physical planning ... to form a natural focus for the whole University community' (Johnson 1973a: 13).
11 Andrews was part of a team involved in the masterplanning of this satellite of the University of Toronto, which involved working on a site with significant areas of remnant vegetation that were to be preserved as part of a network of green spaces, and earmarked as a teaching tool (Taylor and Andrews 1982: 32).
12 See Moulis and Russell.
13 Further information on the idea of the environmental subject informing pedagogy, see Jo-Anne Ferreira, 1999/2000: 31–35.
14 Thyer completed a M.Sc. Thesis in the SAES at Griffith in 1981 on the effects of trampling on the Griffith campus.
15 Johnson undertook an international study tour to visit campuses during 1972.

Bibliography

Apostel, L., Berger, G., Briggs, A. and Michaud, G. (1972), *Interdisciplinarity: Problems of Teaching and Research in Universities*, Organisation for Economic Cooperation and Development (OECD), Paris.

Birrell, J. (1966), *New University at Mt Gravatt, Site Planning Report*, St. Lucia: University of Queensland.

Boyden, S. (1970), 'Environmental Change: Perspectives and Responsibilities,' in J. Evans and S. Boyden (eds.), *Education and the Environmental Crisis: Reports of the Australian Academy of Science*, No.13: 9–22, Canberra: Australian Academy of Science.

Braddock, R., Fien, J. and Rickson, R. (1994), 'Environmental Studies: Managing the Disciplinary Divide,' *The Environmentalist*, 14 (1): 35–46.

Carter, R.L. and Simon, B. (2010), 'The History and Philosophy of Environmental Education,' in A.M. Bodzin, B. Shiner Klein and S. Weaver (eds.), *The Inclusion of Environmental Education in Science Teacher Education*, 3–16, Netherlands: Springer.

Catterall, C.P. and Wallace, C.J. (eds.) (1987), *An Island in Suburbia: The Natural and Social History of Toohey Forest*, Nathan: Institute of Applied Environmental Technology, Griffith University.

D. J. Dwyer and Associates (1973), *Griffith University: Landscape Report*, Queensland.

Ekistics Editors (1976), 'Environment-based Environmental Education,' Ekistics, 41 (246): 257-262.

Ferreira, J. (1999–2000), 'Learning to Govern Oneself: Environmental Education Pedagogy and the Formation of an Environmental Subject,' *Australian Journal of Environmental Education*, 15/16: 31–35.

Franks, D., Dale, P., Hindmarsh, R., Fellows, C., Buckridge M. and Cybinski, P. (2007), 'Interdisciplinary Foundations: Reflecting on Interdisciplinarity and Three Decades of Teaching and Research at Griffith University, Australia,' *Studies in Higher Education*, 32 (2): 167–185.

Gough, A. (2001), 'For the Total Environment: Bill Stapp's Contribution to Environmental Education,' *Australian Journal of Environmental Education*, 17: 19–24.

Gough, A. (2012), 'The Emergence of Environmental Education Research: A "History" of the Field,' in R.B. Stevenson, M. Brody, J. Dillon and A.E.J. Wals (eds.), *International Handbook of Research on Environmental Education*, 13–22, London: Taylor & Francis Group.

Greenall, A. and Womersley, J. (eds.) (1977), *Development of Environmental Education in Australia – Key Issues*, Canberra, ACT: Curriculum Development Centre.

Griffith University Faculty of Environmental Science (1996), *The Evolution of Environmental Sciences: The First Twenty-Five Years*, Griffith University: Nathan.

Griffith University Site and Buildings Committee, Meeting Agenda 11/74, 31 October, 1974. Document 0771/74.

Jackson, J.B. (1973), Correspondence to Roger Johnson, 27 August 1973, Griffith Archives, Johnson Papers.

Johnson, R. (1973a), 'A Case Study: Site Planning for Griffith University, Brisbane,' *Planning for Uncertainty*, The Centre for Continuing Education, The Australian National University.

Johnson, R. (1973b), Correspondence to J. B. Jackson, 5 September 1973, Griffith Archives, Johnson Papers.

Johnson, R. (1973c), Griffith University Site Planning Report, Griffith University.

Johnson, R. (1979), *The Green City*, Melbourne: Macmillan.

Johnson, R., Ragusa, S. and Thyer, N. (1981), 'Griffith University and its Landscape,' *Landscape Australia*, 3(1): 40–50.

Linder, M. (2012), 'Disciplinarity,' in J. Ockman and Rebecca Williamson (eds.), *Architecture School: Three Centuries of Educating Architects in North America*, Cambridge, MA and American Collegiate Schools of Architecture, Washington, DC: MIT Press.

Moulis, A. and Russell, G. (2015), 'John Andrews International Educational Projects in Queensland 1972–1980', in P. Hogben and J. O'Callaghan (eds.), *Proceedings of the Society of Architectural Historians, Australia and New Zealand: 32, Architecture, Institutions and Change*, 425–34, Sydney: SAHANZ.

McCrea, E.J. (2006), *The Roots of Environmental Education: How the Past Supports the Future,* Environmental Education and Training Partnership, University of Wisconsin.

Notteboom, B. (2017), 'Of Strangers and Junkyards: Landscape Magazine Between Lived Experience and Systems Theory,' *OASE: Tijdschrift voor Architectuur*, 98: 43–49.

'Problem Solvers for Our Tomorrow', *The Courier Mail*, 11 June 1973, page unknown.

Quirk, N. (1996), *Preparing for the Future: A History of Griffith University 1971–1996*, Nathan: Boolarong Press and Griffith University.

Ragusa, S. (2017), Oral History Interview with Susan Holden, 5 December, 2017. Brisbane.

Richardson, S.S. (1979), *Parity of Esteem*, Belconnen: Canberra College of Advanced Education.

Robins, L. (1998), *Defending the Little Desert: The Rise of Ecological Consciousness in Australia*, Melbourne: Melbourne University Press.

Rose C.W., Arthington, A.H., Connell D.W. and Rickson, R.E. (2017), 'Environmental Studies at Griffith University: A Brief History of the Foundation Years,' *Proceedings of the Royal Society of Queensland*, 122: 59–65.

Rose, C. and Thoms, P. (1993), 'Interview with Calvin Rose', in *An Oral History of Griffith University: Interviews by Patience Thoms*.

Sachs, A. (2018), *Environmental Design: Architecture, Politics, and Science in Postwar America*, Charlottesville and London: University of Virginia Press.

Saniga, A. and Holden, S. (2022), 'Identity in Landscape' in A. Saniga and R. Freestone (eds.), *Campus: Building Modern Australian Universities*, Nedlands: UWA Publishing.

'School of Environmental Design, Canberra: Architects: Eggleston MacDonald & Secomb with Roger Johnson,' *The Architectural Review*, 1 May 1979: 302–303.

Scott, F.D. (2004), 'On the "Counter-Design" of Institutions: Emilio Ambasz's Universitas Symposium at MoMA,' *Grey Room*, 14: 46–77.

Scrivano, P. and Lobsinger, M.L. (2009), 'Experimental Architecture and Progressive Pedagogy: Scarborough College,' *Architecture and Ideas*, 8: 4–19.

Simpson, R. (1967), 'A University in the Suburbs,' *Architecture in Australia*, October: 821–834.

Snow, C.P. (1959), *The Two Cultures and the Scientific Revolution*, London: Cambridge University Press.

Stapp, William B. (1970), 'A Strategy for Curriculum Development and Implementation in Environmental Education at the Elementary and Secondary Levels,' in J. Evans and S. Boyden (eds.), *Education and the Environmental Crisis: Reports of the Australian Academy of Science No.13*, 23–37, Canberra: Australian Academy of Science.

Stapp, William B. (1971) 'An Environmental Education Program (K-12), Based on Environmental Encounters,' *Environment and Behaviour*, September: 263–283.

Sullivan, F.E. Jr and Schlesinger, W.H. (1972), 'The Environmental Education Act: Where Do We Stand Now?' *BioScience*, 22 (6): 361–363.

Taylor, J. and Andrews, J. (1982), *Architecture a Performing Art*, Toronto and Melbourne: Oxford University Press.

Thyer, N. (1981), *Trampling Effects and Management Strategy in a Dry Sclerophyll Forest of South-east QUEENSLAND*, Griffith University, School of Australian Environmental Studies (M.Sc. Thesis).

Trumbull, R. (1970), 'Drilling for Oil Poses a New Threat to the Great Barrier Reef,' *The New York Times*, 4 September: 10.

UNESCO-UNEP (1976), 'The Belgrade Charter,' *Connect: UNESCO-UNEP Environmental Education Newsletter*, 1 (1): 1–2.

van den Broek, B. (1969), *Native Plants of Brisbane,* Queensland Institute of Technology, Department of Planning and Landscape, Brisbane (Dip. Thesis).

Watson, D. (2016), *The Bush: Travels in the Heart of Australia*, Melbourne: Penguin.

Willett, J. (1983), 'Talk to AES staff,' Griffith University Archives (unpublished transcript).

10

REVISITING ENVIRONMENTAL LEARNING

Cities, issues and bodies

Isabelle Doucet

In their book *Streetwork. The exploding school*, published in 1973, Colin Ward and Anthony Fyson share their ideas on how education can engage with the world outside the school, through classroom innovation and through moving outside the classroom and into the urban environment and communities. Colin Ward, an important theorist of anarchism, writer, and editor in post-war Britain who had also worked as a teacher and for several architecture firms, together with the geographer and teacher, Anthony Fyson, published the book when working as education officers for the Town and Country Planning Association (TCPA), described as an 'all-party, non-sectarian voluntary organisation' in the United Kingdom dedicated to issues of town and country planning (Ward and Fyson 1973: Preface). They proposed an 'environmental education' whereby environmental concerns would permeate all school subjects and learners could engage with issues and problems as they unfold in the 'real world'. Learning within the classroom but also while exploring, walking, and mapping the city, while being in the community, visiting museums and so on, was believed to generate an understanding of how real-world issues, including spatial planning, neighbourhood renewal, and housing, work. The authors argued that *learning* about such issues could be empowering in that it could prepare children and young adults to eventually take charge of the *shaping* of their own environment. They argued that, rather than passive observers, the users of the city could then become active contributors to the decision-making and shaping of their environment. This emphasis on the active users of the city becomes clear only two pages into *Streetwork:* 'What should our aim be in environmental education? To educate for mastery of the environment: nothing less than that' (Ward in Ward and Fyson 1973: 2).[1] The *built* environment in particular was considered of central importance to questions of social and political change, as Myrna Margulies Breitbart (2014: 177) reminds us in her recent revisiting of Ward's ideas on radical pedagogy and planning: 'Housing, public spaces, urban streets, parks, and unclaimed land were not to be "read" so much for their design, as for what could be learned about the socio-economic and political activities they support or inhibit'.

DOI: 10.4324/9781003201205-14

Ambitions in the direction of 'environmental education' can be contextualised within the education unit at the TCPA, where both Fyson and Ward worked at the time when *Streetwork* was written.[2] As Dennis Hardy (1991: 119) has argued, environmental education formed a key part of the TCPA's efforts towards facilitating participation of the public and community action. During their time at the TCPA, Ward and Fyson published, in addition to *Streetwork*, the *Bulletin of Environmental Education* (*BEE*), the journal of the TCPA's education unit that offered a hands-on guide aimed at teachers and schools seeking to contribute to what Tim Ivison (2019: 84) called 'the cultivation of a new kind of popular engagement with the built environment'.[3] In 1978, Ward also published *The Child in the City* (Ward 1978). Whereas *BEE* offered 'a forum to advance both the intellectual and the technical resources of (…) participatory democracy' (Ivison 2019: 85), and *Streetwork* offered ideas on how to set up successful environmental education, *The Child in the City*, through both text and extensive documentary photography by Ann Golzen and others, provides an in-depth study of the everyday (street) life experience of urban children.[4]

Addressing questions of both education and the built environment, environmental education seems to offer a good starting point for responding to *Architectural Education Through Materiality*'s ambitions to study novel approaches in architectural education through a focus on the agency of material objects.[5] If we extend environmental education to the *architectural* classroom, it can point to different pedagogical tools than those typically associated with education in the architectural classroom (the 'studio' or 'atelier'), such as drawings, physical and digital models, collages, sketches, and online collaborative design tools.[6] Efforts to expand the boundaries of the school of architecture and additionally include neighbourhoods and communities can be found in meanwhile well-established practices in user-based design, community architecture, participatory design, and 'live projects'. Such approaches often demand different representational tools, which, in addition to drawings, sketches, and models, also include less 'jargony' and less 'technical' devices such as interactive maps, games, storyboards, walking tours, community charettes, audio-visual materials, and so on. Ward and Fyson draw explicit attention to innovative pedagogical tools, but their down-to-earth, hands-on advice for teachers reminds us also of the importance of mundane, easily overlooked, material supports for environmental learning: suitable locales for community-based learning, notebooks, local newspapers, and sometimes, simply, having access to transport.

Ward's emancipatory ideas on education would also find resonance with his writings on architecture and town planning, addressing topics including housing, playgrounds, self-management, and mutual aid, as expressed, for example, through his enthusiasm for the user-driven architectures of Giancarlo De Carlo, Walter Segal, Lucien Kroll, and John Habraken among others.[7] His writing and lecturing on the role of the architectural profession and the empowerment of users to manipulate their own (urban, built) environment, can help in understanding Ward's appeal for architects exploring the boundaries of their practice.

Environmental education can be placed in line with the observed broader interest among educators in the 1970s in both teaching *about* the environment (environment as a subject) and rethinking education away from classrooms *into* the environment (environment as 'an educative medium') (Ward 1995a: 21). Not just teachers but also urban designers were developing an interest in the potential of the city as a learning environment. In *Streetwork* (Ward and Fyson 1973: 6) and also in lectures, Ward cited a project that I myself have also studied, called 'Metro/Education', and which, in part, sparked the idea about looking closer into environmental education for this chapter in *Architectural Education Through Materiality*.[8] Published in book form by architects/urban designers, Michel Lincourt and Harry Parnass in 1970, *Metro/Education* proposed environmental learning spaces for a newly created university in Montreal, Canada (for more details, see Lincourt and Parnass 1970; Doucet 2019). Rather than proposing the construction of new university buildings, the designers suggested to reprogramme the available and often-underused spaces of downtown Montreal. Combining a systemic analysis of the existing uses of space (especially underused spaces such as cinemas in the daytime, offices in the evening) with a close reading of everyday life in the city (illustrated by photographs by Pierre Gaudard), the design 'project' takes the shape of a flexible learning environment connected to the central metro lines of Montreal, known for its vast network of pedestrianised underground corridors, allowing one to move freely between the metro and all kinds of underground and above-ground facilities such as shops, offices, cinemas, and museums. Ward's appreciation of Metro/Education is unsurprising when considering his own work at the crossroads of educational reform and architecture and urban design.

It is appealing to revisit, today, the environmental education promoted in projects such as *Metro/Education*, *Streetwork*, and *The Child in the City*, not just as a means of discussing the educational role of material agents, objects, and the city itself, but also, and importantly, for its empowering potential. Not only is it arguable that the child's perspective on the city can add refreshing perspectives that can complement the expert views of planners and architects, but when children and young adults take part in environmental education, they can also learn about the forces that are at work in the conceptualisation, design, and decision-making regarding the built environment. In recent discussions in architecture and urban design, this proves relevant again, particularly in discussions on the social production of architecture. For example, in the introduction to their 2017 edited volume *The Social (Re) Production of Architecture*, Doina Petrescu and Kim Trogal start by identifying a new political moment in global capitalism characterised by 'a crisis of reproduction', namely one in which the political struggle has become one of 'how we sustain ourselves and our world' (Petrescu and Trogal 2017: 1). Faced with such a condition, and drawing on Henri Lefebvre's work on the 'right to the city', the editors emphasise the importance of the fact that 'all citizens have the right to shape their societies in and through its spaces' (Petrescu and Trogal 2017: 3) but that, to achieve this, participation is no longer enough. Instead, Petrescu and Trogal (2017: 3–4) call for more rights for citizens; actual rights, such as to housing, but also 'rights of imagination' and 'the right to play'. It seems to me that Ward's work on environmental education could speak to such ambition. Indeed, as also Tim Ivison (2019: 87) posits when wondering about the liberating effects of participation: 'Perhaps it is time for a new environmental education'.

But revisiting environmental education and reclaiming emancipatory forces connected to the city and urban education does not come without some cautionary notes. As feminist scholars, among others, have argued, the subjectivities displayed in urban studies deserve critical scrutiny when these work on the assumption of a 'universal' human subject with little differentiation made according to, for example, gender, race, class, sexuality, citizenship status, or ethnicity. As we will learn later in this chapter, Ward did provide us with clues to issues of gender and subjectivity, both already during the 1970s and more recently, which I will take as an opportunity to begin this dialogue between environmental education and

192 Isabelle Doucet

gender/subjectivity. I hope to use this discussion as a speculation on what to look for and on which elements to be attentive to, when revisiting exciting emancipatory efforts. In what follows, I will take two aspects of environmental education (its material make-up and gender/subjectivity) as prompts to speculate on the empowering potential of environmental learning for architectural pedagogy, today.[9]

Material agency in environmental education

In the opening chapter of *Streetwork*, environmental education refers to a way of teaching that 'can enhance the pupils' understanding of, and concern for, their environment' (Ward in Ward and Fyson 1973: 1). Understood in a broad sense, for example, human habitat, the countryside, pollution, and exploitation of resources (Ward in Ward and Fyson 1973: 2), *Streetwork* focused on the *urban* environment because, so it was argued, the majority of children lived in cities, and also because resources about teaching related to the natural environment and the countryside were argued to be already available (Ward and Fyson 1973: Preface).[10] Posited as an alternative to 'fieldwork' typically used in geography teaching, 'streetwork' aimed at offering an 'issue-based approach' centring on political and social issues, poverty, spatial planning, and other concerns affecting local communities (Fyson in Ward and Fyson 1973: 16).[11] As a more affective form of education, it was hoped that it would prepare pupils 'for their future roles as participators in environmental decision-making' (Fyson in Ward and Fyson 1973: 15). Self-management was central to this, in that environmental teaching was argued to 'enable people to become masters of their own environment' (Ward 1995a: 38) and to demystify the presumed 'specialised and exclusive wisdom' of the environmental professions (including architecture and planning) (Ward 1995a: 37).[12] And what better place to start than the street? Despite having provided a source for learning for generations of urban children, the street was now believed to be largely overlooked by professionals of the built environment, citizens, and children alike (Ward in Ward and Fyson 1973: 17–18).[13] In reclaiming the resourceful and creative child encountered in the history of cities as well as in the global city, the street was again being promoted as a place for learning (Ward 1995b).[14] To realise environmental learning, a whole range of physical and material agents are mobilised that are not typically considered in classroom education. Broadly speaking, I recognise two types: tools and resources that support environmental education and the materiality of the city itself, including the homes and neighbourhoods of the child (Ward in Ward and Fyson 1973: 3).

Material supports for environmental education as described in *Streetwork* included books, reports, local studies, filming equipment, and educational informational bulletins that can inspire teachers. In particular, Chapter 7 'The streetwork teacher', written by Ward, and Chapter 16 'Sources and resources', written by both authors, offer a wealth of advice and lists possible sources for teachers, including ordnance maps, aerial photographs, and other material available in local libraries, in the schools, or from the local authorities. As far as issue-based education focusing on local issues and problems is concerned, local newspapers and all kinds of neighbourhood and grassroots journals were deemed excellent resources. One tool discussed in detail is the educational 'town trail', modelled onto the popular 'nature trail' (Fyson in Ward and Fyson 1973: 43).[15] Similar to how countryside trails were hoped to help people reconnect with nature, urban trails could reconnect urban dwellers with the urban environment. Town trails, however, aimed at a critical rather than picturesque experience, inviting individuals 'to think critically and deeply' about everyday life in the city, amongst other ways by also exploring less pleasant or forgotten spaces (Fyson in Ward and Fyson 1973: 44–46).[16]

Acting as a rich and exciting 'open book' (Ward 1995a: 25; reference to Bernard Rudofsky), the city, and more specifically the urban street, was *itself* to be discovered.[17] This capacity of the city was argued to be already evident in how children appropriate cities as their playground, often leading to conflicts with adult users of the city (one example in the book is that of kids playing on escalators). Environmental education could therefore thrive on learning 'through contact with *the thing itself* and not with a two-dimensional version of it in the classroom' (Ward 1995a: 25, italics in original). As Ward argued in *The Child in the City*, the child's view, characterised by a more direct and embodied engagement with the city, was seen as particularly fruitful and diversifying.[18] Ward believed that the city offered experiences through encounters with both buildings and other humans, such as the 'street characters' found throughout the history of cities (Ward 1978: 180). The built environment/buildings did not include just architectural marvels but also housing projects, industries, and businesses, making it possible to learn about topics such as industrial heritage and the national economy.[19] In order to reach such places, 'mobile urban studies centres' were suggested, for example, in the shape of converted buses (Ward and Fyson 1973: 77). More permanent 'Urban Studies Centres' located within communities were envisioned as a key component for environmental education, and even museums could become mobilised, for example, as repositories for documentation about a place (Ward 1995a: 29–30).[20] *The Child in the City* provided an interesting example of a teacher who invited an architect to come talk to her class about buildings, after which she took the children on a neighbourhood tour. The drawings and models they made of their neighbourhood were exhibited, and the children eventually ended up doing a carnival dressed up as buildings, trees, street crossings, and so on (Ward 1978: 181), ultimately becoming the full embodiment of 'the things themselves'.[21] The wealth of practical information, sources, resources, and examples, provided in *Streetwork*, should at the same time not distract from the authors' central ambitions that the book should first and foremost be 'a polemical book; not a source book' (Ward and Fyson 1973: Preface).

Gendered experiences of the city

> Girls soon learn to take up as little space as possible to be allowed within the category "female". Boys soon learn that they can prove their "boyness" by taking up lots of room, particularly outside on the street.
>
> *(Boys 1984: 41)*

In her depiction of the social conditioning of girls and boys in the city, Jos Boys, a founding member of the Matrix feminist architecture collective, expresses important reservations with regard to the empowering and liberating potential of the city (that also Ward and his colleagues sought to promote). Feminist and gender-focused scholars—in architecture, urban studies, planning, urban history, and geography, among other fields—have indeed highlighted that the urban experience is not the same for all users of the city, particularly not for girls and women. They took issue with the essentialisms and universalisms that often underpinned urban studies, in which the human becomes largely represented by men and, as the editors of *The Sex of Architecture* argued, through the filters of 'long-suspect "truths"': that man builds and woman inhabits; that man is outside and woman is inside; that man is public and woman is private [...]' (Agrest, Conway, and Weisman, 1996: 11). They took issue with the fact that cities, consequently, largely operate by and for men and do not create equal opportunities for men and women (pioneering works in architecture include Agrest, Conway, and Weisman, 1996, Matrix 1984; Colomina 1992; in urban planning among other Greed 1994: 35–40; Miranne and Young 2000).[22] That the 'city of men' prevails until today is vividly argued in Leslie Kern's book *Feminist City* (2020 [2019]: 8): 'As a woman, my everyday urban experiences are deeply gendered. My gender identity shapes how I move through the city, how I live my life day-to-day, and the choices available to me'. If opportunities for women to drift, wander, and get lost in the city are limited, the ambitions of environmental learning are then also curtailed.[23]

Ward may not have engaged extensively with such limitations (at least not in the works I consulted for this chapter), but he did bring the problem of the man-made city to the attention of the reader, notably by pointing out the different social conditioning of girls and boys. From the outset in *The Child in the City* Ward cautions that the urban child pictured in his book is male. In the foreword to the book, Ward (1978: viii) expresses this caution in the shape of an apology: 'There is a final apology to be made. I have referred to the generalised child as *he*, when I meant *he* or *she*, since I can scarcely use the word *it*.' While explaining that it was, at the time, conventional practice to use the male pronoun to depict all genders , Ward clarifies that he actually often did refer to boys: 'I have been made conscious in compiling this book that very often when I use the word *he*, this is what I mean. Boys *do* experience, explore and exploit the environment much more than girls do.' (Ward 1978: viii). When returning to the issue throughout the book (e.g. Chapter 3 'How the child sees the city' and Chapter 15 'The girl in the background'), Ward (1978: 29) questions the supposed 'innate differences' between boys and girls as the sole explanatory factor. Instead, he cites the different social conditioning of girls and boys, including the expectations that girls will help out with housework and look after younger siblings while boys can explore urban street life (Ward 1978: 152–154) and champions a plurality of users and uses of the city that extend beyond the viewpoint of 'the adult, male, white-collar, out-of-town car-user' (Ward 1978: 25).[24]

Even if Ward suggested more equal opportunities for exploring the city (e.g. through a fairer distribution of family tasks), he warned against encouraging girls to behave more like boys, for this would replicate 'the triumph of aggressive masculinity as the quality the child's peers most admire' (Ward 1978: 163).[25] That this was a problem for girls in the city but a problem also for anarchist efforts becomes clear in a conversation with David Goodway (Ward and Goodway 2014 [2003]: 118), when Ward stated: 'the kinds of antisocial behaviour that makes our fellow-citizens unable to accept the concept of an anarchist society are predominantly male activities'. Ward would, perhaps unsurprisingly, cite the women's movement as a key contributor towards greater freedom in society and an important ally to the anarchist cause (Ward and Goodway 2014 [2003]: 118; Ward 2004: 71).[26]

Embodied Learning: when cities become classrooms

In many ways, feminist thinkers have shown ways to overcome these obstacles to environmental learning, including by suggesting specific, situated, and embodied (rather than generic) practices and experiences and a focus on the transformative potential of everyday practices.[27] How can one account for the embodied and affective aspects of urban learning when engaging with real-world issues, when mobilising local stakeholders, travelling on buses, wandering the city? Let us return for a moment to the classroom itself as a place where such questions have been addressed, among others by the feminist theorist and activist writer, bell hooks.

In her book *Teaching Community. A Pedagogy of Hope* (2003), bell hooks introduces the 'classroom without boundaries' as a form of democratic and pluralist education. Democratic education is argued to take place *within* as much as *outside* the institutionalised classroom, whereby teaching 'seeks to re-envision schooling as always a part of our real world experience, and our real life' (hooks 2003: 41). hooks draws attention to the bodily and material agencies that introduce power mechanisms into the classrooms and that therefore can hamper pluralist and democratic education. In a published conversation between herself, and Ron Scapp, a philosopher, and both university professors, hooks describes the impact of both the spatial configurations that establish and govern teacher–learner relationships (e.g. teaching from behind an elevated lectern, classroom seating in rows) and the physical presence of teachers and learners including the self-consciousness that comes with this. In their conversation, Scapp (in: hooks 1994: 138) explains: 'When you leave the podium and walk around, suddenly the way you smell, the way you move become very apparent to your students.'

Emphasising pluralism and embodiment breaks with the illusion that hooks describes, namely that teachers produce 'neutral, objective facts, facts that are not particular to who is sharing the information' (hooks 1994: 139) while it also encourages students to champion difference during their studies and future professional practices. As Leslie Kanes Weisman poignantly asked, more than two decades ago, in the context of the education of architects (Weisman 1996: 279): 'How will students be sensitized to "difference" when they are encouraged to suppress their own gender, race, and class identities in the process of becoming "professional"?'[28]

In architecture, situated and embodied learning has become firmly embedded in a feminist ethos for architectural practice, research, and education.[29] In architecture education, the agency of things, bodies, and subjectivities is articulated in numerous works dedicated to feminist pedagogy. Kim Trogal addresses issues of difference in the education of architects by drawing attention to the often-invisible mechanisms that can hamper good learning processes. Trogal (2017: 240) highlights the important question asked in feminist pedagogies as to 'Who is in the room?' but she also encourages teachers and learners to push this question further by asking about the 'Elephant in the Room'. In reference to a project with the same name, initiated by Trogal with Anna Holder and Julia Udall at the Sheffield School of Architecture, and as discussed by Trogal (2017), the 'elephant in the room' points to unspoken and less visible subjectivities that can affect our capacity to have a fulfilling learning experience, including language barriers and differences in how we value character traits such as humility and boldness. Their approach pushes the attention for subjectivities and bodies to also include issues that are difficult to discuss and, importantly, to approach these difficult issues not just as contextual factors to pedagogy but *in and for themselves* worthy of becoming 'the subject of inquiry and action' (Trogal 2017: 248).

If we extrapolate these sensitivities back again to the scale of the city, I am reminded of Ward and Fyson's issue-based approach to environmental learning and especially of how such an approach encourages the discussion of difficult questions and subjectivities. In inviting people to engage with real-world 'issues', environmental education encourages them to become aware of their own (social, political) positionality and subjectivity in the world, especially in areas where they would not expect to have agency, and it invites them to recognise emancipatory potential in that awareness. This can, in my view, be demonstrated by means of a telling experience by a teacher in Sheffield, as discussed in *The Child in the City* (Ward 1978: 185). An initial interest among children and their teacher in a peculiar house (i.e. different to the surrounding terraced houses) led to a visit to the house to meet its owner followed by a visit to the library to learn more about the history of the house. Soon, the children learned not just about the history of the building but also that it was scheduled for demolition in order to create parking space. This took them onto an unexpected path where they gradually found themselves picking up the fight against the demolition of a local building, which taught them how to learn from local history, how to organise action, and how to approach and mobilise relevant stakeholders. With this example, Ward shows how taking initiative, individually and collectively, and fighting a cause, has the capacity to nurture the kind of collective learning and action that is often also encouraged in feminist approaches to pedagogy and critical practice.[30] That collective learning involves conscious practising of lowering the boundaries between those in power and those not, those teaching and those learning, is shown beautifully by bell hooks: 'When I enter the classroom at the beginning of the semester the weight is on me to establish that our purpose is to be, for however brief a time, a community of learners *together*.' (hooks 1994: 153, Emphasis in original). The appreciation of learning together is also important for architecture, in which it can refer to both the collaborative development of spatial solutions (as in participatory design or community development) and the valuing of collaborative design processes, including the crediting of teamwork as opposed to merely celebrating individual authors of a design.

Imagining change through environmental learning

Considering the continued interest in the empowering forces of everyday uses of the city, as exemplified by DIY urbanism, tactical urbanism, temporary use, and so on, and based upon calls for new imaginations with regard to practices of care and empowerment, it becomes particularly relevant to revisit the opportunities for 'environmental learning' again today. Beginning such a revisit from the vantage point of a feminist ethos can place some cautionary notes and open up exciting questions for future research.

In response to the ambitions of *Architectural Education Through Materiality*, an initial takeaway is that when drawing attention to the materiality of pedagogy, it is not sufficient to highlight those representational tools already central to the conventions of design pedagogy. One must also include everyday mundane practices and the positionalities of both teachers and learners. Suitable tools for learning can contribute to *collective* imaginations of future scenarios (for cities, for buildings). Developing the capacity to imagine new or different scenarios collectively can offer hope and empowerment. Myrna Margulies Breitbart (2014: 179) argued that, for Ward, 'cultivating the imagination' was essential, which was expressed through the value he attached to 'the power of *visual examples* to act as educational vehicles that move people to think outside the box.' (Breitbart 2014: 179, italics in original).[31]

A second takeaway is that we should continue to take seriously the struggle to resist generalist assumptions regarding the users of cities and bodies in classrooms (including cities) and that we should be cautious with expectations regarding the empowering potential when revisiting and reclaiming pedagogical practices. As Ward already indicated in the 1970s and feminist scholars have repeatedly pointed out, *specific* bodies and their subjectivities and positionalities make for *specific* learning opportunities. Any emancipatory outcome depends on such specificities and is therefore not to be taken for granted.

By means of this chapter, my intention was to begin a conversation around issues of material agency, empowerment, and subjectivity when revisiting environmental education as proposed by Ward and also in conjunction with Fyson and colleagues. I aimed to begin this dialogue by drawing from some of the key publications on environmental education and by engaging with some of Ward's hints and pointers with regard to the gendered limitations and needs of environmental learning. As I began engaging with such issues, more questions emerged,[32] and possible routes for future research began to develop. I have become particularly keen to uncover the intellectual and professional connections between Ward, Fyson, and feminist collectives, and individuals, of the time.[33] Also, how can questions of environmental education be revisited in dialogue with discussions on more-than-human worlds and posthumanism, such as in the field of the environmental humanities? What do collaborative action and embodied presence mean in a more-than-human environment, and how can designers develop learning processes for new forms of collaboration between humans and non-humans and for caring for more-than-human worlds? Awaiting opportunities to study these questions, I hope that this chapter has already whetted its readers' appetite to revisit environmental education in order to address questions regarding materiality in architectural education and that it has provided some exciting new possible directions to explore.

Acknowledgements

While taking full responsibility for the contents of this chapter, I am grateful for stimulating discussions with the editors of this volume at different stages during the process; with Tahl Kaminer, Simon Sadler, and Tim Stott as part of our preparations for a conference paper presented at 2020 European Architecture History Network conference held in Edinburgh; and with Helena Mattsson. Meike Schalk provided most useful feedback on a draft of this paper at a time when such input was both welcome and needed. Bri Gauger shared relevant references in the area of planning with me.

Notes

1 In the book's Preface, the authors explain how they wanted to avoid a 'magisterial "we"' and, therefore, wrote the book in first person. Most chapters were written by either Ward or Fyson; a few were written by both. The first chapter, 'Whose environment?' (pp. 1–9), was written by Ward.
2 Ward was employed as a principal officer between 1971 and 1979 together with Fyson. Other colleagues at the TCPA included Rose Tanner and later also Eileen Adams. The TCPA's Education Unit had been established in response to the so-called Skeffington Report of 1969 that had criticised the lack of public participation in planning processes. A detailed historical discussion of the Education Unit and environmental education at the TCPA is provided by Hardy 1991 (especially chapter 8: 'Campaign Profiles'). For further historical context see also Worpole 2014, Ivison 2019, and Perez-Martinez 2020 (the latter publication, and its many insights and further references, I sadly discovered only as this chapter went into copyediting!).

198 Isabelle Doucet

3 Parts of *Streetwork* had originally been published in *BEE* (Ward and Fyson 1973: Preface). For more information about *BEE* (which I have not consulted for this chapter), see Hardy (1991), and through recent discussions in architecture, see, for example, Ivison (2019) and Perez-Martinez (2020).

4 In the foreword to the book, Ward (1978: viii) emphasised the importance of the photographs for the book. For a discussion of the photographs in this work, see also Thomson 2014. By contrast, *Streetwork* contains no images, and only few illustrations, notably Sherry Arnstein's ladder of participation and two of Ebenezer Howard's garden cities diagrams.

5 David Goodway (2006: 318) placed *Streetwork* and *The Child in the City*, together with Ward's 1988 book *The Child in the Country,* in a special category called 'education *and* the environment'. For further discussions on Ward and education, see Ward (1995, published talks) and Burke and Jones (2014, edited volume dedicated to Ward's work on education).

6 I am thinking, for example, of software allowing for shared digital drawing boards used by architecture students for distance learning in design education during COVID-19.

7 For a good introduction to Colin Ward, see Goodway (2006). A selection of key texts is provided by Wilbert and White (2011). In architecture, see, for example, Ward (2000).

8 Ward cited Metro/Education in his 1987 lecture 'Places for Learning' and 1992 lecture 'Growing Up in Meaner Cities', both published in Ward (1995: 92–107) (cited on p. 105) and pp. 119–130 (cited on p. 119), respectively. Another project regularly mentioned is the Philadelphia Parkway Program. I should disclose here that, while a range of exciting global examples exist, I personally speak from my experience studying cases located in Europe, North America, and Australia.

9 I deliberately call this a 'speculation' as it is an early effort as part of a wider ambition to study gender aspects in Colin Ward's work on environmental learning, instigated through my participation in a recent collaborative revisiting of *The Child in the City* with Tahl Kaminer, Simon Sadler, and Tim Stott, on the occasion of a jointly written conference paper with title 'The Anarchist Child: Four Readings of *The Child in the City*' presented at the 2020 European Architecture History Network conference held in Edinburgh in 2021.

10 The notions of 'streetwork' and 'exploding school' were in fact an urban reinterpretation of what already existed in the countryside. Ward (in Ward and Fyson 1973: 5) refers to the 1970 report by the Council of Environmental Education, titled 'Countryside in 1970'.

11 Chapter 2 'Streetwork' (pp. 10–16) was written by Fyson.

12 Self-management was firmly embedded in Ward's anarchist approach to education and spatial planning, as theorised in *Anarchy in Action* (Ward 2008 [1973]). In a chapter dedicated to education called 'Schools No Longer', Ward (2008 [1973]: 106) expresses his belief, following William Godwin, Paulo Freire, Paul Goodman, Ivan Illich and other 'de-schoolers', that national, compulsory education is counter-productive and 'profoundly anti-educational'.

13 Chapter 3 'The freedom of the street' (pp. 17–23) was written by Ward.

14 Ward's appreciation for everyday street life related to the writings of among others, Bernard Rudofsky, Paul Goodman, Jane Jacobs, and Kevin Lynch, all cited as influences in *Streetwork*.

15 Chapter 6 'A trail for every town?' (pp. 40–47) was written by Fyson.

16 The authors were here inspired by Kevin Lynch (see Chapter 5 in Ward and Fyson 1973).

17 Ward (1995a: 25, no reference provided) cites Bernard Rudofsky's observation that, historically, for the child, the street offered 'an open book, superbly illustrated, thoroughly familiar yet inexhaustible.'

18 The chapter 'How the child sees the city' (in Ward 1978: 22–31) draws from environmental psychology represented by cognitive mappers like Kevin Lynch (*The Image of The City*) and the educational theories of so-called 'developmentalists' like psychologist Jean Piaget, and especially draws also from the critiques at the address of these approaches.

19 The 'Sources and resources' chapter in the book (pp. 122–136) lists several architecture periodicals including AD, AJ, AR, Built Environment, RIBA Journal, and Survey.

20 Urban Studies Centres were modelled on or compared to the already established rural field centres, supported by rural councils and counties (Ward and Fyson 1973: 78). The chapter 'Streetwork centres' (pp. 72–80) was jointly authored. For a discussion of Urban Studies Centres see Perez-Martinez (2020), and Hardy (1991).

21 Another great example is the collaboration between Eileen Adams and Ward on the Art and The Built Environment project (1976–1979) testing environmental education through collaborations

with schools, where they aimed at producing art works based on critical readings and explorations of the city (for a recent discussion see Adams 2014).

22 Many other important works could be added here, but such more comprehensive discussion would be beyond the scope of this paper.

23 A recent collection of essays that I have only begun exploring, and may be of interest to the reader, is the volume *Contentious Cities. Design and the Gendered Production of Space,* edited by Jes Berry, Timothy Moore, Nicole Kalms, and Gene Bawden (2021, Abingdon and New York: Routledge). The book explores ongoing issues with gendered productions of space, with a specific focus on the role of radical design practice towards more inclusive cities, drawing on, among others, feminist and queer scholarship.

24 Ward discusses at length the critiques at the address of, for example, Kevin Lynch and Jean Piaget. Feminists have also challenged the containerisation of user-groups, including that of 'women', calling instead for being attentive to class, ethnicity, race, citizenship status, sexuality, and so on (see, e.g., Greed 1994; hooks 2000; Arruzza et al. 2019).

25 In the chapter dedicated to education called 'Freedom in education', in *Anarchism: A Very Short Introduction,* Ward (2004: 51–61) refers several times to the importance, for some but not all anarchist educators, to not separate girls and boys in education, and to teach them the same subjects.

26 A discussion of Ward's personal and intellectual connections with feminism and the women's movement is beyond the scope of this paper and will be the subject of future research. One particularly interesting connection is the vibrant London environment of women's groups and collectives committed to feminist perspectives on the built environment during the 1980s, including Matrix and the Women's Design Service, and the numerous community development initiatives of the 1970s, where women's collectives also often found a voice (see, e.g. the detailed discussion in Berglund 2018). I thank Meike Schalk for pointing me in this direction.

27 Breitbart (2014) draws an interesting connection between Ward and feminist/emancipatory writings and practices in architecture and urban design such as those by Doina Petrescu and muf.

28 I was reminded of this important quote via Lori Brown (2011: 1).

29 Among many excellent references, see Brown (2011), Frichot et al. (2018), Rendell (2018), Stead (2014), and Schalk et al. (2017), and see also the thematic issue I produced with Hélène Frichot (Doucet and Frichot 2018).

30 In her 2018 article 'Only Resist: a feminist approach to critical spatial practice', Jane Rendell (2018) identifies key components of feminist spatial practice: collectivity, subjectivity, alterity, performativity, and materiality (Rendell 2018). Some of these seem to resonate (albeit not always explicitly or fully developed) with the ambitions of environmental education and with Perez-Martinez's (2020) appreciation of aspects of 'peer learning' and collaborations among and between community members and professionals in the workings of Urban Studies Centres in the UK.

31 I find it exciting that Breitbart weaves connections between Ward and Rebecca Solnit's valuing of 'getting lost' (in her 2005 book *A Field Guide to Getting Lost*) and I am myself particularly interested in Solnit's work on the power and hope that can reside in stories and storytelling, as in *Hope in the Dark* (Solnit 2004) and, more recently, *Whose story Is This?* (Solnit 2019).

32 For example, how should we consider environmental education in contemporary and historical contexts where children are, or have been, using the city in creative and inventive ways, by necessity rather than by choice (also opening up questions related to child poverty and child labour)? Several contributions in Burke and Jones (2014) address this issue, including Sinha and Burke's testing of *Streetwork* and *The Child in the City* in their study of street children in New Delhi; and Pat Thomson's (2014: 170) cautionary notes with the revisiting of the documentary photographs in *The Child in the City*, pointing to the risk of nostalgia (celebrating the creativity of children while making abstraction of their poor living conditions) and of approaching the material 'as a narrative of an inequality now in the past.'

33 See endnote 26. This also connects to questions of historiography. For example, Helena Mattsson and Meike Schalk's (2019) work on 'action archives' has shown how innovative methods such as 'witness seminars' with historical actors can provide environments for collective, embodied, and dynamic learning, writing and rewriting of histories.

Bibliography

Adams, Eileen (2014) 'Education for participation.' In Burke, Catherine and Ken Jones, eds. *Education, Childhood and Anarchism. Talking Colin Ward*. Paperback edition 2016. Abingdon and New York: Routledge, pp. 57–71.

Agrest, Diana, Patricia Conway, and Leslie Kanes Weisman, eds. (1996) *The Sex of Architecture*. New York: Harry N. Abrams Inc.

Arruzza Cinzia, Tithi Bhattacharya, and Nancy Fraser (2019) *Feminism for the 99 Percent. A Manifesto*. London and Brooklyn, NY: Verso.

Berglund, Eeva (2018) 'Building a real alternative: Women's design service.' *Field Journal*, 2(1), 47–62.

Boys, Jos (1984) 'Women and public space.' In: Matrix *Making Space. Women and the Man-Made Environment*. London and Leichhardt: Pluto Press, pp. 37–54. Reprinted in 1985.

Breitbart, Myrna Margulies (2014) 'Inciting desire, ignoring boundaries and making space: Colin Ward's considerable contribution to radical pedagogy, planning and social change.' In: Catherine Burke and Ken Jones, eds. *Education, Childhood and Anarchism. Talking Colin Ward*. Paperback edition 2016. Abingdon and New York: Routledge, pp. 175–185.

Brown Lori, A. (2011) 'Introduction.' In: Lori Brown, ed. *Feminist Practices. Interdisciplinary Approaches to Women in Architecture*. Farnham and Burlington: Ashgate, pp. 1–15.

Burke, Catherine, and Ken Jones, eds. (2014) *Education, Childhood and Anarchism. Talking Colin Ward*. Paperback edition 2016. Abingdon and New York: Routledge.

Colomina, Beatriz, ed. (1992) *Sexuality & Space*. New York: Princeton Architectural Press. Princeton Papers on Architecture (Volume 1).

Doucet, Isabelle (2019) 'Metro/Education Montreal (1970): Rethinking the urban at the crossroads of megastructures, systems analysis and urban politics.' *Architecture & Culture*, 7(2), pp. 179–196.

Doucet, Isabelle, and Hélène Frichot, eds. (2018) 'Resist, Reclaim, Speculate: Situated Perspectives on Architecture and the City.' Special issue *Architectural Theory Review*, 22(1).

Frichot, Hélène, Catarina Gabrielsson, and Helen Runting, eds. (2018) *Architecture and Feminisms: Ecologies, Economies, Technologies*. New York: Routledge.

Goodway, David (2006) 'Colin ward.' In: *Anarchist Seeds Beneath the Snow. Left-Libertarian Thought and British Writers from William Morris to Colin Ward*. Liverpool: Liverpool University Press, pp. 309–325.

Greed, Clara H. (1994) *Women and Planning. Creating Gendered Realities*. London and New York: Routledge.

Hardy, Dennis (1991) *From New Towns to Green Politics. Campaigning for town and country planning 1946-1990*. London, New York, Tokyo, Melbourne, Madras: Chapman & Hall. Taylor & Francis Group e-Library edition 2005.

hooks, bell (1994) 'Building a Teaching Community. A Dialogue.' In: *Teaching to Transgress. Education as the Practice of Freedom*. New York and Abingdon: Routledge, pp. 129–165.

hooks, bell (2000) *Feminism is for Everybody. Passionate Politics*. London: Pluto Press.

hooks, bell (2003) *Teaching Community. A Pedagogy of Hope*. New York and Abingdon: Routledge.

Ivison, Tim (2019) 'Exploding school. Planning, participation and the Bulletin of Environmental Education.' In: Dirk van den Heuvel, Soscha Monteiro de Jesus, and Sun Ah Hwang, eds. *Proceedings of the Architecture and Democracy 1965–1989: Urban Renewal, Populism, and the Welfare State Symposium*. Delft and Rotterdam: TU Delft and Het Nieuwe Instituut, pp. 83–90.

Kern, Leslie (2020 [2019]) *Feminist City*. London and Brooklyn, NY: Verso. First published in 2019 by Between The Lines, Toronto.

Lincourt, Michel and Harry Parnass (1970) *Metro/Education*. Montreal: Université de Montréal (UdeM), Faculté de l'Aménagement.

Matrix (1984) *Making Space. Women and the Man-Made Environment*. London and Leichhardt: Pluto Press. Reprinted in 1985.

Mattsson, Helena, and Meike Schalk (2019) 'Action Archive. Oral History as Performance.' In Janina Gosseye, Naomi Stead, and Deborah van der Plaat, eds. *Speaking of Buildings. Oral History in Architectural Research*. Hudson, NY: Princeton Architectural Press, pp. 94–113.

Miranne, Kristine B., and Alma H. Young, eds. (2000) *Gendering the City. Women, Boundaries, and Visions of Urban Life.* Lanham, MD and Oxford: Rowman & Littlefield Publishers, Inc.

Perez-Martinez, Sol (2020) 'Deschooling architecture.' *E-Flux*, https://www.e-flux.com/architecture/education/322673/deschooling-architecture/ (accessed 22 April 2021).

Petrescu, Doina, and Kim Trogal, eds. (2017) *The Social (Re)production of Architecture. Politics, Values and Actions in Contemporary Practice.* Abingdon and New York: Routledge.

Rendell, Jane (2018) 'Only resist: a feminist approach to critical spatial practice.' *Architectural Review*, 19 February 2018, published online: www.architectural-review.com (accessed 30 November 2018).

Schalk, Meike, and Therese Kristiansson, and Ramia Maze, eds. (2017) *Feminist Futures of Spatial Practice. Materialisms, Activisms, Dialogues, Pedagogies, Projections.* Baunauch: AADR Art Architecture Design Research, an imprint of Spurbuchverlag.

Solnit, Rebecca (2016 [2004]) *Hope in the Dark. Untold Histories. Wild Possibilities.* Edinburgh and London: Canongate Books. First published by Canongate in 2005. Originally published in 2004 by New York: Nation Books.

Solnit, Rebecca (2019) *Whose Story Is This? Old Conflicts, New Chapters.* Chicago, IL: Haymarket Books.

Stead, Naomie, ed. (2014) *Women, Practice, Architecture. 'Resigned Accommodation' and 'Usurpatory Practice'.* New York: Routledge.

Thomson, Pat (2014) 'The photograph as "witness".' In Catherine Burke and Ken Jones, eds., *Education, Childhood and Anarchism. Talking Colin Ward.* Paperback edition 2016. Abingdon and New York: Routledge, pp. 157–172.

Trogal, Kim (2017) 'Feminist Pedagogies. Making transversal and mutual connections across difference.' In: Meike Schalk, Thérèse Kristiansson and Ramia Mazé, eds. *Feminist Futures of Spatial Practice. Materialisms, Activisms, Dialogues, Pedagogies, Projections.* Baunauch: AADR Art Architecture Design Research, an imprint of Spurbuchverlag, pp. 239–251.

Ward, Colin (1978) *The Child in the City.* London: The Architectural Press Ltd.

Ward, Colin (1995) *Talking Schools. Ten Lectures by Colin Ward.* London: Freedom Press.

Ward, Colin (1995a) 'Education for Mastery of the Environment.' In *Talking Schools. Ten Lectures by Colin Ward.* London: Freedom Press, pp. 21–38. Lecture held at the UNESCO/UNEP course on Urban Education, London, 1977.

Ward, Colin (1995b) 'Schooling the city child.' In *Talking Schools. Ten Lectures by Colin Ward.* London: Freedom Press, pp. 71–83. Lecture held at the National Short Course on Urban Education, George Washington University, 10 July 1979.

Ward, Colin (2000) 'Anarchy and architecture: A personal record.' In Jonathan Hughes and Simon Sadler, eds., *Non-Plan: Essays on Freedom, Participation and Change in Modern Architecture and Urbanism.* Oxford and Woburn, MA: Architectural Press, an imprint of Butterworth-Heinemann, pp. 44–51.

Ward, Colin (2004) *Anarchism. A Very Short Introduction.* Oxford and New York: Oxford University Press.

Ward, Colin (2008 [1973]) *Anarchy in Action.* London: Freedom Press, first published by Freedom Press in 1982, and originally by George Allen & Unwin in 1973.

Ward, Colin, and Anthony Fyson (1973) *Streetwork. The exploding school.* London and Boston, MA: Routledge & Kegan Paul Ltd.

Ward, Colin, and David Goodway (2014 [2003]) *Talking Anarchy.* Oakland, CA: PM Press, originally published with Five Leaves Publications, 2003.

Wilbert, Chris, and Damian F. White, eds. (2011) *Autonomy, Solidarity, Possibility. The Colin Ward Reader.* Edinburgh, Oakland, Baltimore, MD: AK Press.

Worpole, Ken (2014) 'On the street where you live: Colin Ward and environmental education.' In Catherine Burke and Ken Jones, eds., *Education, Childhood and Anarchism. Talking Colin Ward.* Paperback edition 2016. Abingdon and New York: Routledge, pp. 46–54.

PART 4

Learning by technologies
Audio-visual transmissions

11

IN THE EYE OF THE PROJECTOR

Wölfflin, slides and architecture in postwar America

Rajesh Heynickx

During the first decades of the 20th century, the Swiss art historian Heinrich Wölfflin (1864–1945) constantly improved his method to determine the prevailing style of a given period. This not only happened behind his desk but also in the lecture halls of universities in Berlin (1901–1912), Munich (1912–1924) and Zürich (1924–1934). In delivering his lectures, he was one of the first to use twin parallel projectors.[1] The double projection of slides allowed him to compare the formal characteristics of artworks from different periods. Without using many references outside the projected art works, he started to measure the side-by-side images against five notorious pairs of contrary concepts. These binary modes of visual imagination, like, for example, 'open' versus 'closed' forms, or 'linear' versus 'painterly', offered a formalist criterion to differentiate styles through time.

Wölfflin's pioneering use of the lantern projector or skiopticon – coming from the Greek words 'skia' (shadow) and 'opsis' (view or picture) – testifies to art history's efforts to become an ordered, systematic discipline. What the microscope had been for biologists, the skiopticon, used in art history courses from the early 1890s on, was for art historians.[2] The slide, Max Schmid claimed in 1896, 'collapsed the distance of time, it (has) made the past artwork a new creation of our era' (Schmid 1897). Through illuminated reproductions of art works, art history acquired a systematic descriptive system. Therefore, from the end of the 19th century on, the lecture room could grow into more than just a place for transmitting information. The lantern projector would give it a new appearance: that of an experimental theatre or laboratory (Vogt 1994; Karlholm 2010).

Wölfflin's dual-slide projections formed a basis for the comparative formalism enshrined in his 1915 *Principles of Art History*. This study on the shift in the nature of artistic vision between the art of the 16th and 17th centuries, built around the juxtaposition of Renaissance and Baroque art works, became foundational for a whole discipline (Levy and Weddigen 2020). 'Wölfflin's teachings have become self evident', Hanspeter Landolt wrote in 1944, and he continued: 'his concepts are common property and most scholars are no longer aware of their origins' (Landolt 1944). More than five decades after that statement, when reflecting on the role of images in 20th-century aesthetics, Karen Lang identified these origins in a

DOI: 10.4324/9781003201205-16

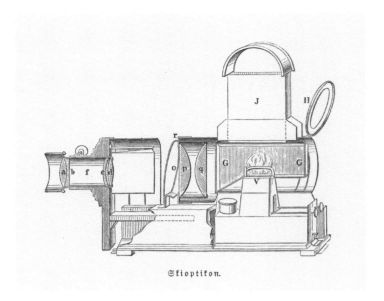

FIGURE 11.1 Sciopticon (Laterna magica, or magic lantern) – an early type of image projector, the ancestor of the modern slide projector. It was widespread throughout Europe from the 17th to the 20th century and became a mass medium in the 19th century. Wood engraving, published in 1897 (Getty Images).

footnote: 'dual slide projection could be considered as art history's complementary technological protocol' (Lang 2006: 24).

In what follows, we will scrutinize this protocol and illuminate how binary comparisons seeped into the foundations of art history. More specifically, we will dissect the imprint Wölfflin's lecture hall achievement left on scholars of European descent, all teaching architectural history in postwar America. By focusing on these 'transplanted' architects, critics and historians, we will clarify how intellectual norms and models were launched or contested through slideshows.

A performative triangle

It is tantalizing to turn first to direct witnesses of what happened in Wölfflin's lectures and to come as close as possible to the apparatus his self-assured manner of delivery depended on. One observer, the painter and art historian Wolfgang Born, living and teaching in New York from 1937 on, waxed lyrical when in the mid-1940s he reflected on his class attendance of two decades earlier:

> It was the most exciting intellectual spectacle I have ever experienced. In the darkened room, the tall figure of the professor appeared as a black silhouette. He stood next to the slide machine in the back of the auditorium, very calm, his unforgettable head … slightly raised. Halting and terse words came from his mouth, stimulated by the picture which appeared on the screen and elucidated their significance with uncanny accuracy…
> *(Born 1970)*

FIGURE 11.2 Wölfflin's 1915 *Kunstgeschichtliche Grundbegriffe. Das Problem der Stilentwickelung in der neuern Kunst* is one of art history's most influential works. This is a spread from a facsimile: the new English translation published by Yale on its one-hundredth anniversary in 2015 (Levy 2015).

As we can learn from this and other *memoires*, the lectures rested on a performative triangle consisting of speaker, audience and image (Landsberger 1924: 92–94). The skiopticon undergirded Wölfflin's scientific authority and helped to spread the methodological assumptions of his formalist gaze among listeners/viewers who often became prolific instructors themselves (Nelson 2000; Eisenhauer 2006). For example, the roots of the comparative analysis cherished by scholars like the Renaissance specialist Rudolf Wittkower, who studied under Wölfflin in Munich, and the architectural historian and theorist Colin Rowe, who studied under Wittkower, have to be situated in Wölfflin's slide lectures. Just like Wittkower who taught at Columbia University over the course of many years, Rowe became a prominent lecturer at American universities. From there, they both exercised an enormous influence on architects and historians (Ackerman 1989; Engel 2016; Martinez 2018).

The approach Rowe developed during the 1960s and 1970s at Cornell University grounded in a dialogue between literary texts, images and diagrams, all of which had been kept widely separated by conventional historians. This approach was fully in line with his 1947 essay 'The Mathematics of the Ideal Villa'. In that essay, written under Wittkower, diagrammatic similarities in the proportions and dispositions of plans and elevations, offered a trans-historical critique of both Palladio's and Le Corbusier's villas. In a 1976 addendum to the essay, Rowe laid bare the origins of that comparison:

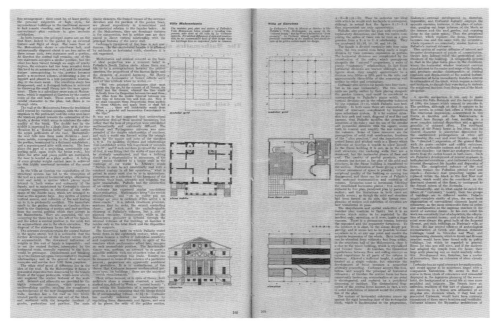

FIGURE 11.3 Spread from Rowe's 1947 essay 'The Mathematics of the Ideal Villa' (Rowe 1947).

> A Wölfflian style of critical exercise (though painfully belonging to a period c. 1900) might still possess the merit of appealing primarily to what is visible, and of, thereby, making the minimum of pretences to erudition and the least possible number of references outside itself.
>
> *(Rowe 1976: 16)*

Anthony Vidler recognised in this statement Rowe's 'claim for accessibility' (Vidler 2008: 63). In a similar way, others linked this confession with Rowe's innovative use of diverse sources, breaking away from art history's 'claims of autonomy' (Crinson and Williams 2019: 63). Both interpretations share something: they foreground Rowe's deep interest in visual immediacy. That was also why Sigfried Giedion lauded the formalist approach of Wölfflin in his 1941 study *Space, Time and Architecture*. His *Doktorvater*, he wrote, had brought 'the meaning and sense of a work of art or a building with a directness' (Giedion 1941: 36). Clearly, in the pairs of contrasting images which formed the conceptual backbone of Giedion's influential history of modern architecture, Wölfflin's projections that many years earlier had held the Zürich auditorium spellbound, resonated.

When Wölfflin found this study in his mail in October 1942, he wrote in his thank you letter to Giedion that the English language prevented him of fully grasping it. But the 'inner connection' and 'discipleship' Giedion had raised charmed the old scholar. It was for him a 'hand-shake from the realms of the young' (Sekler 1990: 272–273). That was a reaction Giedion had hoped for. His handwritten message to Wölfflin in *Space, Time and Architecture* was the following: 'In memory of joint studies'.[3]

FIGURE 11.4 In his 1941 landmark volume *Space, Time and Architecture*, Sigfried Giedion paired images of two iconic spirals: Vladimir Tatlin's Monument to the Third International (1919–1920) and Francesco Borromini's dome for Sant'Ivo alla Sapienza (Built in 1642–1660). The values shared between the baroque age and the modern were thus encapsulated on a single page spread.

Undeniably, it is far too simple to unearth the impact of Wölfflin's projections by directly linking a humming device in the back of a lecture room with articles or books written by those who derived (almost) direct inspiration from the Swiss art historian. Next to being a linchpin of methodological premises, Wölfflin's projections also reached those who would fiercely oppose formalist comparisons. Influential art historians like Frederik Antal and Ernst Gombrich noticed a 'magic sphere' when attending Wölfflin's lectures; yet, they would turn away from it and founded their own schools, respectively, fostering social and psychological approaches to art perception.[4] And, already in 1915, the year that Wölfflin published his programmatic *Principles of Art History*, the young Erwin Panofsky stated that Wölfflin was incapable of producing a thorough understanding of any work of art. Based as it was on *a priori* categories, the founder of iconology argued that the Wölfflinian system would never offer real explanations. It was in deep need of a metahistorical sensitivity.[5] Walter Benjamin, who attended Wölfflin's lectures in Munich that same year, intensely disliked the art historian's performance. In a letter to his friend Fritz Radt, he noted: '(Wölfflin) does not see the artwork, he feels obliged to see it, demands that one sees it, considers his theory a moral act'.[6]

Looking back on those who rejected or imitated Wölfflin's performance, the projector might be called a prime example of 'epistemological technology', a tool for fabricating meaning.[7] Wölfflin, and so many other users of projectors, wanted to communicate and codify insights. By closely looking into two cases in postwar America, we will explore that process in more detail. One entry has already been mentioned: the promotor of modernist architecture Sigfried Giedion, lecturing at Harvard in 1938–1939. Yet, I will start with focussing on a rather forgotten *émigré*, the architect, theoretician and historian Paul Zucker who taught at Cooper Union and the New School for Social Research in New York from the 1940s until 1969.

Training the eye

When musing about the history of latern projection, Heinrich Dilly wrote that the skiopticon or *Lichtbildwerfer* always fell together with one simple, basic act, namely '*werfen*', throwing images on a wall. Still, he added, every projection equally implied a far more complex '*entwerfen*': German for 'making a plan' or 'to outline' (Dilly 1995). The plan Paul Zucker unfolded in his course 'Styles through the Ages' at the New School in the 1950s and 1960s was that of a vast survey of Western art history, one paying attention to both colors and forms, and the way people of other places and times – from Pompeian fresco painters to Mondrian – saw their world. This broad scope seems to have brought about Zucker's incapacity to compose a concise abstract of his course for the annual programme brochure, something that would drive the faculty administration repeatedly nervous. In an internal memo of 1967, the dean, Allen Austill, had to pour oil on troubled waters: 'he (i.e. Zucker) is an old-timer who's done a lot for the school, but is difficult and complicated'.[8]

From his part, Zucker had quickly become frustrated with students' poor slide identification during examinations. 'The students are able to think and articulate independently but are very slow in visual memory', he wrote to Austill in 1967.[9] Two decades earlier, in his essay 'Teaching History of Art in our Visual Chaos', Zucker pointed at the cause of poor visual memory: the flood of visual stimuli produced by publicity posters, newspaper photos and magazine covers. Modern media had hollowed out men's 'capacity of perception'. But, this 1946 lamentation also opened up to a remedy: 'We must jostle the misguided, the dull, the uninterested from their accepted visual patterns acquired through daily experience, and we must lead them towards a gradual understanding and knowledge of real artistic values' (Zucker 1946: 103). In a later essay, dating from 1962, that path was further specified: 'systematic, unrushed education through carefully selected books and lectures by devoted professionals' (Zucker 1962: 27).

At the moment Zucker tried to put this ideal into practice, Wölfflin was never far away. Although he was not a direct student, Zucker engaged actively with Wölfflin's work. *Principles of Art History* was shelved as assigned-reading. Furthermore, Zucker's own 1950 study, *Styles in Painting. A Comparative Study*, an off-shoot of his slide lectures, was clearly modelled on Wölfflin's *opus famosum* and even marketed as its innovative reiteration. (Figure 11.5 and Figure 11.6)

With its introductory statement that the improvement of modern man's comprehensive response to art depended on an immediate, unspoiled awareness of art, and subsequently required the practicing of a careful visual dissection, this book showed how much Zucker was caught up in the 'pedagogical spirit' of Wölfflin's work. For the neo-Kantian Wölfflin, the visual immediacy of art, that is, the shape, arrangement and rhythm of forms present, was essential to reorientate the hazy vision of the bourgeois museumgoer or tourist (Levy 2015: 19–21). Similarly, in the lecture room on 66 West 12th Street New York, Zucker's voice-over, with his distinctive accent, slowly drew the students' gaze into the projections by unpacking the content and context of buildings and paintings.

FIGURE 11.5 Spread from Paul Zucker's 1950 *Styles in Painting. A Comparative Study* (Zucker 1963).

Zucker's conviction that modern man's visual intellect was in need of a reconfiguration, aligns with his defense of creative pursuit and artistic imagination. At the Cooper Union, he invariably aired the idea that architecture students lacked exactly that. Blinded by technological progress, their design work had come in the grip of a 'functionalist expressionism' (Zucker 1959a: 13–15, 19–20, 23 & 28). Still, from the 1940s on, Zucker also started to argue that it was possible to go beyond this myopia (Zucker 1942–1943). Architectural design had to concern itself more with aesthetic issues of space, volume, symbol and abstraction, so that the problem of *what* to build would supersede the contemporary hyperfocus on *how* to build. The *aesthesis* of the participative user had to prevail on technical know-how:

> The function of architecture as an element of any future comprehensive civilization will be determined to a much greater degree by the attitude of those who look at and walk through the buildings than by that of those who design and construct them.
>
> *(Zucker 1944: 30)*

Zucker was in favour of an architectural theory falling together with aesthetics. Clearly, during the first half of the 20th century, in studies by household names like Alois Riegl, August Schmarsow and Wölfflin, this equation had been a common phenomenon. Yet, in the early 1940s, when Zucker gave his first courses on American soil, it had become outstripped

FIGURE 11.6   A publicity brochure for Paul Zucker's *Styles in Painting. A Comparative Study* (New York, Cooper Union Archives, 'Zucker box').

by other voices, like that of Walter Gropius. Their approach toward architecture was centered around architecture's structural relations to a social or a material world, consequently putting much less emphasis on how the perceptual experience of seeing could orientate architectural design (Moravansky 2007: 48–49).

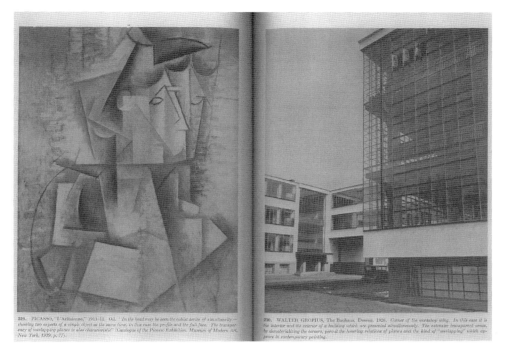

FIGURE 11.7 Spread from Giedion's 1941 *Space, Time and Architecture*: the famous juxtaposition of Picasso's *L'Arlésienne* (1911–1912) and Gropius's Bauhaus Building (1925–1926).

For Zucker, it was evident who had to be blamed for that shift: Sigfried Giedion. The success of Giedion's 1941 study *Space, Time and Architecture* which, as a journalist correctly noted, had rapidly become 'a bible – the book, often the only one, North American architecture students were encouraged to read, or ever did read, on architectural history' (Anonymous 1948; Tallack 1994), was a thorn in the flesh for him. In a 1951 article on architectural theories in the Modern Movement, Zucker omitted Giedion's study on space (Zucker 1951). A direct attack was another option. In 1945, he opened an article on the aesthetics of space in architecture, sculpture and city planning by strongly criticizing a famous juxtaposition Giedion had used in *Space, Time and Architecture*, namely that of Picasso's *L'Arlésienne* (1911–1912) and Gropius's Bauhaus Building (1925–1926). (Figure 11.7)

When mentioning this juxtaposition, Zucker identified the cubist painting wrongly. Spreading the idea that Giedion presented a misleading comparison seemed to be the only thing that really mattered:

> For example, it is virtually not true that a cubistic painting by Braque (sic) and a modern building by Gropius show identical space concepts. The aesthetic concepts underlying both are utterly dissimilar, even beyond the fact that the painting shows reproduced space while the building creates real space. The similarity lies only in the rhythmic organization imposed on the projected and on the penetrable space of painting and building, respectively.
>
> *(Zucker 1945: 12)*

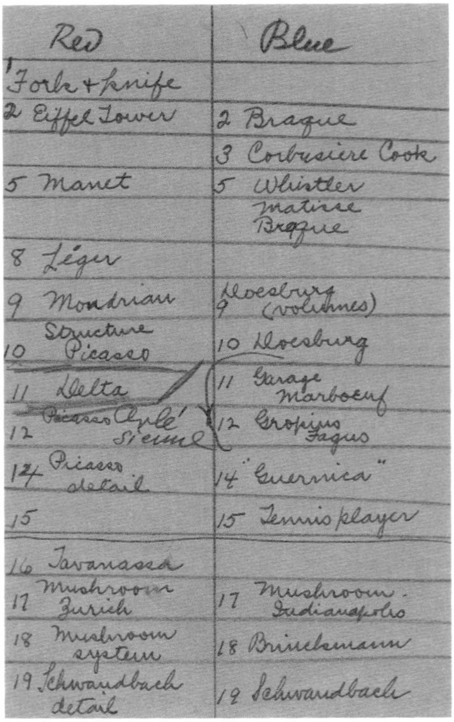

Red	Blue
1 Fork + knife	
2 Eiffel Tower	2 Braque
	3 Corbusiere Cook
5 Manet	5 Whistler Matisse Braque
8 Léger	
9 Mondrian	9 Doesburg (volumes)
10 Structure Picasso	10 Doesburg
11 Delta	11 Garage Marboeuf
12 Picasso Arlé Siemel	12 Gropius Fagus
14 Picasso detail	14 "Guernica"
15	15 Tennis player
16 Javanassa	
17 Mushroom Zurich	17 Mushroom Indianapolis
18 Mushroom system	18 Brinckmann
19 Schwandbach detail	19 Schwandbach

FIGURE 11.8 Giedion's list of slides for his lecture on 'American and European Industry' at Yale University, indicating the juxtaposition of images by means of two projectors (red and blue), ca. November 1941 (gta Archive/ETH Zurich, Nachlass Sigfried Giedion).

In a footnote of the same text, Zucker refers to *Space, Time and Architecture*, yet without giving any page indication. Hence, one could say that the incorrectly determined juxtaposition functioned as a *pars pro toto*: Zucker identified Giedion's complete study with this specific way of situating and explaining art works through comparison. And, indeed, in Giedion's 1938–1939 lectures at Harvard, and also in the course he gave at Yale in 1941, these kind of comparisons had taken center stage (Harbusch 2015: 598). (Figure 11.8)

Giedion's projections, which would constitute the palimpsest of *Space, Time and Architecture*, were composed out of the 500 large glass slides Giedion had brought across the Atlantic. Giedion had informed Gropius, his host at Harvard, that this material came from the most remote corners from Europe, and that it would be new 'even for those who know all the pictures' (Sekler 1990: 268). Presenting rare images was one thing, combining them another. Where, for Giedion, the juxtaposition of a Picasso painting and a Gropius building entailed an act of outmost adequate reasoning, for Zucker, it was nothing more than a treacherous short-cut he loved to criticize during meetings with students at Cooper Union.

Crossing a nebulous terrain

Giedion, the 'ghostwriter of the Modern Movement' (Heynen 2012: 70), seems to have been a nemesis for Zucker, a rival he could hardly defeat. The role of the slide projector in

FIGURE 11.9 Paul Zucker, participating in a debate at Cooper Union in New York, somewhere in the 1960's. The caption of this image, published in a student periodical, reads as follows: 'Cooper Union places great emphasis on "The ability to think". It considers the selection of its Faculty as one of the most important factors in developing this ability' (Undated picture (New York, Cooper Union Archives, 'Zucker box')).

this contention cannot be underestimated. Once the projector was loaded with slides, both Zucker and Giedion succeeded in conveying – with varying success – their ideas and approaches. Both followed the path of etching side-by-side comparisons in the minds of their audience. For Zucker, slides were like pearls in a necklace: by comparatively tying them together, they generated a historical panorama from which a cultural consciousness could be distilled. The argumentative order of comparing and contrasting, so present in his articles and lectures, carried the argument that, through time, the built environment incarnated people's changing ways of expressing feelings.

With that purpose in mind, Zucker would, for example, write a broad historical study on market places in which he unravelled the dynamics of empathy through multiple ages.[10] When unearthing such an old line stemming back centuries, it was for him clear that history had a probing lesson in store: 'feeling into' the aesthetic values of the built environment in one's own time was the right antidote to the numbing technocracy of the rational functionalism defended by Giedion.

Just like the scissors and glue he utilized when putting together the manuscript of *Space, Time and Architecture*, Giedion's projections helped to cut and paste a *Zeitgeschichte*. While ordering his slides for his 1938 lectures, he wrote to Gropius: 'My angle of direction is this: every building should be treated in such a manner that, even without pointing it out, the image of our own period appears by its side'. In other words, the calibration point in the comparisons Giedion fabricated was the own era, a period in search for a consciousness of itself (Sekler 1990: 268). Or, to paraphrase Giedion's notorious mantra, the production of insights with the help of the projector in 1938 at Harvard's Fog Art Museum illustrates how also in architectural historiography mechanization took command.

Zucker's longing for a cultural archive and Giedion's focus on contemporariness were part and parcel of diverging agendas: the promotion of the Modern Movement versus a

THE JOURNAL OF AESTHETICS AND ART CRITICISM

and transparency; *third,* the unification of surface which makes it appear not as a supporting system in itself but merely as an enclosing skin for a definite volume.

Some examples may prove our point of view:

A) Proof of the change in the conception of space: juxtaposition of landscape photographs between 1840 and 1870 and of modern landscape photographs. Juxtaposition of sculptures of the 19th century and of modern sculptures from Maillol to Archipenko.

B) Proof of the development of technical forms and their influence on architecture: forms of the locomotive, of the airplane, and of the steamer in their historical sequence. Examples of modern architecture adopting their forms: Dutch, German and Scandinavian buildings between 1920-30.

C) Proof of the influence of modern technical structures upon contemporary painting: Leger, Sheeler.

D) Proof of the parallel feeling as to the disintegration of space into different planes and as to transparency: juxtaposition of modern paintings from Braque to Picasso and of corresponding modern buildings and interiors.

E) Proof of the independency and freedom of modern architects as to the choice of their artistic means in spite of identical functional needs and structural suppositions. Variant forms of bridges, plants, silos, railway stations, etc., under equal conditions.

Construction changes into expression. In this way modern architecture becomes a subject of humanism. To what extent, only *one* man can prove, the engineer! He will be able to tell us how far the final shape of modern buildings has changed from the mere execution of constructive elements of tension, pressure and calculated masses.

Oliver Cromwell said, "A man never goes quite so far as when he does not know where he is going." So did modern architecture! Based upon the expression of rational conditions and functional needs, it became as independent, free and even emotional as any work ever created by man — therefore approachable from the humanistic point of view.

26

FIGURE 11.10 Spread from Paul Zucker's article 'The Humanistic Approach to Modern Architecture' in which the key arguments were undergirded by comparisons (Zucker 1942–1943).

humanist plea for the importance of 'feeling into' for designers and people in general. In both cases, a better understanding of the role and function of the projector can help to traverse what Braden Engel termed as the 'nebulous terrain' between how historians and critics aesthetically experienced buildings and their 'subsequent epistemological presentation' (Engel 2012: 80). Yet, when one wants to embark on a trip through that terrain of knowledge formation, the instructive Zucker–Giedion case should trigger two forms of travel advice.

FIGURE 11.11 1961: Sigfried Giedion at work in the studio of Swiss bookseller and publisher Hoepli, designing the Italian edition of *Space, Time and Architecture. The Growth of a New Tradition*, which was originally published by Harvard University Press in 1941 (gta Archive/ETH Zurich, Nachlass Ulrich Stucky).

First travel tip: take enough time to research how images were accumulated and controlled. Whereas it has been demonstrated how 20th-century buildings changed irrevocably and substantially through their interaction with photography in print media (Zimmerman 2014), the practices which marked the (re)ordering of photographic or other images with the help of non-printed media, especially in educational contexts, still needs more attention. Although ephemeral in nature, projections transformed the way students started to see the world and how they acted on it accordingly. Through projections, ideas and images were merged into powerful narratives. As our analysis of the Zucker–Giedion case demonstrates, slide shows can help to disclose this incubation and dissemination of architectural knowledge. Slide shows were formative moments *par excellence*. Moreover, they played a crucial role in how we began to understand the evolution of modern architecture. For example, by relying on detailed lecture notes, Catalina Mejia Moreno could demonstrate how Walter Gropius' 1911 latern slide lecture 'Monumentale kunst und Industriebau' introduced a series of traded photographs of North and South American Silos into the discourse of 20th-century modern architecture. This corrects a persistent idea, namely that a set of printed media following a 1913 article by Gropius gave birth to this highly important *translatio studiorum* (Rabaté 2007: 75–77). As Moreno proves, the introduction of the silos took place two years earlier *in* the 1911 projection (Moreno 2014–2015).

Second travel advice: watch out for Wölfflin. The projector clearly opened up a space in which varied discourses were elaborated and transmitted. Yet, the number of theoretical or methodological debates, which was set in motion by Wölfflin's work or teaching practice, is remarkable. In an introductory essay to the 100th anniversary edition of *Principles of Art History* from 2015, Evonne Levy called Wölfflin's blockbuster 'art history's crucible and its Pandora's box' (Levy 2015: 1). The same qualification applies to the slide projector itself; with that difference, it both diffused and amplified the ideas of its pioneering operator. Zeynep Çelik Alexander has beautifully analyzed how Wölfflin's use of the projector fit in an exploration of the disciplinary boundaries between art and science at the beginning of the 20th century. It propelled a new way of knowing, which she termed as 'kinaesthetic knowing': the production of reliable knowledge through the interaction of the body of the listener/

viewer with the world. The projector bypassed 'the matrix of logic and language' and supported an immediate and intimate apprehension of the world. Yet, this immediacy of looking became also larded with Wölfflin's spoken performance, so that a knowledge steeped in facts ('*wissen*') and a familiarity with visual phenomena ('*kennen*') interlocked. This fusion had a double advantage: it offered a rigid control and, at the same time, facilitated the rise of experience as a direct, alternative mode of knowledge (Çelik Alexander 2017: 63–96).

In postwar America, both Zucker and Giedion capitalised on this 'kinaesthetic knowing'. With their projections, both wanted to intermingle their optic perceptive processes with factional knowledge of the shapes and forms of art works or buildings. While doing that, with albeit different agendas in mind, they drew the problem of perception further into the orbit of modern architectural historiography. They proved, as Herman Bauer once stated, that nowhere in art history, one can observe greater confusion than in the interrelation of psychological and historical categories articulated by Wölfflin and what came after him (Bauer 1976: 102). What Zucker and Giedion did in their lecture rooms helped to ramify Wölfflin's achievements. The art historian, standing next to a projector and who was often only visible against a slightly brighter background, had an impact. His silhouette casted a long shadow.

Notes

1 For a sharp analysis of the use of slide projectors in art history courses during the last decade of the 19th century, one has to rely on the seminal work of the German historian Heinrich Dilly. His most recent insights have been brought a corrective to the often repeated, yet wrong idea that Wölfflin was the 'inventor' of twin parallel projection (Dilly 2009).
2 The German scholar Herman Grimm (1828–1901) was among the first to use lantern slides in his lectures (Langmead 2018). He accepted the chair in the newly created discipline of history of art (Lehrstuhl für Kunstgeschichte) in Berlin in 1872 and remained there the rest of his life. He was succeeded by Wölfflin, who inherited his collection of slides (Grimm 1892).
3 Giedion's inscription in the copy of *Space, Time and Architecture* he sent to Wölfflin was the following: "Zu alter Schülerschaft Immer Ihr ergebener." This book is kept in the library of the University of Zürich, Wölfflin Collection.
4 Both established their own 'school'. Antal, who made mention of the 'magic sphere' in Wölfflin's auditorium, became known for his contributions to the social history of art. Gombrich made name with his work on the psychology of perception. For their reflections on Wölfflin, consult Gombrich (1971: 92) and Antal (1949: 49–52 & 73–75).
5 Published in 1915, Panofsky's essay 'The Problem of Style in the Visual Arts' in fact contested Wölfflin's December 1911 lecture to the Prussian Academy of Sciences (Levine 2013: 154–155).
6 Walter Benjamin wrote this in a ferocious letter to his friend Fritz Radt (dated "Munich, November 21, 1915" and "Munich, December 4, 1915") cited in full by Gershom Scholem in a 1980–1981 essay entitled 'Walter Benjamin und Felix Noeggerath' (Scholem 1983).
7 This concept was developed by the art historian and semiotician Donald Preziosi. He used it to indicate that museums rely on stagecraft and dramaturgy in order to convey specific messages. The slideprojector, I argue, does the same in the classroom (Preziosi 2003).
8 Internal memo by Austill, to Abel Reuben, January 21, 1966. Archives of the New School for Social Research in New York.
9 Letter by Paul Zucker to Allen Austill from February 1, 1967. Archives of the New School for Social Research in New York.
10 In his 1959 *Town and Square. From the Agora to the Village Green*, Zucker argues that the square is more than a mere void in the urban fabric. By unravelling a continuous development from Greece and Rome, through the Middle Ages and the Renaissance to the 17th and 18th centuries, he defends the idea that it results from how people experienced and shaped spatial relations in the world they inhabited. The square, he contends, "represents actually a psychological parking place within the civic landscape" (Zucker 1959b: 1–2).

References

Anonymous (May 17 1948), "The Shape of Things" in: *Time*, LI/20, p. 112.

Ackerman, J.S. (1989), 'Rudolf Wittkower's influence in the History of Architecture,' *Source*, 8 (4) and 9 (1): 87–90.

Antal, F. (1949), 'Remarks on the Method of Art History I–II,' *Burlington Magazine* (91): 49–52 and 73–75.

Bauer, H. (1976), *Kunsthistorik. Eine kritische Einführung in das Studium der Kunstgeschichte*, Munich: Beck.

Born, W. (1970), 'Heinrich Wölfflin, 1864–1945,' in A. Werner (ed.), *The Drawings of Albrecht Dürer*, New York: Dover, vii.

Çelik Alexander, Z.Ç. (2017), *Kinaesthetic Knowing. Aesthetics, Epistemology, Modern Design*, Chicago, IL and London: The University of Chicago Press.

Crinson, M. and Williams R.J. (2019), *The Architecture of Art History. A Historiography*, London/New York/Oxford/New Delhi/Sydney: Bloomsbury Visual Arts.

Dilly, H. (1995), 'Die Bildwerfer. 121 Jahre kunstwissenschaftliche Dia-Projektion,' in *Zwischen Markt und Museum. Beiträge der Tagung "Präsentationsformen von Fotografie" am 24. und 25. Juni 1994 im Reiß-Museum der Stadt Mannheim*, Göppingen: Rundbrief Fotografie, Sonderheft 2, 39–44.

Dilly, H. (2009), 'Weder Grimm, noch Schmarsow, geschweige denn Wölfflin … Zur jüngsten Diskussion über die Diaprojektion um 1900,' in C. Caraffa (ed.), *Fotografie als Instrument und Medium der Kunstgeschichte*, Berlin: Deutscher Kunstverlag, 91–116.

Eisenhauer, J.F. (2006), 'Next Slide Please: The Magical, Scientific, and Corporate Discourses of Visual Projection Technologies,' *Studies in Art Education*, 47(3): 198–214.

Engel, B. (2012), 'Nebulous terrain,' *PLAT 2.0, Journal of Rice University School of Architecture*, 2 (1): 78–93.

Engel, B.R. (2016), 'Ambichronous Historiography: Colin Rowe and the Teaching of Architectural History,' *Journal of Art Historiography*, online: https://arthistoriography.files.wordpress.com/2016/05/engel.pdf (accessed 25/03/2021)

Giedion, S. (1941), *Space, Time and Architecture: The Growth of a New Tradition*, London and Cambridge, MA: The MIT Press.

Gombrich, E. (1971), *Norm and Form: Studies in the Art of the Renaissance*, London: Phaidon.

Grimm, H. (1892), 'Die Umgestaltung der Universitätsvorlesungen über Neuere Kunstgeschichte durch die Anwendung des Skioptikons,' *Beiträge zur deutschen Culturgeschichte*, Berlin: Verlag von Wilhelm Herz, 276–395.

Harbusch, G. (2015), 'Work in Text and Images. Sigfried Giedion's Space, Time and Architecture, 1941–1967,' *The Journal of Architecture*, 20 (4): 596–620.

Heynen, H. (2012), 'Modernity and Community. A Difficult Combination,' in R. Heynickx and T. Avermaete (eds.), *Making a New World. Architecture & Communities in Interwar Europe*, Leuven: Leuven University Press, 69–78.

Karlholm, D. (2010), 'Developing the Picture: Wölfflin's Performance Art,' *Photography and Culture*, 3 (2): 207–215.

Landolt, H. (1944), 'Heinrich Wölfflin. Zum 80. Geburtstag des grossen Kunstgelehrten,' *Luzerner Tagblatt*, 143.

Landsberger, F. (1924), *Heinrich Wölfflin*, Berlin: Elena Gottschalk.

Lang, K. (2006), *Chaos and Cosmos. On the Image in Aesthetics and Art History*, Ithaca, NY and London: Cornell University Press.

Langmead, A. (2018), 'Art and Architectural History and the Performative, Mindful Practice of the Digital Humanities,' *The Journal of Interactive Technology & Pedagogy* 12, available online: https://jitp.commons.gc.cuny.edu/art-and-architectural-history-and-the-performative-mindful-practice-of-the-digital-humanities/ (Accessed 25/03/2021)

Levine, E. (2013), *Dreamland of Humanists. Warburg, Cassirer, Panofsky and the Hamburg School*, Chicago, IL: and London: The University of Chicago Press.

Levy, E. (2015), 'Wölfflin's Principles of Art History (1915–2015): A Prolegomenon for Its Second Century,' in H. Wölfflin, *Principles of Art History: The Problem of the Development of Style in Early Modern Art*, trans. J. Blower, ed. E. Levy and T. Weddigen, Los Angeles, CA: Getty Research Institute, 1–46.

Levy, E. and Weddigen, T. (eds.) (2020), *The Global Reception of Heinrich Wölfflin's Principles of Art History*, New Haven, CT: Yale University Press.

Martinez, R.M. (2018), 'The Methodological Approaches of Colin Rowe: The Multifaceted, Intellectual Connoisseur at La Tourette,' *Architectural Research Quarterly*, 22 (3): 205–213.

Moravansky, A. (2007), 'Architectural Theory: A Construction Site,' *Footprint*, 1 (1): 47–56.

Moreno, C.M. (2014–2015), 'The "Corporeality" of the Image in Walter Gropius' Monumentale Kunst und Industriebau Lecture,' *Intermédialités: histoire et théorie des arts, des lettres et des techniques*, 24–25, online article. Available here: https://www.erudit.org/en/journals/im/2014-n24-25-im02279/ (Accessed 25/03/2021)

Nelson, R.S. (2000), 'The Slide Lecture, or The Work of Art History in the Age of Mechanical Reproduction,' *Critical Inquiry*, 26 (3): 414–434.

Preziosi, D. (2003), *Brain of the Earth's Body: Art, Museums, and the Phantasms of Modernity*, Minneapolis: University of Minnesota Press.

Rabaté, J.M. (2007), *1913: The Cradle of Modernism*, Malden, MA: Blackwell Publishers.

Rowe, C. (1947), 'The Mathematics of the Ideal Villa: Palladio and Le Corbusier compared,' *Architectural Review*, 101 (march): 101–104.

Rowe, C. (1976), *The Mathematics of the Ideal Villa and Other Essays*, London and Cambridge, MA: The MIT Press.

Schmid, M. (1897), 'Das Skioptikon in kunstgeschichtlichen Unterricht,' in *Offizieller Bericht über die Verhandlungen des kunsthistorisches Kongresses zu Budapest. 1–3 Oktober 1896*, Nuremberg: Stich, 46.

Scholem, G. (1983), *Walter Benjamin und sein Engel. Vierzehn Aufsatze und kleine Beitrage*, Frankfurt/M.: Suhrkamp.

Sekler, E.F. (1990), 'Sigfried Giedion at Harvard University,' *Studies in the History of Art*, 35: 265–273.

Tallack, D. (1994), 'Sigfried Giedion, Modernism and American Material Culture,' *Journal of American Studies*, 28 (2): 149–167.

Vidler, A. (2008), *Histories of the Immediate Present. Inventing Architectural Modernism*, Cambridge, MA: MIT Press.

Vogt, A.M. (1994), 'Der Kunsthistoriker im Halbdunkel: der Übergang von der Zeichnung zur Projektion in der Vorlesung,' in *Zeitschrift für schweizerische Archäologie und Kunstgeschichte. Revue suisse d'art et d'archéologie. Rivista svizzera d'arte e d'archeologia. Journal of Swiss archeology and art history*, 51 (2): 100–103.

Zimmerman, C. (2014), *Photographic Architecture in the Twentieth Century*, Minneapolis: University of Minnesota Press.

Zucker, P. (1942–1943), 'The Humanistic Approach to Modern Architecture,' *The Journal of Aesthetics and Art Criticism*, 2 (7): 21–26.

Zucker, P. (1944), 'The Role of Architecture in Future Civilization,' *The Journal of Aesthetics and Art Criticism*, 3 (9–10): 30–38.

Zucker, P. (1945), 'The Aesthetics of Space in Architecture, Sculpture and City Planning,' *The Journal of Aesthetics and Art Criticism*, 4 (1): 12–19.

Zucker, P. (1946), 'Teaching History of Art in Our Visual Chaos,' *College Art Journal*, 4 (2): 98–105.

Zucker, P. (1951), 'The Paradox of Architectural Theories at the Beginning of the "Modern Movement",' *The Journal of the Society of Architectural Historians*, 10 (3): 8–14.

Zucker, P. (1959a), *A Platonic Discourse about Some Philosophical Problems of Art (X), between a Young Man, the Student (Y), and Paul Zucker, the Author (Z)*, New York: The Cooper Union Art School. New York.

Zucker, P. (1959b), *Town and Square. From the Agora to the Village Green*, New York: Columbia University Press.

Zucker, P. (1962), 'Popcorn, Pretzels & Rembrandt,' *Cooper Union Alumni News (Founder's Day Yearbook Issue)*, 25–27.

Zucker, P. (1963), *Styles in Painting. A Comparative Study*, New York: Dover Publications.

12

WIRELESS ARCHITECTURE

Robert Cummings's early radio broadcasts

John Macarthur and Deborah van der Plaat

Radio is not the most obvious medium for teaching architecture, yet 'the wireless' was historically important in the dissemination of modern architecture. This is because both radio and modernist architecture claimed to be part of the epoch of a technologically driven modernity. It is also the case that the wireless was a novel social technology – the use of radio broadcasts to a wide audience asked new questions about citizenship, education and culture, including architecture. The advent of broadcast radio in the 1920s and 1930s and the new forms of collective life and imagination that it made possible roughly coincide with the formal professionalisation of architecture and with its entry into the universities. In this chapter, we explore the early career of Robert Percy Cummings (1900–1989), the first professor of architecture at the University of Queensland, Australia and, probably, the first person in Australia to explain modernist architecture to the wider public in radio broadcasts from 1933. The Australian Broadcasting Commission (later Corporation) followed John Reith's model for the British Broadcasting Corporation as an independent public service and a training in liberal concepts of the citizen. The listener's ability to have and to share opinions about matters of which the whole nation was informed was understood to be a basis for political franchise in a democracy. In this model of liberal education, the arts and culture played a large role, connecting individual affects with shared cultural forms. That architecture played a role in this project along with aural forms such as music and literature is perhaps surprising. But it seems that the distance and abstraction of vocal descriptions of modern architecture, made it more accessible and less contentious than modernist music and poetry in the early 20th century. Cummings, again following British examples, saw speaking architecture on the wireless as building the social license for architecture's professionalisation and elevation from building trade to the university.

The archive of Cummings's talks

Cummings's radio talks were early parts of a repertoire of lectures, illustrated with slides when delivered in person, that he developed for four decades over his career from architect

DOI: 10.4324/9781003201205-17

and part-time technical college teacher, to university lecturer, leader of the professional institute and then foundation professor of architecture. Cummings's archive includes transcripts of some 80 lectures which were often reworkings of material around four themes: the principles and history of Architecture; the economics of housing; the civic functions of the Arts and its cultivation of the good citizen; and the necessity of a plan in a modern city and nation. Unfortunately, there are no known recordings. The passage of time and the success of the ideas that Cummings promoted mean that his talks appear to be plodding presentations of now familiar ideas (apart from the occasional praise in the 1930s of the Nazis and the Soviet Union on account of their central planning). His lectures are neither particularly original nor interesting in their manner of address, and it is noticeable how little his ideas developed in 40 years. They repeat the arguments for modernist culture as an historical inevitability and as an expression of a wider modernity, but Cummings tempers this with a careful nationalism, the idea that geography and climate ought to be causal in cultural formation and that a truly Australian architecture will come about. Modernity allows Cummings to suggest that there is a way to develop architecture in Australia despite its lack of historically developed built environment – building towards the future rather than out of the past. Meanwhile, the importance given in the series to the long history of Western architecture in far-away Europe suggests that this new architecture will not be too shocking and honour its British patrimony. If the lectures have a value now it is as useful documents of a time when architects such as Cummings were introducing a version of modernist architecture, one greatly mediated through British architectural discourse, to a conservative Australian public. The greater interest of the early radio lectures is not in their content in itself, but their medium, in the way that the novel technology enabling a "broad cast" of knowledge seems to have encouraged Cummings to seek a new relation between professional expertise, the university and the public's knowledge and appreciation of architecture as a civic virtue.

The archive of Cumming's lectures includes talks marked as being for radio and those for public speaking events which are annotated for slide projection. After Cummings was appointed to UQ, he built a substantial library of 2¼ square glass plate slides, largely copied from books, and later a 35-mm colour slide collection of his own photography on travels to Europe and America in the 1950s. These still exist, and it is possible to match images against some of the lectures. For the radio talks to schools in the 1930s, it is likely that booklets of images were made and circulated, but we have been unable to find copies of these. Undoubtedly, Cummings felt the deficits of wireless education, and in his first series in 1933, he spoke with enthusiasm of the coming of television, experimental broadcasts of which were on-going in Brisbane at the time[1] (Cummings 1933).

There is however little attempt in Cumming's wireless talks to describe in words the experience of architecture to make up for this spatio-visual deficit. Palazzo Strozzi is "expressive of strength, solidity and protection"; "Versailles shows the splendour and extravagance of the period" (Cummings 1936), and while "Functionalism can be overdone, but no one will deny that the simplicity of plain well-proportioned surfaces combined with the use of materials carefully selected for their texture and colour, give a distinctive quality of beauty" (Cummings 1936). The radio talks do not attempt the kind of ekphrasis that one might expect. They differ little from the public lectures with their notes for 'slide', where, we assume, Cummings left the script and spoke extempore to the image. For the listening public, there are a list of buildings, places, architects and stylistic terms, linked by concepts of social, climatic and technological determination. The wireless talks strip architecture back to questions of cultural competency, to the recognition of these names by the educated listener, and the impression given to others that it is necessary to gain cultural capital in architecture before one could understand and feel what Cummings's adjectives meant.

Cummings education and architectural education

The story of Cummings career (Cummings 1977) tells us how he came to be on the radio and also allows us to see that the logic of that engagement is not particular to him and tells us a wider story about architecture, modernity and the cultural mission of public broadcasting.[2] Born in Brisbane to a middle-class family, Cummings started his architectural career at age 14 working as a draftsman prior to enrolling in a building course at the Central Technical College (CTC) in 1916. CTC was essentially a trade school with part-time courses suiting working students, although it had a successful visual arts programme and, in 1918, began a diploma course in architecture. Queensland being a relatively poor state was late in founding its University in 1909 with limited degree courses and aspiring architects from wealthy families went to Sydney where architecture was taught in the University. Cummings graduated from CTC in 1923 and won the Wattle Day Scholarship which was intended to provide artistic education for Queenslanders in Britain.[3] Cummings chose to study at the Architectural Association (AA) in London, where several Australian and New Zealand servicemen had spent some time on demobilisation programmes in 1919, including Bruce Lucas who was by then teaching at CTC and was later to be Cummings's partner in practice (Willis 2013).

At the farewell held for Cummings at Finneys Café in 1924, the award was described by the architect and scholarship committee member, C F Whitecombe, as an opportunity for a Queensland architect to come into 'contact with the best of teachers and the most brilliant of students'. On his return, it was hoped that he would 'influence… all the young students which were to follow in his profession' (Anon 1924: 18–19). It was argued that such international exposure would help the local architectural community develop a style suited to its own unique needs.

Cummings entered the AA in September 1924 in the third year of a five-year course and graduated with a diploma and an Associate Membership of the Royal Institute of British Architects in 1927. In his second year, Cummings was awarded the Henry Jarvis Scholarship from the RIBA, and in 1927, he secured the prestigious Rome Scholarship in Architecture, with a competition design for "An Empire Centre in a Capital City". After a short visit to Queensland, he entered the British School at Rome where he devoted two years of his scholarship to research and restoration work and mixing with the painters, sculptors, engravers and art historians who made up the School. In 1929 and 1930, Cummings taught with Verner Rees, the AA third-year master, with the intention of teaching on his return to Brisbane. Rees was a part of the modernist faction in the ideological disputes at the AA at this time, and Cummings was influenced by him and Howard Robertson, author of influential books on architectural composition and Frank Yerbury, the School's secretary and photographer. Robertson and Yerbury's books later became part of Cumming's curriculum at UQ (Robertson 1924, 1932; Yerbury 1931). Cummings went to the 1925 *Exposition internationale des arts décoratifs et industriels modernes* in Paris where he would have seen Robertson's British Pavilion along with buildings by Mallet-Stevens, le Corbusier and Melinkov. In 1929, he joined Yerbury's tour of modern work in Germany (Anon 1929: 216). Robertson, by then Principal of the AA was one of Cummings's referees for his successful application for a post at UQ in 1935.[4]

When Cummings returned to Brisbane in December 1930, he arrived into a slow rolling controversy about architectural education. The State of Queensland had made architecture a registered profession in 1928, but there were concerns as to the quality of training, and in 1933, Leslie Wilkinson, Professor of Architecture at the University of Sydney, advised the national registration board not to accredit the CTC until it could be brought up to university standard (Freeland 1971). Cummings had been involved in meetings about an architecture course at The University of Queensland shortly after his return in 1931. By 1935, he was teaching some architecture courses in the Engineering faculty and became the first full-time Lecturer appointed to teach the diploma of architecture in 1937. Delayed by the war, Architecture finally became its own Faculty in 1949 and commenced its degree program in 1953, with Cummings taking the inaugural Chair in Architecture in 1955. Cummings not only led the formation of architecture at UQ, he managed the process by which CTC and UQ shared staff, students and facilities until each developed into distinct programmes and CTC became part of the new Queensland Institute of Technology in 1965, the year of Cumming's retirement.

In the 1930s, architecture was changing it social status and its status as form of knowledge. Legislation defining architecture as a 'closed' profession of registered experts was paralleled by its entry into the university as an intellectual discipline within the timeless universe of knowledge. Cummings's life work was to set up architectural education in a university context, where its claims to intellectual rigor could be validated and its potential socio-economic leadership established. Placing architectural education in the university was also a statement of social class, separating the architect from the builder and the apprenticeship and trade school night classes that were common and remained so while full-time university education was the province of the well-to-do.[5] From his own middle-class, trade school education, Cummings aimed to push architecture up the social hierarchy into the university, but also outward. The wireless talks are significant in showing that he considered professional education in the university as one part of a spectrum of the dissemination of architecture that spanned from the education of children to architecture as a form of civic knowledge that ought to be shared by all citizens. Cummings saw the education of the public in architecture as a process parallel to and underpinning registration, its social license. In a lecture to the New South Wales Institute of Architecture in 1950, he blamed the lack of success of registration in gaining greater control of the built environment by architects on a failure to build a broad public understanding of the value of architecture.

Wireless broadcast and Australia

Wireless telegraphy was becoming competitive in Australia around the turn of the 20th century, but it was some decades before voice radio could be broadcast to a wide audience. In Brisbane, the young Cummings may have heard experimental radio broadcasts, but the first full program on station 4QG did not commence until 27 July 1925 nearly a year after his departure for London (Carty n.d.). Unusually, 4QG was set up by the Government of Queensland in 1925 as a public broadcaster, preceding both the Australian Broadcasting Commission (1932) and its model the British Broadcasting Corporation (1927), although both had earlier lives as semi-public consortia of broadcasters. 4QG was subsumed into the ABC on the 1 July 1932 (Inglis 1983). Broadcasting was of compelling interest for its potential in socio-economic matters from education to crop and weather reports, and in Queensland, the somewhat dictatorial Premier William Forgan Smith used 4QG to cement the hegemony of his Labor party. Music dominated early radio but talks played an important role. Many of these were solicited from academics, and in its first years, the ABC set up committees at the state universities, at Queensland involving school principals, to shape the programming. The prominence of educative talks was part of radio's civilising mission, but it was also a result of the political pressure of newspaper proprietors to strictly limit news content, and even to control when the short news bulletins were read so as not to compete with evening newspapers (Inglis 1983: 13–14). These social and political uses of radio and its commercial repercussions should also be seen in the frame of geo-politics and the shifting structures of the British Empire. The British Government and the BBC saw the military strategic and cultural uses of radio as Empire matters, while Australia and the other "Dominions" of former settler colonies saw radio as a force for independent nationalism. The growing sense of national identity, within an expanded realm of international communication that radio fostered in Australia, was somewhat at odds with the Empire. Cummings adventures in radio need to be seen in this wider image of rapid technological change, rising nationalism, and the slow unravelling of the British Empire. His experience is perhaps typical of British educated Australian academics who spoke on the ABC, balancing deference to cultural patrimony with sense of what modernism and the wireless would bring. But Cummings's talks also give us an insight into how architecture played into the culture and politics of early broadcast.

Architecture on the BBC and at the AA

When Cummings arrived in London in September 1924, the BBC was the British Broadcasting Company, a nationalised consortium of radio manufacturers and the General Post Office which, in 1922, had grasped control of a potential clash of commercial broadcasters competing for frequencies. It was not to become the British Broadcasting Corporation with its public service mandate until 1 January 1927. Early broadcasts were made live from regional transmitters and to an extent focused on talks as the signal quality was not very good for music. Nevertheless, it is astonishing how much architecture was spoken about in the first decade of broadcast radio. The earliest notice of such a talk was Scottish Arts and Crafts architect George Washington Brown speaking to the topic "What about Architecture?" out of 5SG Glasgow on 18 December 1923. By the time Cummings left the UK, in late 1930, there are 175 talks which address architecture in BCC records.[6] Early significant talks were those of Professor CH Reilly who had set up the first university School of Architecture in Britain at Liverpool in 1904. Reilly spoke on 'Modern Architecture' out of Manchester in April and May 1925, then on the same topic from London in September 1925 largely opposing European modernists, but in a 1926 broadcast on Eric Mendolsohn, he had begun to change his mind (Powers 2000: 5). By 1926, there was capacity to relay signal, and Vernon Constable gave a series of seven lectures on the history of architectural styles from the Egyptians to the Renaissance that went out across England. Cummings's key teacher at the AA Howard Robertson made his first broadcast on the history of London buildings on 8 May 1925 from London 2LO.

Shundana Yusaf who has studied the sweep of the BBC's architecture talks from 1927 to 1945 states that: "Architecture-related topics were presented four and a half times more often than visual arts (painting and sculpture combined) and almost twice as often as literature" (Yusaf 2014: loc 1740). The BBC's emphasis on architecture is consistent with the first Director John Reith's aim for broadcast to be a training in citizenship, not so much imparting expert knowledge but ways and manners of thinking especially for the broader public who might otherwise be intimidated by expertise. Reith and the BBC drew on social liberal political philosophies in which self-improvement and personal freedom were the basis of redistributive politics of opportunity rather than material welfare (Yusaf 2014: loc 487). It was this same progressive cultural and social liberalism that drove the agenda of the principal architecture journal of the time the *Architectural Review* (Macarthur 2020). The accessibility of the built environment as a topic of description and conversation and architecture's combination of practical and aesthetic matters allowed for a story telling mode. Although the BBC's commissioned content was tightly scripted and edited by the Corporation, these were 'talks' rather than lectures and intended to have the familiar tone of a conversation in the home. Some critics of modernism such as Clough Williams-Ellis and Reginald Blomfield were invited onto the wireless to encourage listeners to take active points of view. Nevertheless, it is clear that the BBC was pushing modernism in all its forms, and arguments about modernist architecture being the outcome of technological change made it a crucial tool. Modernist architecture was a much more convenient vehicle for the BBC's view of cultural civics than the heat raised in discussion of modern literature or music.

In Cummings's last months at the AA, he would have listened to prominent teachers, and members of the AA make a detailed argument for modernism in the series "Today and Tomorrow in Architecture": over five successive Tuesday evenings in May and June with the BBC's magazine *The Listener* publishing a supplementary pictorial guide (Anon 1930b). Humphrey Pakington argued the limits of historical styles. Howard Robertson surveyed the modern architecture of Europe. Maurice Webb described the Chicago steel-framed skyscrapers. Harold Tomlinson, the economic efficiency of the new architecture, and RA Duncan concluded the series by arguing for modernist architecture as a necessary outcome of the forces of modernity that would lead to a culture that was scientific and collectivist.

Public intellectuals of many fields other than architecture spoke on the wireless, and for Cummings, the most significant of these was the art and culture critic Herbert Read who dominated the airwaves in 1930 with 51 Wednesday evening talks on art, culture and society. Read covered topics that included the work of individual historical and contemporary artists; art and manufacturing; Neolithic, naïve and children's art; psychoanalysis; architecture and sculpture; architecture and engineering; scholasticism and art; etc. Some of these talks became the basis for his book *The Meaning of Art* of 1931. Read's 1925 book *Education through Art* was an explicit revival of Frederick Schiller's 18th-century idea that personal growth through aesthetic awareness was necessary training in civic and political judgement. These ideas were widely understood in Brisbane. In 1941, the Art Gallery established art classes for children in which painter Vida Lay applied what she described as a 'universal language of art'. She explained her views at the University of Queensland Duhig lecture, 'The rudiments of the language of art', delivered in 1940. Her later pamphlet, *Art for All* (c.1946), made an urgent plea to combat the ugliness and monotony of the modern world through imagination and a pleasing environment. C M B Homrigh cited Read's *Art and Industry* in his Duhig Lecture 'Art – Its Place and Value in Education,' of 1946. Cummings placed a copy of Read's *Art and Industry* prominently in a photograph of his own attempt at industrial design, a Perspex-legged coffee table and milled aluminium ash-tray made later in Brisbane. When Cummings developed the curriculum of the UQ architecture school, Howard Robertson's book on modern architectural composition was the chief text book in design, and Read's *Art and Industry* was prominent in reading lists. We can surmise that Cummings's radio talks were inspired by his AA peers and teachers and that his plan to teach architecture at university included from the beginning a commitment to educate the public in a cultural citizenship that included architecture.

Cummings left London when the Depression was news, but building had not yet stopped and arrived in October 1930, a Brisbane with 30% unemployment and no work for architects. He expected some degree of acclaim from the profession and exhibited his Rome Prize drawings but experienced something of the "tall poppy syndrome", perhaps partly on account of the *moderne* stripped classical style of his project. His first public lecture after his return was in October 1931 to the progressive women's club the Lyceum. He spoke to the topic "Modern Tendencies in Architecture" (Cummings 1931). It was this lecture which became the culmination and high point of his six-part series on the history of architecture for the newly formed ABC going out on 4QG weekly in late October and November of 1933. From Cummings's notes, there seemed to have been 11 of the talks prepared for radio from 1933 to 1939, several repeated multiple times. The 1933 series was in the Evening programme intended for adult listening. The ABC's programme at the time was divided between evening programs for adults, with broadcasts for schools and light entertainment during the day. In 1935, he spoke of the "Importance of the Study of Art and Architecture" in the evening program and he spoke on architecture in broadcasts for senior high school students in Art and then again in series with Daphne Mayo and the painter Vida Lahey in 1937.

In the radio talks, Cummings argued that architecture was the 'matrix of civilization' (a phrase borrowed from William Lethaby) arguing that it had reflected the time and place of the society it served and was presently out of step with the 20th century. Nevertheless, Cummings consoled his audience with the admission that culture was an evolutionary process and (following Lethaby) that it was "impossible to ignore the traditions of its past". In terms of what he may have heard in Britain, the 1933 series combined the historical overview of Vernon Constable's 1927 BBC series with a compacted version of his AA teachers' series on modernism from 1930. Following the dominant British opinion, Cummings advocated Dutch and Scandinavian modernism for Australia despite his apparent interest in German and French modernism. He was particularly taken with Eric Mendelsohn's talks at the AA and on the BBC (Cummings 1977: 77), but Cummings students in the 1960s remember his lectures on modernism being "Dudock, Dudock, Dudock" (the architect Willem Marius Dudock),[7] and Cummings and Bruce Lucas's award winning First Church Christ Scientist, (1941) bears out the idea that he did not move on from this English version of Dutch brick modernism. Our interest in these talks, however, lies not in their content but their medium, the novelty of which made much of Cummings's argument for him. For most of Cummings's listeners, in 1933, it would have been the first time that they had heard architecture on the wireless and the first time they heard of modern architecture.

The earliest note of an Australian radio talk on architecture is of P A Oakley FRVIA speaking in 1928 on 3LO Melbourne.[8] In 1930, 2UW Sydney broadcast a series encouraging the aesthetic appreciation of architecture with Leslie Wilkinson, James Peddle, B J

Waterhouse, and James Nagle (Anon 1930a: 8). We have found mention of eight other talks in the 1930s. The most substantial seemed to have been a 1933 series on architecture and planning out of 6WF Perth. Also, in 1933, University of Sydney Professor Leslie Wilkinson gave a series for the University Extension Board on 2BL.[9] In New Zealand, in 1933, there was a series "An Introduction to the Understanding of Architecture" which included a lecture by the Professor RA Lippincott.[10] We can find no record of the content of any of these talks or series. Cummings was not alone in talking architecture on the wireless in 1933, but he was certainly among the first and has left us the only substantial record. In 1937, when the ABC set up its first national talks programme relayed to the "national" stations in each capital and their regional relay stations, Wilkinson the senior authority on architecture in the country gave the first lecture "Why not a Typical Australian House?" in a series "Architecture at Home and Abroad" (which has also left no record beyond its title). Cummings was not only early in getting himself on air, but it is also significant that he was as unusually junior to appear in public at this level when compared to Wilkinson or Lippincott in New Zealand. Wilkinson was a proponent of neo-Georgian architecture, and the idea of a Mediterranean style Australian house is most likely what his talk proposed. At a time when the question of what modern architecture should be was still a matter of what an appropriate style would be, Cummings spoke of structural rationalism, functionalism and Le Corbusier, even as he admitted, the latter was too radical for Queensland tastes. Given the fragmented wireless network in 1933, it is highly likely that neither Cummings nor the Queenslanders who listened to him knew that he was an outlier in Australia with his up-to-date London views.

How Cummings came to be on the radio is also interesting. He was already involved with the University having been appointed in 1932 to manage the University Public Examinations in Art for Schools when he was commissioned by Henry Alcock, McCaughey Chair of History and Economics at UQ later that year as part of a process where, in each State, committees were formed at universities involving academics and schools administrators to provide speakers for the nascent talks programs of the new ABC (Cummings 1977: 98). The UQ-based Educational Broadcast Committee was formed in November 1932 only months after the ABC was formed on 1 July. The committee was chaired by Alcock, and David Felsman was the ABC's talks organiser, but instrumental in the UQ committee as it developed was Bevil Molesworth, Lecturer in Economics who had previously run the University's extension for adult learning through the Workers Education Association from 1921 (Consandine 2000). Molesworth, a UQ graduate, became involved with the Workers' Education Association in Britain when undertaking post-graduate studies at Baliol College Oxford and was an early enthusiast for radio-based education. In 1934, Molesworth travelled to study the educational scope of radio and on his return published *Adult Education in England and America* in 1935, which had a particular focus on radio. He became the Queensland director of talks and then first ABC national director of talks in 1937. Cummings route to the air would have been similar to many other academics except that it happened early in Queensland on account of its Government radio station, the difficulties of providing education to its dispersed population and Molesworth and Cummings personal experience of the Reith-ian project.

Minutes of the UQ committee in 1933 contain a review of the first year and a note on the character of the talks and the kinds of lecturer to be invited. Personality, enthusiasm, accuracy and variety were sought. No one soliciting for appearances was to be accepted.

Professional radio presenters were banned, and any claims by influential persons to appear were not to be entertained. These minute comments are probably recording the words of Alcock. We get another sense of the significance of radio for the University at the time where Cummings describes the collegiate atmosphere he found there: "...the Professors were men of scholarship and standing, working not only in their specialised fields but in community organisations of Art, Theatre, Radio and other cultural activities" (Cummings 1977: 98). Cummings's enduring community interest was in the Art Gallery where he served as a Trustee and in other capacities for 30 years from 1937, so it is interesting in his 1967 reminiscences he puts Radio with Art.[11]

The autonomy of the ABC was of great concern to Alcock who was one of the academics around the ABC Chairman William James Cleary who were opposed to the extent of censorship of the Lyons Federal Government and adamant that the Commission be independent. The real or apparent politicisation of the ABC was a great concern then as now. In August 1937, Prime Minister Lyons was incensed that the ABC refused to broadcast Premier Forgan Smith and himself speaking at the opening of the Brisbane Agricultural Exhibition as Cleary had banned any talk by politicians to be broadcast so close to the election to be held in October (Thomas 1978). Cummings's British education, professional standing and, presumably, the personable, enthusiastic but authoritative voice that the committee desired, made him a suitable candidate to be invited onto the radio and subsequently into the University of Queensland where he was appointed lecturer 18 months later by a committee chaired by Alcock. No small part of that invitation to speak on the radio was his topic: architecture, providing a valuable demonstration to the public of technology driving social progress and cultural improvement, at a time when the University had decided to admit the profession to its halls.

There's an art to listening in...

We have argued that there is little of the experience of architecture in Cumming's talks, but we can conclude by considering what the experience of listening to such radio talks was like in the 1930s. We can recover some of the novelty of early radio listening by recalling odd facts, such as the need to instruct the public that they need not open their doors and windows to let the radio waves in (Inglis 1983: 7). In Australia, uniquely and bizarrely, from November 1923 to July 1924, wireless receivers were licensed and sold as 'sealed sets' pretuned to one frequency only so that the content was purchased with the receiver. Receivers and licenses were relatively expensive, and radio was not a universally accessible medium until the 1940s. In 1928, there were 270,000 licenses, or 4% of the population, but half of the licenses were in more closely settled Victoria where it is estimated that only 21% of households would have had a wireless receiver [Inglis 1983: 9]. More important was the fact that relation of speaker and listener was strikingly different to when it later became a ubiquitous medium.

Cummings's early talks were live to air from the top floor of the Taxation Building on George Street which was surmounted by two massive masts and strung aerials.[12] The broadcast audience was at once the totality of the public who were able to catch the signal, but also small groups gathered around the receiver, family and neighbours, school class rooms, lunch rooms in workplaces and so on. While the signal was geographic or even ionospheric for short-wave broadcasts, the voice of the broadcast talks was in a conversational tone and volume suited to the room.

The BBC and ABC insisted that talks be tightly scripted and read despite being a representation of extempore discussion. Molesworth described the delivery of the BBC news readers:

> The events of the day are not just read from a list. They are told as a tale by a friend—an intimate and sympathetic friend who is there to explain, to help and to educate. (And all in the best of English spoken in as delightful a voice as one could wish to hear.)
>
> *(Anon 1935a: 11)*

What is at stake here for early theorists of radio education is the problem of distracted listening, of the radio becoming a familiar background noise that could be soporific. Popular musical entertainment on the wireless was in serious competition with its role as an educational medium, but this extended beyond the content of programming, entertaining or educational to the mode of listening into which the wireless was training its listeners. The sonorous and intimate address of the talk's speaker could not by itself make for critical listening. As M J McDonald explained in *The Queenslander* in 1936, "There's an art in listening-in and the radio user must do his part – he can turn a programme into a stream of noise". The answer to this problem was 'listening groups'. Already a social experience, early radio listeners in groups could be made self-critical by being led and organised. This was Molesworth's important finding from his 1934 studies of the BBC, where from 1928 on, educated middle-class persons were being encouraged and trained to form listening groups who would meet in preparation prior to a broadcast talk and continue after to discuss it.

David Goodman has researched the history and character of these listening groups and the particular kind of civic education that they enacted (Goodman 2016a,b). The liberal political philosophy of public broadcast was set against the dangers of propaganda and of reinforcing existing viewpoints that arose from reading partisan newspapers. The membership of listening groups was intended to be heterogenous in background and opinion, and the topics of talks were to open points of argument. The groups were thus a training in individual critical thinking in a circumstance where judgements had to be articulated and differences respected. The leaders were not there to guide the group to a correct opinion but rather to inculcate the kinds of conduct desirable in a democracy. Brisbane's *Sunday Mail* in 1936 explained that 'The chief purpose of group discussion will be to stimulate individual thought on modern world affairs' (Anon 1936). Listening groups were finally part of the national talks program in 1939, and by 1944, there were nearly 4,000 people registered as members of groups, which went on to be a part of the ABCs activity until 1953 (Goodman 2016b: 635). This then is the ethos of the radio talk in the period. Cummings's talks on architecture shared a space with topics like "Will the World Follow the Soviets?" While architecture may have been a less useful topic than geo-politics in training in democratic debate, this is the context that we seek to recover in this chapter – a moment when architecture was climbing into the ivory tower of academe it was also attempting to be a part of civic education.

Queensland educators and broadcasters were well aware of listening groups before they were officially begun with the national talks programme in 1939. The *Brisbane Telegraph*, which was particularly keen on listening groups, in 1930, reported that the BBC had 700 listening groups for its talks programme (Anon 1930a: 3). In March 1933, *The Telegraph* reported Reith's address to the third National Conference of Group Leaders and Group

Listeners. Brisbane's *The Week*, in 1933, interviewed Major W T Conder, the Manager of the one-year old ABC, and expressed frustration that he would not commit to forming listening groups (Anon 1933: 6). In 1936, ABC staff were sent to workplaces in the southern state of Victoria to organise listening groups around lunchtime broadcasts, but there is no record of this in Queensland. *The Telegraph* made a long report of Molesworth's findings on adult education and listening groups on his return in 1934, and a very flattering profile in 1937 as he was leaving Brisbane following his appointment as national Broadcast talks controller (Anon 1935a: 16). In 1933, prior to Moleworth's visit to Britain and the USA, he reported to the UQ Education Broadcast Committee about the idea of 'listening circles' and the need to investigate them.

There is no record of listening groups being formed for Cummings 1933 series or his later radio talks. It is curious, however, that when the Adelaide *News* advocated listening groups in 1931, its principal example was the BBC's "Today and Tomorrow in Architecture," the series commissioned from the AA in 1929–1930 that Cummings would have heard. The *News* reported "two of the speakers in the series arranged a lecture with lantern slides of the buildings mentioned. It attracted a large audience of those who had listened to the broadcast" (Anon 1931: 9). There were certainly listening groups for Cummings, Mayo and Lahey's schools talks, guided by teachers trained in the art curriculum, with books and some special visual guides. We do not know if formal listening groups were formed for Cummings evening lectures for adults, certainly, it was within the aims and means of the local Workers Educational Association (WEA 1923) in which Molesworth was active and the CTC Diploma Course in architecture which ran evening classes. But we could also imagine the informal setting of a middle-class improving family gathered around the wireless with a family friend who was an architect or builder, prepared to guide a conversation aided by a copy of Banister Fletcher's *A History of Architecture on the Comparative Method*. Cummings talks can read as dry and a little condescending, heavy with names and an intention to impress on the listener the importance of architecture and those with knowledge about it. But in the discourse of the time, it is clear that the talk was intended as only part of wireless education, and there is no reason to doubt that some listeners connected Cummings words with their lived experience of the built environment, a disposition to culture and an imagination of a better world. Arguably, what was most at stake in Cummings's wireless talks is not architecture, but the shifting relation of common knowledge and licensed expertise that broadcast brought about. At the same time that a detailed examinable knowledge became a legislated requirement to practice as an architect, architecture also became something that the educated public should be able to make judgments about in a liberal democracy.

Notes

1 Val McDowell made the first TV broadcast in Australia in Brisbane in 1929 and was making experimental broadcasts at the time of Cummings's lectures. McDowell was broadcasting daily for an hour from 1935 when Cummings was on air.
2 Also see: Sinnamon (2007); Rowe (2011); Carty n.d. and van der Plaat (2012).
3 The first of the Wattle Day scholarships had gone to the sculptor Daphne Mayo in 1919. Cummings worked with Mayo and the painter Vida Lahey in radio talks for the school curriculum and in the foundation of the Queensland Art Gallery. His advocacy for architecture in the arts is the subject of a paper in preparation by the present authors.
4 Applications for the Lectureship in Architecture, Notes for the Assistance of the Vacation Committee of the Senate prepared by H Alcock, n.d, The University of Queensland Archives.

232 John Macarthur and Deborah van der Plaat

5 While not a part of the university system, the Architectural Association School of Architecture was heavily class marked by its full-time curriculum and was the destination of Oxbridge graduates wishing to study architecture, such as Geoffrey Scott had before WWI. See Cunningham (2001).

6 We have consulted the archive of the BBC Radio Times. Available at https://genome.ch.bbc.co.uk

7 Rex Addison, a student of Cummings in the 1960s, in person communication.

8 The ABC's records and the *Australian Wireless Weekly* are not conveniently searchable as the BBC's archives. Nevertheless, with the assistance of ABC archives staff (thanks Guy Tranter) and Trove's searchable newspaper archive, it is possible to have a good impression of architecture on the wireless in Australia in the 1930s. Oakley's talk was reported in the *Otago Daily Times*, as New Zealand took shortwave relays of Melbourne stations (thanks Robin Skinner). Other early talks that we have found include: In March 1931. Frank Heyward FRAIA spoke on to Tasmania on "Architecture in the Home". In 1933, the *Daily News* of Perth reports plans for radio talks including architecture and town planning; and that year, E Cohen spoke on "The Style of Architecture as applied to modern building" and R Summerhayes spoke on "Domestic Architecture" on 6WF out of Perth. Walter Bunning spoke on "Design in Architecture" in December 1939, out of 2BL, and may have continued to appear, but the next record we can find of him is in 1944 talking about training in Town planning for architects in the post-war era. There were early architecture broadcasts in New Zealand, Stanley W Fearn ARIBA in 1928. Prof R K Knight in 1931, and in 1933, R A Lippincott was a speaker in series "An Introduction to the Understanding of Architecture".

9 The Maitland Daily Mercury Wed 8 March 1933, p. 3; "British Architecture in the 19th C" Radio Programmes, Manawatu Standard, 8 March 1933, p. 4. Professor L H Wilkinson will tell listeners about "Architecture", No. 2, "British Architecture in the 19th century" (thanks Robin Skinner).

10 'Broadcasting', Stratford Evening Post, 25 August 1932, p. 8.

11 Cummings role in the visual arts in Brisbane from his early associations with Mayo and Lahey is the subject of another paper under preparation by the present authors. Cummings other great interest was bush walking and nature conservation through his long association and work for Binna Burra Lodge in the Lamington National Park.

12 The ABC set up its first recording facilities in Sydney in 1935. Carty "Australian Radio Time Lines" Cummings writes that he later recorded lectures at the ABC's Queen Street studios, but it is unclear what years those were Cummings (1977: 98–99).

References

Anduaga Egaña, Aitor. 2009. *Wireless and Empire Geopolitics, Radio Industry, and Ionosphere in the British Empire, 1918–1939.* Oxford and New York: Oxford University Press, 2009.

Anon. 1924. "Wattle League's Farewell." *Courier Mail*, Tuesday 1 July.

Anon, 1929. *The Architectural Association Journal*, vol. XLV, no. 512, October.

Anon. 1930a. *Telegraph*, Tuesday 3 March.

Anon. 1930b. *The Listener*, April.

Anon. 1931. *News*, Adelaide, Monday 27 July.

Anon. 1933. *Week*, Brisbane, Wednesday 21 June.

Anon. 1935a. "Cinema and Radio 'Queensland Lagging Behind'." *Telegraph* Brisbane, Tuesday 15 January.

Anon. 1935b. *Telegraph*, Tuesday 15 January, p. 11.

Anon. 1936. "ABC to Introduce Discussion Group Broadcasts." *Sunday Mail* (Brisbane), July 5,10.

Anon. 1937. *Telegraph*, Saturday 22 May, p. 16.

Carty, Bruce. n.d. *Australian AM Radio History*. Self-published PDF available internet.

Consandine, Marion. 2000. "Molesworth, Bevil Hugh (1891–1971)." *Australian Dictionary of Biography*, National Centre of Biography, Australian National University.

Cummings, Robert Percy. 1933. "Modern Tendencies in Architecture." Unpublished lecture, Cummings Archive, Private Collection.

Cummings, Robert Percy. 1936. "Some Aspects of Present Day Architecture." Unpublished lecture, 25th June 1936, Cummings Archive, Private Collection.

Cummings, Robert Percy. 1937. "The Renaissance." ABC Radio talk to Senior Students 4QG 9th February 1937, Unpublished lecture, Cummings Archive, Private Collection.

Cummings, Robert Percy. 1977. "Mostly from the Diaries of R P Cummings." Unpublished manuscript, Fryer Library, The University of Queensland, F2350.

Cunningham, Colin. 2001. "A Case of Cultural Schizophrenia: Ruling Tastes and Architectural Training in the Edwardian Period." *Architectural History* 44 (Essays in Architectural History Presented to John Newman): 64–81.

Fletcher, Banister. 1905. *A History of Architecture on the Comparative Method: For the Student, Craftsman & Amateur.* 5th ed. rev. and enl. ed. London: Batsford.

Freeland, J M. 1971. *The Making of a Profession: A History of the Growth and Work of the Architectural Institutes in Australia.* Sydney: Angus & Robertson.

Goodman, David. 2016a. "A Transnational History of Radio Listening Groups 1: The United Kingdom and United States." *Historical Journal of Film, Radio and Television* 36, no. 3: 436–465.

———. 2016b "A Transnational History of Radio Listening Groups II: Canada, Australia and the World." *Historical Journal of Film, Radio and Television* 36, no. 4: 627–648.

Inglis, K S. 1983. *This Is the ABC The Australian Broadcasting Commission 1932–1983.* Melbourne: The University of Melbourne Press.

Macarthur, John. 2020. "The Smell of Politics: Hubert De Cronin Hastings and Liberalism in Architectural Discourse." *GTA Papers 4: Grand Gestures,* no. 4: 22–45.

Macarthur, John, & Deborah van der Plaat. 2012 "Cummings, Robert." In *The Encyclopaedia of Australian Architecture,* edited by Philip Goad and Julie Willis, 184–185. Port Melbourne, Vic., Australia: Cambridge University Press.

McDonald, M J. 1936. "There's an Art in Listening-in and the Radio User must do His Part–He can Turn a Programme into a Stream of Noise." *Queenslander,* Thursday 24 September, p. 11.

Minutes of the Broadcast Talks Committee. 1934. University of Queensland Archive.

Molesworth, B. H. 1935. *Adult Education in America and England.* Melbourne: Melbourne University Press.

Moreno, Joaquim, Tim Benton, and Nick Beech. 2018. *The University Is Now on Air, Broadcasting Modern Architecture.* Edited by d'Architecture Centre Canadien. Heijningen: Montréal: Jap Sam Books, Canadian Centre for Architecture.

Potter, Simon J. 2008. "Who Listened When London Called? Reactions to the BBC Empire Service in Canada, Australia and New Zealand, 1932–1939." *Historical Journal of Film, Radio and Television: BBC World Service, 1932–2007: Cultural Exchange and Public Diplomacy* 28, no. 4: 475–487.

Potter, Simon J. 2020. *Wireless Internationalism and Distant Listening: Britain, Propaganda, and the Invention of Global Radio, 1920–1939.* First edition. ed. Oxford: Oxford University Press.

Powers, Alan. 2000. "C. H. Reilly: Regency, Englishness and Modernism." *The Journal of Architecture* 5, no. 1: 47–64.

Read, Hebert. 1919. *Art and Industry: The Principles of Industrial Design.* London: Faber and Faber.

Read, Herbert. 1925. *Education through Art.* London: Faber and Faber.

Read, Herbert. 1931. *The Meaning of Art.* Harmondworth: Penguin

Robertson, Howard. 1924. *The Principles of Architectural Composition.* London: Architectural Press

Robertson, Howard. 1932. *Modern Architectural Design.* London: The Architectural Press.

Rowe, Charles. 2011."Robert Percy Cummings and the Story of Queensland Architecture." The University of Queensland.

Schiller, Friedrich. 1967 [1794]. *On the Aesthetic Education of Man.* Translated by E M Wilkinson and LA Willoughby. Oxford: Oxford University Press.

Sinnamon, Ian. 2007 "Cummings, Robert Percy (1900–1989)." *Australian Dictionary of Biography,* vol. 17 (Melbourne: Melbourne University Press), 280–281.

Thomas, Alan. 1978. "The Politicisation of the ABC in the 1930s: A Case Study of 'the Watchman'." *Politics* 13, no. 2: 286–295.

Willis, Julie. 2013. "The Architectural Association and the Architectural Atelier." *Proceedings of the Society of Architectural Historians, Australia and New Zealand:* 30, Open, Griffith University, Gold Coast.

Workers' Educational Association of Queensland. 1923. *What the W.E.A. Is.* Brisbane: The Association.

Yerbury, F. R. 1931. *Modern Dutch Buildings: With Photographs Specially Taken by the Author.* London: Ernest Benn.

Yusaf, Shundana. 2014. *Broadcasting Buildings: Architecture on the Wireless, 1927–1945.* Cambridge, MA: The MIT Press.

13

THE CAPTIVE LECTURER

James Benedict Brown

This chapter is a critical reflection on my relationship as a university teacher with the act of recording one's teaching. While this chapter was conceived before the Covid-19 pandemic as a history of lecture capture in the university, it has necessarily evolved as a result of the highly changed circumstances under which it has been written. The personal and the professional have become conflated. Before the pandemic, I actively hampered attempts to record my teaching. I forcibly turned wall-mounted cameras away from the room, affixed post-it notes on camera lenses and unplugged microphones. Now, I am taking steps to actively (and perhaps permanently) record my teaching for dissemination in non-linear and non-traditional form.

The pre-history of video in and of the university is one of the fascinating pedagogical experiments. Hidden in the service ducts of Denys Lasdun's 1960s' campus for the University of East Anglia (UEA), the university deployed a closed-circuit television network to broadcast science experiments and lectures directly from laboratories and studios into students' accommodation (Sanderson 2002: 116). The Open University (OU), meanwhile, extended the reach of the university nationwide, using late-night off-air hours of broadcast television channels to transmit learning materials from the new city of Milton Keynes to students all over the country. The recent reappraisal of the design courses delivered by the OU by the Canadian Centre for Architecture (CCA, 2018) has prompted historians of architectural education to explore the formative role of lecture capture and its precedents in design education.

But whereas these early uses of video were driven by pedagogical and political agendas, the more recent history of video in the university can be read as a feature of the spread of neoliberalism in higher education. This chapter avoids charting a material evolution of the technology, the technology, but instead explores the ways in which ways in which both technology and pedagogy have driven forward the creation of new hybrid spaces of learning, in which the apparent materialities and immaterialities of on- and off-line spaces are merged.

DOI: 10.4324/9781003201205-18

The camera in the classroom

Lecture capture is a broad term for technology that facilitates the digital recording, archiving and dissemination of lectures. Lecture capture allows students to watch and re-watch teaching events anywhere with an internet connection in their own time and at their own pace. As the technology began to become established in higher education, Whatley and Ahmad (2007) demonstrated that summary video lectures could possibly support students' learning as part of a hybrid in-person and online education. When James Kadirire surveyed the landscape of lecture capture technologies in 2011, a number of competing software platforms were already available, including Echo 360, Panopto, Camtasia Relay, Mediasite and Tegrity (Kadirire 2011). These platforms competed to offer education providers with the most unified user-experience, offering automatic recording of classroom teaching through multi-track video recordings taken from cameras, the visual material being projected by the teacher and the dialogue between teacher and student captured by microphones. The rapid pace of technological development in video, audio and data processing technologies all contributed to increased possibilities of the medium. The quality of digital cameras increased while the average cost decreased. The availability and speed of server storage made the archiving of large video files more practical. Most importantly, the quality and market penetration of consumer laptops, tablets and smartphones improved rapidly, allowing students to access recorded lectures on a variety of devices and in almost any location.

Lecture capture prompted an existential crisis in teachers who advocated – perhaps uncritically – the perceived superiority of proximal learning. What if no-one comes to my lecture? Will students skip my early morning classes? Will the provision of recorded lectures lead to a noticeable reduction in student attendance in class? Or will the additional engagement offered by digital tools in classrooms (such as audience response clickers) help to restore attendance interaction and learning?

The impetus towards expanding lecture capture was driven by favourable student feedback. A 2014 study of pharmacy students in a Canadian university that analysed user analytics of recorded lectures and surveys of staff and students found that while faculty did not make a particular active educational use of their recorded lectures, students did (Marchand, Pearson and Albon 2014). Lecture capture provides students with opportunities for alternative, even heightened, engagement in learning. By studying the viewing statistics of lectures that were recorded over two years using lecture capture as part of an undergraduate economics course at a British university, Elliott and Neal (2016) isolated data that indicated the number of distinct students who watched recordings, the frequency with which they watched recordings, the average length of viewings as well as the time of the day when lectures were viewed. They concluded that students value lecture recordings, making more extensive use of the recordings than had previously been identified. But amidst a field of emerging pedagogical research that attributed either increased student attainment or reduced student engagement to the technology of lecture capture, the implementation of the technology became a point of confrontation between teachers and the academy.

The author in the classroom

In 2015, I started working in a large multi-faculty post-1992 university.[1] Thirty years earlier, while I was still a child, the Jarratt Report had articulated how universities should begin to operate like corporate enterprises, aiming for efficiency in the production of graduates and demonstrating value for money. In the three decades before I joined the university as a teacher, higher education in Britain had travelled far down to the path towards marketisation and privatisation. Enrolling in an architecture degree in 2001, I had been amongst the first cohorts of students to pay tuition fees for my university education. As I completed a Master's degree and continued into doctoral research, the role of the universities was changing. Under the administrations of both Conservative and Labour governments, universities were shifting their focus from educating students to developing competencies in future workers, reproducing neoliberal capitalist relations of production (Maisuria and Cole 2017). In 2009, oversight of universities in Britain was re-allocated from the government Ministry of Education to the Department for Business, Innovation and Skills. Prospective students were now encouraged to think of themselves as consumers choosing from the different products of competing departments and universities (Vernon 2018).

The consequences for my job as a university teacher were profound. As a Lecturer and then Senior Lecturer, I spent about as much time on in-class teaching as I did on student recruitment activities, delivering dozens of open-day presentations and interviewing applicants. The recruitment process was a bizarre indictment of the marketised university. The Conservative government of David Cameron had removed the cap on university recruitment, meaning that higher education institutes were now free to enrol as many students as we (or rather our management) wanted. While this was presented to voters as the administration of a kind of social justice, the real motivation of these marketising reforms was '(i) the expansion of the market to have a greater number of consumers; and linked to this, (ii) the fact that individual providers of HE are pitted more directly in competition in a dog-eat-dog environment where, in the conditions of reduced government funding, the losers that fail to attract ever increasing numbers of students will be susceptible to closure' (Maisuria and Cole 2017: 606). Few of our prospective students realised that they held all the cards. Many had travelled hundreds of miles, chosen their best clothes and presented often beautiful (and always laboriously prepared) portfolios of their creative work from secondary education without knowing that if I rejected an applicant, the decision would be reviewed personally (and likely revoked) by the Dean of Faculty. I was not interviewing these young people: rather, I had been instructed to sell our course and our university to them in order to try and persuade them to enrol here instead of with any of our competitors. The 2017 Teaching Excellence Framework (TEF) was on the horizon, and the importance of recruiting, retaining and satisfying students was being impressed on us. We responded by recruiting more students, retaining more students who might otherwise have failed modules and courses and working harder to satisfy their expectations of this consumerist experience.[2]

In 2015, the British government announced a reduction in the state subsidy for the Disabled Students Allowance (DSA). The change meant that, from the start of the 2016/2017 academic year, universities rather than central government were responsible for funding the provision of support for disabled students, including classroom notetakers, scribes and proof-readers (Havergal 2016). In response to these changes, my employer announced a wide-reaching initiative that required lecturers to use classroom technology to video-record all their teaching (Grove 2016). This initiative, which was facilitated by a £110 million bond to be invested in new buildings and new technologies, was billed as an opportunity to widen participation and remove barriers to engagement in higher education. British universities were looking for new ways to distinguish themselves in a crowded marketplace of higher education provision. The adoption of new technologies in the classroom was one way in which universities could attract students, with our proprietary video platform appearing in promotional materials and undergraduate prospectuses. But the initiative provoked a dispute between the University and the trades union representing academic staff. The dispute centred on the refusal of the university to guarantee that recordings would not be used for the purposes of performance management. The intellectual rights of lecturers were also unclear. Once recorded and archived, a lecture was the property of the University; yet, the teacher appeared to remain liable for its content including, for example, copyright infringement through the use of music or video in a lecture (*ibid.*). These disputes centred on authorship, but they were set against a diminishing landscape of employment terms and conditions. The ratio of teachers to students in British universities had declining for many years: from one teacher for every 10 students in 1980 to one for every 12 in 1990 and one for every 17 in 2000. Teacher salaries had remained stagnant in real terms over the same period (Vernon 2018: 272–273). My employer's excursion into the bond market had leveraged our financial position beyond any previous precedent. Through my recruitment activities, I knew that the recruitment and retention of students was essential for our continued financial security. Lecture capture appeared to many teachers to be another way to drive financial efficiencies from academic workers. The university could employ a teacher for one hour but capture that academic labour for limitless reproduction and re-use.

The peculiar spatial requirements of architectural education provided my colleagues and I with a brief stay of execution. The Royal Institute of British Architects (RIBA) mandates that 50% of the curriculum of a professionally validated course must be delivered through 'design studio projects' (Brown 2020). On a pedagogical level, our unpredictable and often unscheduled flow between individual and group tutorials, desk-crits and wall-crits, independent and directed study all made video recording of sessions impossible. Our open-plan studios were not conducive to the cameras and microphones, all of which had been designed with axial classrooms and lecture theatres in mind.

A survey of lecture capture policies in 149 British universities between 2015 and 2016 found a marked increase in the number of HEIs using some form of lecture capture (Ibrahim, Howarth and Stone 2020). Whereas 31% of British universities surveyed in 2011/2012 had some form of provision, policy or plan to develop lecture capture, by 2014/2015, this had risen to 75%. Justifications given by HEIs included student demand, the pedagogical benefits of lecture capture for revision and obligation to meet the needs of students with learning or language difficulties. There was extensive evidence of other British universities, like mine, employing technologies known as lecture capture as a solution to the reduction in state aid for students with disabilities as well as an important mechanism to meet statutory obligations.

The confrontation between the academy and its faculty members regarding intellectual property and performance evaluation was problematised by the way in which the hardware appeared when staff returned from the summer vacation. Lecture capture entered the classroom suddenly, borrowing hardware and technologies first developed for fly-on-the-wall television. In the phraseology of the union dispute, these small devices not only represented an Orwellian Big Brother but they also physically resembled the cameras used by the syndicated TV show *Big Brother* to discretely capture the interactions and dialogue between candidates who had auditioned to spend their several months living under a perpetual televisual gaze. Norman K. Denzin theorised the effects of cinema on the voyeuristic gaze in society (Denzin 1995), and it was not long before others began to recognise the voyeuristic implications of reality television (Baruh 2009). The cameras used in reality television were controlled remotely by the editors, producers and directors who exercised editorial control. When *Big Brother* first appeared on Dutch and then British television screens, the fully enclosed sets in which participants lived for the duration of the broadcast were constructed with hidden passages in the walls, wide enough for a camera operator and studio camera to be manoeuvred behind a pane of one-way glass. The material space of the *Big Brother* house was a mediated construction, a kind of pseudo-space not of genuine inhabitation but of continual surveillance and performativity. The hidden nature of the camera placed participants in uncertain fields of view, with no way of knowing precisely where the camera was pointed. As camera technology evolved over successive seasons of *Big Brother*, the materiality of surveillance was compressed, and the walls regained more familiar depth. Individual cameras no longer needed human operators on set. They could be hung from the ceiling and could be operated remotely, turning and pivoting with the use of small motors. A new generation of reality and so-called 'scripted reality' television entertainment was on the horizon, with small motorised and remote-controlled pan-tilt-zoom (PTZ) cameras entering the space of the doctor's surgery (*GPs: Behind Closed Doors*, Channel 5, 2014 to date), the veterinarian (*The Supervet*, Channel 4, 2014 to date) and the zoo (*The Secret Life of the Zoo*, Channel 4, 2006 to date). Hanging or sitting in corners of workplaces and consultation rooms, these devices had less in common with television cameras used to broadcast (literally, to *cast* broadly) and more in common with closed-circuit security cameras used to police behaviour and record misdemeanour for retrospective sanction. As camera technology advanced, so too did video storage. Cameras no longer filled cassette tapes. Hard drives and servers displaced the materiality of video storage and access to some unseen and inaccessible server room.

In the university, however, the technology was not so sophisticated. The lecturer was obliged to use a software interface to press 'record' and that was it. Most cameras were installed in a fixed position, directed towards the lectern or the front of the classroom. This led to the problematic rule that, in many teaching spaces, teachers were forbidden to move away from the lectern. The field-of-vision of the camera and reach of the microphone were so limited that they could not capture itinerant teachers, often the ones who worked hardest to engage their students by moving throughout the teaching space. While employing the very latest technological developments in hardware and software, my university was an early adopter of technology that did not yet have the capacity to move or follow its subject. Lecture capture could not reflect the unpredictable spatial relationships of critical pedagogy, in which teachers and students collaborate to challenge the implicit student–teacher dynamic embodied by the front-facing classroom. As high-end equipment from television had trickled down into academia, so too were rapid developments in camera technology spreading in the consumer market. As action cameras such as the GoPro became ever smaller and ever more adaptable, so too peripheral devices like drones and handheld gimbles gave producers of web video cameras that could follow and track movements. Inquiries as to this possibility in our classrooms were rejected: the university had invested in these cameras, and we were to stand where we were told.

Without the certainty that recordings of lectures and interactions between teachers and students would not be used for performance evaluation or disciplinary procedures, the material presence of these small devices represented an immaterial presence in the classroom.

The recording was preserved in servers and backed up in ways that the teacher could not erase. The interactions between teacher and student were liable to remain on record *ad infinitum*. The content being delivered and the manner in which it was being delivered were eligible for judgment not only against contemporary standards but also those as-yet unimagined in the future. The presence of the camera and the instant and eternal availability of every lecture not only invoked Bentham's *panopticon* but also contributed to an emergent culture of self-policing. Teachers and students were reminded of the analogy by the name of the lecture capture software we used: *Panopto*.

Although my teaching duties were centred on the design studio, I was not excused from the obligation to engage with lecture capture. University policy dictated that, in the first year of operation, first-year undergraduate lectures must be recorded. Subject to a successful first year, lecture capture would be extended to other groups. I chose the path of mischievous resistance. If possible, I took the opportunity to the turn wall-mounted cameras in such a way that they could not see me or my students. Post-it notes would mysteriously find their way onto camera lenses. Microphones (if shoogled in just the right way) would become detached from their bases. The use of certain software packages foiled the ability of Panopto to record what was being projected on screen. I reminded my students of the importance of good attendance in class and the anecdotal evidence that students with better attendance achieved better grades. These tactics might have led me to some kind of chastisement, but I never found out. Towards the spring of 2017, I resigned.

The camera in the bedroom

I was in my first year as an Associate Professor in Umeå University in northern Sweden when, in the first quarter of 2020, everything changed (Jandrić et al. 2000; Crosbie and Salama 2020). In the months immediately after the closure of university campuses due to the coronavirus pandemic, I wrote how colleagues in my discipline had passed through all five stages of the Kübler-Ross model of grief: denial, anger, depression, bargaining and acceptance (Kübler-Ross 1969). I wrote:

> we spent the first two months of the year in a politically-sanctioned period of denial. When it became apparent that the virus was not contained to a specific geographic region or demographic, our governments instigated restrictions and our universities closed. At that point, we entered the phase of anger. Some made it to bargaining and then depression. Those who made it out the other side are emerging with a lukewarm glow of acceptance: we are all distance educators now.
>
> *(Brown 2020)*

The initial reaction of those in education was generally focused on the application of unfamiliar technologies to existing pedagogical structures. We also had to re-appraise our relationship with the quotidian technology we had all begun to take for granted. Apart from occasional international Skype calls, few of us were familiar with the capacity of the computer to connect us visually with an entire class. Many of my students and colleagues had followed the recommendations of tech bloggers, journalists and even the FBI director Mark Comey who, in 2016, admitted to sticking tape over his laptop's webcam (Kaste 2016). Our cameras were unharnessed, the sticky residue of black electrical tape rubbed away in confusion and disbelief. Teachers and students alike had to quickly familiarise themselves with previously obscure software packages such as Zoom and Microsoft Teams.

The first instinct for teachers was to try and restore a sense of continuity, re-creating material spaces of learning in an immaterial realm. But serious social and psychological frontiers were collapsing both for teachers and students. Jesse Stommel writes how:

> The boundaries between the personal and the professional have blurred. Some of our most private spaces are now on camera. Some of our most private moments are recorded: joys, tragedies, exhaustion, bewilderment. And our children, animals, and partners are surprise guests for meetings, classes, and keynotes ... When our cat died of hypertrophic cardiomyopathy in July, I could not keep that loss private – because so much of my public life has been let into my home.
>
> *(Stommel 2020a)*

Students, meanwhile, were no less spared from the effects of this intrusion to their personal spaces. In the United States of America, academics reported the widespread incidence of students joining online classes from inside their cars. Student bodies and non-profits promoting access to education report that students in low-income households, with poor internet connectivity or close proximity to family members in substandard accommodation are increasingly driving to public WiFi hotspots and studying in car parks (Flaherty 2020).

For many educators and academic administrators, the live video connection between student and teacher was a requirement to demonstrate active engagement in class. The inequalities these demands reveal and heighten students' vulnerabilities. The right of teachers to require that students turn on their cameras during synchronous online teaching versus the right of students not to do so is an emergent concern, one that is different from yet that also echoes the concerns of lecturers forced to record their lectures. Can we or should we compel our students to turn on the camera? Stommel wrote elsewhere:

> Many students face very specific challenges at home: housing insecurity, domestic violence, lack of access to internet or other technology, physical disability, chronic and acute illness. We can't assume all students (or staff) can simply join our communities from home. We have to build with an understanding of these challenges and, even where learning remains fully (or mostly online), we have to continue to make space on college campuses for students who have no other homes from which to "shelter" in place.
>
> *(Stommel 2020b)*

While the Covid-19 pandemic prompted a rapid take up of distance learning technologies, their emergence in the preceding two decades did not go unnoticed. A rich seam of academic practice is documented by theorists who defined the evolution from critical pedagogies (in the tradition of Paulo Freire, Henry Giroux, bell hooks, etc.) to critical digital pedagogies. In *An urgency of teachers: The work of critical digital pedagogy*, Sean Michael Morris writes about the mutuality of teacher and student presence in the classroom, regardless of whether it formed through a video connection or not. The teacher's presence

> ... is not simply showing up to call on raised hands, answer questions, or deliver PowerPoint lectures. Presence is human, all-too human, because education is human, and

learning is a problem that humans must solve. And a teacher's presence must welcome students' presence so that the community can begin to answer the questions education demands we address.

(Morris and Stommel 2018)

Invoking the principles of critical pedagogy – that student and teacher are co-creators of the curriculum and co-learners in the classroom – it became possible to imagine that while everything had changed, we had to find a way to show our students that we still had that same connection.

Teaching design online

In the northern spring of 2020, architecture schools around the world moved from their teaching from proximate to distance, and the signature pedagogy of the design studio had to be dragged along with them. The Covid-19 pandemic accelerated the confrontation between architecture educators and the possibilities of online learning. In *Educating the Reflective Practitioner* (1987), Donald Schön refers to the four learning constructs of design studio. Setting Schön's learning constructs to one side, I prefer to describe design studio in architecture education as a conflation of four very different dimensions. First, the design studio is a physical space in the university. Second, the design studio is a period of time in the teaching calendar: an indeterminate catchall for the time when a student is expected to be present and engaging in either self-directed or directed learning. Third, the design studio can be understood as a large field of both teaching method and pedagogies. These are not the same thing. The fourth and final characteristic dimension of the design studio is its culture (Brown 2020). It is a mistake to assume that *physical* presence is required in all four dimensions of the design studio. Lev Vygotsky's concept of a *zona blizhaishego razvitiia* (zone of proximal development, ZPD) is easily misinterpreted by studio advocates as a physical space in which the student, through close supervision by the teacher, becomes capable of demonstrating new skills without assistance. Vygotsky's ZPD suggests that there is a conceptual distance between what a student cannot do, what she can do with the support of a more knowledgeable other and what she can do unaided. It is easy to read Donald Schön's celebration of the architecture design studio and draw the conclusion that this is the ideal environment in which a student can make their own path between what cannot and can be done, thanks to the physical proximity of the tutor and fellow students, both of whom can look over her shoulder and offer opinions or suggestions. While the design studio can indeed be a special place where design 'stuckness' is resolved (Sachs 1999), I do not believe that physical proximity to other students solving their own design problems makes that process any easier.

The design studio is architecture's 'signature pedagogy' (Larson 1977; Peel 2011; Crowther 2013). It was fatally theorised by Donald Schön (1985 and 1987), whose extrusion of the master–pupil relationship only began to be corrected many years later by Webster (2005) and others. How we adapt this problematic pedagogical framework to distance learning will be a matter of great importance. Advocates point to the social and peer-to-peer learning that are characteristic of design studio pedagogies, which distance learning cannot match. Yet, there are precedents for learning design at a distance. Just a few years before the unimaginable relocation of architecture education online, in 2017, the CCA in

Montréal staged a retrospective of 'A305: History of Architecture and Design, 1890–1939', a third-year undergraduate arts course offered by the OU between 1975 and 1982. The exhibition and accompanying events celebrated the forward thinking of the curriculum, one which used a mix of printed and televised content to support students studying the subject at distance. Today, the OU continues to offer a range design courses equivalent to one, two or three-years full-time proximate study, notably a BA/BSc (Honours) in Design and Innovation. Studying the social interaction and peer learning of students in this very programme, Lotz, Jones and Holden (2015) established that social interaction and peer-to-peer learning is not only possible in a fully online studio, it is something that actively constructed through a hierarchy of student engagement in a virtual learning environment.

The pre-Covid introduction of lecture capture to university campuses (justified for political, economic or even pedagogical reasons) presaged some of the moral, ethical and pragmatic dilemma that would appear during the adaptation to pandemic teaching. The danger with the deployment of any innovation in the classroom is that it is driven by technology rather than pedagogy. Writing about the relative merits of traditional studio spaces and a new digital interactive workspace, Arvola and Artman conclude 'that most of these attempts at creating interactive spaces for creative collaboration have been guided more by what can be done than by what should be done' (2008: 82). But what happened in the first months of 2020 was quite different. Whereas the growth of lecture capture was driven by the increasing quality and affordability of digital video and audio recording, pandemic teaching was driven by a pedagogical challenge. Educators were faced with no alternative but to replace proximal teaching with online teaching. It was time to repurpose the technology to our own ends.

Liberating the captive lecturer and student

In September 2020, I offered a new interpretation of the undergraduate History of Architecture courses at Umeå School of Architecture. Although the year began with a complex plan for reducing the density of staff and student occupation of our building and limited in-person teaching for design courses, a pre-existing condition made it undesirable for me to teach on campus.[3] I chose instead to work from home. I was faced with the opportunity to re-imagine almost everything about the courses I was about to teach. With no choice but to teach online, I confronted my distrust of the camera head-on and attempted to decolonise my curriculum in both form and content. Less than five years after I proactively chose to obscure classroom video cameras and walk throughout the classroom, in vain attempts to foil the lecture capture system, I found myself actively engaging with the idea of video recording my lectures. Mindful of my own anecdotal experience of student engagement with recorded lectures at universities (which tended to show a sharp drop-off in viewers after about 20 minutes), I used my laptop and smartphone to record a series of video 'chapters', distinguished from traditional one- or two-hour long lectures by a shorter and more online-appropriate duration of 10–20 minutes. Each chapter introduced one or maybe two ideas or concepts. Pre-recording the chapters allowed students to access them asynchronously in either dedicated independent study hours or during their own time. Synchronous teaching was limited to three- or four-hour seminars, held over Zoom, which discussed the content of the video chapters and the reading list distributed by PDF or eBook. The seminars were structured around tasks and smaller digital breakout rooms. The process of preparing this teaching was long, tedious and challenging. Whereas I might not have written down every word of my lectures before, I felt the need to have a script to refer to. Slides had to be recomposed with images that had identifiable authors and Creative Commons licenses. Clicking 'record' and watching the little green light adjacent to my laptop's webcam illuminate seemed to dissolve the confidence I used to find in the lecture theatre. Countless chapters were started and then abandoned as I stumbled over words or mis-cued my images.

Having informed students in advance that we would make no attempt at in-person teaching (while colleagues teaching design proposed hybrid classes where both proximate and online attendance were supported), the response from students was broadly positive, and for the first time in many years, I did not dread the outcomes of the forthcoming student evaluations (which turned out to be incredibly supportive and positive). Mixing asynchronous (pre-recorded) and synchronous (live) video content heightened the qualities of the live interactions between teachers and students. Mindful of the unimaginable diversity of student living conditions, I did not require students to turn on their cameras, although when breakout rooms closed and students returned to deliver their short summative presentations, it was a pleasure to see that the smaller and more intimate peer-to-peer environment of the breakout rooms returned a delightful mosaic of students' faces sitting in a colourful array of rooms and contexts.

The materiality of immaterial spaces of learning

In *Neoliberalism on the Ground Book Subtitle: Architecture and Transformation from the 1960s to the Present*, Kenny Cupers, Catharina Gabrielsson and Helena Mattsson (2020) set out to demonstrate the ways in which the 'concrete everyday' of architecture and the built environment is connected to the abstract economic theories and policies of neoliberalism. This chapter has reflected on the 'concrete everyday' of teaching architecture in higher education in two very different intensities of the neoliberal university. Emigrating (or 'Brexiting') from the United Kingdom to Sweden allowed me to exchange the neoliberal university for a social democratic model of free higher education – one in which I am now, effectively, a civil servant of the Swedish state. Yet, I have not been able to escape from the material consequences of neoliberal forces. Despite widespread belief outside Sweden of this country being some kind of social democratic utopia, Cupers, Gabrielsson and Mattson demonstrate the exact opposite with several notable Swedish examples.

In his account of the emergence of the neoliberal university in Britain, James Vernon writes how

> universities are the product of historically specific and always changing rationales for which conditions of emergence are as contingent as they are structural. In Britain the neoliberal university was not the consequence of any grand plan or class interest. It took shape gradually as the technologies of marketization, privatization, and financialization were deployed by a variety of actors to solve what were identified as specific problems, often problems created by the preceding wave of "reforms".
>
> *(Vernon 2018: 280)*

Regardless of context or political system, neoliberal processes can be found in universities everywhere, and they are precisely not democratising. Reinhold Martin writes how 'neoliberalism entails in most accounts an usurpation of democratic procedures that is dedicated to enhancing the sovereignty of allegedly autopoietic markets' (Martin, in Cupers, Gabrielsson and Mattsson 2020: 409–410). Regardless of the field of study, 'neoliberalism entails the reshaping of regimes charged with supplying cultural meaning' (*ibid.*: 415–416).

When I first proposed this chapter to the editors of this book in the summer of 2019, the Covid-19 pandemic was unimaginable. To paraphrase Crosbie and Salama (*op.cit.*), there is now an opportunity. In a world shaped by the climate emergency and the stubborn resistance of institutions to address systemic racism and sexism, we have demonstrated that we are capable of doing things differently – even from within the neoliberal university. Since the cost and logistics of travel are no longer an obstacle, we can invite guest speakers from global institutions to deliver content relating to our own institutional blind spots. I was able to invite experts from abroad to deliver guest lectures on the history of Chinese and Indian cities, for example, without the financial and environmental costs of flying the speaker to northern Sweden. Freed from the spatial constraints of the lectern and the line-of-sight of the camera in the lecture theatre, I am now free to use a smartphone or a laptop to take my students for a walk. Recalling the highly confrontational introduction of lecture capture technologies to the university, I remember the problematic way in which technology appeared to be making demands on us to change our pedagogical approaches. But now, based on student feedback, providing my students with pre-recorded video chapters does not appear to have undermined the quality of my teaching. Recording chapters outside the classroom (sometimes using a smartphone camera on location) removed any suggestion that the video was in any way inferior to an equivalent classroom experience. This is not a secondary recording of a moment in time that you missed; this is an original text to be absorbed in whatever way you choose, as many times as you like. The legal consequences of recording one's teaching have not gone away. The precise legal relationship between the university and sessional lecturers who record their lectures, for example, remains to be determined.

This chapter is part confession and part speculation, prompted by teaching in times of pandemic. When I recall how teaching from my living room quickly conflated my personal and professional lives, I remember how dramatically lecture capture had disrupted my confidence as a teacher. By demanding the right to keep digital copies of my teaching practice, university management revealed that an implicit purpose of the technology was to police behaviour, dissuade dissent and to maximise the economic efficiency of my academic labour. The camera was just a material component of a panoptic environment that suddenly enveloped the campus. The video camera in the lecture theatre was a menacing presence: an uninvited observer, a silent participant in the class who never raised their hand or asked a question, but who remembered everything that was ever said by a teacher or student.

How has video, both pre- and post-pandemic, changed our understanding of physical space of higher education? Early pedagogical experiments in analogue video – such as those at UEA in Norwich and the OU in Milton Keynes – are exceptional. They emerged in the white heat of the post-war British university, manifesting themselves at the intersection between pedagogy, ideology and technology. The arrival of digital cameras in the neoliberal university was part of a technocratic mechanism reflecting the power dynamics of the newly marketised university. They were a material trace of the menacing immateriality of surveillance, seized by managerial actors in the supposed cause of differently abled students who, for example, had lost the right to a state-supported note taker. While this chapter is a personal account of the concern of the teacher, it should not be overlooked that the consequences for the rights of the student are still unclear. By agreeing to attend a class in a lecture-capture-equipped teaching space, students faced yet another barrier to raising their hand and entering into a dialogue with a teacher.

How, then, has video challenged us to undertake new pedagogical experiments? When Covid forced us to abandon the physical spaces of learning, architecture educators were amongst the most vocal in their complaints about the loss of a material studio experience. The signature pedagogy of architecture education is defined by the space of the design studio. Most of our pedagogical successes, errors and conflicts take place in the design studio. We defend it to the last, fighting cost-cutting and defending the rights of architecture students to effectively own a heated, illuminated and networked workspace on campus for the duration of their university studies. Few students in other disciplines outside the arts have ever held such expectations. Do we defend this right because the material space of the studio is necessary? Or are we so resistant to change that we cannot imagine an alternative? My responsibility to teach classroom-based history courses liberated me from some of those expectations, but countless universities have found ways to teach creative disciplines online – and many – such as the OU – were doing it for a long time before the pandemic struck.

The material space of architecture education does not have to be as proximal as we might believe. The materiality of our digital interfaces, the materiality of our places of residence or places of study have not been dissolved. A rural farmhouse with its flickering fireplace is as material as the cramped one-room apartment or kitchen table occupied by the student. The materiality of our private lives is multiplied and projected outwards in a supposed immaterial online space of learning. Online teaching is not immaterial.

Notes

1 A former polytechnic university, granted 'full' university status by the Further and Higher Education Act of 1992, one of the intentions of which was to abolish of the hierarchical binary between universities and polytechnics.
2 Students report overall satisfaction on their university education via the National Study Survey (NSS), taken at the end of the graduating year. While satisfaction remains an elusive variable (Senior, Moores, & Burgess 2017) and while the factors affecting grade inflation in higher education are complex (Bachan 2017), a clear connection has been drawn between the award of higher grades and greater student satisfaction (Maisuria & Cole op cit.: 609).
3 At the time of writing (January 2021), *Folkhälsomyndigheten* (the public health agency of Sweden) has not endorsed the use of face masks in all but healthcare settings and during rush hours on public transit, recommending instead that individuals take collective responsibility for maintaining 1.5 metres social distancing. Proximate teaching of design studio has continued throughout the pandemic for first and final year students according to these recommendations.

References

Artman, H. and Arvola, M. (2008). Studio life: The construction of digital design competence. *Nordic Journal of Digital Literacy*, 3(02), 78–96.

Bachan, R. (2017) Grade inflation in UK higher education. *Studies in Higher Education*, 42(8), 1580–1600.

Baruh, L. (2009) Publicized intimacies on reality television: An analysis of voyeuristic content and its contribution to the appeal of reality programming. *Journal of Broadcasting & Electronic Media*, 53(2), 190–210. Available at https://www.doi.org/10.1080/08838150902907678

Brown, J.B. (2020) From denial to acceptance: A turning point for design studio in architecture education. *Distance Design Education* (online). https://distancedesigneducation.com/2020/05/11/from-denial-to-acceptance-a-turning-point-for-design-studio-in-architecture-education/

Canadian Centre for Architecture (CCA). (2018) The University Is Now on Air: Broadcasting Modern Architecture. Exhibition: 15 November 2017 to 1 April 2018.

Crosbie, M.J. and Salama, A.M. (2020) *Educating Architects in a Post-Pandemic World.* [online] Common Edge. Available at: https://commonedge.org/educating-architects-in-a-post-pandemic-world/ [Accessed October 14, 2020].

Crowther, P. (2013) Understanding the signature pedagogy of the design studio and the opportunities for its technological enhancement. *Journal of Learning Design*, 6, 18–28. Available at: https://www.jld.edu.au/article/view/155 [Accessed August 2, 2020].

Cupers, K., Gabrielsson, C. and Mattsson, H. (2020). *Neoliberalism on the Ground: Architecture and Transformation from the 1960s to the Present.* Pittsburgh, PA: University of Pittsburgh Press.

Denzin, N. K. (1995) The cinematic society: The voyeur's gaze. *Sage*, 34.

Elliott, C. and Neal, D. (2016) Evaluating the use of lecture capture using a revealed preference approach. *Active Learning in Higher Education*, 17(2), 153–167. Available at: https://doi.org/10.1177/1469787416637463 [Accessed October 10, 2020].

Flaherty, C. (2020) Parking lot Wi-Fi is a way of life for many students. [online] Available at: https://www.insidehighered.com/news/2020/05/08/parking-lot-wi-fi-way-life-many-students [Accessed October 13, 2020].

Grove, J. (2016, July 28) Disability cuts lead to universal lecture capture policy. Available at https://www.timeshighereducation.com/news/disability-cuts-lead-to-universal-lecture-capture-policy [Accessed September 6, 2020].

Havergal, C. (2016, July 13) Government confirms cuts to disabled students' allowance. Available at: https://www.timeshighereducation.com/news/government-confirms-cuts-disabled-students-allowance [Accessed September 6, 2020].

Ibrahim, Y., Howarth, A. and Stone, I. (2020) Lecture capture policies: A survey of British universities. *Postdigital Science & Education*. Available at: https://doi.org/10.1007/s42438-020-00102-x [Accessed October 13, 2020].

Jandrić, P., Hayes, D., Truelove, I. et al. (2020) Teaching in the age of Covid-19. *Postdigital Science & Education*. Available at: https://doi.org/10.1007/s42438-020-00169-6 [Accessed October 13, 2020].

Kadirire, J. (2011). The pedagogy of lecture capture. *Networks*, 14(14), 1–8.

Kaste, M. (2016) Why the FBI director puts tape over his webcam, *NPR*, 8 April. Available at: https://www.npr.org/sections/thetwo-way/2016/04/08/473548674/why-the-fbi-director-puts-tape-over-his-webcam?t=1610819569749 [Accessed January 16, 2021].

Kübler-Ross E. (1969) *On Death and Dying.* Abingdon: Routledge.

Kuhn, S. (2001) Learning from the architecture studio: Implications for project-based pedagogy. *International Journal of Engineering Education*, 17(4–5), 349–352.

Larson, M.S. (1979) *The Rise of Professionalism: A Sociological Analysis.* Berkeley, CA: University of California Press.

Lotz, N., Jones, D. and Holden, G. (2015) Social engagement in online design pedagogies. In: Vande Zande, R., Bohemia, E. and Digranes, I. (eds.), *Proceedings of the 3rd International Conference for Design Education Researchers.* Aalto University, pp. 1645–1668. Available at: http://oro.open.ac.uk/43592/1/SocialEngagementLxD2015Lotz.pdf [Accessed October 12, 2020].

Maisuria, A. and Cole, M. (2017) The neoliberalization of higher education in England: An alternative is possible. *Policy Futures in Education*, 15(5), 602–619.

Marchand, J.P., Pearson, M.L. and Albon, S.P. (2014) Student and faculty member perspectives on lecture capture in pharmacy education. *American Journal of Pharmaceutical Education*, 78(4). Available at: https://www.ajpe.org/content/ajpe/78/4/74.full.pdf [Accessed October 14, 2020]

Morris, S.M. and Stommel, J. (2018) An urgency of teachers: The work of critical digital pedagogy, Hybrid Pedagogy Inc. Available at: https://hybridpedagogy.org/an-urgency-of-teachers/ [Accessed March 4, 2021].

Peel, D. (2011) Signature pedagogies and the built environment. *Journal for Education in the Built Environment*, 6(2), 1–7. Available at: https://doi.org/10.11120/jebe.2011.06020001 [Accessed October 14, 2020].

Raaper, R. and Olssen, M. (2015) Mark Olssen on neoliberalisation of higher education and academic lives: An interview. *Policy Futures in Education*, 14(2), 147–163.

Sachs, A. (1999) "Stuckness" in the design studio, *Design Studies* 20(2), 195–209.

Sanderson, M. (2002) *The History of the University of East Anglia, Norwich*. London: Hambledon & London.

Schön, D. (1985) *The Design Studio: An Exploration of its Traditions and Potentials*. London: RIBA Publishing.

Schön, D. (1987) *Educating the Reflective Practitioner: Toward a New Design for Teaching and Learning in the Professions*. Hoboken, NJ: Jossey-Bass.

Senior, C., Moores, E. and Burgess, A.P. (2017) "I Can't get no satisfaction": Measuring student satisfaction in the age of a consumerist higher education. *Frontiers in Psychology*, 8, 980.

Stommel, J. (2020a) *Care Is a Practice; Care Is Pedagogical*. [online] Academe. Available at: https://www.aaup.org/article/care-practice-care-pedagogical [Accessed October 13, 2020].

Stommel, J. (2020b) *How to Build an Online Learning Community: 6 Theses*. [online] Jesse Stommel. Available at: https://www.jessestommel.com/how-to-build-an-online-learning-community-6-theses/ [Accessed October 14, 2020].

Vernon, J. (2018) The making of the neoliberal university in Britain. *Critical Historical Studies*, 5(2), 267–280.

Webster, H. (2005) The architectural review: A study of ritual, acculturation and reproduction in architectural education. *Arts and Humanities in Higher Education*, 4(3), 265–282. Available at: https://doi.org/10.1177/1474022205056169 [Accessed October 13, 2020]

Whatley, J. and Ahmad, A. (2007) Using video to record summary lectures to aid students' revision. *Interdisciplinary Journal of E-Learning and Learning Objects*, 3(1), 185–196.

INDEX

Note: *Italic* page numbers refer to figures and page numbers followed by "n" denote endnotes.

Acheson, Arthur 127, 134, 138–140
Acheson, Elizabeth 138–140
Action for Cities 91, 96
Actor-Network Theory 4, 12n3
Adams, Eileen 197n2
Adult Education in England and America (Molesworth) 228
'After Modernism' 50, 51n8
A.H.10.93 257 Contra-construction for Palladio painting 46
Aicher, Otl 58
Albers, Josef 38, 51n13; *Interaction of Color* 45
Alexander, Christopher 124
Alexander, Zeynep Çelik 1, 4, 131
Amâncio d'Alpoim Miranda 'Pancho' Guedes 8, 69
Ambasz, Emilio 184; *The Formulation of a Design Discourse* 6
American Institute of Planners (AIP) 88
American Society of Planners and Architects 100
Andrews, John 175–177, 181, 184, 186n11
Anker, Peder 137
Anschauung 7
Arab–Israeli War 151
Architectonic Space (van der Laan) 21, 33
architects: American 87; data graphics in education of 85–102; early modern 75; modernist and avant-garde 38; neo-avant-garde 117; professional competencies of 88; South African 69; 'transplanted' 206
Architectural Association (AA) 54, 107, 126; architecture on 225–229

Architectural Association School of Architecture 232n5
Architectural Design (AD) 135
architectural education 223–224
'architectural intellectuality' 5
architectural modernism 44
Architecturalö Education Through Materiality 190–191, 196
Architectural Principles in the Age of Humanism (Wittkower) 45
Architectural Review 226
architecture: at the AA 225–229; on the BBC 225–229; body as an ultimate form of 149–162; and the city 32–35; experiencing 32–35
archive of Cummings's talks 221–223
Art and Industry (Read) 226–227
Arte Povera 10, 162n1
Associati, Archizoom 162n1
Australia 164; Dutch and Scandinavian modernism for 227; environmental education in 186n5; expansion of tertiary education in 10; higher education system in 185n1; new post-war universities in 166; post-war campus designs 180; reform of higher education policy in 185; and wireless broadcast 224–225
Australian Broadcasting Commission 221, 224
Australian Universities Commission (AUC) 185n1
Australian Wireless Weekly 232n8
author, in classroom 236–240

Baker, Herbert 76
Bauhaus model 5

250 Index

Beaux-Arts system 5
Bender, Tom 130, 131
Benjamin, Walter 6, 218n6; 'The Work of
  Art in the Age of Mechanical Reproduction'
  117
von Bertalanffy, Ludwig 135
Big Brother 238
Bill, Max 55, 57, 58, 61–62
body: as an inventory 152–153; as an ultimate
  form of architecture 149–162; in different
  global tools workshops 153–154; as a tool
  152–153
Body group workshops 154–159
Bollnow, Otto Friedrich: *Mensch und Raum
  (Human and Space)* 32
Bonet, Antonio 59
Bossche School 21
Bourdieu, Pierre 160
Boyarsky, Alvin 107, 126
Boyden, Stephen 168
Boyer, M. Christine 99
Brand, Stewart 128
Branzi, Andrea 149, 150
Bray, Ted 164, 166–171, 186n4
Breitbart, Myrna Margulies 189, 196, 199n27
Breuer, Marcel 87, 100
Brisbane Telegraph 230
British Broadcasting Company (BBC) 225;
  architecture on 225–229
British Broadcasting Corporation 221, 224
British Empire 225
van den Broek, Barbara 172–173
Brown, George Washington 225
Brown, Trisha 158
Brownlea, Arthur 169
Bulletin of Environmental Education (BEE) 190,
  198n3
Bürdek, Bernhard E. 60
bush campus: as design and pedagogical concept
  164–185; as design concept 170–174; as
  pedagogical concept 174–180
Buti, Remo 162n1

Caine, Graham 126, 133, 139, 142
Cambridge Collage 106–124, 121–123;
  Cambridge 108–115; Cambridge Collage
  121–123; collage 115–118; Dalibor Vesely
  106–108; phenomenology and design method
  119–120
camera: in the bedroom 240–242; in the
  classroom 236
Cameron, David 237
Campe, Jim 131, 143n1; *Natural Energy Designer's
  Handbook* 135
campus: bush campus 164–185; Ulm campus
  55, 62, 65
Canadian Centre for Architecture (CCA) 12, 235

Canizaro, V. B. 131
Can Our Cities Survive? 87
captive lecturer and student, liberating 243–244
Carl, Peter 111–112, 114–115
Carlson, C. Eric 101
Casabella 149, 152, 154
Catholic neo-scholastic theology 21
Catholic theology 20
Celant, Germano 162n1
change and environmental learning 196–197
Chiari, Giuseppe 162n1
The Child in the City (Ward) 190–194, 196,
  198n5
Chuene, Alpheus 74
church architecture: course in 20–22; Dom Hans
  van der Laan 20–22
cities: becoming classrooms 194–196; gendered
  experiences of 193–194
classical hermeneutics 3
classrooms: author in 236–240; camera in 236;
  cities becoming 194–196
Clough, Richard 184
collage 115–118
Colomina, Beatriz 1, 5, 128
Complexity and Contradiction (Venturi) 49
Conceptual Art movements 10, 161
Congrès International de l'Architecture Moderne
  (CIAM) 87
Cook, Peter 106–107
course in church architecture 20–22
Courtauld Institute of Art 62
Covid-19 pandemic 198n6, 235, 241, 242, 245
critical theory 50
critique: on the Ulm institute 59–62; on Warburg
  institute 62–64
Cuff, Dana 6
Cullen, Gordon 76
Cummings, Robert Percy 11; archive of
  Cummings's talks 221–223; early radio
  broadcasts 221–231; education and
  architectural education 223–224
Cupers, Kenny: *Neoliberalism on the Ground Book
  Subtitle: Architecture and Transformation from the
  1960s to the Present* 244
curriculum reform at Harvard 87–89

Dalisi, Riccardo 154, 162n1
Daston, Lorraine: *Objectivity* 4
data graphics: in education of architects and
  planners 85–102; at Harvard Graduate School
  of Design 85–102
De Carlo, Giancarlo 190
decolonial education 68–79
DeMars, Vernon 181
Denzin, Norman K. 238–239
Dernie, David 115, 122
Derrida, Jacques: *Les contemporains* 50

Deschooling Society (Illich) 6, 149, 161
design: cultures 4; functionalist 8, 65; neoclassical 45; pedagogies 2; teaching online 242–243; tools of creative 1
Dewey, John 6
Dilly, Heinrich 210, 218n1
disciplinary disruption, parallel narratives of 164–185
Dorfles, Gillo 149
Douglas Tartan 19
Dreyfuss, Henry: *The Measure of Man: Human Factors in Design* 163n17
Dudok, Willem 76

Eckbo, Garett 184
Eclectica 73–76
Eco, Umberto 149
ECOL Operation House 126
'Ecosystem Ecology' 135
Educating the Reflective Practitioner (Schön) 242
Education through Art (Read) 226
Eisenman, Peter 41, 43, 44, 46, 117
Ekistics 183
embodied learning 194–196
environmental design 180–185
environmental education: development of 168, 186n5; material agency in 192–193; and TCPA 190; and UNESCO 167
environmentalism and interdisciplinary education 166–170
environmental learning 189–197; cities become classrooms 194–196; embodied learning 194–196; gendered experiences of the city 193–194; imagining change through environmental learning 196–197; material agency in environmental education 192–193
Erlebte Raum (Experienced Space) 32
Esherick, Joseph 181
'expanded hermeneutics' 3
experiential learning 9, 129–131

Fabro, Luciano 162n1
Façon Classique 20
Feminist City (Ker) 194
54 Alma Street Darlington 138
Fisher, John O. 103n14
Fletcher, Banister: *A History of Architecture on the Comparative Method* 231
The Formulation of a Design Discourse (Ambasz) 6
Framingham: Your Town, Your Problem report 90
Frankfurt School 108
Franks, D. 168, 185
Freire, Paolo: *Pedagogy of the Oppressed* 6
From wooden blocks to Scottish tartans. Dom Hans van der Laan's reconciliation of rational patterns and spatial experience (Voet) 7–8
Frost, Christian 115, 122

Froud, Daisy 1
Fuller, Buckminster 128
Fyson, Anthony 189; *Streetwork. The exploding school* 189–193, 198n3, 198n4, 198n5

Gabrielsson, Catharina: *Neoliberalism on the Ground Book Subtitle: Architecture and Transformation from the 1960s to the Present* 244
Gadamer, Hans-Georg 64
Gallison, Peter: *Objectivity* 4
Gänshirt, Christian 1, 7
Gaus, John Merriman: *The Graduate School of Design and the Education of Planners* 88
gendered experiences of the city 193–194
Gestalt Psychology 120
Getty, Scott 140
Geysen, Frans 41
Giedion, Sigfried 11, 49–50, 208, 210, 214–215; *Space, Time and Architecture* 49, 208, *209, 213,* 213–214, 215, 217
Gilbert, Creighton 66n4
Global Tools body workshops 149–151
Golzen, Ann 190
Gombrich, Ernst 63–64, 66n6, 218n4
Goodman, Paul 130
Goodway, David 198n5
Goossens, Wim 43
The Graduate School of Design and the Education of Planners (Gaus) 88
Graves, Michael 76
Green, Cedric 74
The Green City (Johnson) 185
Grey Douglas Tartan 29
Griffith University 164–166; aerial photograph of *171;* campus under construction *174;* expansion of 185; fieldwork on and off campus as an aspect of learning for SAES students *179;* first four Schools at *169*
Grimm, Herman 218n2
Gropius, Walter 54, 87, 100, 131, 212
Grosvenor, Ian 2, 4, 39
Grumman Corporation 137
Gubser, Michael 108
Guedes, Pedro 71, 79, 80n7

Habermas, Jurgen 108
Habraken, John 190
Hadid, Zaha 117
Hardoy, Jorge Ferrari 59
Hardy, Dennis 190
Harriss, Harriet 1
Harvard Graduate School of Design: curriculum reform at Harvard 87–89; data graphics in education of architects and planners at 85–102; objectives in Harvard planning problems 89–102; objects in Harvard planning problems 89–102

252 Index

Harvard planning problems: objectives in 89–102; objects in 89–102
Heidegger, Martin 106
Heiselberg, Edward 91
Henry, Reg 164
hermeneutics: classical 3; expanded 3; Ihde's criticism of 3; material 2–4; modern 106; philosophical 63–64
Herzog & De Meuron 1
Hewes, Gordon W. 63
Heynen, Hilde 6, 49
A History of Architecture on the Comparative Method (Fletcher) 231
Holloway, Dennis 132, 138
Homage to the Square painting series 45
hooks, bell: *Teaching Community. A Pedagogy of Hope* 195
Hoppenbrouwers, Alfons 8, 38–51; into the classroom 43–50; painting as searching 41–43; rethinking space and time 48–50; 'revolution' of spatial concepts 44–48; social biography of the object 39–40; studio visit 40–41; visual pedagogy 38–51
Horn, Rebecca 156
Hudnut, Joseph 88, 89, 100
Husserl, Edmund 106, 107, 115

Ihde, Don 3
Illich, Ivan 128, 130; *Deschooling Society* 6, 149, 161
Ilse, John 138
Ilyenkov, Evald 153
Inghilleri, Paolo 157
Integrated Household System 137
Interaction of Color (Albers) 45
Italian Radical Architecture 149
Italian Radical design movement 159
Ivison, Tim 191

Jackson, J. B. 180–181
Jacob, Mary Jane: *The Studio Reader* 41
James, Colin 'Col' 127
Jencks, Charles 49
John Moffat Building 68–69, 71–74, 78
Johnson, Henrietta 74
Johnson, Roger 170; *The Green City* 185
Jonas, Kurt 78
Journal of the American Institute of Planners 91, 102

Kadirire, James 236
Kaiser, David 12
Kallipoliti, Lydia 137
Kern, Leslie: *Feminist City* 194
'kinaesthetic knowing' 131
Kingery, David W. 3
Koffka, Kurt 120

Köhler, Wolfgang 120
Kostof, Spiro 6
Kroll, Lucien 190
Kurchan, Juan 59

van der Laan, Dom Hans 7–8, *19,* 19–35; *Architectonic Space* 21, 33; course in church architecture 20–22; experiencing architecture and the city 32–35; reconciliation of rational patterns and spatial experience 19–35; Scottish Tartan 29–32; teaching spatial superposition 22–29; from wooden blocks to Scottish Tartans 19–35
Lacaton & Vassal 1
Landolt, Hanspeter 205
Landscape magazine 180, 183
Lang, Karen 205
Laprade, A. 22
L'Artisan et les Arts Liturgiques 20
Lasdun, Denys 235
Latimer, Elspeth 115
Latour, Bruno 3
learning: embodied 194–196; experiential 9, 129–131; materiality of immaterial spaces of 244–246
Le Corbusier 41, 43, 44, 50, 76, 223, 228
lecture capture: author in the classroom 236–240; camera in the bedroom 240–242; camera in the classroom 236; liberating captive lecturer and student 243–244; materiality of immaterial spaces of learning 244–246; teaching design online 242–243
Lefebvre, Henri: *The Production of Space* 51n17; *The Right to the City* 51n17
Le Nombre Plastique 21–22
Lesák, František 156
Les contemporains (Derrida) 50
The Limits to Growth (Club of Rome) 135
Lissitzky, El 38
The Listener 226
Loschke, Sandra Karina: *Materiality and Architecture* 1
L'Ouvrier Liturgique 20
Lubar, Stephen 3
Lutye, Edwin 68

Mackenzie, Bruce 184
Mackintosh, Charles Rennie 74
Magris, Roberto 154
Maldonado, Tomás 57, 61–62, 65
'the mangle of practice' 5
Marcuse, Herbert 108
Martienssen, Rex 76
material agency in environmental education 192–193
material hermeneutics 1–12, 3; objects absorbed into processes 5–7; pedagogical turn 5–7

Materialities of schooling: Design-technology-object-routines (Lawn and Grosvenor) 12n2
materiality: of immaterial spaces of learning 244–246; of schooling 2–3
Materiality and Architecture (Loschke) 1
The Mathematics of the Ideal Villa (Rowe) 45
Mattsson, Helena: *Neoliberalism on the Ground Book Subtitle: Architecture and Transformation from the 1960s to the Present* 244
May, John 1, 4
McDonald, M. J. 230
McDowell, Val 231n1
McEwen, Frank 71
McGill University's Minimum Cost Housing Group (MCHG) 126–127, 130, 133–134
McHarg, Ian 183
The Meaning of Art (Read) 226
The Measure of Man: Human Factors in Design (Dreyfuss) 163n17
Mendini, Alessandro 10, 152, 154
Mensch und Raum (Human and Space) (Bollnow) 32
Merleau-Ponty, Maurice: *Phenomenology of Perception* 120
Meyerson, Martin 100
model 1–2; Bauhaus model 5; Beaux-Arts system 5; functionalist 59; 'laboratory' 103n14; 'lifeboat' model of interdisciplinarity 176–177; Meyer-led Bauhaus 62, 65; pedagogical 5; urban diagrammatic 8, 35
Modern Movement 48–49, 50, 51n17
Moholy-Nagy, László 38
Molesworth, Bevil 228, 230–231; *Adult Education in England and America* 228
Molière, Granpré 32
Morris, Sean Michael: *An urgency of teachers: The work of critical digital pedagogy* 241
Mosconi, Davide 152, 154
Mother Earth News 135
Muybridge, Edward 157
MVRDV 1

Natural Energy Designer's Handbook (Van der Ryn and Campe) 135
neo-Marxism 5
neo-Thomism 35n3
Nietzsche, Friedrich 119
Noia, Nazareno 10, 152
Nouvelle théologie 20
NRPB Urbanism Committee 85

Objectivity (Daston and Gallison) 4
objects: of experimentation 130–133; in Harvard planning problems 89–102; social biography of 39–40
Ockman, Joan 12
Odum, Eugene 135

Olsen, Donald 181
On Adam's House in Paradise: The Idea of the Primitive Hut in Architectural History (Rykwert) 63
Open University, in United Kingdom 12
Oppenheim, Dennis 156
Order out of Chaos (Prigogine) 49
Ortega, Alvaro 127, 132
Orwell, George 11
Our Cities, Their Role in the National Economy report 85–87, 94–95, 103n11

Padovan, Richard 33, 36n10
painting as searching 41–43
Palladio, Andrea 44–45
Panofsky, Erwin 209
Papanek, Victor 128
parallel narratives of disciplinary disruption 164–185
passages 71–73; as relations 76–78
Patočka, Jan 106–108
Pawley, Martin 107
pedagogical turn 5–7
Pedagogy of the Oppressed (Freire) 6
Perkins, George Holmes 88, 99
Perrault, Palladio 41
Pesce, Gaetano 10, 152
Pestalozzi, Johann Heinrich 7
Petrescu, Doina 191
Pettena, Gianni 153
phenomenology 5; and design method 119–120
Phenomenology of Perception (Merleau-Ponty) 120
Pichler, Walter 156
Pickering, Andrew 5
planners: activism of emerging community 79; American 87; data graphics in education of 85–102
planning problems 85–102
Plastic Number 22, *23,* 29–30
postpassage 79
Povera, Arte 162n1
Prague Spring 106
Prigogine, Ilya: *Order out of Chaos* 49
Principles of Art History (Wölfflin) 205, 209–210, 217
The Production of Space (Lefebvre) 51n17
Progressive Architecture 131
Proust, Marcel 50

The Queenslander 230

Radical Architecture movement 10
Radical Pedagogies 1
Raggi, Franco 10, 150–151, 152, 156
Ragusa, Sam 170
rationalism 5
rational patterns and spatial experience 19–35

Read, Herbert: *Art and Industry* 226–227; *Education through Art* 226; *The Meaning of Art* 226
reconciliation: of rational patterns 19–35; of spatial experience 19–35
Renaissance architecture 65n1
'revolution' of spatial concepts 44–48
Ricci, Leonardo 149, 162n4
Rickson, Roy 164
Riegl, Alois 66n5
Riello, Giorgio 2–3
The Right to the City (Lefebvre) 51n17
van der Rohe, Mies 50
Rose, Calvin 169, 186n3
Rousmaniere, K. 13n6
Rowe, Colin 11, 49; *The Mathematics of the Ideal Villa* 45; *Transparency: Literal and Phenomenal* 45
Royal Institute of British Architects (RIBA) 238
Ruskin, John 143n3
Rykwert, Joseph 8, 53–65, 106–107; alienation at Ulm 54–55; covert references 58–59; critique on the Ulm institute 59–62; critique on Warburg institute 62–64; haptic experience within educational settings 56–59; *On Adam's House in Paradise: The Idea of the Primitive Hut in Architectural History* 63

Sadler, Simon 152
Sash, Cecily 73
Savioli, Leonardo 149
Scapp, Ron 195
Schiller, Frederick 226
Schlemmer, Oskar 158
Schmid, Max 205
Schön, Donald: *Educating the Reflective Practitioner* 242
Schumacher, E.F.: *Small is Beautiful* 129
Science and Technology Studies 4
'scientific operationalism' 65
Scottish Tartan 20, 29–32, 31, 35
Second World War 57
Segal, Walter 190
Sereni, Dario 157
The Sex of Architecture 194
Shanken, A. M. 102n3
Sint Lucas Institute for Architecture in Brussels 8
The sitting position—A question of method lecture 8
Slutzky, Robert 51n13; *Transparency: Literal and Phenomenal* 45
Small is Beautiful (Schumacher) 129
Smith, Dean 115, 121–122
Smith, William Forgan 225
Smithson, Alison 73
Smithson, Peter 73
Snow, C. P. 169
social biography of object 39–40

The Social (Re) Production of Architecture (Petrescu and Trogal) 191
Society of Latin Liturgy 31
South Africa: framing transitional objects for decolonial education in 1980s 68–79; introducing Eclectica 73–76; passage 71–73; passages as relations 76–78; passing Pancho 68–71; postpassage 79
The South African Architectural Record 76
Space, Time and Architecture (Giedion) 49, 208, *209, 213,* 213–214, *215,* 217
space and time 48–50
Space Electronic 163n19
spatial concepts 44–48
spatial superposition, teaching 22–29
Spreafico, Marina 157
Stanek, Lukasz 51n17
Stapp, William 167, 186n5
Stengers, Isabelle 49
Stephenson, Gordon 99
Stieber, Nancy 48
Stommel, Jesse 241
Stowell, Fran 139
Streetwork. The exploding school (Ward and Fyson) 189–193, 198n3, 198n4, 198n5
structuralism 5
student design-build projects (1970s): no white coat boffins 133–135; and objects of experimental lifestyles 126–142; pottering about to sounds of Zappa and Lennon 141–142; process of people living together 135–139
studio 2–3, 5–6, 40–41; abstract geometric painting in 38; drawing and collage-making in 9; fine arts 72
The Studio Reader (Jacob) 41
Styles in Painting. A Comparative Study (Zucker) 210, *211, 212*
Surrealism 120
Sydney Autonomous House 127
Sydney Morning Herald 139–140
Synthetic Cubism 120

Tafuri, Manfredo: *Theories and History of Architecture* 6
Tanner, Rose 197n2
Task by *American City* 101
teaching: design online 242–243; spatial superposition 22–29
Teaching Community. A Pedagogy of Hope (hooks) 195
The Telegraph 230–231
Tendenza movement 149
Theories and History of Architecture (Tafuri) 6
Thomas, Helen 64
Thornton, Nicole 178
tools 1, 4, 7, 50, 85, 89, 123–124, 138, 159–162

Town Planning Review 97
Transparency: Literal and Phenomenal (Slutzky and Rowe) 45
Trogal, Kim 191, 195
Tschumi, Bernard 117

Ulm School of Design (Hochschule für Gestaltung) 8; critique on 59–62; Joseph Rykwert's object lesson at 53–65
Undercurrents 135
Urban Action Group 73
An urgency of teachers: The work of critical digital pedagogy (Morris) 241
US Environmental Education 183

Vaccari, Franco 153, 162n1
Vandenbreeden, Jos 51n6
Van der Ryn, Sim 143n1; *Natural Energy Designer's Handbook* 135
Van Eyck, Aldo 43, 71, 73, 75, 79
Venturi, Robert 73; *Complexity and Contradiction* 49
Vesely, Dalibor 9, 106–108
Villa Rotunda 45
Villa Stein 44
visual pedagogy 38–51

Waeyenberghe, Marleen van 40
Wagner, Martin 85
Warburg Institute 53–54, 58; critique on 62–64
'Warburg Method' 62–65, 66n4
Warburg School 8
Ward, Colin 189; *The Child in the City* 190–194, 196, 198n5; *Streetwork. The exploding school* 189–193, 198n3, 198n4, 198n5

Warsaw Pact 106
The Week 231
Wertheimer, Max 120
Western modernity 151
Western philosophy 4
Whitecombe, C. F. 223
White Rose Group 57
Whole Earth Catalog 135
'whole personality' 65n3
Willett, John 164, 166
Wilson, Harold 108
wireless architecture 221–231; architectural education 223–224; architecture on the BBC and at the AA 225–229; archive of Cummings's talks 221–223; Cummings education 223–224; wireless broadcast and Australia 224–225
wireless broadcast and Australia 224–225
Wittkower, Rudolf 11, 53–54, 62, 65n1; *Architectural Principles in the Age of Humanism* 45
Wölfflin, Heinrich 11, 66n5, 205–218; crossing a nebulous terrain 214–218; performative triangle 206–210; *Principles of Art History* 205, 209–210, 217; training the eye 210–214
'The Work of Art in the Age of Mechanical Reproduction' (Benjamin) 117
World War II 128, 164

Yom Kippur War 151
Yusaf, Shundana 226

Zodiac 54
Zucker, Paul 11, 210–218; *Styles in Painting. A Comparative Study* 210, *211, 212*

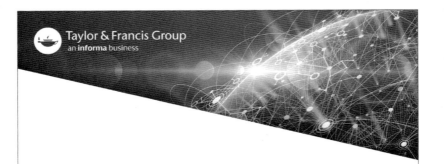